EPIDEMICS AND THE LAW FROM PLAGUE TO THE PRESENT

This collection of essays presents a socio-legal history of epidemics from the medieval period to the present day.

Building on previous studies of infectious diseases undertaken by social historians of medicine, this collection explores the histories of epidemics and disease by looking at the legal measures deployed against them.

Whilst previous works have considered the mechanisms by which legal change occurs, the social and political assumptions on which new laws and new legal structures are premised and the social changes which follow, this book focuses on the way in which historical actors understood law to be a complex means of responding to disease and the way in which that law shaped (and limited) the responses which could be made to disease.

Taking an interdisciplinary approach, it features contributions from scholars across a range of academic disciplines who consider the wider implications of epidemics and disease beyond the obvious health effects. The collection focuses first on regulatory responses such as the quarantine laws and border policies in the eighteenth century, the framing of 'disease' in the Colonial Immigration Acts in the nineteenth century and the ethics of public health in the twentieth century in Great Britain. It then goes on to consider developments in broader legal doctrine which themselves resulted from social and/or legal responses to disease, including the centralisation of labour regulation in the wake of the Black Death, property disputes about leper houses, pest houses and fever hospitals, and the prosecution of medical professionals for disease transmission in 19th century England.

Methodologically all the chapters are historical, but a range of approaches has been taken, from quite traditional doctrinal legal history through socio-legal history to traditional political and social history, to bring the history of epidemics and the legal measures deployed against them in to sharp focus.

Epidemics and the Law from Plague to the Present

Edited by
Emily Gordon
Charles Mitchell
and
Ian Williams

•HART•
OXFORD • LONDON • NEW YORK • NEW DELHI • SYDNEY

HART PUBLISHING

Bloomsbury Publishing Plc

Kemp House, Chawley Park, Cumnor Hill, Oxford, OX2 9PH, UK

1385 Broadway, New York, NY 10018, USA

Bloomsbury Publishing Ireland Limited, 29 Earlsfort Terrace, Dublin 2, D02 AY28, Ireland

HART PUBLISHING, the Hart/Stag logo, BLOOMSBURY and the Diana logo are trademarks of Bloomsbury Publishing Plc

First published in Great Britain 2025

A catalogue record for this book is available from the British Library.

A catalogue record for this book is available from the Library of Congress.

Library of Congress Control Number: 2025937165

ISBN: HB: 978-1-50998-444-2
ePDF: 978-1-50998-446-6
ePub: 978-1-50998-445-9

Typeset by Compuscript Ltd, Shannon

For product safety related questions contact productsafety@bloomsbury.com

To find out more about our authors and books visit www.hartpublishing.co.uk. Here you will find extracts, author information, details of forthcoming events and the option to sign up for our newsletters.

CONTENTS

PART III
LONGER-TERM LEGAL AND SOCIAL CONSEQUENCES OF INFECTIOUS DISEASE

LIST OF CONTRIBUTORS

Professor Alison Bashford FBA is Scientia Professor in History and Director of the Laureate Centre for History & Population at the University of New South Wales, Sydney and Emeritus Vere Harmsworth Professor of Imperial and Naval History at Cambridge University.

Professor Roberta Bivins is a Professor of History at Warwick University.

Dr Alex Chase-Levenson is an Associate Professor of History and Public Health at Binghamton University, State University of New York.

Dr Tom Crook is a Reader in Modern British History at Oxford Brookes University.

Dr Lorren Eldridge is a Fellow in Law at Queens' College Cambridge and an Assistant Professor in Private Law at Cambridge University.

Professor Jonathan Garton is a Professor of Law at Warwick University.

Dr Emily Gordon is a Fellow of St John's College Cambridge.

Professor Charles Mitchell KC (Hon) FBA is a Professor of Law at University College London.

Dr Joe Sampson is an Assistant Professor in Legal History at Cambridge University.

Professor Chantal Stebbings is Emeritus Professor of Legal History at Exeter University, and a Visiting Fellow in the Centre for Tax Law at Cambridge University.

Dr Katherine D Watson is a Reader in History at Oxford Brookes University.

Dr Janet Weston is an Assistant Professor in the Centre for History in Public Health at the London School of Hygiene and Tropical Medicine.

Dr Ian Williams is an Associate Professor of Law at Oxford University and Fellow of St John's College Oxford.

PART I

Introduction

1

Socio-Legal Histories of Infectious Disease

EMILY GORDON, CHARLES MITCHELL AND IAN WILLIAMS*

I. Introduction

Social crises are agents of legal change and epidemics are a prime example. Many questions arise about the mechanisms by which legal change occurs, the social and political assumptions on which new laws and new legal structures are premised, and the social changes they effect – or prevent, by reinforcing the status quo. However, while the interplay between infectious diseases and the law has been investigated by historians of medicine and public administration it has been rather neglected by legal historians. For this book we therefore asked scholars from all these disciplines to discuss how the law has been used as a response to epidemics, how these have affected the evolution of legal ideas and legal structures, how they have influenced social and political ideas and relations, and how these legal and social developments have themselves affected one another. In this chapter we introduce the book by bringing out some themes that emerge from the following chapters (in Part II) and contextualise the contributors' work by undertaking a survey of the existing scholarship (in Part III). This has proved to be something of a quixotic project as the literature is large and multi-faceted, but we hope that this overview will enable future researchers to identify starting points for their own work and see connections between the contributions of other scholars working in a variety of disciplines.

* For their helpful comments on a draft of this chapter we thank Roberta Bivins, Tom Crook, Lorren Eldridge, Chantal Stebbings, Katherine Watson and Janet Weston; and for valuable research assistance we thank John (Ching Jack) Choi. We alone are responsible for any errors. All webpages cited in this chapter were last accessed on 26 November 2024. This book is based on papers which were presented and discussed at a conference in September 2023 at the UCL Faculty of Laws. We thank all of the conference participants for their contributions.

II. Complexity Revealed

An important theme running through the chapters in this book is that law is not a value-neutral, easy-to-use tool for converting policy into action once scientists and political leaders have decided what to do. Law is, and always has been, a highly adaptable instrument for responding to infectious diseases – and many other social crises for that matter. But it would be a mistake to imagine that it is a well understood and unproblematic tool. It works in complex and sometimes unpredictable ways to produce effects which may or may not be those which policymakers intend. Different policies may pull in different directions and the laws designed to implement them can cut across one another. Law can also be used by other actors to obstruct policy implementation in ways that policymakers may find frustrating. Many social and political histories of the fight against infectious disease offer significant insights into the formation, content and application of law, but many are premised on instrumentalist conceptions of law in the service of public health.[1] There are more questions to be asked about the interplay between law and infectious disease than such histories suggest.

The chapters in this volume show how complex this can be. Some provide new perspectives on the utility of law; others show how it has been used to challenge, and even frustrate, responses to disease. We have divided them into two, rather loosely differentiated, groups. The main focus of the chapters in the first group is on the use, or non-use, or abuse of law as a regulatory response to immediately pressing public health needs. The chapters in the second group are more concerned with the interrelationship between law and infectious disease, from the impact of existing legal doctrines and norms on medical and social responses to disease, through to the more diffuse, and sometimes unexpected, longer-term effects on legal and social relationships of legal and social responses to epidemics.

Regulatory responses to diseases are discussed in the chapters by Joe Sampson (chapter two), whose topic is the early seventeenth-century plague, and Tom Crook (chapter four), who considers infectious diseases in the Victorian period. Both examine ways in which the creation of broadly framed legal powers to respond to diseases led to significant local variations in the actions of those empowered. In relation to the plague of 1603, Sampson highlights that although some powers were expressly granted by the central authorities, much discretion was left to local actors, in particular justices of the peace. They took their own initiative in selecting and implementing measures in (and possibly with) their own communities. In the context of an emergency response, this granting of discretion was not always seen as problematic. Sampson observes that while other, and formally similar, interventions by state agents were complained about and challenged as conflicting

[1] *cf* Anne Kirkland, 'Beyond Law as a Tool of Public Health: Vaccines in Interdisciplinary Sociolegal and Science Studies' (2023) 18 *Anuual Review of Law and Social Science* 179.

with wider legal principles, measures taken in response to the plague went unchallenged. Sampson suggests that the challenges posed by a threatening epidemic may explain the absence of criticism of both the central and local authorities at that time.

Other chapters problematise the use of law as a regulatory response to diseases. Several authors make clear that legal measures, ostensibly for disease control and public health, were not always driven by these issues. Janet Weston (chapter seven) notes that measures severely restrictive of personal liberties were proposed to prevent the spread of HIV and AIDS and that these were motivated by hostility to social groups which were most at risk of infection. For Roberta Bivins (chapter six), meanwhile, the 'health inspection clause' in the Commonwealth Immigrants Act 1962, which permitted medical testing and exclusion on medical grounds of migrants at the border, had much less to do with protecting public health from the threat of diseases such as smallpox or tuberculosis than it did with preventing undesired (legal) immigration to the United Kingdom.

This kind of 'hijacking' of health measures is likely to limit their efficacy as tools against infectious disease; and this is an area in which legal historians working beyond the history of law and health can make important contributions, understanding these ostensibly health-focused interventions as part of a (much) longer history of the use of the law against marginalised communities in many different contexts. As Alison Bashford's chapter (chapter five) shows, the 'borrowable' nature of written law had a role to play in the normalisation or globalisation of health clauses in immigration legislation. Bashford points out that many post-colonial statutes concerning immigration and border control were based directly on older, colonial legislation which had been implicitly (and sometimes explicitly) race-based. Moving from legislation to the law in action, Katherine Watson's chapter (chapter 11) indicates that there was a greater willingness to prosecute female midwives who had transmitted disease in the course of attending patients than there was to prosecute male physicians who had done the same. This unequal application of the criminal law undermined its effectiveness as a tool for the protection of public health.

Rejecting the notion that law is simply an uncomplicated means to a regulatory end, Crook's chapter draws out the distinction between the active and latent authority of law. In nineteenth-century Britain, the law was rarely invoked actively, to bring the force of the state down on individuals who failed to comply with public health requirements. The more important role played by law as an instrument of public health policy was through the use of its latent authority to convince, persuade, and ultimately threaten, people to act as required. From this perspective, legally imposed vaccine mandates were not attacks on individual choice, but guidance from the legislature as to the correct choice to be made, ignored only by those predisposed to reject the views of central authorities. A similar role for law is identified by Weston in the contexts of both tuberculosis at the start of the twentieth century and HIV/AIDS at its end. She highlights contemporary views that the law could be used to codify wider social norms, communicating those to the ignorant or unwilling, without any particular intention or desire on the part of those making the law that it should be applied. Their intention, in other words, was to use law as a communicative tool, shaping behaviour not through sanctions but by taking advantage of law's status as a particular form of normative text.

This use of the law as a means to persuade could be manipulated. Bivins shows that legally mandated health checks at the border in twentieth-century Britain were thought by medical professionals to be of questionable value in securing public health objectives, but were important for the Government which sought to maintain support for immigration from parts of the world which were widely viewed by British citizens as riven by disease. Nineteenth-century manufacturers of quack medicines also exploited the way in which invocations of legal authority could influence opinion, as discussed by Chantal Stebbings in chapter 10. She shows how the formality of a legally-mandated revenue stamp gave the impression to prospective purchasers that official approval had been given for ineffective, and often dangerous, medications. Public officials and lawmakers were aware of this problem, but in the context of nineteenth-century endemic diseases which were seen as a fact of life, and given the popularity of some products, they considered that the revenue's gain from selling the stamps outweighed the possible harm which might be caused to tax-paying purchasers using the products.

While law is a tool, it is not one created solely for the purpose of addressing diseases. Many chapters engage with the challenges and consequences of employing existing law in the struggle against disease. Using existing law, rather than bespoke responses to disease, brought with it values, ideas and approaches previously developed in the law in very different contexts. To some extent, at least, the effect was to shape legal engagement with epidemics. Consequently, as Weston argues, twentieth-century British lawmakers were reluctant to make rules in the public health field which conflicted with the existing values and norms of the legal system, a reluctance which was only overcome by lawmakers stating that new legislation was not meant to be used. A conflict with wider legal norms thus inhibited a response to diseases until that conflict was resolved through presentation of it as purely theoretical.

When there were attempts to use existing legal doctrine to address the spread of disease, such doctrine was not always helpful. Watson shows that attempts to use criminal prosecution to punish medical professionals for transmitting infectious disease to patients rarely met with success. Among the factors limiting the usefulness of the criminal law in this context was the law's historical approach to, and conceptualisation of, what constituted infliction of an 'injury', as well as its insistence on the offender having acted with a particular mental state. These rules involved concepts which had been developed in different contexts and proved to be ill-adapted for use in addressing the problem of negligent transmission of infectious disease.

Even where there had been express legislation or other regulatory rules about diseases, Bashford's contribution highlights that such laws sometimes remained unchanging even after changes in the political, medical and social contexts in which they had to be applied. Sometimes this stasis was a deliberate choice (as in the postcolonial statutes discussed by Bashford), but on other occasions law simply did not change at the same pace as the contexts in which it operated. A similar problem is discussed by Alex Chase-Levenson in chapter three, who examines the practices of Mediterranean authorities upon which Britain relied. These operated a unique legal system of lazarettos which had originally been designed to exclude plague, even as plague declined as a matter of practical concern. It should not be assumed that this seeming ossification was due to the conservatism and slackness of lawmakers, for as Chase-Levenson writes, it was not unreasonable of them to keep safeguards in place against possible future epidemics, given the limited medical understanding of the causes of infectious disease which existed at that time. This was an ongoing issue for all those who sought to make plans against future disease outbreaks; another example is discussed by Jonathan Garton and Charles Mitchell in chapter nine in their study of seventeenth-century pesthouses created to guard against future plague outbreaks which never came, raising questions about the proper use of the property 200 years later.

Important (and ostensibly unrelated) legal ideas and values could be instrumentalised to impede responses to disease. Sometimes this was as simple as individuals using proceedings in the tort of nuisance to block the disposal of sewage and other waste from cities to the detriment of property-owners in the vicinity, or the building and operation of isolation hospitals from which it was feared that infection would spread into the neighbouring community. These are variously discussed by Crook and Garton and Mitchell, who suggest among other things that the success enjoyed by litigants reflects the high value assigned to property rights in the English legal system, albeit that such litigants considered that they were acting legitimately to protect themselves, and their neighbours, from being forced to bear the high cost of measures implemented for the benefit of the community at large.

Garton and Mitchell's chapter nine also discusses how legal responses to epidemics, and their social consequences, caused significant developments to take place in the wider law (and more specifically the law affecting charities and property). This general theme is brought out in chapter eight, where Lorren Eldridge discusses the creation and enforcement of labour legislation enacted in the aftermath of the population decline after the Black Death. This is well-covered ground in medieval history scholarship and there is a broad consensus that the legal response was mostly conservative: its goal was to maintain pre-plague structures despite the death of a massive proportion of the population. But Eldridge discusses the very significant impact of these emergency reactions to an unprecedented pandemic on the long-term intellectual development of English law, not just on employment law, but on wider principles of contract law and the law governing personal status. While other scholars have highlighted the role of medical practice in preserving attitudes towards race and slavery in the wider British empire, Eldridge's chapter suggests that legal changes in relation to the Black Death cut across the law on personal status in order to prioritise what would now be called the law of contract.

III. Infectious Diseases and the Law

Many scholars have previously studied laws enacted as a direct response to epidemics and laws which have emerged in their social, economic and legal aftermaths. Significant work has been done by social historians of medicine, feminist historians, historians of empire and postcolonialism, historians of public administration, historical geographers and contemporary public policy theorists, legal epidemiologists and public health ethicists. For the legal historian it is illuminating to read and reflect on these bodies of scholarship, for although their primary focus is on the social, economic and political impacts of infectious disease, the literature also has much to tell us about law, the social and economic context of its formation, its doctrinal content and its downstream effects on later social and legal changes.

This material is much too large for us to attempt a comprehensive and detailed account. Our less ambitious goal is to identify and summarise recurring points of interest to legal scholars that appear in the literature. We recognise that characterising researchers as belonging to one discipline or another can be reductive, and that there are many overlaps between the concerns and interests of scholars whose work we review. Indeed, one of our goals is to point out these overlaps, and to suggest that the socio-legal history of infectious disease has emerged as a field of enquiry in itself, to which scholars from many disciplines have already made important contributions. A further goal of this chapter is to map out this field, identify accounts of the major issues and suggest possible lines of further enquiry.

A. Law and Medicine

It has often been observed that decisions to enact laws in response to diseases, and the content of these laws, are affected by scientific understandings (or misunderstandings) of the diseases. For instance, Matthew Daly and others have discussed how the mistaken belief that leprosy (Hansen's disease) is highly communicable led to the enactment of laws in nineteenth-century Hawaii, empowering its Board of Health to identify, detain, and confine anyone 'deemed capable of spreading the disease'.[2] Similar measures were taken by British colonial administrators of

[2] Matthew Daly, 'Medical Necessity as a Necessity for Crimes against Humanity: An Examination of the Molokai Transfers' (2007) 24 *Arizona Journal of International and Comparative Law* 645. See too

the 1800s, based on the same misapprehension and also on the belief that strict segregation laws had been enforced in medieval England, as a result of which the disease had been eradicated. The latter belief was also mistaken, as demonstrated by Carole Rawcliffe in her study of the subject,[3] prompting Margaret Brazier's comment that:

> For those who argue that we should learn from history and are inclined to cheer the use of history in law-making relating to medicine, the trouble is much of what is believed about the laws relating to the treatment of lepers in medieval England is wrong.[4]

On the same general theme, Alison Bashford has observed that the emergence of germ theory in the late 1800s led to the discovery that tuberculosis is contagious and thus a threat to the community, leading Australia, Britain and Germany to accept state responsibility for treating the disease in the early 1900s.[5] As Peter Baldwin has written, however, the political implications of germ theory in late nineteenth- and early twentieth-century Europe were 'neither unambiguous nor invariant': liberals did not always prefer sanitarian approaches focused on the improvement of living standards for the poor, nor did conservatives always favour the more authoritarian approaches of quarantine and vaccination.[6] Similarly, progressives in early twentieth-century America favoured anti-spitting laws to reduce the spread of tuberculosis despite their coercive content;[7] and in present-day America, as Kunihiko Yoshida has observed,

> the Right wing has supported more libertarian arguments related to Covid regulations, while Left-wing groups have paradoxically supported strong public health control through such measures as travel restrictions, quarantine requirements, mask-wearing,

Alexander Cheung, 'How Stigma Distorts Justice: the Exile and Isolation of Leprosy Patients in Hawai'i' (2018) 10 *Asian Bioethics Review* 53; Kerri Inglis, 'Leprosy and the Law: The "Criminalisation" of Hansen's Disease in Hawai'i, 1865–1969' in Catherine Stanton and Hannah Quirk (eds), *Criminalising Contagion: Legal and Ethical Challenges of Disease Transmission and the Criminal Law* (Cambridge, Cambridge Univerity Press, 2016). *cf* Shelja Gautam and Khegesh Gautam, 'The Perception of Incurability: Leprosy, Discrimination, and the Medical Truth' (2018) 36 *Boston University International Law Journal* 249 (discussing why India was slow to repeal its Lepers Act 1898).

[3] Carole Rawcliffe, *Leprosy in Medieval England* (Woodbridge, Boydell Press, 2006). At 5 Rawcliffe writes of the 'fantasies and misapprehensions about "the medieval leper" propagated during [the nineteenth century] when microbiologists, colonial administrators and evangelicals turned to the past for evidence to support their own campaign for mandatory segregation'.

[4] Margaret Brazier, *Law and Healing: A History of a Stormy Marriage* (Manchester, Manchester University Press, 2023) 27.

[5] Alison Bashford, *Imperial Hygiene: A Critical History of Colonialism, Nationalism and Public Health* (Basingstoke, Palgrave Macmillan, 2004) 64; and sources she cites at fn 26.

[6] Peter Baldwin, *Contagion and the State in Europe, 1830–1930* (Cambridge, Cambridge University Press, 1999) ch 6, esp 545–48.

[7] Jeanne E Abrams, '"Spitting Is Dangerous, Indecent, and against the Law!" Legislating Health Behavior' (2013) 68 *Journal of the History of Medicine and Allied Sciences* 416. Other coercive measures implemented during the progressive era are discussed in Michael Willrich, '"The Least Vaccinated of Any Civilized Country": Personal Liberty and Public Health in the Progressive Era' (2008) 20 *Journal of Policy History* 76. On 'sanitationist' and 'quarantinist' pathways in the US, see also John Fabian Witt, *American Contagions: Epidemics and the Law from Smallpox to COVID-19* (New Haven, CT, Yale University Press, 2020).

> and social distancing, despite the risk that support for such measures could become a target of Foucauldian critiques of biopower.[8]

Although 'heroic' histories of medical and scientific discovery can give a different impression, changes in scientific thinking usually do not happen all in one go: old and new theories often run in parallel and this can slow down the development of new policies and law premised on a new theory because policymakers do not immediately give up on the old one. Miasmatic theories of the causes of cholera, for example, were slow to yield to germ theories and for a time acceptance of the new idea was partial and complex – both theories 'could and did co-exist' in the thinking of a single person.[9]

A different phenomenon occurs with the outbreak of new diseases about which little is initially known. When insufficient information is available to assess the risks of infection, policymakers may respond with measures that may later appear in hindsight, with the benefit of better information and more accurate scientific understandings, to have gone too far, or not far enough, in their sacrifice of individual liberties[10] – this is a major theme of the public policy reviews of public health responses to COVID-19 which are now underway around the world. New technologies may also make it possible to achieve better medical outcomes, but at the same time they may create new ethical and social challenges – examples being the modern-day collection and analysis of personal data on a massive scale, and use of citizen location and contact tracing systems, offering the potential to control the spread of diseases more effectively, but only at the cost of personal privacy and other civil liberties.[11]

Another point again is that once laws are in place, political obstacles can stand in the way of bringing them to an end, despite changes in the underlying medical science which establish that they are ineffective or counter-productive: this was the case, for example, in the US and Japan in the twentieth century, where isolation

[8] Kunihiko Yoshida, 'A Comparative Study of Socio-Legal Scenarios in the COVID-19 Pandemic: Focusing on Asian Responses' (2023) 10 *Asian Journal of Law and Society* 57, 60–61.

[9] Alison Bashford, 'Tuberculosis & Economy: Public Health & Labour in the Early Welfare State' (2002) 4 *Health and History* 19, endnote 17. See also Michael Worboys, *On Spreading Germs: Disease Theories and Medical Practice in Britain, 1865–1900* (Cambridge, Cambridge University Press, 2000): there were many germ theories of disease and these were developed and used in different ways in veterinary medicine, surgery, public health and general medicine.

[10] On the implications of this for public choice theory see Mark Koyama, 'Epidemic Disease and the State: Is There a Tradeoff between Public Health and Liberty?' (2023) 195 *Public Choice* 145.

[11] Kat Albrecht and Brian Citro, 'Data Control and Surveillance in the Global TB Response: A Human Rights Analysis' (2020) 2 *Law, Technology and Humans* 107; Tiffany Li, 'Privacy in Pandemic: Law, Technology, and Public Health in the COVID-19 Crisis' (2021) 52 *Loyola University Chicago Law Journal* 767; Michael Cederblom, 'Welcome to the Digital Age: Reinventing Contact Tracing and the Public Health Service Act for a Modern Pandemic Response' (2022) 31 *Annals of Health Law and Life Sciences* 101. See too Ebi Robert and Felix Eboibi, 'Global COVID-19 Technology Contact Tracing, Rights to Privacy and Cybercrime Perpetration' (2023) 29 *Computer and Telecommunications Law Review* 85; Michelle Miao, 'Coded Social Control: China's Normalization of Biometric Surveillance in the Post COVID-19 Era' (2024) 19 *Washington Journal of Law, Technology & Arts* 53.

policies for leprosy, and isolation facilities, were preserved long after they had been proven to be scientifically unnecessary.[12]

The causal flow could also go the other way. Civil and criminal laws have been deployed to challenge or marginalise therapeutic practices of which policymakers disapprove. For instance, Helen Tilley has argued that persistent efforts were made in colonial Africa to rid official medical spheres of theories about health and disease that invoked nonmaterial causes and definitions of bodies and landscapes that rested on vital energies and animating spirits[13] – although Heather Bell has written that the participation of women and native Africans as medical personnel in delivering health programmes demonstrates the tenuousness of colonial power in practice,[14] and Mari Webel has suggested that native African strategies to mitigate disease played a part in shaping colonial disease prevention programmes.[15]

Medical and therapeutic practices can also be indirectly influenced by legal constructs such as 'personhood' which encode social hierarchies. Consider the argument by Arnab Dey that medical approaches to cholera, kala-azar, and malaria infection were affected by the legal distinction between indentured and non-indentured labourers in nineteenth-century Assam tea plantations.[16] Another example is the legal distinction drawn between 'aliens' and 'citizens' which underpinned racialised practices of border screening programmes adopted across the British Empire, and the Commonwealth, aimed at smallpox, tuberculosis and other diseases.[17]

Laws enacted in response to infectious disease have often been attributable to multiple causes, not all of them medical. For instance, concerns about moral purity have been a driver, and frequently a more significant driver than public health concerns, of many laws enacted to combat venereal disease;[18] the UK Contagious

[12] Hajime Sato and Janet Frantz, 'Termination of the Leprosy Isolation Policy in the US and Japan: Science, Policy Changes, and the Garbage Can Model' (2005) 5 *BMC International Health and Human Rights* 3.

[13] Helen Tilley, 'Medicine, Empires, and Ethics in Colonial Africa' (2016) 18 *AMA Journal of Ethics* 743; Helen Tilley, 'Medical Cultures, Therapeutic Properties, and Laws in Global History' (2021) 36 *Osiris* 1. See too Deepak Kumar, 'Unequal Contenders, Uneven Ground: Medical Encounters in British India, 1820–1920' in Andrew Cunningham and Bridie Andrews (eds), *Western Medicine as Contested Knowledge* (Manchester, Manchester University Press, 1997).

[14] Heather Bell, *Frontiers of Medicine in the Anglo-Egyptian Sudan, 1899–1940* (Oxford, Oxford University Press, 1999).

[15] Mari Webel, *The Politics of Disease Control: Sleeping Sickness in Eastern Africa, 1890–1920* (Athens, OH, Ohio University Press, 2019). *cf* Dennis Awuah, *British Colonial Strategies to Control the Influenza Epidemic of 1918 to 1919 in Ashanti* (Illinois State University MSc thesis, 2002), available at https://ir.library.illinoisstate.edu/cgi/viewcontent.cgi?article=2512&context=etd.

[16] Arnab Dey, 'Diseased Plantations: Law and the Political Economy of Health in Assam, 1860–1920' (2018) 52 *Modern Asian Studies* 645.

[17] Alison Bashford, 'The Great White Plague Turns Alien: Tuberculosis and Immigration in Australia, 1901–2001' in Flurin Condrau and Michael Worboys (eds), *Tuberculosis Then and Now: Perspectives on the History of an Infectious Disease* (Montreal and Kingston, McGill-Queen's University Press, 2010); *cf* Becky Taylor, 'Immigration, Statecraft and Public Health: The 1920 Aliens Order, Medical Examinations and the Limitations of the State in England' (2016) 29 *Social History of Medicine* 512.

[18] Judith Walkowitz, *Prostitution and Victorian Society: Women, Class and the State* (Cambridge, Cambridge University Press, 1980); Suzann Buckley and Janice Dickin McGinnis, 'Venereal Disease

Diseases Acts 1864–1886 are a much discussed example. Similarly, pilgrim traffic between India and the Middle East was monitored by British and French imperial authorities in the late 1800s as much out of security as out of sanitary concerns.[19] Again, border screening measures have been adopted by many countries to avoid paying the cost of health problems emanating from other countries, a consideration that continues to shape immigration laws around the world.[20] Such laws are out of tune with the International Health Regulations (IHR) 2005 which recognise that cross-border pandemics are a global problem for which effective and just solutions are to be found through international co-operation rather than the self-serving actions of individual states. But of course the immigration laws of many states long pre-date the 2005 version of IHR, and in fact the early history of international treaty-making in the area of global health itself illustrates the general point being made here, since the International Sanitary Conventions agreed between 1892 and 1926 aimed to curb the spread of diseases from Asia to Europe (cholera, then plague and yellow fever) and their purpose was 'protecting Europe without unduly hindering trade'; only later did the focus shift from 'self-protection against external threats' to 'safeguarding the public's health in every region of the world'.[21]

and Public Health Reform in Canada' (1982) 63 *Canadian Historical Review* 337; Constance Backhouse, 'Nineteenth-Century Canadian Prostitution Law: Reflection of a Discriminatory Society' (1985) 28 *Social History* 387; Dorothy Chunn, 'A Little Sex Can Be a Dangerous Thing: Regulating Sexuality, Venereal Disease, and Reproduction in British Columbia, 1919–1945' in Susan Boyd (ed), *Challenging the Public / Private Divide: Feminism, Law, and Public Policy* (Toronto, University of Toronto Press, 1997); Lesley Hall, 'Venereal Diseases and Society in Britain, from the Contagious Diseases Acts to the National Health Service' in Roger Davidson and Lesley Hall (eds), *Sex, Sin and Suffering: Venereal Disease and European Society Since 1870* (London, Routledge, 2001); Philippa Levine, *Prostitution, Race and Politics: Policing Venereal Disease in the British Empire* (London, Routledge, 2003); Pamela Cox, 'Compulsion, Voluntarism, and Venereal Disease: Governing Sexual Health in England after the Contagious Diseases Acts' (2007) 46 *Journal of British Studies* 91; Scott Wasserman Stern, 'The Long American Plan: The US Government's Campaign against Venereal Disease and Its Carriers' (2015) 38 *Harvard Journal of Law and Gender* 373; Christina Firpo, *Black Market Business: Selling Sex in Northern Vietnam, 1920–1945* (Ithaca, NY, Cornell University Press, 2020) ch 2.

[19] William Roff, 'Sanitation and Security: The Imperial Powers and the Nineteenth Century Hajj' (1982) 6 *Arabian Studies* 143; Michael Low, 'Empire and the Hajj: Pilgrims, Plagues, and Pan-Islam under British Surveillance, 1865–1908' (2008) 40 *International Journal of Middle East Studies* 269; Saurabh Mishra, *Pilgrimage, Politics, and Pestilence: The Haj from the Indian Subcontinent 1860–1920* (New Delhi, Oxford University Press, 2011); Valeska Huber, *Channelling Mobilities: Migration and Globalisation in the Suez Canal Region and Beyond, 1869–1914* (Cambridge, Cambridge University Press, 2013) chs 6 and 7; James Casey, 'Sacred Surveillance: Indian Muslims, Waqf, and the Evolution of State Power in French Mandate Syria' in James Fichter (ed), *British and French Colonialism in Africa, Asia and the Middle East: Connected Empires across the Eighteenth to the Twentieth Centuries* (London, Palgrave Macmillan, 2019).

[20] Richard Coker and Alan Ingram, 'Passports and Pestilence: Migration, Security and Contemporary Border Control of Infectious Diseases' in Alison Bashford (ed), *Medicine at the Border: Disease, Globalization and Security, 1850 to the Present* (Basingstoke, Palgrave Macmillan, 2006). See too Polly Price, 'Infecting the Body Politic: Observations on Health Security and the "Undesirable" Immigrant' (2015) 63 *University of Kansas Law Review* 915, esp 933–34.

[21] Lawrence Gostin and Rebecca Katz, 'The International Health Regulations: The Governing Framework for Global Health Security' (2016) 94 *Milbank Quarterly* 264, 266. See too Norman

B. Effectiveness of Laws

Different laws work in different ways, making them more or less suitable vehicles to implement different policies. Short-term solutions focused on individuals (isolation of the infected sick,[22] contact tracing / partner notification,[23] mask-wearing[24]) may call for one type of law; another may be better suited to longer-term solutions focused on the wider community (public collection and disposal of refuse,[25] immigration controls,[26] vaccination programmes,[27] surveillance, data collection

Howard-Jones, *The Scientific Background of the International Sanitary Conferences, 1851–1938* (Geneva, World Health Organisation, 1975); Mark Harrison, 'Disease, Diplomacy and International Commerce: The Origins of International Sanitary Regulation in the Nineteenth Century' (2006) 1 *Journal of Global History* 197; David Fidler, 'Public Health and International Law: The Impact of Infectious Diseases on the Formation of International Legal Regimes, 1800–2000' in Andrew Price-Smith, *Plagues and Politics: Infectious Diseases and International Policy* (Basingstoke, Palgrave, 2001); David Fidler, 'From International Sanitary Conventions to Global Health Security: The New International Health Regulations' (2005) 4 *Chinese Journal of International Law* 325; Valeska Huber, 'The Unification of the Globe by Disease? The International Sanitary Conferences on Cholera, 1851–1894' (2006) 49 *Historical Journal* 453; Flavia D'Abramo, 'The Past and Present of Pandemic Management: Health Diplomacy, International Epidemiological Surveillance, and COVID-19' (2021) 43 *History and Philosophy of the Life Sciences* 1.

[22] Richard Coker, 'Civil Liberties and Public Good: Detention of Tuberculous Patients and the Public Health Act 1984' (2001) 45 *Medical History* 341; Bashford (2004) (n 5) ch 5; Nola Ries, 'Quarantine and the Law: The 2003 SARS Experience in Canada (A New Disease Calls on Old Public Health Tools)' (2005) 43 *Alberta Law Review* 529; John Booker, *Maritime Quarantine: The British Experience, c. 1650–1900* (Aldershot, Ashgate, 2007); Kira Newman, 'Bubonic Plague and Quarantine in Early Modern England' (2012) 45 *Journal of Social History* 809; Shin-Rou Lin, 'A Costly Illusion?: An Empirical Study of Taiwan's Use of Isolation to Control Tuberculosis Transmission and Its Implications for Public Health Law and Policymaking' (2013) 13 *Asian-Pacific Law & Policy Journal* 107; Krista Maglen, *The English System: Quarantine, Immigration and the Making of a Port Sanitary Zone* (Manchester, Manchester University Press, 2014); Alex Chase-Levenson, *The Yellow Flag: Quarantine and the British Mediterranean World, 1780–1860* (Cambridge, Cambridge University Press, 2020) ch 5; Euan Roger, '"To Be Shut Up": New Evidence for the Development of Quarantine Regulations in Early-Tudor England' (2020) 33 *Social History of Medicine* 1077.

[23] Jon Andrus et al, 'Partner Notification: Can it Control Epidemic Syphilis?' (1990) 112 *Annalas of International Medicine* 542; Ronald Bayer and Kathleen Toomey, 'HIV Prevention and the Two Faces of Partner Notification' (1992) 82 *American Journal of Public Health* 1158; Lawrence Gostin and James Hodge Jr, 'Piercing the Veil of Secrecy in HIV/AIDS and Other Sexually Transmitted Diseases: Theories of Privacy and Disclosure in Partner Notification' (1998) 5 *Duke Journal of Gender Law and Policy* 9; Allan Brandt, 'The History of Contact Tracing and the Future of Public Health' (2022) 112 *American Journal of Public Health* 1097.

[24] Mark De Vitis and David Carter, 'The Law and the Limits of the Dressed Body: Masking Regulation and the 1918–19 Influenza Pandemic in Australia' in Carl Stychin (ed), *Law, Humanities and the COVID Crisis* (London, University of London Press, 2023); Anna Garus-Pakowska and Maciej Pakowski, 'The Obligation to Use Face Masks in Public Spaces as a Public Health Measure and Permissible Limits on Civil Liberties' (2023) 44 *Journal of Public Health Policy* 110.

[25] Deborah Brunton, 'Regulating Filth: Cleansing in Scottish Towns and Cities, 1840–1880' (2015) 42 *Urban History* 424; Jane Stevens Crawshaw, *Cleaning Up Renaissance Italy: Environmental Ideals and Urban Practice in Genoa and Venice* (Oxford, Oxford University Press, 2023) ch 5.

[26] All the contributions in Bashford (2006) (n 20); Roberta Bivins, *Contagious Communities: Medicine, Migration and the NHS in Post War Britain* (Oxford, Oxford University Press, 2015) ch 1.

[27] Sanjoy Bhattacharya et al, *Fractured States: Smallpox, Public Health and Vaccination Policy in British India, 1800–1947* (New Delhi, Orient Longman, 2005); Kevin Malone and Alan Hinman,

and analysis by public health agencies[28]) or infrastructure projects (lazaretti and pesthouses,[29] sewerage systems,[30] bath houses,[31] isolation hospitals[32]). Some policies require public spending, others not; some laws are coercive and mandatory (compulsory quarantine, compulsory vaccination, compulsory notification of infection, criminalisation of disease transmission), others are enabling and permissive (opt-in vaccination, legal validation of property-holding structures to fund healthcare provision). As Scott Burris and his co-authors have written of the wide range of legal strategies used in modern times to address public health challenges,

> Law, informed by epidemiology and behavioral sciences, can be used to set specific standards of conduct, change social norms, and structure the default choices available in everyday life. Law can do this through many legal devices, including statutes, regulations, orders, guidelines, and taxes, and it can be invoked at the local, state,

'Vaccination Mandates: The Public Health Imperative and Individual Rights' in Richard Goodman et al (eds), *Law in Public Health Practice*, 2nd edn (New York, NY, Oxford University Press, 2007); Stanley Williamson, *The Vaccination Controversy: The Rise, Reign, and Fall of Compulsory Vaccination for Smallpox* (Liverpool, Liverpool University Press, 2007); Deborah Brunton, *The Politics of Vaccination: Practice and Policy in England, Wales, Ireland and Scotland, 1800–1874* (Rochester, NY, University of Rochester Press, 2008); Gareth Millward, *Vaccinating Britain: Mass Vaccination and the Public Since the Second World War* (Manchester, Manchester University Press, 2019); Malte Thießen, 'Security, Society, and the State: Vaccination Campaigns in 19th and 20th Century Germany' (2021) 46 *Historical Social Research / Historische Sozialforschung* 211; Kay Wilson and Christopher Rudge, 'COVID-19 Vaccine Mandates: A Coercive but Justified Public Health Necessity' (2023) 46 *University of New South Wales Law Journal* 381.

[28] For eg, the registration of plague deaths in Milan after 1452, which were not 'the first attempts to register a city's deaths', but were unique until the 1800s, insofar as 'university-trained physicians – not parish priests, other clerics, or gravediggers – evaluated the corpses, gathered the reports of symptoms, and pronounced the cause of death': Samuel Cohn Jr and Guido Alfani, 'Households and Plague in Early Modern Italy' (2007) 38 *Journal of Interdisciplinary History* 177, 178. See also Graham Mooney, *Intrusive Interventions: Public Health, Domestic Space and Infectious Disease Surveillance, 1840–1910* (Rochester, NY, University of Rochester Press, 2015); Jacob Steere-Williams, 'Performing State Medicine During its "Frustrating" Years: Epidemiology and Bacteriology at the Local Government Board, 1870–1900' (2015) 28 *Social History of Medicine* 82; Matthew Newsom Kerr, *Contagion, Isolation, and Biopolitics in Victorian London* (Basingstoke, Palgrave Macmillan, 2017).

[29] Jane Stevens Crawshaw, *Plague Hospitals: Public Health for the City in Early Modern Venice* (Aldershot, Ashgate, 2012); Andrew Wells, 'Urban Governance, Economic Intervention, and the Plague in Bristol, England, 1665–66' in Mohammad Gharipour and Caitlin DeClercq (eds), *Epidemic Urbanism: Contagious Diseases in Global Cities* (Bristol, Intellect, 2021); Aaron Columbus, '"To Be Had for a Pesthouse for the Use of this Parish": Plague Pesthouses in Early Stuart London, c 1600–1650' (2022) 51 *Urban History* 125.

[30] David Sunderland, '"A Monument to Defective Administration?" The London Commissions of Sewers in the Early Nineteenth Century' (1999) 26 *Urban History* 349; James Hanley, 'The Metropolitan Commissioners of Sewers and the Law, 1812–1847' (2006) 33 *Urban History* 350; Jamie Benidickson, *The Culture of Flushing: A Social and Legal History of Sewage* (Vancouver, University of British Columbia Press, 2007).

[31] Tom Crook, '"Schools for the Moral Training of People": Public Baths, Liberalism and the Promotion of Cleanliness in Victorian Britain' (2006) 13 *European Review of History* 21.

[32] Gwendoline Ayers, *England's First State Hospitals and the Metropolitan Asylums Board 1867–1930* (London, Wellcome Institute of the History of Medicine, 1971); Anthony Wohl, *Endangered Lives: Public Health in Victorian Britain* (Cambridge, MA, Harvard University Press, 1983) 77–82 and 119–27; William Anderson, *Fever Hospital: A History of Fairfield Infectious Diseases Hospital* (Melbourne, Melbourne University Press, 2002); Margaret Currie, *Fever Hospitals and Fever Nurses – A British Social History of Fever Nursing* (Abingdon, Routledge, 2005) ch 2.

> and federal levels. This complex matrix of legal options and actors invites innovation, creativity, and sophistication.[33]

This leads to questions about the role played by law as a tool for policy implementation. It might be asked of laws whether, and if so how – and why – they have made a difference, and answering these questions requires consideration of such matters as 'why people obey the law, how and to what extent penalties drive compliance, the impact of laws on norms, social modelling, and how peer attitudes shape understanding of legal rules'.[34] Research into such questions has been relatively neglected by epidemiologists in the modern public health field,[35] and a lack of data inevitably means that the further back in time one goes, the less likely it becomes that answers can be confidently given.[36] An associated question is how one might measure the 'success' or 'failure' of policies and their translation into law (where laws have been enacted to implement an agreed policy[37]). In many cases, policymaking and lawmaking expertise cannot be pulled apart, and assessed separately, from the medical expertise which informs particular measures. Nor can one assess 'success' and 'failure' in this context without first deciding how policymaking and lawmaking *ought to be* conceived and measured, ie one needs a theory of 'good governance' to identify a set of assessment criteria.[38]

[33] Scott Burris et al, *The New Public Health Law: A Transdisciplinary Approach to Practice and Advocacy*, 2nd edn (New York, NY, Oxford University Press, 2022) 81 and ch 6 generally.

[34] Scott Burris et al, 'The "Legal Epidemiology" of Pandemic Control' (2021) 384 *New England Journal of Medicine* 1973, 1974. For socio-legal and psychological theories of compliance, see Danqi Guo et al, 'Emotions, Crisis, and Institutions: Explaining Compliance with COVID-19 Regulations' (2024) 18 *Regulations and Governance* 177, and the literature cited there. On methodological approaches to legal epidemiology, see Matthew Jay, 'Legal Epidemiology, Evidence-informed Law and Administrative Data: New Frontiers in the Study of Family Justice' in Naomi Creutzfeldt et al (eds), *Routledge Handbook of Socio-Legal Theory and Methods* (London, Routledge, 2019); Mathieu Poirier et al (eds), 'Principles and Methods of Global Legal Epidemiology' (2022) 76 *Journal of Epidemiology & Community Health* 828; Alexander Wagenaar et al (eds), *Legal Epidemiology: Theory and Methods*, 2nd edn (London, Wiley, 2023).

[35] ibid 1973. But for studies focused on infectious disease, see eg, Aaron Siegler et al, 'Law Everywhere: A Causal Framework for Law and Infectious Disease' (2020) 135 (1st supp) *Public Health Reports* 25S; Matthew Kavanagh et al, 'Law, Criminalisation and HIV in the World: Have Countries that Criminalise Achieved More or Less Successful Pandemic Response?' (2021) 6 *BMJ Global Health*; Angus Wong and Laura Balzer, 'State-Level Masking Mandates and COVID-19 Outcomes in the United States: A Demonstration of the Causal Roadmap' (2022) 33 *Epidemiology* 228.

[36] *cf* Paul Slack, 'The Response to Plague in Early Modern England: Public Policies and Their Consequences' in John Walter and Roger Schofield (eds), *Famine, Disease and the Social Order in Early Modern Society* (Cambridge, Cambridge Univerity Press, 1991) 179: 'the historian can never be certain whether it was good management or good fortune which prevented a serious outbreak of plague in any particular instance. There were simply too many variables involved in mortality and morbidity differentials'.

[37] Whether this has been done, and if so, how effectively it has been done, are also questions which merit investigation, as in eg Brian Citro, 'Activating Law and Human Rights to End Tuberculosis: An Empirical Assessment of Ten Countries' Fulfillment of United Nations Commitments' (2024) 21 *Indiana Health Law Review* 1.

[38] Considered in eg Kathleen Tierney, 'Disaster Governance: Social, Political, and Economic Dimensions' (2012) 37 *Annual Review of Environment and Resources* 341; International Federation of Red Cross (IFRC) and Red Crescent Societies, *Law and Disaster Preparedness and Response*

One law might be intended to control behaviour by sanction, forcing citizens into compliance; another might aim to change behaviour by altering citizens' perceptions of social norms with which they wish to align themselves.[39] Which kind of law should be preferred may turn on political considerations in addition to effectiveness, and whether laws of either type have achieved their goals must be judged by different metrics.[40]

There are different reasons why a failure to deliver desired outcomes might be attributed to technical failures by policymakers and lawmakers. Policies may have been misguided owing to misunderstandings about the nature and scale of a problem, as in the case of British responses to the 1918–19 influenza epidemic, both at home and in the colonies.[41] A more recent example is Thabo Mbeki's policy of AIDS denialism in South Africa, which is widely believed to have caused several hundred thousand excess deaths; only after litigation to enforce victims' constitutional rights to health did the South African Government implement effective prevention and treatment programmes.[42] Laws promulgated by Jair Bolsanaro's administration in Brazil in response to COVID-19 are thought to have had a similarly disastrous effect, undermining existing public health measures such as social distancing in a quest for herd immunity, promoting unproven and ineffective therapies, and delaying the provision of vaccines.[43] Laws can also be counterproductive in ways that were predictable from the outset, as in the case of laws to criminalise non-disclosure of HIV infection which have increased stigmatisation of the infected, causing them to conceal their condition and deterring them from accessing treatment and care.[44] Laws may also be bound to fail because they

Multi-Country Synthesis Report (IFRC, 2019); Simon Deakin and Gaofeng Meng, 'The Governance of Covid-19: Anthropogenic Risk, Evolutionary Learning, and the Future of the Social State' (2020) 49 *Industrial Law Journal* 539.

[39] Cass Sunstein, 'On the Expressive Function of Law' (1996) 144 *University of Pennsylvania Law Review* 2021.

[40] See further Fortuna Casoria et al, 'Perceived Social Norm and Behavior Quickly Adjusted to Legal Changes during the COVID-19 Pandemic' (2021) 190 *Journal of Economic Behavior and Organisation* 54.

[41] Sandra Tomkins, 'The Failure of Expertise: Public Health Policy in Britain during the 1918–19 Influenza Epidemic' (1992) 5 *Social History of Medicine* 435; Maura Chhun, '"A Good Winter Rain Will Put Everything Right": The British Government in India's Response to the 1918 Influenza Pandemic and Famine' (2019–20) 19 *Middle Ground Journal*; David Arnold, 'Death and the Modern Empire: The 1918–19 Influenza Epidemic in India' (2019) 29 *Transactions of the Royal Historical Society* 181.

[42] Nicoli Nattrass, *Mortal Combat: AIDS Denialism and the Struggle for Antiretrovirals in South Africa* (Scottsville, University of KwaZulu-Natal Press, 2007); Pride Chigwedere et al, 'Estimating the Lost Benefits of Antiretroviral Drug Use in South Africa' (2008) 49 *Journal of Acquired Immune Deficiency Syndrome* 410; Mark Heywood, 'South Africa's Treatment Action Campaign: Combining Law and Social Mobilization to Realize the Right to Health' (2009) 1 *Journal of Human Rights Practice* 14.

[43] Fernando Luiz Abrucio et al, 'Combating COVID-19 under Bolsonaro's Federalism: A Case of Intergovernmental Incoordination' (2020) 54 *Brazilian Journal of Public Administration* 663.

[44] Patrick Michael Eba, 'HIV-Specific Legislation in Sub-Saharan Africa: A Comprehensive Human Rights Analysis' (2015) 15 *African Human Rights Law Journal* 224; Matthew Weait, 'Limit Cases: How and Why We Can and Should Decriminalise HIV Transmission, Exposure, and Non-Disclosure' (2019) 27 *Medical Law Review* 576; Kavanagh et al (n 35); Kyle Kirkup, 'Law's Sexual Infections' (2023) 46 *Dalhousie Law Journal* 609 (on the 2019 recommendation by the Canadian House of Commons Standing Committee on Justice and Human Rights that HIV non-disclosure should be removed

are premised on action being taken by state agencies which lack the necessary powers, as occurred in Britain following the enactment of the Cholera Act 1832, which failed to provide Local Boards of Health with summary jurisdiction to deal with nuisances;[45] or because they are premised on the provision of funding that will never arrive, as in early twentieth-century Accra, where 'sanitary regulation, taxation, and Town Council politics placed the responsibility for implementing colonial visions on townspeople who could not afford it',[46] or on social conditions that do not exist, as in modern-day Nigeria, where crowded accommodation and lack of running water made it impossible for many people to comply with isolation and handwashing orders designed to curb the spread of COVID-19.[47]

Laws may have been poorly drafted and use vague concepts that leave too much to the individual discretion of state officers, producing uncertainty and inconsistency of application, as occurred under the regime created in England by the Statute of Labourers 1351, enacted to address labour shortages after the Black Death.[48] Poor drafting may also leave those to whom rules apply uncertain of their effect, as in the case of British laws criminalising the transmission of HIV,[49] and of Australian stay-at-home orders during the COVID-19 pandemic which produced 'nonsensical and unworkable' results when applied to people living in strata title apartments.[50] Or governments may issue a series of orders, some framed as 'laws', others as 'guidelines', producing a complex set of rules the legal status of which is uncertain, as occurred in Britain during the COVID-19 pandemic.[51]

from sexual assault laws and its further recommendation that a new offence be created for the non-disclosure of all infectious diseases); Sean Bland, 'Decriminalizing Disease: A Health Justice Approach to Infectious Diseases and Criminal Law' (2024) 77 *Arkansas Law Review* 441. *cf* Joseph Lelliott et al, 'Pandemics, Punishment, and Public Health: COVID-19 and Criminal Law in Australia' (2021) 44 *University of New South Wales Law Journal* 167. Punishment of soldiers who contracted venereal disease during World War I had similar effects: Leo van Bergen, 'The "Prick Parade": The First World War and Venereal Disease' in Leo van Bergen and Eric Vermetten (eds), *The First World War and Health: Rethinking Resilience* (Leiden, Brill, 2020) 195.

[45] Fraser Brockington, 'Public Health at the Privy Council 1831–34' (1961) 16 *Journal of the History of Medicine and Allied Sciences* 161, 179–80. The Privy Council was also slow to give Local Boards of Health powers to compel parish vestries to pay for town improvements and temporary hospitals: Ann-Marie Akehurst, 'Complacency, Confusion, and the Mismanagement of Cholera in York, England, 1832' in Gharipour and DeClercq (n 29).

[46] Jennifer Hart, *Making an African City: Technopolitics and the Infrastructure of Everyday Life in Colonial Accra* (Bloomington, IN, Indiana University Press, 2024) 33.

[47] Opeyemi Yetunde Omotuyi, 'Responding to the Covid-19 Pandemic: Implications for Law and Development in Nigeria' (2021) 2 *Law and Social Justice Review* 109.

[48] Mark Bailey, *After the Black Death: Economy, Society, and the Law in Fourteenth-Century England* (Oxford, Oxford University Press, 2021) 82 and 209.

[49] Catherine Dodds et al, 'Responses to Criminal Prosecutions for HIV Transmission among Gay Men with HIV in England and Wales' (2009) 17 *Reproductive Health Matters* 135. *cf* Patrick Michael Eba, 'Towards Smarter HIV Laws' (2016) 24 *Reproductive Health Matters* 178.

[50] Cathy Sherry, 'All about the Land: The (Mis)Application of Public Health Orders to Strata Schemes during the Delta Variant COVID-19 Outbreak in Sydney, Australia' (2023) 45 *Sydney Law Review* 279.

[51] Tom Hickman, 'The Use and Misuse of Guidance during the UK's Coronavirus Lockdown', posted 9 September 2020 at: https://papers.ssrn.com/sol3/papers.cfm?abstract_id=3686857; John Sorabji and Steven Vaughan, '"This Is Not A Rule": COVID-19 in England and Wales and Criminal

Laws may have been transplanted from one jurisdiction to another, something which has frequently been done for prosaic and pragmatic reasons: in David Schorr's words, lawyers 'are not a particularly creative bunch' and when asked

> to draft a legal document – contract, will, deed, regulation, statute, or any of the other products for which society relies on lawyers – professionals will rarely start with a blank slate … [but] will typically copy from a similar document that has already been used for similar purposes.[52]

How well this works out in practice may then depend on the degree to which the social context for which laws were designed varies from the social context of the jurisdiction into which they are transplanted: consider, for example, the nineteenth-century regulation of prostitution across Britain and its Empire.[53] Existing rules designed in one socio-political context to meet one type of situation may also be pressed into service to meet a new situation for which they are a poor fit, a feature of some legal responses to COVID-19 – though they may have worked well enough in the short term.[54] An example is the Epidemic Diseases Act 1897, originally enacted by the British colonial Government to tackle a plague outbreak in Bombay (Mumbai),[55] which fell short in various ways as a legal regime on which the prevention and control of epidemics could be grounded in the modern era. The Act empowered (and was invoked by) Indian state governments to take such coercive powers as were required to combat a 'dangerous epidemic disease', without defining 'dangerous' or 'epidemic' or safeguarding the constitutional and human rights of citizens; following a review by the Indian Law Commission, an overhaul has now been recommended.[56]

C. Law and Social Norms

Laws introduced in response to infectious disease may be predicated on, and reinforce, social norms and stereotypes, or they may react against, and change, them. Laws may or may not resonate with public opinion and may be met by popular apathy, enthusiasm or resistance, sometimes by all three when public opinion is divided. Questions may then arise about the function of law and its justifications:

Justice Governance via Guidance' (2021) 12 *European Journal of Risk Regulation* 143; Joe Tomlinson et al, *Law and Compliance During Covid-19* (London, Nuffield Foundation, 2022).

[52] David Schorr, 'Horizontal and Vertical Influences in Colonial Legal Transplantation: Water By-laws in British Palestine' (2021) 61 *American Journal of Legal History* 308, 309.

[53] Philip Howell, *Geographies of Regulation: Policing Prostitution in Nineteenth-Century Britain and the Empire* (Cambridge, Cambridge University Press, 2009).

[54] Dean Knight, 'Stamping out COVID-19 in New Zealand: Legal Pragmatism and Democratic Legitimacy' [2021] *Public Law* 241.

[55] Chinmay Tumbe, *Age of Pandemics (1817–1920): How They Shaped India and the World* (Noida, Harper Collins, 2020) ch 3.

[56] Law Commission of India, *Report No 286: A Comprehensive Review of the Epidemic Diseases Act, 1897* (Government of India, Law Commission of India, February 2024).

does and should law reflect existing social behaviours and expectations; does and should it shape these and point them in different directions?

Many historians of empire have argued that the power to make laws designed to address epidemics has been used as a tool of imperial control, to endorse and reinforce racial constructs, and that this has exacerbated tensions between imperial rulers and the ruled.[57] For example, Alison Bashford has observed that vaccination reform required administration and bureaucracy and knowledge of statistics and demography; vaccination programmes therefore provided a means for the collection of information, and were thus 'one of the mechanisms through which British as well as colonial populations were rendered governable'.[58] A similar point is made in Rohan Deb Roy's study of imperial responses to malaria epidemics in South Asia, where the consolidation of knowledge about disease outbreaks and the colonial extraction of information about the locality happened simultaneously and converged to stereotype the Burdwan division of West Bengal as a malarial landscape on the map of the British empire.[59]

Neglect, under-funding and poor decision-making by rulers (colonial or otherwise) leads to anger and resentment among the ruled, and bad decision-making results in bad law – or in no law when law is needed. This theme has been developed by many historians of empire. For example, it has been argued that the failure of the colonial Government to institute quarantine measures in Western Samoa in response to the 1918–19 influenza pandemic was the main cause of an uprising there;[60] that a lack of interest, accompanied by the desire to avoid expenditure, led to a muted and delayed response to plague outbreaks in colonial India;[61] and that public health budgets regarded as acceptable by colonial rulers in Africa would have been thought far too low if applicable to their home countries and this despite the fact that mortality and morbidity rates were much higher in sub-Saharan Africa than elsewhere.[62]

[57] These and associated themes are explored in eg Maynard Swanson, 'The Sanitation Syndrome: Bubonic Plague and Urban Native Policy in the Cape Colony, 1900–1909' (1977) 18 *Journal of African History* 387; Radhika Ramasubban, 'Imperial Health in British India, 1857–1900' in Roy MacLeod and Milton Lewis (eds), *Disease, Medicine and Empire* (London, Routledge, 1988); Megan Vaughan, *Curing Their Ills: Colonial Power and African Illness* (Stanford, CA, Stanford University Press, 1991); David Arnold, *Colonizing the Body: State Medicine and Epidemic Disease in Nineteenth Century India* (Berkeley and Los Angeles, CA, University of California Press, 1993); Mark Harrison, *Public Health in British India: Anglo-Indian Preventive Medicine 1859–1914* (Cambridge, Cambridge University Press, 1994); Anil Kumar, *Medicine and the Raj: British Medical Policy in India, 1835–1911* (Walnut Creek, CA, AltaMira Press, 1998); Bhattacharya et al (n 27).

[58] Bashford (2004) (n 5) 33.

[59] Rohan Deb Roy, *Malarial Subjects: Empire, Medicine and Nonhumans in British India, 1820–1909* (Cambridge, Cambridge University Press, 2017) ch 3.

[60] Ryan McLane, 'Influenza and Quarantine in Samoa' in Alison Bashford (ed), *Quarantine: Local and Global Histories* (London, Palgrave, 2016).

[61] Chase-Levenson (n 22) 231–35.

[62] Helen Tilley, 'Medicine, Empires, and Ethics in Colonial Africa' (2016) 18 *American Medical Association Journal of Ethics* 743, 745–46.

Laws have perpetuated social tendencies to stigmatise, scapegoat and 'other' minority groups. They include the poor[63] and the victims of particular diseases, for example, leprosy,[64] tuberculosis,[65] COVID-19,[66] HIV/AIDS (including gay men also facing discrimination for their sexuality[67]) and gonorrhea (including prostitutes also facing discrimination for other reasons). Of the Contagious Diseases Act 1864, enacted in response to the latter, Judith Walkowitz wrote that it was 'the high water mark of an officially sanctioned double standard of sexual morality, one that upheld different standards of chastity for men and women and carefully tried to demarcate pure women from the impure'.[68] The legislation instituted inspection and medical treatment for female prostitutes, but not for male soldiers with whom they had sexual relations. This was abandoned by many army regiments as an inefficient means of reducing venereal disease that was 'unpopular' with the men.[69]

Casting blame on racial groups for infectious diseases also has a long history.[70] 'Othering' has resulted in the framing of diseases as a racialised problem to which racialised policies and laws are the answer. Immigration laws have been ostensibly designed to exclude sufferers from particular diseases on public health grounds

[63] Dorothy Porter, '"Enemies of the Race": Biologism, Environmentalism, and Public Health in Edwardian England' (1991) 34 *Victorian Studies* 159; Kevin Siena, *Rotten Bodies: Class and Contagion in Eighteenth-Century Britain* (New Haven, CT and London, Yale University Press, 2019); Debolina Dey, 'Pathologizing Poverty: The Metaphor of Contagion from the New Poor Law to Public Health' (2020) 9 *Journal of Interdisciplinary History of Ideas* 5.1.

[64] Daly (n 2); Cheung (n 2); Bashford (2004) (n 5) ch 4.

[65] International Human Rights Clinic, University of Chicago Law School, *Tuberculosis, Human Rights and the Law: A Compendium of Case Law* (January 2017), available at www.southernafricalitigationcentre.org/wp-content/uploads/2017/03/TB-Human-Rights-and-the-Law-Case-Compendium.pdf; Matthew Kavanagh et al, 'Tuberculosis, Human Rights, and Law Reform: Addressing the Lack of Progress in the Global Tuberculosis Response' (2020) 17 *PLoS Medicine*.

[66] Lelliot et al (n 44).

[67] Matthew Weait, 'Unsafe Law: Health, Rights and the Legal Response to HIV' (2013) 9 *International Journal of Law in Context* 535. See too John Nkengasong and Jirair Ratevosian, 'Legal and Policy Barriers for an Effective HIV/AIDS Response' (2023) 401 *Lancet* 1405.

[68] Walkowitz (n 18) 70.

[69] Myna Trustram, 'Distasteful and Derogatory? Examining Victorian Soldiers for Veneral Disease' in London Feminist History Group (eds), *The Sexual Dynamics of History* (London, Pluto Press, 1983) 153, 158.

[70] Kim Yi Dionne and Fulya Turkmen, 'The Politics of Pandemic Othering: Putting COVID-19 in Global and Historical Context' (2020) 74 *International Organization* 213; Dušan Ristić and Dušan Marinković, 'Biopolitics of Othering during the COVID-19 Pandemic' (2022) 9 *Humanities and Social Sciences Communications* 409 and sources cited there. For case studies, see eg, Nayan Shah, *Contagious Divides: Epidemics and Race in San Francisco's Chinatown* (Los Angeles and Berkeley, CA, University of California Press, 2001); Lewis Darwen et al, '"Irish Fever" in Britain during the Great Famine: Immigration, Disease and the Legacy of "Black '47"' (2020) 44 *Irish Historical Studies* 270; Angela Gover et al, 'Anti-Asian Hate Crime During the COVID-19 Pandemic: Exploring the Reproduction of Inequality' (2020) 45 *American Journal of Criminal Justice* 647; Karma Chávez, *The Borders of AIDS: Race, Quarantine, and Resistance* (Seasttle, WA, University of Washington Press, 2021); Barbara Pfeffer Billauer, 'Politicization and Pariah-Tization of Epidemics – A Recipe for Legal and Policy Disaster: Comparing the 1892 Cholera Epidemic with the Handling of COVID-19' (2024) 24 *Journal of Law in Society* 25.

but have discriminated against racial groups in practice.[71] Consider, for instance, the measures taken against leprosy on the west coast of Canada in the late 1880s and early 1900s, discussed by Renisa Mawani, who has written that the disease was 'so profoundly "raced" that it came to be known in popular and medical discourse as a "Chinese disease"'; the results were 'legally mandated and coercive systems of containment targeting those "unfit" and "undesirable" [Chinese] immigrants thought to be infected'.[72] Another example is the racialised discourse of nineteenth- and twentieth-century colonial officials in South Africa and their mobilisation of 'health' to justify the planning and development of racially segregated urban settlements resulting in the creation of suburban white neighbourhoods and African townships.[73]

Laws may be met by popular hesitancy or pushbacks. The reasons include popular misapprehensions about the causes of disease and reasons for treatments, mistrust of medical professionals, reluctance to pay for new measures, dissatisfaction with incompetent officials and resentment caused by heavy-handed interference in citizens' private lives.[74] For instance, popular rioting during the British cholera epidemic of 1831–32 was variously triggered by fears that doctors

[71] Howard Markel, '"Knocking out the Cholera": Cholera, Class, and Quarantines in New York City, 1892' (1995) 69 *Bulletin of the History of Medicine* 420 and sources cited at 424, fn 7; Bashford (2004) (n 5); Coker and Ingram (n 20); Bivins (n 26) ch 1; Kavita Sivaramakrishnan, 'Yellow Fever, Quarantine and the Jet Age in India: Extremely Far, Incredibly Close' in Bashford (2016) (n 60); John Chircop, 'Lazarettos as Border Filters: Expurgating Bodies, Commodities and Ideas, 1800–1870s' in Sevasti Trubeta et al (eds), *Medicalising Borders: Selection, Containment and Quarantine since 1800* (Manchester, Manchester University Press, 2021).

[72] Renisa Mawani, '"The Island of the Unclean": Race, Colonialism, and "Chinese Leprosy" in British Columbia, 1891–1924' [2003](1) *Law, Social Justice, and Development Journal* <http://www2.warwick.ac.uk/fac/soc/law/elj/lgd/2003_1/mawani/> last accessed 24 July 2025; for racialised measures against bubonic plague in San Francisco and smallpox in western Canada in the same period, see respectively Charles McClain, 'Of Medicine, Race, and American Law: The Bubonic Plague Outbreak of 1900' (1988) 13 *Law & Social Inquiry* 447; Kristin Burnett, 'Race, Disease, and Public Violence: Smallpox and the (Un)Making of Calgary's Chinatown, 1892' (2012) 25 *Social History of Medicine* 362; and for racialised measures against leprosy elsewhere see Zachary Gussow, *Leprosy, Racism, and Public Health: Social Policy in Chronic Disease Control* (Boulder, CO, Westview Press, 1989); Alison Bashford and Maria Nugent, 'Leprosy and the Management of Race, Sexuality, and Nation in Tropical Australia' in Alison Bashford and Claire Hooker (eds), *Contagion: Historical and Cultural Studies* (London, Routledge, 2001); Stephen Snelders, *Leprosy and Colonialism: Suriname Under Dutch Rule, 1750–1950* (Manchester, Manchester University Press, 2017).

[73] Swanson (n 57); Susan Parnell, 'Creating Racial Privilege: The Origins of South African Public Health and Town Planning Legislation' (1993) 19 *Journal of Southern African Studies* 471; Paul Maylam, 'Explaining the Apartheid City: 20 Years of South African Urban Historiography' (1995) 21 *Journal of Southern African Studies* 19; George Pavlich, 'Plaguing Segregations: Paradigms of Rule at the Cape of Good Hope' (2023) 38 *Canadian Journal of Law and Society* 335. *cf* Liora Bigon, 'A History of Urban Planning and Infectious Diseases: Colonial Senegal in the Early Twentieth Century' [2012] *Urban Studies Research*, available at https://onlinelibrary.wiley.com/doi/10.1155/2012/589758; Regina Campinho, 'Hoping for Catastrophe: Epidemic Threat and Political Ambition in Colonial Macao's Early Attempts at Urban Sanitation, 1885–1900' (2019) 30 *Traditional Dwellings and Settlements Review* 33.

[74] Roy McLeod, 'Law, Medicine and Public Opinion: The Resistance to Compulsory Health Legislation, 1870–1907' [1967] *Public Law* 107 and 189; Margaret Hamilton, 'Opposition to the Contagious Diseases Acts, 1864–1886' (1978) 10 *Albion* 14; Graham Mooney, 'Public Health Versus Private Practice: The Contested Development of Compulsory Infectious Disease Notification in Late Nineteenth-Century Britain' (1999) 73 *Bulletin of the History of Medicine* 238.

were engaged in Malthusian plots to reduce the size of the population, or that doctors were scheming to acquire bodies for anatomical dissection, or by resentment that Irish wakes were banned as the authorities sought to bury the bodies of cholera victims quickly.[75] During the Hong Kong plague epidemic in 1894, volunteers were sent to find the corpses of victims and carry them away to special cemeteries in violation of Chinese religious beliefs and practices, prompting families to conceal the bodies of their dead relatives.[76] Resistance of this kind was attributed by colonial officials to 'native prejudice', though the label 'conscientious objection' might have been used in their home countries – a point well made by Jack Jin Gary Lee and Lynette Chua in their account of resistance to smallpox vaccination in the Straits Settlements in the late 1800s and early 1900s.[77]

Nineteenth-century British sanitary inspectors met with non-cooperation, escalating to hostility and abuse; temporary fever hospitals built in the same period were torn down by angry and fearful crowds; both were challenged in the courts by businessmen and property-owners who sought to protect their economic interests or private enjoyment of their property.[78] Vaccination programmes have often met with popular resistance during their history, although they have also enjoyed popular endorsement.[79] Mask-wearing laws were widely flouted in Europe, North America and Australia during the 1918–19 influenza and COVID-19 pandemics,[80]

[75] Various chapters in Michael Holland et al (eds), *Cholera and Conflict: 19th Century Cholera in Britain and its Social Consequences* (Leeds, [Thakray] Medical Museum Publishing, 2009).

[76] Robert Peckham, 'Spaces of Quarantine in Colonial Hong Kong' in Bashford (2016) (n 60). Disruption of traditional burial practices by regulatory measures is also discussed in Vanessa Harding, 'Burial of the Plague Dead in Early Modern London' in Justin Champion (ed), *Epidemic Disease in London* (London, Centre for Metropolitan History, 1993); Heather Conway, 'Death Rites Disrupted: Coronavirus, "Lockdown" Laws and the Altered Social Ritual of the Funeral' (2023) 74 *Northern Ireland Legal Quarterly* 211; Natalie Banta Lynner, 'Death in a Pandemic: Funeral Practices and Industry Disruption' (2023) 70 *UCLA Law Review* 154.

[77] Jack Jin Gary Lee and Lynette Chua, 'Smallpox Vaccination and the Limits of Governing through Contagion in the Straits Settlements, 1868–1926' (2023) 45 *Law and Policy* 331. Compare the 'conscience clauses' in the British Vaccination Acts 1898 and 1907, discussed in Nadja Durbach, 'Class, Gender, and the Conscientious Objector to Vaccination, 1898–1907' (2002) 41 *Journal of British Studies* 58.

[78] Tom Crook, 'Sanitary Inspection and the Public Sphere in Late Victorian and Edwardian Britain: A Case Study in Liberal Governance' (2007) 32 *Social History* 369; Matthew Newsom Kerr, 'Sites of Complaint and Complaining: Fever and Smallpox Hospitals in Late Victorian London' in Jonathan Reinarz and Rebecca Wynter (eds), *Complaints, Controversies and Grievances in Medicine: Historical and Social Science Perspectives* (London, Routledge, 2015); Samuel Cohn, Jr, *Epidemics: Hate and Compassion from the Plague of Athens to AIDS* (Oxford, Oxford University Press, 2018) ch 13.

[79] Dorothy Porter and Roy Porter, 'The Politics of Prevention: Anti-vaccinationism and Public Health in Nineteenth-century England' (1988) 32 *Medical History* 231; Nadja Durbach, '"They Might as Well Brand Us": Working-Class Resistance to Compulsory Vaccination in Victorian England' (2000) 13 *Social History of Medicine* 45; Williamson (n 27); Brunton (n 27); Rebekah McWhirter, *'Lymph or Liberty': Responses to Smallpox Vaccination in the Eastern Australian Colonies* (University of Tasmania PhD thesis, 2008), available at https://figshare.utas.edu.au/articles/thesis/Lymph_or_Liberty_Responses_to_Smallpox_Vaccination_in_the_Eastern_Australian_Colonies/23210159/1; Michael Willrich, *Pox: An American History* (New York, NY, Penguin, 2011); Werner Troesken, *The Pox of Liberty: How the Constitution Left Americans Rich, Free, and Prone to Infection* (Chicago, IL, University of Chicago Press, 2015).

[80] Janice Dickin McGinnis, 'The Impact of Epidemic Influenza: Canada, 1918–1919' (1977) 12 *Historical Papers / Communications Historiques* 120, 126; Brian Dolan, 'Unmasking History: Who

although in contrast mask-wearing has historically been embraced in East Asian countries, a disparity that is often attributed to different cultural and social attitudes towards the practice.[81] Circulation of health misinformation has contributed to public panics and has significantly undermined vaccination (and other public health) programmes, as has recently been the case with the MMR (measles, mumps and rubella) vaccine in countries including Britain, Italy and the US.[82] Publication of imaginary conspiracy theories about the causes of infection and governmental responses can be particularly damaging during epidemics, when fear, anxiety and paranoia can quickly proliferate,[83] rendering people vulnerable to misinformation; and for the same reasons, eruptions of quackery have also occurred, as during the influenza pandemics of 1889–92 and 1918–20, not to mention the recent COVID-19 pandemic.[84] Counter-measures have included the dissemination of well evidenced public health information[85] and the passing of laws that prohibit the publication of health misinformation, although these have encountered definitional problems as well as freedom of expression and ethical constraints.[86]

Was Behind the Anti-Mask League Protests During the 1918 Influenza Epidemic in San Francisco?' (*Perspectives in Medical Humanities*, UC Medical Humanities Consortium, 19 May 2020), available at https://escholarship.org/uc/item/5q91q53r; Leo Kahane, 'Politicizing the Mask: Political, Economic and Demographic Factors Affecting Mask Wearing Behavior in the USA' (2021) 47 *Eastern Economic Journal* 163; Garus-Pakowska and Pakowski (n 24).

[81] Mitsutoshi Horii, 'Why Do the Japanese Wear Masks? A Short Historical Review' (2014) 14 *Electronic Journal of Contemporary Japanese Studies*, available at www.japanesestudies.org.uk/ejcjs/vol14/iss2/horii.html; Christos Lynteris, 'Plague Masks: The Visual Emergence of Anti-Epidemic Personal Protection Equipment' (2018) 37 *Medical Anthropology* 442; Yong Yang et al, 'Coronavirus Disease 2019 Pandemic: What Does Wearing Masks Mean?' (2020) 133 *Chinese Medical Journal* 2749; Heewon Kim and Hyungsub Choi, 'COVID-19 and the Reenactment of Mass Masking in South Korea' (2021) 43 *History and Philosophy of the Life Sciences*, available at https://link.springer.com/article/10.1007/s40656-021-00400-y.

[82] Millward (n 27) ch 5; Johnathan Bowes, 'Measles, Misinformation, and Risk: Personal Belief Exemptions and the MMR Vaccine' (2016) 3 *Journal of Law and the Biosciences* 718; Linda Fentiman, *Blaming Mothers: American Law and the Risks to Children's Health* (New York, NY, NYU Press, 2017) ch 9; Marco Rizzi and Katie Atwell, 'Giving Bad Science the Stamp of Approval: Policy and Legal Consequences of a Vaccine Scare in Italy' (2024) 45 *Public Health Reviews*, available at www.ssph-journal.org/journals/public-health-reviews/articles/10.3389/phrs.2024.1606756/full. A related phenomenon is the fear-inducing representation of 'new' infectious disease threats in global news and entertainment media: Nichola King, 'Mediating Panic: The Iconography of "New" Infectious Threats, 1936–2009' in Robert Peckham (ed), *Empires of Panic: Epidemics and Colonial Anxieties* (Hong Kong, Hong Kong University Press, 2015).

[83] Philip Strong, 'Epidemic Psychology: A Model' (1990) 12 *Sociology of Health and Illness* 249. The severity of disease outbreaks and the magnitude of the panicked reactions they trigger are not always commensurate: David Arnold, 'Disease, Rumor, and Panic in India's Plague and Influenza Epidemics, 1896–1919' in Robert Peckham (ed), *Empires of Panic: Epidemics and Colonial Anxieties* (Hong Kong, Hong Kong University Press, 2015).

[84] Ian Freckelton, 'COVID-19: Fear, Quackery, False Representations and the Law' (2020) 72 *International Journal of Law and Psychiatry*, available at www.sciencedirect.com/science/article/pii/S0160252720300704.

[85] *cf* Molly Walker Wilson, 'Effective Public Health Communication in a Post-COVID-19 America: Lessons from Behavioral Science' (2024) 28 *Lewis & Clark Law Review* 109.

[86] Melinda Mills and Jonas Sivelä, 'Should Spreading Anti-vaccine Misinformation Be Criminalised?' (2021) 17 *British Medical Journal* fn 272; João Marecos et al, 'Health Misinformation and Freedom of Expression: Considerations for Policymakers' (2023) 18 *Health Economics, Policy and Law* 204.

Levels of compliance with government rules can increase as a result of panic, anxiety, and sadness flowing from the actual and perceived threat of epidemics, but they can also decrease as a result of anger, loneliness, and impatience.[87] Public panics can also lead to social unrest,[88] and to vigilantism and violence by one social group against another. For instance, outbreaks of yellow fever in nineteenth-century America led citizens and militias in uninfected areas to take unnecessary and overreaching 'shotgun quarantine' measures. These were given official imprimatur by state and town governments and, most unusually in the constitutional history of the US, this prompted calls from state politicians for Congressional intervention. However, the ensuing political and legal controversy faded when effective medical treatment measures were discovered and implemented.[89]

D. Law, Government and Politics

In recent times, the question whether autocratic or democratic states have a better track record in responding to epidemics has been brought into focus by comparisons between the Chinese Government's responses to COVID-19 and those of democratic states.[90] Some political theorists have argued that old democracies are likelier than new democracies and authoritarian regimes to have the strong institutions needed to make public policy and implement it into law effectively while maintaining safeguards for civil liberties;[91] and that although autocratic states have stronger powers to impose coercive measures they are hobbled by their lack of effective systems through which to receive and send information.[92] However, the unsatisfactory quality of broadly but vaguely drafted emergency powers used by

[87] Danqi Guo et al, 'Emotions, Crisis, and Institutions: Explaining Compliance with COVID-19 Regulations' (2024) 18 *Regulation and Governance* 177.

[88] Rebecca Cordell et al, 'Disease and Dissent: Epidemics as a Catalyst for Social Unrest' (2023) 3 *Global Studies Quarterly* 1, though noting that 'perceived opportunities for unrest are influenced by the scale and scope of the disease outbreak, and particularly lethal disease outbreaks may … offset the incentives for collective mobilization'.

[89] Polly Price, 'Epidemics, Outsiders, and Local Protection: Federalism Theater in the Era of the Shotgun Quarantine' (2016) 19 *University of Pennsylvania Journal of Constitutional Law* 369. *cf* Tiarne Barratt and Alison Bashford, 'Lines of Hygiene: Pandemic Border Control in Australia, 1919' (2022) 53 *Australian Historical Studies* 284.

[90] See, eg, Yexin Mao, 'Political Institutions, State Capacity, and Crisis Management: A Comparison of China and South Korea' (2021) 42 *International Political Science Review* 316; Shupeng Lyu et al, 'One Pandemic, Two Solutions: Comparing the US-China Response and Health Priorities to COVID-19 from the Perspective of "Two Types of Control"' (2023) 11 *Healthcare* 1848.

[91] John Gerring et al, 'Democracy and Human Development' (2012) 74 *Journal of Politics* 1. *cf* Mihail Chiru, 'The Resilience of Parliamentary Oversight during the COVID-19 Pandemic' (2024) 47 *West European Politics* 408, 410: '[t]he scholarship analysing the fate of parliaments during the pandemic seems to concur that parliaments were marginalized more and lost power at the expense of governments in European countries in which democracy was less consolidated'.

[92] Matthew Kavanagh, 'Authoritarianism, Outbreaks, and Information Politics' (2020) 5 *Lancet Public Health* e135. See also Jacques Delisle and Shen Kui, 'Lessons from China's Response to COVID-19: Shortcomings, Successes, and Prospects for Reform in China's Regulatory State' (2020) 16 *University of Pennsylvania Asian Law Review* 66.

democracies during the COVID-19 pandemic,[93] and the weak oversight of delegated legislation used to enact control measures,[94] suggest that such claims should not be taken at face value. Additionally, as Kunihiko Yoshida has argued, the key elements that have posed challenges in controlling COVID-19 have included the nature of a country's social structure, ie whether its society was individualistic or communally and collectively oriented, a distinction that cuts across political differences, as some societies of the latter type support democratic governments (such as Japan and South Korea) while others are ruled by dictatorships (such as Cambodia and China).[95]

Few epidemiological studies have been undertaken to test such arguments empirically. Collection of data for comparative purposes is fraught with difficulties[96] and another reason, in JP Ruger's words,

> must certainly stem from the complexity of the health-politics nexus and the difficulty of identifying independent and interactive influences in both directions. The relationship can be defined in many ways, ranging from the study of political systems (e.g. democratic or authoritarian, legislative and executive governance, proportional or majoritarian electoral systems, constitutional structure); culture (e.g. political values); institutions (e.g. centralized or fragmented, presidential or parliamentary, responsiveness to citizenry, political parties); state capacity (technical and administrative capacity, level of corruption); and philosophy, to more nuts-and-bolts political process factors, such as personal politics (e.g. political leadership, powerful personalities, presidential tactics), political strategy and interest group representation (e.g. its strength or weakness in a political system).[97]

[93] Katie Lines, *18 Months of COVID-19 Legislation in England: A Rule of Law Analysis* (London, Bingham Centre for the Rule of Law, 2021); House of Lords Select Committee on the Constitution, *COVID-19 and the Use and Scrutiny of Emergency Powers, 3rd Report of Session 2021–22* (HL Paper 15, 2021); Janet McLean, *NZLC SP23: The Legal Framework for Emergencies in Aotearoa New Zealand* (Wellington, Te Aka Matua o te Ture / New Zealand Law Commission, 2022).

[94] Pritan Dey and Julian Murphy, 'Pandemic Parliamentary Oversight of Delegated Legislation: Comparing the Performance of Westminster Systems' (2021) 15 *ICL Journal* 465; Daniella Lock et al, 'Delegated Legislation in the Pandemic: Further Limits of a Constitutional Bargain Revealed' (2023) 43 *Legal Studies* 695. On the use of delegated legislation generally, see Michael Taggart, 'From "Parliamentary Powers" to Privatization: The Chequered History of Delegated Legislation in the Twentieth Century' (2005) 55 *University of Toronto Law Journal* 575; Jeff King, 'The Province of Delegated Legislation' in Elizabeth Fisher et al (eds), *The Foundations and Future of Public Law; Essays in Honour of Paul Craig* (Oxford, Oxford University Press, 2020).

[95] Yoshida (n 8) 60–61. *cf* Lesley Jacobs, 'Rights and Quarantine During the SARS Global Health Crisis: Differentiated Legal Consciousness in Hong Kong, Shanghai, and Toronto' (2007) 41 *Law & Society Review* 511: public health officials in Toronto were less likely than those in Hong Kong and Shanghai to favour individual rights over community health security when formulating quarantine laws during the SARS epidemic.

[96] On the 'politics of pandemic data' relating to COVID-19 deaths, see Scott Greer et al, 'Introduction: Explaining Pandemic Response' in Scott Greer et al (eds), *Coronavirus Politics: The Comparative Politics and Policy of COVID-19* (Ann Arbor, MI, University of Michigan Press, 2021) 6–8.

[97] JP Ruger, 'Democracy and Health' (2005) 98 *QJM: An International Journal of Medicine* 299, 299. See too Holly Jarman, 'State Responses to the COVID-19 Pandemic: Governance, Surveillance, Coercion, and Social Policy' in Greer et al (n 96). But *cf* Alvaro Franco et al, 'Effect of Democracy on Health: Ecological Study' (2004) 329 *British Medical Journal* 1421; and other contributions to this *British Medical Journal* issue.

In democratic states, laws which constrain individual freedoms for the common good are always controversial and coercive laws responding to infectious disease are no exception.[98] Lawmakers, and the public whom they serve, have struggled with the question of whether such laws are 'worth it', and in Alison Bashford's words, public health has long been

> a significant domain for the working out of different understandings of the responsibilities and rights of government, of subjects and citizens, and indeed (perhaps especially) of non-subjects and non-citizens. Compulsory vaccination and compulsory isolation raised questions about the legitimacy of government forcing citizens and subjects to submit to either, or both.[99]

A further consideration is that lawmakers around the world, whether democratic or not, now commonly defer to the technical expertise of medical scientists and public health administrators to a greater degree than in the past.[100] No doubt this can largely be attributed to the nineteenth- and twentieth-century professionalisation of medicine, enhanced kudos of doctors generated by advances in medical science and proliferation of 'scientific' language and rhetoric,[101] although on occasion political calculations may also have played a part.[102] One result has been that, for better or for worse,[103] the scientific wisdom of the day has become embedded

[98] Felice Batlan, 'Law in the Time of Cholera: Disease, State Power and Quarantines Past and Future' (2007) 80 *Temple Law Review* 53; Ashlee Beazley, 'Contagion, Containment, Consent: Infectious Disease Pandemics and the Ethics, Rights, and Legality of State-Enforced Vaccination' (2020) 7 *Journal of Law and the Biosciences* 1; Keith Ewing, 'Covid-19: Government by Decree' (2020) 31 *King's Law Journal* 1; Yee-Fui Ng and Stephen Gray, 'Wars, Pandemics and Emergencies: What Can History Tell Us about Executive Power and Surveillance in Times of Crisis?' (2021) 44 *University of New South Wales Law Journal* 227.

[99] Bashford (2004) (n 5) 51. For different perspectives on this general theme, see also Christine Crudo Blackburn, '"Greater Good" versus Civil Liberties in the United States: Tuberculosis and Seattle's Firland Sanatorium' (2017) 38 *Journal of Public Health Policy* 482; Michael Cederblom, 'Towards Action and in Pursuit of Scofflaws: Shifting the Framework of Pandemic Public Health Punishment from Theory to Pragmatism' (2022) 9 *Lincoln Memorial University Law Review* 80; Tom Crook, 'Afterword: From Asiatic Cholera to COVID-19 – The Many Publics of Modern Public Health' in Alex Mold et al (eds), *Publics and Their Health: Historical Problems and Perspectives* (Manchester, Manchester University Press, 2023).

[100] But not always: compare this assessment of the Trump administration's failure to form and implement effective measures to tackle the COVID-19 epidemic in the US: 'government [cannot] function properly [in response to public health emergencies] when past and present political interventions have rendered its scientific experts fearful, timid, politicized, demoralized, and ineffectual': Barry Sullivan, 'Lessons of the Plague Years' (2022) 54 *Loyola University of Chicago Law Journal* 15, 42.

[101] For an introductory account of this topic, see Keir Waddington, *An Introduction to the Social History of Medicine* (Palgrave Macmillan, Basingstoke, 2011) ch 3.

[102] For an argument that it suits populists to rely on technocratic, and particularly scientific, expertise because these can be ued to depoliticise issues and at least partially shield them from direct political accountability, see Raphaël Girard, 'Accountability, Populism and Expertise: The UK Government's Response to COVID-19' [2021] *Public Law* 707.

[103] Tomkins (n 41); *UK Covid-19 Inquiry Module 1: The Resilience and Preparedness of the United Kingdom – A Report by The Rt Hon the Baroness Hallett DBE Chair of the UK Covid-19 Inquiry* (HC 18, 2024) para 6.52, finding that 'The scientific advice received by the UK government … was not subject to sufficient external challenge by either ministers or officials.'

in policymaking, and this has affected the way in which policy is made, because, in Tsung-Ling Lee's words:

> The rise of technocracy reflects a utilitarian calculus that seeks to preserve the greater good. ... [This] moves the public discourse away from an individualist framing of rights and carves out space for solidarity through institutionalizing processes that shape a shared identity. ... [From] a human rights perspective, a technocratic approach as a pandemic response is not necessarily a bad thing; it might be desirable insofar as protecting the right to life and health is concerned. ... [But] a technocratic government tends to perceive the population as monolithic ... [and] as a technocratic approach prioritizes the right to life and health above other human rights, it is underpinned by a heavy utilitarian undertone. Viewing the pandemic through a utilitarian lens neglects the fact that the pandemic has a disparate impact on different population groups ...[104]

Other concerns besides public health have also influenced the thinking of policymakers, including the likely impact of measures on a state's economy and its relations with other states. So Tim Carter has written of nineteenth- and twentieth-century British thinking about quarantine that it was seen to be 'both very disruptive to trade and alarming to the crew and passengers';[105] he also notes the argument that 'quarantine only remained on the statute book until 1896 to enable Britain to be in a position to retaliate against any other countries that imposed it in ways that adversely affected British trading interests'.[106]

Another example discussed by Daniel Flecknoe is the unwillingness of American military leaders in the World War I 'to prioritize public health over war-winning objectives'; despite the known benefits of isolating influenza victims, therefore, '[p]atriotic parades and other ceremonial military-civilian gatherings went ahead' and 'troop ships continued to set sail'.[107]

The role played in policy formation by interest groups with their own agendas can also be significant, their impact varying according to whether they succeed in capturing the ear of government. Strong groups determined to maintain the status quo can slow down the introduction of new measures for long periods. For example, it seems this is why a nationwide cattle slaughter campaign was not put in place in Britain until the 1950s, although it had been widely accepted since at

[104] Tsung-Ling Lee, 'The Rise of Technocracy and the COVID-19 Pandemic in Taiwan: Courts, Human Rights, and the Protection of Vulnerable Populations' (2021) 22 *German Law Journal* 1115, 1116–17.

[105] Tim Carter, *Merchant Seamen's Health, 1860–1960: Medicine, Technology, Shipowners and the State in Britain* (Woodbridge, Boydell Press, 2014) 70.

[106] ibid 79. Similar examples are discussed in Mark Harrison, 'The Great Shift: Cholera Theory and Sanitary Policy in British India, 1867–1879' in Biswamoy Pati and Mark Harrison (eds), *Society, Medicine and Politics in Colonial India* (London, Routledge, 2018); Julia Mansfield, 'Quarantine Diplomacy: Public Health and Transatlantic Commerce during the Yellow Fever Pandemic of 1793–1805' in Jacob Steere-Williams and Blake Scott (eds), *Port Cities of the Atlantic World: Sea-Facing Histories of the US South* (Columbia, SC, University of South Carolina Press, 2023).

[107] Daniel Flecknoe, 'Un-remembered but Unforgettable: The "Spanish Flu" Pandemic' in van Bergen and Vermetten (n 44) 222–23.

least the early 1930s that 40 per cent of the milking herd was infected with bovine tuberculosis.[108]

When decisions have been made to implement coercive laws, the questions arise whether policymakers have always put the same considerations in the balance and weighed them off in the same way; and how their decisions, and the implementation of these decisions through law, have affected social attitudes regarding the costs and benefits of individualism and collectivism, civil liberties and state power.[109] Ideas about the use of laws constraining individual freedoms have tended to align with contemporary ideas about the role to be played by the state in social welfare provision. For example, Gareth Millward has written of the introduction of the poliomyelitis vaccine programme in the UK that members of the public themselves demanded that the state should make immunisation services available to all, and that the programme 'was created and expanded not entirely due to administrative or epidemiological measurement, but on what various branches of government believed would be popular with the wider public'.[110] More complicatedly, when it came to the vaccine for pertussis (whooping cough) in the 1970s, popular pushback against the vaccine was 'rooted in anxieties about the role of the welfare state' and there was much discussion of 'the provision of financial compensation to the victims of vaccine damage'.[111] Thus citizens 'demanded that the state should provide protections [against the disease], but also that citizens should be protected against state actions'.[112]

Social and political perceptions of these issues have differed across time and place. Michael Zeheter has pointed out significant differences of approach

[108] Peter Atkins, 'Lobbying and Resistance with Regard to Policy on Bovine Tuberculosis in Britain, 1900–1939: An Inside/Outside Model' in Condrau and Worboys (n 17). Bovine TB remains a significant animal health problem in Britain where efforts to combat and eliminate the disease are affected by a complex set of ecological, socio-economic and socio-cultural factors: Philip Robinson, 'Framing Bovine Tuberculosis: A "Political Ecology of Health" Approach to Circulation of Knowledge(s) about Animal Disease Control' (2017) 83 *Geographical Journal* 285; on this topic see also Patrick Bishop, 'Badgers, Bovine Tuberculosis and the Role of Science in the Formulation of Welsh Environmental and Agricultural Policy' in Patrick Bishop and Mark Stallworthy (eds), *Environmental Law and Policy in Wales: Responding to Local and Global Challenges* (Cardiff, University of Wales Press, 2013).

[109] Jim Jose and Kasey McLoughlin, 'John Stuart Mill and the Contagious Diseases Acts: Whose Law? Whose Liberty? Whose Greater Good?' (2016) 34 *Law and History Review* 249; Knight (n 54).

[110] Millward (n 27) 115–16.

[111] ibid 151.

[112] ibid 150. See also Wendy Parmet, 'Pandemics, Populism and the Role of Law in the H1N1 Vaccine Campaign' (2010) 4 *Saint Louis University Journal of Health Law & Policy* 113: popular distrust of vaccination is exacerbated by mandatory vaccine laws that exclude or limit state and manufacturer liability. On modern compensation schemes for vaccine injury, see Richard Goldberg, 'Vaccine Damage Schemes in the US and UK Reappraised: Making Them Fit for Purpose in the Light of Covid-19' (2022) 42 *Legal Studies* 576; Duncan Fairgrieve et al, 'Comparing No-Fault Compensation Systems for Vaccine Injury' (2023) 31 *Tulane Journal of International and Comparative Law* 75. See also John Winter et al, 'Toward a Global Solution on Vaccine Liability and Compensation' (2019) 74 *Food and Drug Law Journal* 1. On the question of whether and, if so, on what basis compensation should be payable for loss suffered by those subject to compulsory isolation orders, see Margaret Battin et al, 'Compensation and the Victims of Constraint' in Margaret Battin et al, *The Patient as Victim and Vector: Ethics and Infectious Disease* (Oxford, Oxford University Press, 2009).

towards the control of cholera in nineteenth-century Quebec City and Madras (Chennai): in the former, the colonial administration emulated British precedent and sought to develop similar institutions that allowed authorities to impose quarantines and make sanitary improvements; in the latter, the provincial government sought to exploit the colony for profit and was reluctant to commit its resources to measures against cholera that would alienate the city's inhabitants, something it began to do only after the Indian rebellion in 1857 when concern rose in Britain over the health of its troops in India, and a mission of sanitary improvement was begun.[113]

Administrative initiatives have a tendency towards mission creep and increase of state power and the escalation of epidemics from local to national scale can result in centralising efforts to shift power from local to national administrations. Sometimes these efforts succeed, sometimes not. Such fights are often part of a bigger history of power struggles between federal and state governments. Jerrold Michael has written, for example, that in late nineteenth-century America, 'where the growing cities, ports, and rapidly spreading poverty provided fertile grounds for mass outbreaks of cholera, typhoid, yellow fever, whooping cough, tuberculosis' and other diseases, arguments about public health policies were subsumed within wider debates about the roles played by local authorities and their federal counterparts, and tensions between 'regional and state interests and national goals'.[114] In Australia, too, attempts were made by the Commonwealth Government after the influenza pandemic of 1918–19 to consolidate its powers at the expense of state governments when dealing with health emergencies.[115]

The outcome of such power struggles is often inconclusive: rulemaking authority becomes dispersed, resulting in polycentric decision-making and layered systems of rules which may lack consistency and may be difficult for state officials and citizens to understand and follow. During COVID-19, competing claims to authority in the United States and Canada arose in relation to many issues, including border closures, imposition of curfews, closure of schools and parks, banning of large public gatherings and so on. Michael da Silva has observed that multiple claims for authority to decide such questions create a 'puzzle': how should such competitions be resolved? He notes that debates about lawmaking authority in the emergency conditions created by epidemics have tended to reflect existing debates, suggesting that such conditions do not generate unique concerns about the allocation of power, albeit that they 'provide extreme examples of the strengths and weaknesses of different allocation options and the cost of different tradeoffs

[113] Michael Zeheter, *Epidemics, Empire, and Environments: Cholera in Madras and Quebec City, 1818–1910* (Pittsburg, PA, University of Pittsburgh Press, 2015).

[114] Jerrold Michael, 'The National Board of Health: 1879–1883' (2011) 126 *Public Health Reports* 123, 123. This is also a theme of Polly Price, *Plagues in the Nation: How Epidemics Shaped America* (Boston, MA, Beacon Press, 2022).

[115] Mark Finnane, 'Governing in a Pandemic: Law and Government in Australia, 1919' (2022) 53 *Australian Historical Studies* 266.

between options'.[116] Where authority should be allocated therefore turns on the balance which should be struck between familiar principles: for example, 'interests in coordination can support federal control and interests in flexibility can support more local control'.[117]

Laws introduced as a response to epidemics (and other social crises) are often framed in an open-ended way (since no one knows how long the crisis will last) and often stay in place after the need for them has passed. A 1999 study of communicable disease statutes in American states found that many were between 40 and 100 years old and although some remained relevant and fit for purpose, many others were marked by redundancy and ambiguity. The authors observed that:

> … old public health statutes that have not been substantially altered since their enactment are often outmoded in ways that reduce both their efficacy and their conformity with modern standards. These laws often do not reflect contemporary scientific understandings of disease, current treatments of choice, or constitutional limits on states' authority to restrict individual liberties. Laws enacted with different diseases in mind, at very different moments in time, may deploy different and inconsistent legal or medical approaches to similar disease control problems. Conversely, older statutes, codifying superannuated methods, may be used by opponents of current public health policies to support a return to 'traditional' policies that many present officials regard as inappropriate.[118]

Similarly, a 2010 study found that 202 laws and decrees relating to communicable disease had been passed in Greece since 1833. Many had fallen into disuse, but had remained in force as they had never been revoked; some had been rendered worse than useless by medical advances and epidemiologic changes, eg a rule that public employees should submit to annual radiography screening for the purposes of tuberculosis control.[119]

[116] Michael da Silva, 'COVID-19 and Health-Related Authority Allocation Puzzles' (2021) 30 *Cambridge Quarterly of Health Care Ethics* 25, 31.

[117] ibid 30. *cf* Martin Gorsky et al, 'Public Health and English Local Government: Historical Perspectives on the Impact of "Returning Home"' (2014) 36 *Journal of Public Health* 546 (English public health decision-making was taken by local government bodies, then transferred to central government in 1974, then partly returned to local government in 2012); Keir Waddington, 'Resistance and Prevention: Rural Local Government and the Fight against Tuberculosis' (2024) 35 *Modern British History* 180 (resistance of early 20th century Welsh county and rural district councils to centralising public health reform); Keir Waddington, '"In Constant Fear of Some Dire Epidemic Breaking Out": Rural Responses to Infectious and Epidemic Disease, 1870-1920' (2024) *Rural History* 211 (measures taken by rural sanitary authorities in late 19th century and early 20th century Wales).

[118] Lawrence Gostin et al, 'The Law and the Public's Health: A Study of Infectious Disease Law in the United States' (1999) 99 *Columbia Law Review* 59, 106. Similar conclusions are drawn in a contemporaneous study of UK legislation: Stephen Monaghan, *The State of Communicable Disease Law* (London, Nuffield Trusts, 2002). And *cf* HC 18 (n 103) para 2.14: at the time of the COVID-19 pandemic, the Civil Contingencies Act 2004 and associated regulations and guidance that set out the framework for civil protection in a nationwide emergency was widely acknowledged by public health specialists and practitioners as being outdated and did not relate to contemporary governmental structures, roles and responsibilities.

[119] Sophia Hatzianastasiou et al, 'Legal Aspects of Public Health: How Law Frames Communicable Disease Control in Greece' (2011) 32 *Journal of Public Health Policy* 445.

When crises are over, governments are always under pressure to move on to the next set of problems, but they should pay more attention to abrogating laws whose time has passed. Population-wide legal restrictions on freedom of association and movement tend to be rolled back quickly as they are socially and economically damaging and unsustainable for long periods, but coercive measures aimed at individuals can remain in place for much longer, with negative consequences for the rights and freedoms of citizens.[120] One reason may be that the question whether an epidemic is 'over' is itself commonly determined by considerations of political expediency rather than by reference to medical understandings of disease. So Regina Jefferies and her co-authors have written that:

> Pandemic episodes are typically considered 'over', not when disease is eradicated but when the biological and socio-economic trajectories of disease conceptually diverge. When disease becomes endemic, social restrictions are eased and the urgency and immediacy of the pandemic threat dissipates, making it possible to return to life as normal.[121] For example, the HIV/AIDS pandemic is considered conceptually 'over', the immediate threat historically consigned to the 1980s, while the now endemic disease continues to disproportionality ravage sub-Saharan Africa and geographically 'Other' regions of the world.[122] This illusion of endemic disease as pandemic ending creates the false perception of disease as something that does indeed end and not only disguises the true, never-ending, ongoing nature of biological disease but also prioritizes Western experiences of disease.[123] This regrettably erases the experiences of those who continue to experience widespread suffering long after policymakers have decided that the immediate threat has passed[124] and may leave in place legal options once considered unthinkable or disproportionate as a line of first response.[125]

[120] Ng and Gray (n 98) 261. See also Nathan Goodman et al, 'Infectious Diseases and Government Growth' (2021) 25 *Independent Review* 537.

[121] Citing Erica Charters and Kristin Heitman, 'How Epidemics End' (2021) 63 *Centaurus* 210.

[122] Citing Jeremy Greene and Dora Vargha, 'Ends of Epidemics' in Francis Gavin and Hal Brands (eds), *COVID-19 and World Order: The Future of Conflict, Competition, and Cooperation* (Baltimore, MD, Johns Hopkins University Press, 2020).

[123] Citing Wenzel Geissler and Ruth Prince, 'Layers of Epidemy: Present Pasts during the First Weeks of COVID-19 in Western Kenya' (2020) 62 *Centaurus* 248.

[124] Citing Patricia Kingori and Catherine McGowan, 'After the End of Ebola' (*Somatosphere*, 19 August 2016), available at https://somatosphere.com/2016/after-the-end-of-ebola.html/.

[125] Regina Jefferies et al, 'Regulating Movement in Pandemic Times' (2023) 20 *Journal of Bioethical Inquiry* 633, 638.

PART II

Direct Regulatory Responses to Infectious Disease

2

Central and Local Legal Responses to the Plague of 1603

JOE SAMPSON*

I. Introduction

Less than a week after his coronation, James VI and I issued a series of Orders to address a fresh outbreak of the plague. The content of these Orders, a recycling of earlier Elizabethan prototypes, was directed to Justices of the Peace. How this audience reacted to the Orders and sought to implement them has been difficult to discern. The Quarter Session reports, themselves limited, give only a partial picture. This chapter focuses on a Memorandum Book of a single Justice of the Peace to provide a snapshot into how central rules were implemented in a locality. It begins with the context within which the Justice was working: the advent of the plague, the particular severity of the 1603 outbreak, and the legal responses taken centrally. It then examines in detail the entries of the Memorandum Book relating to the plague and identifies the key concerns that its author had in regulating his jurisdiction. It ends with a brief exploration of the aftermath of the legal responses to the plague of 1603 and the staid response to the emergency powers deployed.

II. The Plague of 1603

Elizabeth I died in the early hours of 24 March 1603. Her health having taken a deleterious turn in the preceding months, the identification of her successor in James VI of Scotland had already taken place.[1] The proclamation declaring James's right to the crown was issued that same day.[2] Approximately two weeks later,

* Much of this chapter is based on a manuscript in the private collection of John Baker. I am very grateful to him for making its contents available to me, and for his generous assistance with the paper. I am also grateful to the participants in the conference on which this volume is based for their helpful comments, and in particular to Ian Williams for his feedback.

[1] David Willson, *King James VI and I* (London, Jonathan Cape, 1963) 158.

[2] James Larkin and Paul Hughes (eds), *Stuart Royal Proclamations, Vol 1: Royal Proclamations of King James I 1603–1625* (Oxford, Clarendon Press, 1973) proclamation 1. The text, written by Elizabeth's first

on 5 April 1603, the new king began the long trip south from Edinburgh. Stopping regularly to hunt and enjoy the hospitality of his new subjects, he would not arrive in London until 7 May. His coronation followed 11 weeks later, on 25 July.[3]

The same period of four months saw a resurgence of the plague in London. The aptly named Bills of Mortality for London began to be published after several years in abeyance in the week ending 17 March 1603, a week before the passing of Elizabeth. That week saw a relatively high number of deaths in the City of London and its Liberties, with a total of 108 recorded. The following week this dropped to 60, with numbers hovering between 60 and 80 per week for the following month. Of these, an average of four per week were attributed to the plague. By the week of James I's coronation, the number of deaths in the City and Liberties had climbed to 1312, of which 1025 were attributed to the plague. By the middle of August this figure had doubled, and it remained in the mid-2000s per week for over a month. The numbers then dropped to the high hundreds, where they hovered until late in the year, before finally coming down to double digits by December. The plague lingered in the years that followed, but did not return to anything like the 1603 figures during the remainder of James's reign.[4]

To understand the range and severity of the measures taken in quick succession in 1603, we must begin by mapping the advent of the plague in that year. This can be done through Bills of Mortality for London, albeit with some caveats.[5] Bills of Mortality for London appear to be a product of the sixteenth century. Their early history is one of patchy and inconsistent publication, with the occasional single Bill discoverable in the early decades of the century. Consistent publication came at the end of the century, with the first unbroken weekly series running from late 1592 to late 1595, against the backdrop of the London plague of 1592 and 1593. After two years of few deaths attributed to the plague, the series was discontinued. The practice was revived in March 1603, at a time when the plague was causing only a small number of deaths. The practice of publication was institutionalised in 1611.[6]

The collection of data to be used in the creation of Bills of Mortality appears to have been the responsibility of two pairs of women (described in the London

Secretary, had already received James's approval to facilitate the expedient release of the proclamation: John Bruce (ed), *The Secret Correspondence of King James VI of Scotland with Sir Robert Cecil* (London, Camden Society Publications, 1861) lxxvii and 47.

[3] On James's reception as he journeyed south, see Roger Lockyer and Peter Gaunt, *Tudor and Stuart Britain*, 4th edn (Oxford, Routledge, 2018) 297–99.

[4] 1606 had the next highest mortality rate after 1603, with approximately 2000 deaths across the year, or the equivalent of a particularly bad week in the summer of 1603.

[5] Systematic figures are only available for London, although occasional Bills can be found for other towns.

[6] The Worshipful Company of Parish Clerks, who already undertook the process of gathering information and publishing their findings, were placed under an obligation to do so by a charter of 1611. By this time the Bills of Mortality were already among their primary roles: James Robertson, 'Reckoning with London: Interpreting the *Bills of Mortality* before John Graunt' (1996) 23 *Urban History* 325, 328–34.

Orders of 1592 as 'sober Ancient Woemen') referred to as 'searchers' sworn to the task in each parish.[7] The use of searchers was certainly in place in London by 1574, though it is likely to have had an earlier origin.[8] The 1592 London Orders detail the process of the search, with the first pair responsible for viewing the bodies of the recently deceased, and the second pair those as yet living but suspected of carrying the plague. These pairs would then report their findings to the precinct's constable, who in turn informed the alderman and parish clerk. The final recipient of the data then produced the Bill of Mortality. These duties were punitively enforced, with the threat of pillory and corporal punishment hanging over those who made false reports, and deprivation of local pension for dereliction.

The 1592 London Orders do not detail the work to be done by the searchers. It appears likely nothing more than a visual examination would inform the identification of the cause of morbidity, though Boyce notes that had medical practitioners been responsible for the task they would have been unlikely to offer more than this themselves.[9] Given the searchers' lack of medical expertise it would be wise to approach the data provided by Bills of Mortality with a degree of caution, although the striking physical symptoms of the plague make it unlikely that the figures are wholly unreliable.[10] If anything, the risk is likely to be one of under-reporting, because some people would have died from the plague before the telltale buboes had developed. The reverse risk, of a person being identified as a plague-caused death by virtue of buboes when something else killed them, would be slight. Moreover, even if the absolute numbers of deaths caused by the plague are not entirely reliable, the Bills of Mortality provide a keen insight into the *perception* of the severity of the plague as it spread across London.

The Bills of Mortality were published weekly, beginning with figures for the City and Liberties in the week ending 17 March. Fuller figures encompassing the addition of the Outer Parishes began to be published with the week ending 21 July.[11] The 18 weeks before this addition show a sharp upturn in deaths thought to be attributable to the plague in London: from less than 10 per week in the first six weeks, to 424 in the last week before the fuller figures began to be published. The numbers continued to climb from there, with every week between 18 August and 15 September seeing over 2000 deaths in the City and Liberties alone, and closer to 3000 if the parishes were factored in. The overall picture can be

[7] Wilfred Barrett, *Present Remedies against the Plague* (Oxford, Oxford University Press, 1933) xi, quoting *Journal of the London Court of Common Council* entry for 7 September 1592.

[8] Richelle Munkhoff, 'Searchers of the Dead: Authority, Marginality, and the Interpretation of Plague in England, 1574–1665' (1999) 11 *Gender & History* 1, 2.

[9] Niall Boyce, 'Bills of Mortality: Tracking Disease in Early Modern London' (2020) 395 *The Lancet* 1186, 1186.

[10] Though Slack notes that we cannot be entirely confident that the label 'plague' was used solely to refer to those who died of the bubonic plague. It might also have been used to refer to generic bad luck: Paul Slack, *The Impact of Plague in Tudor and Stuart England* (Oxford, Routledge, 1985) 64.

[11] Charles Creighton, *A History of Epidemics in Britain* (Cambridge, Cambridge University Press, 1894) Vol I, 475–76.

summarised with the following two graphs, produced using the statistics extracted from the Bills by Creighton.

Figure 2.1 City and Liberties only, March–July 1603

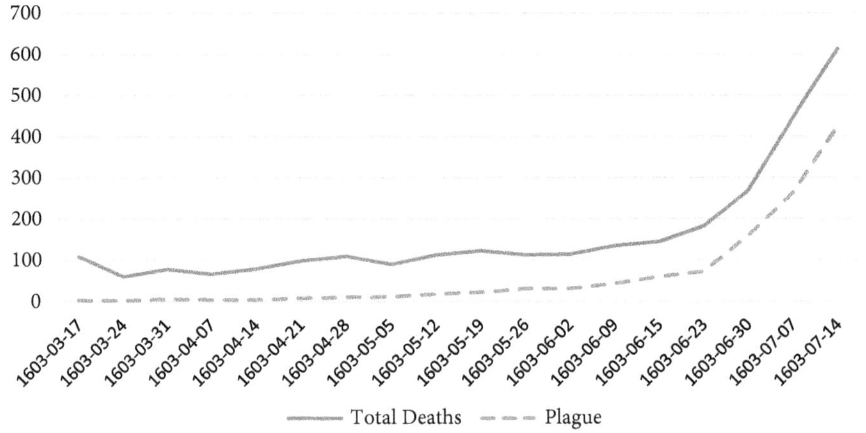

Figure 2.2 City, Liberties and Outer Parishes, July–December 1603

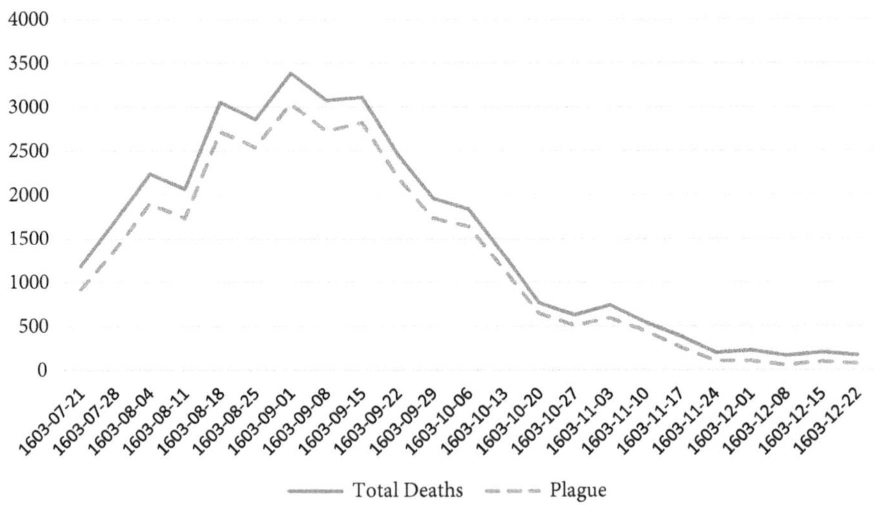

The separation of the data, shown above, into two graphs represents the difference in geography covered by the Bills within 1603. The Bills ending with 14 July 1603 only captured deaths in the City and its Liberties; from 21 July 1603 deaths in the outer parishes were included too. The graphs show clearly that the spike in deaths beginning in June 1603 were seen principally as a consequence of the plague, with the gap between the two lines representing causes of death other than the plague remaining consistently sized. The Bills of Mortality presenting this picture on a weekly basis circulated widely, far beyond London. And it is against this backdrop of an emerging public health crisis that the new monarch approached the capital.

III. First Measures

The earliest measures taken to control the spread of the plague took the form of royal proclamations, and were concerned with controlling access to James himself, perhaps indicating a personal wariness on the part of the new monarch about the risks posed by the plague. The first sign of this is a proclamation dated 29 May 1603 that ordered non-locals to vacate the city.[12] The text is bittersweet, noting the warm hospitality that James had received on his journey south and the continued desire to mark the accession of a new king. It notes, however, that

> we find the sickness already somewhat forward within our City of London, which by concourse of people abiding there is very like to be increased, and imposeth us as well for our peoples' sake, as for the safety of our own person … to prevent by all provident means.[13]

All were commanded to leave the city unless they had 'some special cause of attendance at our court for our service, or for some necessary cause concerning their own estate', in which case permission was granted to remain until the end of the term, at which point an immediate departure was expected.

Soon after, on 23 June 1603, Trinity term was prematurely adjourned. While the reference to the plague in the proclamation of 29 May 1603 was oblique and buried beneath civilities, here it features in the opening line:

> For as much as the infection of the plague is at this present greatly increased and dispersed as well in the cities of London and Westminster, as also in the suburbs thereof, the king's most excellent majesty considering that great peril and danger might ensue [to those in court] … if the people of all sorts, and out of all parts of this realm, should resort or continue together for their suits and causes this instant term …[14]

Three months later, on 16 September 1603, Michaelmas term met the same fate.[15]

Despite these measures, and any apprehensiveness James himself might have felt about the plague, it is clear that not everyone was convinced that it posed a serious risk. The vast quantities of personal correspondence preserved in the State Papers present, when stitched together, vignettes on the continuation of the full business of government while suppressing a pandemic. Take, for example, the saga concerning the entertainment of the newly appointed Spanish ambassador to England told across three letters in 1603 and 1604. The ambassador, Don Juan de Taxis, Count

[12] *Stuart Royal Proclamations, Vol 1* (n 2) proclamation 11.
[13] State Papers Domestic, James I, 1603–1640: SP 14/1 f.231 (in manuscript; printed SP 14/73 fol 21).
[14] State Papers Domestic, James I, 1603–1640: SP 14/73 fol 23.
[15] ibid fol 31.

of Villa Mediana, makes his first appearance in a letter from Sir Lewis Lewkenor to Lord Cecil dated 23 August 1603.[16] In it, Don Juan is described as 'full (according to the Spanish fashion) of leisure and gravity in his gesture and speeches, exceedingly vaunting, and vainglorious in speaking either of his master or of himself'. This unflattering characterisation likely reflects Sir Lewis's thoughts on the new ambassador's plans to arrive with no fewer than 147 retainers at the height of the plague, to the consternation of his hosts. Sir Lewis sought to contain the ambassador, explaining that James had forbade appearances before him other than on urgent and specific business. If this satisfied the Spanish ambassador, such satisfaction was short-lived, particularly when the Spaniard discovered that the ambassador from Paris had been granted an audience. The following month Sir Lewis was forced to arrange bullfighting in Southampton to meet the visitor's expectations.[17]

IV. The Orders

The Spanish ambassador is just one example. The State Papers are replete with correspondence which make it clear that London's upper echelons viewed the plague as creating a risk primarily to their maids and servants. Consequently, it is perhaps not surprising that the measures seen thus far took the form of proclamations, individual commands by the monarch, with a view to limiting royal audiences. However, the most extensive set of measures taken to control the plague were issued in the name of the Privy Council as well as James. These Orders followed less than a week after James's coronation, on 30 July 1603.[18] In content they mirror almost to the word a set of orders issued by the Privy Council under Elizabeth in October 1577, and reissued in 1592 and 1593.

The Orders begin with a blanket delegation of responsibility for their implementation to the Justices of the Peace in each county, who were instructed to gather (so long as they were confident that they were uninfected) and devise a plan for the division of responsibility for the county between themselves.[19] They were further empowered to recruit additional Justices, if so required.[20] Once the geographical division was reached, each was to identify the towns – and indeed

[16] State Papers Domestic, James I, 1603–1640: SP 14/3 fol 63.

[17] ibid fol 132.

[18] The Orders were published as *Orders, thought meete by his Majestie, and his Privie Counsell, to be executed throughout the Counties of this Realme, in such Townes, Villages, and other places, as are, or may be hereafter infected with the Plague, for the stay of further increase of the same London*. The edition used here is that contained in Robert Barker, *Foure Statutes, specially selected and commanded by his Maiestie to be carefully put in execution by all iustices and other officers of the peace throughout the realme: together with a proclamation, a decree of the Starre-chamber, and certaine orders depending upon the former lawes, more particularly concerning the citie of London, and counties adioyning* (London, Robert Barker, 1609) [Trinity College Cambridge VI.10.41[10]].

[19] *Orders* (n 18) 1st Order (Barker, *Foure Statutes* (n 18) 59).

[20] ibid 15th Order (Barker, ibid 67). Note the absence of a specific commission for the newly recruited Justices.

the houses – in which infections were rife, and to have the inhabitants confined.[21] These measures were to be supplemented by the system of viewers already operating in places such as London, which the Orders required to be established in every county.[22] The Justices were also to offer financial relief to those so quarantined, and were empowered to impose a tax and appoint collectors of alms to fund this relief.[23]

A significant element of the Orders concern isolation. Where the viewers attributed a death to the plague, or where a person with the plague was believed to reside, the affected houses were to be locked up for six weeks.[24] The Justices were to appoint individuals to supply the quarantined inhabitants with food and other necessities, themselves to be marked with a white rod so that others could steer clear.[25] Some allowance was made for agricultural workers, who were permitted to tend to their tasks so long as they were clearly marked by their clothing, or by again carrying a white rod, so that others could avoid contact with them.[26] Failure to do so resulted in the offender being put in the stocks besides their home, and their house accordingly marked as being dangerous, with watchmen appointed to oversee compliance. Establishments where people frequented, such as inns or alehouses, were to be closed and their signs taken down if they were found to be infected. Any persons lost to the plague were to be buried in specially designated spaces, and only during twilight when the presence of others was unlikely.[27] All of these measures were reinforced by the expectation of a closely knit information network in the locality. Any hundred where an infection was identified was to report this fact on a weekly basis, and the Justices of the county were ordered to gather every 20 days to ensure the effective implementation of the Orders as a whole.[28] Churchwardens were similarly expected to report infections and deaths on the same timeline of about three weeks.[29]

Finally, punitive sanctions were imposed on any who undermined the efforts to contain the plague. The Orders forbade individuals from saying or publishing anything that suggested it was pointless or else uncharitable to avoid association with the infected, enforced by the threat of imprisonment.[30] The Order targeted both secular and ecclesiastical individuals. Particular attention was paid to an anticipated theological argument: that it was unacceptable to spread the view that

[21] ibid 2nd Order (Barker, ibid 59).
[22] ibid 4th Order (Barker, ibid 61).
[23] ibid 2nd Order (Barker, ibid 59) on relief; 3rd Order (Barker, ibid 60) on taxation; and 6th Order (Barker, ibid 63) on alms.
[24] ibid 5th Order (Barker, ibid 62–63).
[25] ibid 7th Order (Barker, ibid 63).
[26] ibid 5th Order (Barker, ibid 62).
[27] ibid 10th Order (Barker, ibid 65).
[28] ibid 11th Order (Barker, ibid 65) sets out the 20-day requirement for Justices; the 12th Order (Barker, ibid 66) for affected hundreds.
[29] ibid 9th Order (Barker, ibid 64–65).
[30] ibid 16th Order (Barker, ibid 68).

an individual's time of death was predetermined, and so there was no risk in associating with the infected.

Thus far the rules concerned the implementation of specific Orders from the Privy Council, but the Orders also allowed for novelty as the situation developed, and in a strikingly open-ended form:

> [T]he said justices may put in execution any other orders that by them at their general assembly shall be devised and thought meet, tending to the preservation of his majesty's subjects from infection; and to the end their care and diligence may the better appear, they shall certify in writing the said orders newly devised; and if any shall wilfully break and contemn the same, or any of the orders herein specified, they shall either presently punish them by imprisonment or, if the persons contemning them shall be of such countenance as the justices think meet to have their faults known to his majesty or to the Council, they shall charge and bind them to appear before us and the contempt duly certified, that there may be a more notorious sharp example made by punishment of the same by order of his majesty.[31]

Not only is the breadth of the delegation, permitting any measure that can be justified as containing infections, noteworthy, but also the ability to imprison without any central oversight of the measures breached other than in cases of more serious breaches, where the Justices wanted to make an example of the malefactor.

V. Local Implementation

Though the Orders issued in 1603 were not original in their content, their implementation appears to have been taken more seriously by the Justices than earlier versions were by their predecessors. Previously, implementation had been extremely patchy with the Justices of many counties – Shropshire among them – which was thought not to have made significant efforts before 1604.[32] It would appear that the significant burdens placed on Justices by the Orders caused many to imagine that they were really addressed to Justices in other types of locality, and in particular for towns rather than more rural environments.[33] It was only with the Orders of 1603 that the measures began to be enforced in earnest in most of the larger towns, and that data on death rates began to be compiled in counties such as Kent, Devon, Cheshire and Hampshire, with the remainder beginning in the following year.[34] It is telling that leading treatises on the jurisdiction and powers of the Justices of the Peace from the late sixteenth century do not touch on these emergency powers, despite considerable discussion of the limits of the officials' powers.[35]

[31] ibid 14th Order (Barker, ibid 67).

[32] Steve Hindle, *The State and Social Change c.1550–1640* (Basingstoke, Macmillan, 2000) 170.

[33] Slack (n 10) 211–12.

[34] ibid 212, fn 57 provides archival sources for each county.

[35] eg William Lambarde's *Eirenarcha*, first published soon after the first instance of the Elizabethan Orders in 1582, makes no mention of them. Book 1 c 12 contains a sustained discussion of jurisdiction

An insight into the use made of the powers conferred by the 1603 Orders is provided by the Memorandum Book of Anthony Kynnersley, a Justice of the Peace for Loxley Hall in Staffordshire.[36] The entries present a snapshot of the difficulties faced by the local authorities in implementing the central Orders, and in keeping the plague under control. Hindle, in his treatment of the regulation of the plague, suggests that several aspects – particularly those concerning quarantine – were too difficult to implement and enforce.[37] The evidence from Kynnersley's Memorandum Book cuts against this view. While the evidence is one-sided – we can see what Kynnersley ordered, but not how his orders were received – it shows a clear desire to keep the plague under strict control, and a willingness to use coercive measures to ensure compliance.

Kynnersley's entries concerning the plague in 1603 can be divided into four types of response. First, the framework for information-gathering required supplementation during large events that were desirable, such as fairs, for which Kynnersley made a range of additional appointments to augment his network with a view not only to collecting data on the spread of the plague, but also keeping the local population under control. Secondly, much of his official activity focused on supply chains – addressing not only the obvious risk of carriers from outside the locality bringing the plague into town, but also the extent to which businesses represented a risk to compliance. Thirdly, the difficulties faced in ensuring his own officials played their part in upholding the rules. And, finally, the steps taken to stamp out large gatherings that could not be justified.

A. Control

Several of Kynnersley's early orders recorded in his Memorandum Book concern the augmentation of the structures designed to keep the plague under control during a fair at Uttoxeter. The first of these, on 6 September 1603, reads as follows:

> Warders appoynted as followeth. Fyrst in the lane agaynst Mr Mynours howse, four warders whereof one to be a very able person of discretion. Item, att the hend of the highe streate to be vj warders. Item att Smethye Lane end two warders. Item att Tynkers Lane end two warders. Item at the end of Balland Streete agaynst Launtes to be foure warders. Item att Pynfold Lane betwene the bridge and the yate to be vj warders. Item att the Scholehowse Lane end two warders.[38]

The warders were to be located at the ends of several arterial roads around Uttoxeter, suggesting their primary concern was the control of access, as well as

and coercive powers. Later works for Justices that deal with the plague see the origins of related power in Jacobean legislation, eg Michael Dalton, *The Countrey Justice* (London, Society of Stationers, 1618) c XLV cites only 1 Jac 31. Later editions added 21 Jac 28 (continuation).

[36] The manuscript (hereafter JHB MS 2496) is in the private collection of Professor Sir John Baker. I am immensely grateful to him for making his transcriptions available to me.

[37] Hindle (n 32) 171.

[38] JHB MS 2496 (n 36) fol 57v.

keeping an eye on who was travelling into town for the occasion. The warders were further supported by a team of messengers, with the entry continuing:

> Further, that every warder have his messenger, because noe warder shall styrre from his place, and for that day to have victualls brought unto them. And these messengers to foe from the warders to the how[s]keapers where they[r] recett shalbe to be answered for by a token receyved from the hoseholders.
>
> Also that there shalbe one person att every streetes ende that can wryte.[39]

That warders were appointed in pairs is already indicative of a shift system, ensuring that the entry points were kept under constant watch. The further provision of messengers responsible not only for relaying information but for supplying them with necessities only reinforces this perception. The network of warders and messengers ensured oversight and the expedient sharing of information. This structure was then supplemented by two further appointments with a more disciplinary role:

> Also that the bell man doe goe throughe every streete uppon the fayre even and doe geve warninge to every howseholder that they shall apprehend and take all suche suspected persons as shall come throughe any of there backesydes into the towne and bringe them to the constables or thre deputyes to receave condigne punishement for the same.
>
> Further that there be iij whippers att the towne charge appoynted to serche all highe wayes rounde about the towne for to whippe away roages, vacabondes and beggars that use to lye by the highe way sydes begginge.[40]

The role of the trio of whippers is clear, and this is the first of several references to the rogues, vagabonds and beggars thought to be lurking on the highways between towns by whom Kynnersley is particularly troubled, clearly because he believed that they would bring infection into his as-yet unaffected town.[41] The 'bell man' does not appear elsewhere in Kynnersley's memoranda, but he performed much the same role as the whippers within the town's borders: he was tasked with rounding up people who should not have been in the town and taking them before local officials.[42]

These first Orders have one further distinctive quality. They are the only measures recorded by Kynnersley that note community participation and assent. We are told that the measures were 'devysed by Mr Anthony Kynnersley esquyer and consented unto and agreed upon the sixte day of September 1603 generally by the constables and inhabitantes of Uttoxatour aforesaid'.

[39] ibid.

[40] ibid.

[41] The measures taken resonate with legislation from a few years earlier – the 'Acte for punishment of Rogues, Vagabonds and Sturdy Beggars' (39 Eliz I c 4). These three roles are defined in section 2 of the Act, with whipping authorised in section 3.

[42] It may be significant that 39 Eliz I c 4 section 11 provides that 'any two or more Justices of the Peace … shall have full power by authority of this present Acte to heare and determine all Causes that shall growe or come in question by reason of this Act'. Such a provision would appear to authorise further measures to do with turning away itinerants beyond those specified in the Act.

Admittedly, we have only Kynnersley's word for the community's consent to his new regime, but that he sought and recorded it indicates that these measures had a different quality to the others described. In a raft of rules that imposed heavy restrictions on everyday life, these are the norms that took the population the furthest from ordinary life, and imposed the heaviest restriction on the ordinary business of the town. Their purpose was to enable fairs to proceed as they previously had, presumably something collectively desired by the community. But such rules would only be workable if the general populace saw their value and agreed to this additional layer of restriction, so far beyond that envisaged by the central Orders.

This first set of measures has some similarities to steps taken in London. In 1609 Richard Barker published a compilation of legislation and guidance for Justices of the Peace that was principally concerned with the plague, with the late Elizabethan Orders (reissued under James) provided as an exemplar.[43] These too began with a series of appointments: watchmen and searchers, as in Staffordshire, but also dedicated surgeons to assist in the work of the searchers.[44] The London measures also included steps to stave off 'loose persons', with additional prohibitions on 'plaies, beare-baitings, games, singing of ballads, buckler play, or such like causes of assemblies of people', perhaps more of a concern in the metropolis than in smaller provincial towns.[45] By contrast, the London measures did not detail the sort of information network that Kynnersley set up, even for large gatherings such as fairs. The steps taken for the Uttoxeter fair look to have been a local innovation.

B. Supply

The measures taken by Kynnersley also focused on supply chains. This focus can be subdivided into three types of measure: those concerning merchandise entering town, those concerning inns, and those concerning shops. The worries underpinning the first two are obvious enough, insofar as both deal with outsiders entering the town bubble, potentially bringing infection with them.[46] Shops, on the other hand, typically dealt with locals. Here the concern was on how the provision of victuals and alcoholic drink encouraged unsafe gatherings. Kynnersley's measures sought to restrain trade at times where those predisposed towards breaking the rules might find the last bit of encouragement in such disinhibiting wares.

[43] Barker, *Foure Statutes* (n 18) 83–87. These may have been an updated version of the 1582 London Orders.

[44] ibid 79–80.

[45] ibid 86.

[46] In this respect, Kynnersley's measures mirror the advice given in Lodge's influential 1603 treatise on managing the plague to close all cities to traffic: Ákos Tussay, 'Plague Discourse, Quarantine and Plague Control in Early Modern England: 1578–1625' (2020) 61 *Hungarian Journal of Legal Studies* 113, 123, citing Thomas Lodge, *A Treatise of the Plague* (London, V Sims for Edward White, 1603) ch 8, fn 33.

Kynnersley's records contain several measures taken against merchants who had travelled into the locality from London. Indeed, the earliest record of action taken by Kynnersley in response to the plague concerned people travelling to London:

> A precept to dyvers towneshipps directed as followeth. Forasmuche as certeyne of Utcester and Crakemarshe to [t]he greate discontent of theire neyghbours a[n]d damage of the whole cuntrey have notwithstandinge our comaundement to the contrary gone to London and are returned home with dyvers packes of wares out of that infected cytye, we thought good in our discretion for the generall safetye to enclose these carryers for a tyme in a removed place from conversinge with others, and also to make a stay of there wares tyll we might understand what covetous and unhonest mercers and other tradesmen procured the carryers to incur this contempt, which havinge now discovered and desirous to delyver our cuntrey from any further charge of watchinge, and also to delyver the wares to the owners, but before the delyverye thereof thought good to advertys the chief officers and magistrates of every towne where the aforeseyd wares shall come that they may use their owne discretion for the restraynt of any merchantes wares to asinge [?] hymself and also to the better safetye of the who[l]e cuntrye. Geven under our handes and seales [t]he 27 of August 1603.[47]

The reference to an earlier command not to travel to London shows that Kynnersley's memoranda are not a complete record of his actions. His response in this entry is comprehensive: not only were the carriers and their wares isolated, efforts were also successfully made to identify the cause of the carriers' trip to London – the 'covetous and unhonest' businessmen who had enticed the carriers to breach the justice's orders. That Kynnersley was perhaps overstepping and upsetting local people of significance is suggested by a brief entry from the following day:

> 28o Augusti 1603 A precept to the carriers of Utcester and Crakenmarshe. These are to will and require you that notwithstondinge our former warrant to the contrarye, you delyver to this berer Thomas More suche sope and other wares as you have brought from London for hym, and this shalbe your warrant in that behalf. Gyven under our hands die et anno supradictis.[48]

The actions taken on 27 August 1603 were not an isolated incident. To take one further example, he wrote to the constables of Gratwick in the following terms:

> I am geven to understand from the baylies of Stafforde that a carryer of there towne hath bene lately at London and hath brought loadinge from thence, but consideringe of the daungerous infection which ys so greate at this tyme that never the lyke was in any mans memorye, and they havinge a care of there towne wold not suffer hym to unloade, but cause his howse to be shutt up, and as I further understande that that loadinge which they baylies durst not suffer to be in the towne ys brought to your towne of Greatwiche and recetted att Mylwardes howse there, therefore these shalbe in his highnes name to charge and commaund you presently upon the sight hereof that you goe to Mylwards

[47] JHB MS 2496 (n 36) fol 57.
[48] ibid.

> and there make diligent serche and inquirye whether there be any suche packes lefte there or noe, and yf you fynd there be I commaunde you in his highnes name that you cause the doores of his howse to be shutt up and they people safely to be therein kept, not only by the watche but also by the warders, that no further daunger may insue thereof, nether to the towne nor countrye, untyll other course be taken therein. Thus fayle you not hereof, as you will aswere the contrarye att your perill. Loxley, this present Sunday morninge the xj th of September 1603.[49]

It would appear that the officials of Stafford did their job: the merchant was not permitted to unload his wares, and so tried his luck at Gratwick, where he had now taken up residence. Note how Kynnersley made his orders to the constables not solely in his own name, but with the authority of the king. These Orders – to quarantine the merchant and his wares, with the threat of punishment for the officials if they failed to comply – were beyond the scope of the central Orders, which commanded isolation only for '[t]he houses of those so certified to have died of the plague, or where there are understood to be persons sick of the plague'. The basis for Kynnersley's suspicions appears to have been nothing more than the bare fact that the carrier in question had travelled from London, rather than any suggestion that they were symptomatic, much less confirmed as carrying the plague.

That inns would require special regulation requires little explanation.[50] Their business inescapably involved hosting outsiders, and so long as inns were permitted to remain open, they served as an obvious route for the plague to enter the locality. Alehouses provided a similar risk; though their business was not so intrinsically connected with outsiders, they provided a clear forum for the spread of disease once present in town. So it is no surprise that the two were treated together in the central Orders: if an infection was traceable to either establishment, they were to be closed and their signs taken down.[51] Kynnersley grouped inns and 'victualers' together. The latter term was sufficiently broad to refer to alehouses, and that Kynnersley forbade them from hosting strangers suggests it is that business that he had in mind:

> Also that every victualer unbounde that shall lodge any persons shall enter into regognisaunce of x li. that they shall not lodge in their howses any strangers or any other suspected persons for whom they shall geve a token as aforesaid, which come lately from any towne that ys infected in the towne, or other lewde or evill disposed persons that shall commytt any misdemeanours.
>
> Also that every victualer shall have there severall pryvatt marke for which they wilbe answrable, ready (which they mark there bread withall) made in severall tokens, to send to the warders for suche ghestes as they will undertake for.[52]

[49] ibid fol 58.

[50] Joan Kent, *The English Village Constable 1580–1642: A Social and Administrative Study* (Oxford, Clarendon Press, 1986) 32–33 traces the rise of constabulary regulation of alehouses, a trend seen as beginning in 1604 (when legislation empowered constables and churchwardens to enter alehouses when enforcing regulations; the plague Orders appear to be a prototype for such powers).

[51] *Orders*, 5th Order (Barker, *Foure Statutes* (n 18) 62).

[52] JHB MS 2496 (n 36) fol 57v.

These measures struck a balance between service to the local population and wariness of strangers. It again went further than the central Orders, which only carried consequences if an infection actually occurred. Kynnersley's measures were preventative rather than reactive, operating on the assumption that the threat came from beyond the town's boundaries. This perhaps speaks to a particular wariness of the plague on Kynnersley's part, bolstered by further actions taken against alehouses in July 1604, after the worst of the plague had passed, as he thought that several alehouses 'make noe care what strangers they lodge, nor from when they come'.[53]

C. Officials

Kynnersley was naturally reliant on other officials for the enforcement of his rules, and did not receive universal support.[54] In a postscript to his Order to the constables of Gratwick concerning a merchant from London he added a personal threat:

> Constable, I sent you comaundement by Raphe Broughe that there sjould be noe wakes kept, notwithstondinge you doe suffer lewde company to resorte together in this daungerous tyme of infection havinge no regarde of your duetye to our gracious prince nor yett for the safetye of your selves, these shalbe to comaunde you in his highnes name that you suffer noe strangers but suche as be very well knowen unto you, nor any minstrells to drawe lewde company to be in your towne, for the avoydinge of further daunger that may insue thereof. Thus fayle you not etc.[55]

Here we see concern that the constable was allowing disorder to ferment under his watch, coupled with an accusation of disregard for both his official duty to the monarch and his own health. A later entry shows that Kynnersley was willing to follow through on his threats. On 18 September 1603 he wrote to officials in Kingston as follows:

> These shalbe in the kinges majesties name strayghtly to charge and commaunde you that presently upon the receypte hereof that you take Richard Baylye, the constable of your towne, and sett hym in the stockes for that he disobeyed the charge which I gave hym in hys hignes name, that eyther the Londioner which was newly come into the towne should be presently sent fourth or ells that he, his wyef and whole howsehold which did receave her should have his doores shut up and to tended both by watche and warde, that they should nether goe to there neyghbours nor there neyghours unto them. And further I understand that the same Londoiner hath her mother in the towne, which hath recourse unto her. Therefore these shalbe in his highne[ss's] name to commaund you to put her mother into the howse with her, and there they all to be kept as aforesayd a fortnight or more, that we may avoyde the daunger which otherwayes may ensue.

[53] ibid fol 79.
[54] Kent (n 50) 194–96 details the ability of Justices of the Peace to discipline constables.
[55] JHB MS 2496 (n 36) fol 58.

> And further that you kepe the constable in the stockes untyll he doe undertake to see the whole company of them kept together in that howse as aforesaid. Thus fayle you not ec. Loxley, this present Sunday the xviij th of September 1603.[56]

This entry records an early command, again given in the king's name, that Richard Baylye, constable of Kingston, should either chase away a Londoner said to be in his town, or else place the household where they resided under watch to prevent the spread of any potential infection. The constable apparently failed because he allowed the Londoner's mother, who lived in Kingston, to continue going about her business rather than being shut up with her family. For this failure, Kynnersley ordered the constable to be put in the stocks 'untyll he doe undertake to see the whole company of them kept together in that howse as aforesaid'. Here Kynnersley appears to have punished the constable not for violating any of the central Orders – which did not require family members to be isolated where living apart – but for disobeying his personal command.

D. Wakes

Despite Kynnersley's best efforts, and despite the increasing risk posed by the pandemic, it is clear that some in the locality could not be dissuaded from revelry. The Memorandum Book makes several references to 'wakes'. This term initially described the practice of services throughout the night before a feast-day. These events reportedly become a pretext for revelry. Such gatherings were clearly of concern to Kynnersley. An order to a constable in a neighbouring town dated to the middle of September 1603 reads as follows:

> Wheras we are credably enformed of the great dysorder used in deverse constablewyckes of dyvers dysorderly persons and not onley att the wake tymes but also dyvers other tymes, as well att the tyme of devyne service as other tumes, as a nomber of them makinge of love ales without licence, where a great nomber of dysorderly persons do resort and ther are quarrelinge, as also a nomber of roages and mynsteralls ther gather togather to the great dysorder of his majesties subyectes, and now att this instant go about to by great abundance of maulte agaynst the wake tyme, and many of them without lycense, as allso consideringe this dangerous tymes of sicknes wher unto dyverse and sundry infected do and will resort, these are therfor to requere you as also in his majesties name to charge and commaund you that you geve warninge to all the pettye constable within your said hundred that the also geve warninge to all the vytlelers within every ther the constablewyckes that the do not sell any alle duringe the tyme of the wakes ne yet that the said comstables permytt and suffer any other to brew or sell alle not permytted, or sufer any mynstryles to play duringe the wake tyme, and that you have great care of the punyshinge of rogues and vagrant persons accordinge to the statut.[57]

[56] ibid fol 59.
[57] ibid.

This entry grouped wakes together with other types of gatherings, but put wakes at the forefront of the credible rumours of disorder. Kynnersley was clearly affronted by the manner in which people were attending 'without licence', suggesting a gathering without justification. The approach taken was to limit the opportunity for such gatherings to arise in the first place: shops were to be instructed not to sell alcohol during the hours in which wakes were held, a time when minstrels were also not allowed to play music.

The compromise was evidently insufficient. Within a week, Kynnersley issued a further Order to the constable of Leeke:

> These shalbe in his heighnes name strayghtley to charge and commaund you that presently upon the receyt hereof you repare to Marborrowe Chaple and there geve warnynge to Thommas Thornnycraft and Margett Fowell and Frauncis Thrush that the nor any of them shall as this Sunday followynge beinge the xviij th of this present monethe of September that the keepe noe wakes wherby the drawe nor heade of company together consydering this dangerous tyme of infection, and for avoy[d]inge of further inconvenyence that may insue therby, and further I charge and commaund you in his heyghnes name that you suffer no wakes to be keept within your constablewycke whensoever ytt shall happen, neyther yet suffer any mynstrylls or pedlers to play to drawe any company together, for if the will not take warninge se that you punyshe them in the nature of roages. Thus faylle you not as you will answere to the contrary at your perills.[58]

Here the focus was squarely on wakes. And, at the end of September, to the constables within the manor of Horton:

> Whereas wee are geven to understand that divers within your sayde constablewick are purposed to keepe there wakes on Sonnday next, wherunto many lewd and evill disposed personns are accustomed to resort, and many greate misdmeaners committed to the breach of Godes holy saboth, his majesties late proclamation for the abholishing thereof lately publyshed by that meanes contemned, and the whole number of is sayd mayjesties subjects within your constablewick greately indaungered by reason of the infection of sicknes in many places at this presente disperced, these are therefore in his sayd majestyes name straightyly to charge and commaund you and every of you that within every your sayde divitions you sett for the carefull and diligente watch and warde to kepe oute all personns not inhabiting within the parrish of Horton, and allso that you give warneing unto all vittellers and alehousekeepers that uppon that day, namely Sonnday, and the day following they forbeare to receave into there houses any personn not dwellin[g] within the parish aforesayd, and that whomesoever shall offend herein you bring them before one of us to aunswere his contempte, as you and every of you will avoyd the daunger of neglecte of your dwty herein at your perill.[59]

The first of these Orders, to the constable of Leeke, purported to ban all wakes. The missive to the constables of Horton reveals that the problems faced by our Staffordshire justice were occurring nationally. Kynnersley claims that James

[58] ibid fol 60.
[59] ibid fol 61.

had published a fresh proclamation purporting to forbid wakes entirely. If such a proclamation was enacted, this was certainly not its focus. James issued four proclamations in September 1603, concerning: 1) raising and pulling down certain recently erected buildings; 2) the adjournment of part of Michaelmas Term; 3) measures targeting rogues, vagabonds, idle and dissolute persons; and 4) the pression of piracies and depredations upon the sea.[60] Of these, only the third plausibly aligns with the measures taken by Kynnersley. However, it made no reference to wakes. It was instead a complaint that 'of late by the remissenesse, negligence, and connivencie of some justices of the peace' the aforementioned rogues and their ilk 'swarmed and abounded every where more frequently then in times past' – it was a measure focused on the individuals rather than the events.[61] To meet this problem James and the Privy Council had 'assigned places and parts beyond the Seas, unto which such incorrigible or dangerous Rogues should according to the same Lawe be banished and conveyed'. This is not obviously a measure targeting the revelry of wakes.

Viewed in the round, Kynnersley appears to have been committed to protecting his wards against the plague. The central Orders were largely reactive, imposing measures to be taken when a person was identified as (or strongly suspected of) carrying the plague. By contrast, Kynnersley was more proactive, taking steps to ensure the plague did not make it into his towns. It is also noteworthy that the number of entries is relatively slight. Those that are recorded document instances of disobedience, and the necessity of further restrictions (particularly on the supply of alcohol) to ensure no lapses in compliance. But they are spread out across a period of several months, and relatively few. Doubtless they represent an incomplete picture, as any action taken 'on the ground' by constables and other officials would not be recorded in such a way. But the fact that Kynnersley felt compelled to write to his officials on such an infrequent basis suggests that he was under the impression that they were otherwise enforcing his regulations appropriately.

VI. After 1603

The outbreak of plague abated late in 1603, and the exigency felt in Kynnersley's notes declined with it. The following year saw a statutory response to the plague.[62] The legislative process was expedient but not smooth. Although the Bill was first introduced on 11 May 1604 and passed its third reading barely a month later, on 16 June 1604, that five-week period saw the original text rejected outright by the committee scrutinising it.[63] It was the committee's replacement text that

[60] *Stuart Royal Proclamations, Vol 1* (n 2) proclamations 25–28.
[61] ibid proclamation 27.
[62] 1 Jac I c 31.
[63] *Journals of the House of Commons: Volume 1, 1547–1629* 206–7 (introduction of initial Bill, 11 May) 225–26 (rejection by committee 'as not fit to be retained', 25 May) 240–41 (third reading and vote, 15 June).

ultimately passed into law.[64] Unfortunately the basis for the committee's rejection has proved elusive.

The legislation's long title, 'An Acte for the charitable reliefe and ordering of persons infected with the Plague', speaks to a difference in emphasis from the measures of the preceding year. This is reflected in the content, which is significantly narrower than the Orders. The legislation has four main provisions. The principal concern appears to have been taxation, the procedures for which take up over half of the Act's extent. These provisions afforded local officials considerable flexibility in determining the level of levy required to meet the needs of the poor, and empowered them to imprison those who refuse to pay.[65] It also placed on a statutory footing the orders concerning quarantine (and provision for those quarantined), and authorised the use of force to ensure that the infected remained confined.[66] Furthermore, anyone visibly suffering from the plague who was seen travelling or conversing with others was to be treated as a felon, with the usual threat of capital punishment attached.[67] The third provision authorised the appointment of searchers, examiners, watchers, keepers and buriers; the fourth disapplied the legislation from the Universities, Eton, Winchester, and cathedrals.[68]

Clearly absent from this legislation was the blanket delegation of power to Justices of the Peace. There is nothing that comes close to the Orders' statement that Justices could put in place any measures they collectively thought necessary to preserve the health of the locality, and on pain of whatever punishment they thought fit. Similarly absent were the measures concerning common sites of the infection spreading, such as inns. And even the provisions for isolation were noticeably narrower than in the Orders, applying only to those who were infected or shared a dwelling with an infected person.

A question arises about the status of the Orders after the Act of 1604 had been enacted, since the overlap between the two was far from complete. Many of the steps taken by Kynnersley, from impounding cargo to shutting down shops, would have gone beyond what Parliament had authorised if they had been performed in 1604. Yet the Orders continued to be circulated after 1604 as something with which Justices should be familiar. Take, for instance, Robert Barker's 1609 compilation of legislation of significance to Justices of the Peace, appended to which are various other proclamations and orders.[69] The titular *Foure Statutes* end with the Plague Act 1604, which are immediately followed by the 1603 Orders. That the

[64] ibid 226.

[65] 1 Jac I c 31, s 1.

[66] ibid, s 2.

[67] ibid, s 1. Anyone who disregarded quarantine but lacked visible signs of infectious sores would instead be treated as a vagabond, and so evade capital punishment.

[68] ibid, s 4.

[69] Barker, *Foure Statutes* (n 18). That the collection also includes advice from medics about cost-free medicines with a particular focus on the plague suggests its primary goal was to provide a resource for officials on matters arising from the plague.

Orders did not have the status of legislation would have been clear to the readership, but it would also have been clear that Justices of the Peace were expected to attend to them.

The blurring of the boundary between Act and proclamation is all the more curious for its constitutional context. The first decade of the seventeenth century saw repeated skirmishes between monarch and Commons over James's use of proclamations to circumvent the ordinary processes of law-making. That same compilation of statutes ends with James's proclamation against new buildings, and an exemplar decree from Star Chamber dealing with the enforcement of an Elizabethan version of the proclamation.[70] That proclamation would take centre stage in the *Case of Proclamations* in 1610, the culmination of this constitutional conflict.[71]

The petition brought by the Commons listed seven specific objections, underpinned by examples from 16 proclamations.[72] These were: 1) that proclamations were being used to alter points of law, and indeed to make new law; 2) that proclamations were being used shortly after a parliament to enact matters which that prior session had directly rejected; 3) that proclamations touched the freehold livelihood of men; 4) that proclamations enabled Justices (among others) to punish individuals without trial and conviction, without those individuals having the authority to inquire into nor determine such offences; 5) that proclamations were taking the form of penal statutes; 6) that proclamations were enabling the punishment of offenders in courts of 'arbitrary discretion', in the manner of Star Chamber; and 7) that proclamations were acquiring the qualities of precedent, insofar as subsequent proclamations referred to earlier incarnations. The proclamation for raising and pulling down buildings, contained in Barker's 1609 compilation, is used as evidence for the third and sixth complaints.

The 1603 Orders on handling the plague were objectionable in similar terms. They created new frameworks for social regulation, imposed extensive limits on everyday life, allowed for Justices of the Peace to bypass the ordinary processes of criminal justice in punishing individuals, and further to create new offences without oversight. Admittedly they were not proclamations per se, but as with a proclamation they took the form of a unilateral decree given without parliamentary input.[73] And yet they are conspicuously absent from Parliament's complaint, despite their continued circulation.

[70] ibid 107–13. The exemplar decree is dated 29 November 1609.

[71] The tense background is canvassed in the chapters on the Parliament of 1604–1610, and particularly the financial disputes in 1610, in Richard Cust and Andrew Thrush (eds), Conrad Russell, *King James VI and I and his English Parliaments* (Oxford, Oxford University Press, 2011).

[72] Elizabeth Foster (ed), *Proceedings in Parliament 1610* (New Haven, CT, Yale University Press, 1966) Vol II, 260–61.

[73] Slack describes the earlier Elizabethan Orders, which like the 1603 Orders were issued by the monarch and Privy Council, as having 'derived their authority from the royal prerogative unrestrained and undiluted': Slack (n 10) 209.

Given no small degree of constitutional anxiety about the sources of measures, why is it that the Orders of 1603 did not attract similar attention? A range of answers are plausible, and may collectively explain the lack of controversy. First, although the powers conferred on Justices allowed for summary punishment, they were in response to something that could be framed as *malum in se*. In the *Case of Proclamations* a distinction with offences is drawn between *malum in se*, contrary to the common law, and *malum prohibitum*, rendered criminal by an Act of Parliament.[74] The objection to the use of proclamations to create offences was that it stood outside of these two sources. If endangering others through a failure to abide by public health directives could be framed as something inherently wrongful, the objection would be circumvented. Secondly, although the powers are novel in their connection with the plague, they are analogous to existing public order powers conferred by legislation. The Plague Act, and earlier Orders, are often found together with legislation allowing for the arrest, punishment and transportation of vagabonds.[75] Kynnersley's focus on such individuals in 1603 was due to the threat of infection they carried, but his actions could have been justified under vagrancy legislation. Thirdly, the action may have been considered uncontroversially necessary, particularly given the sharp increase in the mortality rate and the absence of a sitting Parliament.

VII. Conclusion

It is difficult to write on the regulation of previous pandemics without drawing comparison with recent experience. As a historical resource, Kynnersley's Memorandum Book is not as fulsome as Daniel Defoe's account of life in London during the Great Plague. It does, however, have the advantage of being contemporaneous with the events it describes. And for legal and social historians, it has particular value. The measures described are timeless, and their contemporary echo hardly needs emphasis. In his entries Kynnersley describes a community struggling as the parameters of everyday life were redefined. In the heightened regulations for the Uttoxeter fair, we can see an eagerness for the continuation of ordinary events. In the punishments doled out to his officials, we can see the difficulties of enforcing pandemic regulations when those who are responsible for the rules do not abide by them. And in his war on wakes, the unusual practice of 'Plague Raves' finds an ancestor.[76] Perhaps the sharpest point of departure between the seventeenth and twenty-first century experiences of pandemic regulation is the controversy those rules have inspired once the worst had passed.

[74] *Case of Proclamations* (1611) 12 Co Rep 7.
[75] eg 39 Eliz I c 4.
[76] For which see, eg, https://dj.dancecult.net/index.php/dancecult/article/view/1227/1044.

3

Epidemic Extraterritoriality and Border Prophylaxis in Western Europe, 1780–1850

ALEX CHASE-LEVENSON

I. Introduction

By their very nature, epidemics are events curtailed by a beginning and an end. The historian Charles Rosenberg has concluded persuasively that even in their tremendous diversity, such events follow a distinct, dramaturgical form – one in which ominous signs and initial administrative blindness give way to panic, social breakdown, and then resolution/atonement.[1] In legal and political terms, epidemics have habitually been seen as fertile moments of experimentation, where the pressing nature of the emergency can lead to bureaucratic and legislative innovation. Epidemics are both 'states of exception', in which typical norms and rights are sometimes suspended, and crucibles of innovation, during which lasting precedents are set. We have only to think of our own experiences during the COVID-19 pandemic to see how both have applied.

Yet, in the late eighteenth and early nineteenth centuries, the permanent quarantine system operating in Western and Southern Europe offers a different way to think about the legal world of epidemics. Though lazarettos (quarantine stations) existed long before and long after this time (and well beyond this space), the coherence they took on as a network of demarcation in the Mediterranean world of this era demonstrates a particular (and formative) instance of legal ambiguity that profoundly shaped the development of international health as a field.

In lazarettos, epidemic disease was always presumed and rarely present. In this way, lazarettos were themselves permanent instantiations of a 'state of exception'. Even in constitutional regimes, the whims of a health board and its rules held the power of life and death over all who passed through. And, also like broader

[1] Charles E Rosenberg, 'What is an Epidemic? AIDS in Historical Perspective' in Charles E Rosenberg, *Explaining Epidemics* (Cambridge, Cambridge University Press, 1992).

epidemics, lazarettos shaped administrative (and reformist) imaginations as further public health innovations unfolded. This influence can be linked to Mediterranean quarantine's scope and scale in this era; in addition to intra-European quarantines based on as little as a rumour of disease, literally every ship, passenger, trade good, and letter proceeding to Western Europe from the Ottoman Empire and North Africa was required to submit to detention in a quarantine station, for periods ranging from about 10 days to over 80, based on the lingering presence of bubonic plague over the Ottoman frontier and across the sea. At one level, this reflected a simple epidemiological barrier: the final major plague epidemics in Western Europe occurred in 1720, in Provence, whereas major Ottoman port cities saw recurrent epidemics until about 1840. At another level, the layering of different kinds of borders (confessional, cultural, political, and biological) freighted this quarantine system with unusual significance.

Indeed, in an era before universal passport controls, proceeding through a lazaretto represented the most intensive form of border regulation possible anywhere in the world. Those who experienced it often had to endure involuntary detention and suffer the indignity of fumigation and of invasive checks to ensure no symptoms of disease were being concealed. Furthermore, quarantine's status as a *national* border was often emphasised by the fusion of customs inspections and quarantine declarations. As the nature of every trade good on board a ship potentially liable to quarantine was of the utmost interest to boards of health (with certain 'susceptible goods', like cotton, seen as particularly in need of fumigation), customs authorities clearly noted the utility of this information, and governments thus fostered a close alliance among these distinct functions of the state. In Britain, for example, quarantine was (rather anomalously) controlled by the Privy Council, yet it was carried out entirely by the Customs Service.

And yet, as much as quarantine stations served as border regimes for the country in which they sat, they collectively came to comprise a transnational institution, a kind of supra-national or civilizational border between East and West. By its practitioners, quarantine came to be recognised as one of the key responsibilities of an advanced nation; its absence could be a source of critique, its presence, a ticket to membership in a transnational club. Those operating within the network of lazarettos possessed what one French quarantine reformer called '*le droit sanitaire de l'Europe*', a right to land one's ships in free pratique (without quarantine) in other European ports.[2]

This 'right' had emerged implicitly; it nevertheless had legal force. Although boards of health had the theoretical power to institute whatever quarantine rules they felt were most appropriate, they all relied on the same system of bills of health, documents whose validity was signified by the signature of *any* European consul. Every nation employing what came to be referred to simply as 'the quarantine

[2] Pierre Ségur-Dupeyron, *Des Quarantaines et des pertes qu'elles occasionent au commerce* (Paris, Madame Huzard, 1833) 23.

laws' relied on the same classification of clean, touched, or foul bills of health, and the parameters of quarantine for each of these levels were undergirded by shared assumptions. Boards of health did not exist or make rules in a vacuum; they constantly corresponded with each other, with diplomats, and with their own national governments. In this way, lazarettos were simultaneously national and international spaces, institutions whose procedures were shaped more by transnational norms than domestic particularities.

Quarantine law constituted an active sphere of national legislating. Britain enacted major quarantine laws in 1753, 1800, and 1825 (with minor changes in between). France revised its sanitary legislation during the Plague of Marseille in 1720, during the Revolution, and then again in 1822. Yet, in almost all ways, national legislation mattered far less in terms of actual practice than the supranational norms I have just described. Such norms were incorporated into quarantine practice by orders from local boards of health, often expressly deputised to act in this way. As such, by the late eighteenth century, the spread of quarantine practice across Western Europe and the sense that it had succeeded at keeping plague away, fostered an understanding that 'the quarantine laws' formed a subject best considered as *ius gentium*, a necessary presence in any 'civilised' nation.[3] These laws were unwritten, an accumulation of shared practices that mattered more than individual national legislation. Just so, by the 1820s, sanitary bureaucrats routinely adverted to 'the Sanitary System of Europe', as a proper noun, to indicate quarantine. As administrators of a universal and customary sphere of practice in states increasingly aware of themselves as epidemiologically implicated, members of boards of health governed a system as transnational colleagues in a way that effaced national distinctions. With the exception of anti-piracy activities coordinated among different nations from the early modern period, epidemic prevention forms one of the earliest and most robust arenas in which such a 'law of the people' was coordinated and applied by bureaucrats in different nations.

In this chapter, I am concerned with the implicit contradiction between lazarettos as markers of a political border (closely allied with customs services) and lazarettos as spaces subject to norms and procedures forged by Continent-wide traditions. I argue that it is precisely such a contradictory situation that enabled a new understanding of international sanitary space, a unique sort of extraterritoriality that was a crucial building block of the norms that undergird modern international health. As a national boundary marker, lazarettos accrued grandeur and formal stakes, but as a site where *ius gentium* ensnared travellers, sailors, and trade goods in a regulatory web with no central authority, lazarettos also lay curiously beyond the nation. Sanitary extraterritoriality was the result, and it

[3] A classical conception that was elaborated in the Medieval and Early Modern periods, *ius gentium* was applied to numerous topics of diplomacy, war, and the law of the sea. It has not been habitually linked to disease control. On the concept in general, see Dante Fedele, '*Ius Gentium*: The Metamorphoses of a Legal Concept (Ancient Rome to Early Modern Europe)' in Edward Cavanagh (ed), *Empire and Legal Thought* (Leiden, Brill, 2020).

constitutes a critical concept in the evolution of international health as a sphere of regulation beyond the nation almost two centuries before the founding of the World Health Organization (WHO).

And so we turn to legislation passed in 1753 by Britain's Parliament, in which these ambiguities were on full display. Two bills addressing quarantine were carried that year, one regarding quarantine practice in general and another regarding the Levant trade. For our purposes, the 'Act for enlarging and regulating trade into the Levant seas' is the more interesting piece of legislation,[4] containing, as it did, a clause stipulating that Britain would henceforth admit ships that had departed from the Middle East with a foul bill of health only if they had performed quarantine already at one of seven foreign lazarettos:[5] Marseille, Malta, Genoa, Venice, Messina, Livorno, or Ancona. This was an extraordinary rule, in which the British Government unilaterally deputised foreign bureaucrats to convert dangerous bodies and trade goods into safe ones.

As John Booker has noted, this was far from the 'temporary expedient' claimed by the eighteenth-century plague writer Patrick Russell; the idea that Britain might admit foul bill ships without initial reception elsewhere in Europe was deeply controversial.[6] In essence then, this constituted the abdication of sovereignty in favour of expertise, a rule that unilaterally deputised foreign boards of health and lazaretto workers to carry out an explicit role in admitting British subjects home. While the idea of partially outsourced passport control seems absurd in the contemporary world, this is certainly what this dynamic amounted to.

It is particularly interesting to note that over the 46 years this rule applied (from 1754 until a Quarantine Act in 1800 finally allowed ships with foul bills to perform quarantine in Britain itself), Britain was at war with France for 20 years, as it had been for much of the first half of the eighteenth century. The inclusion of Marseille on the list of foreign lazarettos licensed to admit travellers to Britain demonstrates a recognition that its reputation as one of the largest and most rigorous quarantine ports outweighed a political concern that its employees might subject British ships to unjustifiable delays. Indeed, there is evidence to suggest that such a practice would have been rare and itself a violation of quarantine norms. When France *did* impose a rule treating British ships as if they always had foul bills of health during a later phase of the Napoleonic Wars, its erstwhile Italian allies severely castigated the decision for its departure from sanitary professionalism.[7]

[4] 26 Geo II, c 18.

[5] Part of the 'quarantine laws' that applied in every nation to mandate the practice was the rule that every ship must carry a bill of health. Bills could be 'clean' (indicating the port of departure had no report of plague), 'touched' or 'suspect' (in case a ship had incidental contact with another ship from an area where plague was reputed to be), or 'foul' (indicating the ship departed from a port city in which there had been verified cases of the plague). The signature of any European consul made a bill of health valid, but the general convention was that a ship should have its bill signed by the local consul from the country in which the ship was flagged.

[6] John Booker, *Maritime Quarantine: The British Experience, c. 1650–1900* (Aldershot, Ashgate, 2007) 173.

[7] See Mongiardini to *Intendants Sanitaires de Marseille*, 30 April 1814. Archives Départmentales des Bouches-du-Rhône, Marseille (ADBR) 200 E 423. On the occasion of the 1814 declaration of

Absent the pressures of war, however, Marseille's quarantine officials were at least as professional as those anywhere else. In fact, it is from Marseille that the most explicit enunciation of lazaretto extraterritoriality emerges. In 1818, the storeroom of one Sieur Poucel, the '*aubergiste*' of the *Lazaret d'Arenc* (Marseille's enormous lazaretto, the only structure in France authorised to receive ships and passengers from the Levant), was raided by inspectors from the city's tax office (the *Octroi*). In choosing to vociferously protest this violation in a legal proceeding, Marseille's *Intendants Sanitaires* explicitly declared the lazaretto to be part of 'the domain of all nations', and emphasised the unprecedented nature of an intrusion into this forbidden space.[8] A perplexed Parisian minister tasked with making a final decision in the case further noted that the Marseille Board insisted that the lazaretto's 'inviolability and independence' were 'set down by a law', and apparently concluded that proceeding based on past practices was the clearest way forward.[9]

These two positions (the British Parliament's willingness to deputise its subjects' sanitisation to foreign lazarettos and the Marseille *Intendance*'s clear enunciation of the world of the lazaretto as 'the domain of all nations') demonstrate that across time and space, an administrative logic was cohering in the late eighteenth and early nineteenth centuries that held that lazarettos were separate from the polities that housed them. Such a logic presupposes a distinction between the national aspects of lazarettos (the connection to customs regimes, their ultimate control by national governments) and the medical aspects, where the ostensibly disinterested task of plague prevention contributed to a sense that professional sanitary responsibility transcended national affiliation.

II. Disease Prevention as a Shared Enterprise

Surely this sort of lazaretto extraterritoriality was based on an understanding of the way epidemics themselves (and particularly bubonic plague) did not respect national borders. Plague was portrayed as the antithesis of civilisation, and, consequently, an antagonist that every 'civilised' country ought to proactively oppose. As one handbill (produced by the Marseille *Intendance Sanitaire* to explain quarantine to French prisoners of war returning from Alexandria after the failure of the Egyptian Campaign) explained the nature of quarantine:

> There are countries that are suspect, as regards public health: those too often afflicted by the plague … [and] those [countries] who communicate with these others, without

the short-lived Genoese Republic, Mongiardini (of Genoa's Magistrato di Sanità) began to write in Italian instead of French (which had been used for the previous seven years, during which the Board of Health of Genoa had been subordinated to Marseille's Board), and wrote that Genoa was immediately dropping all quarantines ordered against ports 'which would not have been suspected, if not for the commerce they maintained with the English nation'.

[8] See 'Procès de Sieur Poucel': ADBR 200 E 18.

[9] See Louis-Emmanuel Corvetto to Vicomte Lainé, 27 February 1818. Archives Nationales (Pierrefitte), F/8/28/1/1.

> taking preservative measures from this essentially contagious evil. Such is the effect of ignorance, despotism, and superstition. ... Everywhere where the rights of man maintain their power, these protective laws are respected. Common interest ensures it is so, as does the severity that accompanies them, and ensures they cannot be violated without punishment.[10]

Civilised modernity, according to these bureaucrats, required both the absence of plague and the presence of quarantine. As another French plague-writer put it, 'the same foyer of corruption which fosters the plague in Egypt and Ethiopia was in France and Italy: enlightened thinkers destroyed it'. This author, writing in 1800, was aware that plague formed the relatively recent past of Europe itself, and (to him) the institution of quarantine over the course of the eighteenth century was clearly the 'miracle' that had caused it to disappear.[11]

Epidemic disease appeared to be a greater menace than ever in this precise era. As I have shown elsewhere, the period from the 1770s to the 1830s represents a high point of epidemic activity, with plague, yellow fever, and cholera all causing devastation in the Middle East, North Africa, the Black Sea region, and Southern Europe.[12] Plague in particular, the original disease to inspire the quarantine laws, went through a major uptick in the 1810s. In 1812, an epidemic in Istanbul killed somewhere between 100,000 and 300,000 people (at least a quarter of the population of the city), in the worst outbreak since the 1780s. Odessa and Aleppo each lost tens of thousands of inhabitants in 1812–13 and 1814 plague epidemics.[13] This particular intensification was clearly linked to the further spread of the disease, which breached quarantine ports in Southern Europe for the last time in that decade. Malta was struck with plague in 1813, Corfu in 1816, and Mallorca in 1820, while the Puglian town of Noja (in what was then the Kingdom of the Two Sicilies) experienced the last outbreak of plague on the (Western half of the) Continent in 1815.

For Western powers (Britain, France, Spain, Austria, and the Italian States) with significant coasts or colonial possessions in the Mediterranean, this represented a major crisis. Because it coincided with the Napoleonic Wars, such a crisis is easy to miss. Yet, one can see it in such things as the three-concentric rings of troops dispatched to guard Noja and shoot anyone on sight if they attempted to leave the plague-stricken town (mirroring almost exactly the French plague-writer JP Papon's insistence on at least two cordons of troops if plague broke out in Europe, and the understanding that 'each man becomes a soldier in such a situation').[14]

[10] 'Proclamation des Conservateurs de la Santé Publique,' 28 Fructidor, An 9 [15 September 1801]. AN (Pierrefitte) F/8/1/Dossier V.

[11] JP Papon, *De la Peste*, Vol I (Paris, Lavillete et Compagnie, 1800) viii–ix.

[12] For a more detailed argument regarding this period as one of public health crisis, see Alex Chase-Levenson, *The Yellow Flag: Quarantine and the British Mediterranean World* (Cambridge, Cambridge University Press, 2020) ch 2.

[13] See Daniel Panzac, *La Peste dans L'Empire Ottomane, 1700–1850* (Leuven, Éditions Peeters, 1985) 359.

[14] Papon (n 11) Vol II, 4.

One can note the terror of the ministers who summoned the French military cordon sent to the Pyrenees to guard the border with Spain during that country's yellow fever epidemics in the early 1800s. In declaring a 'state of siege' along the southern border, the Minister of the General Police asked (in a panicked dispatch): 'what sorts of remedies can oppose such a pressing evil?' before concluding that 'without extreme punishments, one cannot hope to prevent it; all borders will be breached – the sick man stalked by death will be stopped only by death itself'.[15] Finally, one can note the sense of threat it would have taken to induce Britain's relatively hands-off Privy Council to order three ships, arriving from Morocco in 1800 (again, during Spain's yellow fever epidemics) with ostensibly dangerous goat furs as cargo, to 'be forthwith carried out to sea, and there sunk in deep water, under the Direction and Inspection of one of His Majesty's Ships of War'.[16]

Such dramatic language and such extreme policies ensured that Western European countries emerged from the Napoleonic crisis determined to prove their sanitary bona fides. Indeed, the extreme detail with which such bona fides were proved can seem retrospectively ludicrous. Some five years after the end of the plague of Malta, officials on that island were writing memorials to boards of health around the Continent about the disposal of some resurfaced jewels, coins, and papers from the house of someone known to have died during the outbreak. The discovery of these items, worried the Superintendent of Quarantine, could 'destroy the confidence which ought to exist' between quarantine authorities in different ports.[17] The urgency with which that 'mutual confidence' was sought was, in this case, in part about Malta's desire to see ships from those islands received in free pratique (without quarantine) in Italy. But the letter would not have come across as hyperbole in Livorno, because members of boards of health in the post-Napoleonic Mediterranean assumed their foreign interlocutors all understood the fight against epidemic disease (or at least plague and yellow fever) needed to be an international effort, that all Western European states had a basic interest in protecting each other.

One can detect ways in which the 'total war'[18] of the Napoleonic Era encouraged a sense that civilised government and quarantine went hand in hand. When Marseille's board of health published a pamphlet in 1799 accusing the British of conspiring with North Africans to infect France with plague, they vaunted their own faithful application of the quarantine laws as all that could protect 'the general salubrity of Europe' from such an uncivilised attack (the rumour may well have

[15] Report by the Minister of General Police. Undated (but from the context, certainly from 1801). Archives Nationales (Pierrefitte-sur-Seine) F/8/1/VII.

[16] PC Order from 7 January 1800. UK National Archives, Kew (henceforth, TNA) PC 2/154. The fate of the *Mentor*, the *Lark*, and the *Aurora* remained a controversial episode for years.

[17] Robert Grieves to the Governor of Livorno. 18 September 1818. National Library of Malta, Valletta (henceforth, NLM) LIBR 843.

[18] See David Bell, *The First Total War* (Boston, MA, Houghton Mifflin, 2007).

been invented by the Marseille board, to bolster its own prestige).[19] Because the language of sanitary defence and ideological power ran so well together, governments on opposite sides of the conflict found themselves intensifying their commitment to quarantine, especially in the face of the epidemic crisis described above.

This was borne out in many other aspects of quarantine governance. Boards of health corresponded not only with each other, but also directly with diplomats posted in the Middle East and elsewhere; few (or no?) other corporate bodies in any nation in this era would have carried out such a correspondence, at least in such a regular manner. Board members often operated with horizons that looked across the Mediterranean, or towards other quarantine ports more than to their own national capitals, especially by the 1830s, and particularly in France where Parisian ministers often pushed for greater reforms than Marseille's health board members were willing to concede. In the immediate aftermath of the Napoleonic Wars, even the membership of boards of health could be strikingly cosmopolitan, with Britons serving on Genoa's venerable *Magistrato di Sanità*.

It is important to emphasise the degree of authority these bodies had over the specific liminal institution they governed. Boards of health commanded absolute power over all aspects of quarantine justice. They could refuse to admit a ship, or, in rare cases, order a ship to leave the quarantine port. Given that in states like France and Tuscany, a single quarantine station served as the only port of admission for all ships arriving from the Middle East, such a power was equivalent to denying admission to the country as a whole.

It is precisely this sort of power and authority which lent spaces of quarantine the sense of extraterritoriality I am suggesting in this chapter. Decisions over admissibility to national states, powers to segregate, examine, and discipline travellers, decisions to burn cargoes, powers to isolate or punish (even very prominent) individuals who passed through lazarettos, were only occasionally necessary, but demanded clear authority. It is for this reason that in place of a traditional board of health, British law tasked the Privy Council with administering quarantine, long after that body had lost most of its other practical functions. At the Hapsburg-Ottoman frontier, where 'terrestrial' lazarettos detained all travellers, the popular quarantine station at the Rothenthurm Pass was located under a mountain emblazoned with the imperial seal. Yet, as imbued with such significance as they were, these spaces were under the control of bureaucrats who saw themselves as colleagues engaged in a transnational task – at least equally dedicated to norms and customs that had emerged organically among them. It is this fusion of national and international, and the embodied liminality symbolised by the lazaretto (explored in Part III), that created sanitary extraterritoriality – the first iteration of a theme represented today by the WHO and its agents, among others.

[19] L'Administration Sanitaire de Marseille, *Conservation de la Santé Publique* (Marseille, Bertrand and Company, 1799).

An examination of board of health composition and identity shows tremendous variety but a consistent emphasis on one or more of several common themes: grandeur, cosmopolitanism, and expertise. In Marseille, for example, the board of health had a strong corporate identity; uniquely among Mediterranean boards, each member of the *Intendance* signed every outgoing letter (among the hundreds sent each month).[20] Each member went through a nomination process involving a vote by Marseille's City Council, followed by a formal nomination (occasionally going against the Council's wishes) by the Prefect of the Bouches-du-Rhône department, and final approval by the responsible minister in Paris (the Interior Minister during the Empire and Restoration and the Minister of Commerce and Industry under the July Monarchy). All of those involved seem to have valued long experience with Levantine commerce.[21] In addition to those nominated in this fashion, the Board (by the Restoration, this was formally the *Intendance Sanitaire de Marseille*) included two local doctors and the Mayor of Marseille (named an '*Intendant né*' by virtue of his office). The status of the health board was elevated further by the unique presence in Marseille of an 'Agency' of the Ministry of Foreign Affairs (a constant interlocutor with board members in many quarantine matters).

Other ports operated differently. In Genoa, the long-time president of the Magistrato di Sanità was the Marchese di Pallavicini, scion of a storied local aristocratic family. Similarly, in Malta, when the British colonial Government decided to convene a board of health, to better assimilate the colony's quarantine practices with those of neighbouring states, selected among political and medical representatives was a venerable Maltese aristocrat: the Baron Trigona.[22] Such members of boards were clearly intended to create corporate bodies endowed with expertise and pedigree that would be internationally legible.

Through their membership, then, as well as their competencies, boards of health emphasised their international authority. After all, it should be remembered that the expertise granted to members of boards of health must have contributed to their unique responsibility for creating the only international document theoretically accepted worldwide: the bill of health. Again, bills of health were of critical importance in terms of determining the length of any period of quarantine, and were intended to be signed by the consul from the nation of the ship's flag. Yet, at least in many cases, the bills themselves were composed and printed by boards of health in European ports and dispatched subsequently to major ports of departure. In an era when passports were far from universal and, when carried, made out only for particular destinations, a bill of health was perhaps the only indispensable

[20] Each member present at the meeting where the letter was written, that is. Elsewhere, letters were almost always exclusively signed by the president of the board of health.

[21] In records from a group nomination held in the autumn of 1818, the Municipal Council proposed a list of close to a dozen (ranked) possibilities, among whom the Prefect selected only those marked as 'ayant résidé en Levant' (or a specific Levantine city) or 'faisant le commerce du Levant'. See Prefect of the Bouches-du-Rhône to the Interior Minister, 27 October 1818. AN (Pierrefitte) F/8/28/II.

[22] See circular letter from the Maltese Board of Health to the boards of health of the Mediterranean. 6 April 1826. National Archives of Malta, Rabat (henceforth NAM) CSG 03/71.

document universally acceptable (and mandatory) for border-crossing. Certainly, where checking the documents of travellers ever occurred in early nineteenth-century Europe, it was usually in the interior of states (such as at the first inn at which a traveller stopped after crossing a frontier).[23] The bill of health, then, was certainly the only such document to actually be presented *at* a border.

III. The Lazaretto and the Law

Boards of Health were the ultimate governors of all aspects of quarantine. Yet they operated at something of a remove from lazarettos themselves. In Marseille, for example, the water-side offices of the *Intendance* by the Old Port were about one mile south of the forbidding *Lazaret d'Arenc*. When it suited its members to do so, the *Intendance* stressed the inaccessibility of that institution to even their own particular interests. Citing an ambiguous '*loi inviolable à laquelle aucune sort de raison ne peut faire déroger*', one *Intendant* emphasised he was unable to bring even one of his own parents on a tour of the building.[24] This law, in fact, appears to have been reasonably violable, as the same archival dossier in which the above declaration appears carries records of the later visit of Prince Borghese (Napoleon Bonaparte's brother-in-law), who was granted a tour of the lazaretto in 1807 (accompanied by the Mayor of Marseille) at 5am (perhaps to avoid encountering anyone in the halls). The *Intendants* noted to the Interior Minister that they assumed the prohibition against receiving external persons into the lazaretto could not apply to one 'so close' to the emperor.[25]

As this contradictory situation exhibits, lazarettos operated through layers of prohibited access. For a traveller or sailor 'imprisoned' there, a chance touch of someone from another party of travellers could lead to an extension of quarantine. One traveller noted her terror that if a dog she observed running around Malta's lazaretto had brushed against her she might have to suffer through weeks more imprisonment.[26] Travellers felt constantly surveilled by lazaretto guardians. At the parlatorio, an evocative chamber in which potentially infected travellers in quarantine could speak to friends or associates living freely on shore, 'guardians' (the traditional name given to lazaretto guards) stood in between the two groups of people with sticks ready to swat away hands that got too close. One can think of the parlatorio as an analogue to a modern rank of passport control desks, in which

[23] See John Torpey, *The Invention of the Passport: Surveillance, Citizenship, and the State* (Cambridge, Cambridge University Press, 2000) 57–59.

[24] Conservateurs de Santé de Marseille to the Interior Minister. 15 Thermidor, An XII [3 August 1804]. AN (Pierrefitte) F/8/29/VI.

[25] Conservateurs de Santé de Marseille to the Interior Minister. 4 August 1807. AN (Pierrefitte) F/8/29/VI.

[26] Lucinda Griffith, *A Journey Across the Desert from Ceylon to Marseille*, vol II (London, Henry Colburn, 1845) 97.

vigilant guards separate those yet to be admitted from those deemed safely inside the border – the difference, of course, was at the parlatorio there was no possibility of passing to the other side (at least until some days had gone by).

Touch and the avoidance of touch, then, were central preoccupations. Barriers within barriers ensured space for every kind of activity was circumscribed and regulated. Guardians observed every move lazaretto detainees made as they moved through quarantine themselves, one or two assigned to each party of travellers or quarantined ship. Small wonder, then, that the Marseille *Intendance* should have chosen this precise feature to explain the lazaretto to the new arrivals there during the return of Napoleon's *Armée d'Orient* from Egypt in an enormous public notice: 'Those places of reserve known as lazarettos', they wrote, '[are] marked by enclosures and limits'.[27]

This proliferation of barriers was enforced by some generally understood rules. It was clear by the very nature of quarantine that flight from the lazaretto was prohibited, and in the tiny handful of times it was attempted, the consequences were generally severe. In 1819, for example, the register of deliberations of the *Intendance* finds a Sardinian sailor who was imprisoned and recommended for more of 'the most severe' punishments after he swam from the boat on which he had been performing quarantine to the Island of Ratonneau (part of the quarantine apparatus of the city and itself in isolation), solely based on the reasoning that he was '*sans doute*' attempting to reach the city of Marseille.[28] In March 1814, just around the end of Malta's plague epidemic, a lazaretto guardian who had 'openly breached the quarantine' was sentenced to death, only to be pardoned at the last moment on the grounds that his was the first death sentence issued after Malta officially became a British colony.[29]

Absent such cases, however, routine examples of more minor infractions and even more frequent declarations that certain behaviours might violate abstract norms and practices were often couched in legal language. Such language often reveals the presumption of law where none precisely existed, a feature of much discussion surrounding 'the quarantine laws'. The rule forbidding an *Intendant* from bringing even his own parent past the triple walls of the *Lazaret d'Arenc* was expressed as an 'inviolable law', but as I have just shown above, it was not inviolable, and it was not a law either.

This disjuncture between the ubiquitous assumption of universal quarantine laws and the actual justification for lazaretto practices becomes even clearer when we look more minutely at those practices themselves. A norm shared around the Mediterranean, for example, meant that precisely two guardians needed to be present on board for any standard-sized ship performing quarantine, with its crew, in a quarantine harbour. Each bale of merchandise deemed susceptible had a specific procedure for disinfection made so regular that a small change could

[27] 'Proclamation des Conservateurs de la Santé Publique'.
[28] Minutes of the *Intendance*. 20 April 1819. AN (Pierrefitte) F/8/28/II.
[29] See the plaque constructed on the front façade of Malta's lazaretto (still in excellent condition).

generate vast correspondence and hand-wringing (perhaps, once wondered a French minister, lazaretto guardians need only insert their arms in and wiggle two sides of a cotton bale, rather than the requisite three? The answer was no).[30] With the theoretical reputation of *ius gentium* and the resulting sense that a deviation from sanitary norms risked Continent-wide disaster, and in the absence of a clear theoretical framework explaining why any particular quarantine procedure was medically essential, norms and traditions collected legal weight.

It is for this reason that in the 1840s, when the universality that underlay Mediterranean quarantine began to come apart, the sense of betrayal was so complete among boards of health that it seemed like a problem of law and not simply of medical risk. The apparent retreat of plague in coastal Middle Eastern trading cities after the Egyptian plague of 1835, the rise of 'anticontagionist' voices in the early years of the sanitarian movement, and a new eagerness in the French, British, and Austrian governments to take action to reform the system after its failure to stop cholera, all contributed to a steady drumbeat of rule changes that lessened the severity of quarantine or exempted some people, boats, and goods altogether.

In 1841, for example, the French Government (more than a decade after France's initial invasion) forced the Marseille *Intendance* to change its rules to allow ships from Algeria to dock in free pratique (ie, without quarantine). Coming in the midst of a tumultuous relationship between the Minister of Commerce and Industry (Laurent Cunin-Gridaine) and the *Intendants*, which would eventually result in their mass resignation, this episode fundamentally changed the perception that boards of health were solely responsible for the rules of quarantine. There was a clear sense in the aftermath that the Marseille board had lost its good reputation among the more conservative Italian health boards.[31] This is visible, for example, as the Tuscan consul in Marseille grimly forwarded the Governor of Livorno's *Consiglio di Sanità* (board of health) a quotation from a reformist French newspaper, which had suggested 'It is good for the *Intendants* to be made to face this truth: that it is not they who ought to make the law in the Mediterranean.'[32]

The upshot of such a dismissive comment, of course, was that in the era before the 1840s, it clearly *was* the boards of health who 'made the law' in the quarantine spaces of the region. That this was possible shows the previous way national legislation had actually been crafted to enable such independent action. A French Revolutionary-era order of the National Convention, clarifying the new regime's quarantine policy, simply read:

> It is ordered that the Municipalities and Administrative Corps of Corsica and of [France's] Mediterranean coasts … should dedicate themselves to the execution of this

[30] See the correspondence in ADBR 200 E 194 between Laurent Cunin-Gridaine (Minister of Commerce and Industry) and the *Intendance Sanitaire de Marseille*.

[31] This sense is clear in the letter from Augustus Foster to Lord Palmerston, 11 May 1840. Published in *Correspondence Relative to the Contagion of the Plague and the Quarantine Regulations of Foreign Countries, 1836–1843* (London, TR Harrison, 1843) 171.

[32] A Gazzelli to the Governor of Livorno. 23 September 1841. Archivio di Stato di Livorno (ASL) Sanità 302.

> decree and the old laws, which prohibited quarantine from anywhere other than the ports of Marseille and Toulon, and should consult the Marseille Board of Health in all cases which require precautions, [and] to follow exactly the instructions that it might give them.[33]

Decades later, French ministers maintained the same line when petitioned by eminent figures for a reduction in quarantine – it was the Marseille *Intendance* that set the rules.[34] Before the mid-1840s, even when ministers clearly disapproved of decisions taken by the *Intendance*, they emphasised their deference. When an unusually short quarantine for a British diplomat at Trieste induced the *Intendants* to place a quarantine on all ships from Austrian ports, an official at the Interior Ministry wrote to the health board members that he feared their 'evident concern for the interests of public health' had led, in such instances, to 'excessive rigor'. Nevertheless, he emphasised, this was said 'without an intention to disapprove the measure you have taken'.[35] In the event, the advice was completely ignored and Marseille only removed its quarantine on Austrian ports several months later.

Not only did French politicians and bureaucrats defer to boards of health, but they created regulations that increased their authority by funnelling all ships requiring quarantine through two ports (Marseille for ordinary travellers and traders and Toulon for ships of war). This pattern was followed in other states. In Piedmont-Sardinia, for example, the health boards of Genoa and Cagliari were in charge of quarantine administration for the state as a whole, while Livorno's *Consiglio di Sanità* was sometimes referred to as the '*Dipartimento Sanitario*' of the entire Grand Duchy of Tuscany.

In many cases, then, such oversight constituted a vast administrative remit. Livorno itself was home to three major lazarettos (San Rocco, San Jacopo, and San Leopoldo), all located around the same urban waterfront. Genoa's *Magistrato di Sanità* superintended two major lazarettos; the smaller *Lazaretto della Foce* close to the city itself and the much larger *Lazaretto del Varignano* some 100 km away in La Spezia. Marseille's *Intendance*, probably the most powerful board of health in the Mediterranean, oversaw only one lazaretto, but it was truly vast. So large, in fact, was the *Lazaret d'Arenc* that the *Intendants* at one point seriously considered constructing a railway to move goods around it more efficiently.[36] In Spain, boards of health in Port Mahon (where a lazaretto was newly built in the nineteenth century) and Barcelona held similar powers, with only those ports allowed to receive ships with foul bills of health. In all of these states, these preeminent boards of health oversaw the action of much smaller health boards along the coast, which would meet to deal with unusual events like shipwrecks or smugglers, and report

[33] Decree of the National Convention, 17 December 1792 and Decree of the National Assembly 21 July 1792. Quoted in L'Administration Sanitaire de Marseille, *Conservation de la Santé Publique*.

[34] See, eg, Minister of the Interior to the *Intendants*, 7 February 1823. ADBR 200 E (n 7) 298.

[35] Roisbertrand to the *Intendants*. No date, but from context, it is clearly January 1825. ADBR, ibid.

[36] The notes, sketches, and correspondence surrounding this plan can be found in ADBR 200 E 1305.

all activity to the superintending boards. In this way, the entire maritime frontier of Southern Europe was surveilled by health boards, the only such authorities to have that purview.

While further quarantine legislation was passed during the early nineteenth century, boards of health did not lose their power until later. Both France and Britain enacted major revisions to their quarantine laws in the 1820s, for example. France's 1822 law laid out certain rules, such as the death penalty for quarantine infractions, that seem draconian, but in terms of their actual enactment, huge deference was paid to the Marseille *Intendance*. There were, in fact, numerous records of quarantine violations where the punishments were far milder than death. In Britain, the Quarantine Act 1825 laid out an apparently liberal regime, allowing the Privy Council to suspend quarantine for ships from the Levant with clean bills of health. But this seemingly revolutionary change was immediately suspended by the Privy Council's own order-in-council enacting the law, which confirmed nothing would change. The upshot of both laws was that either the *Intendance* or the Privy Council had absolute authority over quarantine justice, quarantine lengths/procedures, and the question of whether there would even be any quarantine at all. In Britain, this meant that quarantine withered away following a Privy Council order ending clean-bill quarantine in 1847.[37] In France, pressure from Parisian ministers forced the *Intendance* to institute similar reforms at roughly the same time. In both countries, changes to national legislation followed changes in practice only *much* later, indicating the way changing assumptions over the limits of *ius gentium* in sanitary spaces, rather than changing national positive law, was most significant. Britain's Quarantine Act 1825 remained on the books until 1894, while France's 1822 Quarantine Law was not repealed until a public health law was enacted under the Fourth Republic, in 1953.[38]

In sum, deference to boards of health (which was also the norm in the Italian States and the Austrian Empire) ensured that there was, until the 1840s, an assumption that such boards did indeed 'make the law' in Mediterranean sanitary affairs. And this was a form of 'the law of civilised peoples' that was all the more real because boards based their regulations on customary practice in other European ports. Constantly in communication with each other, boards tended to act in concert in response to similar threats, to routinely exchange tables of quarantine lengths and descriptions of rules, and to react with retaliatory quarantines when rumours or reports of deviation in other ports were made known to them. Where disagreement with national governments and reformist ministers emerged (particularly in France, but this dynamic was also visible in Italian states like Tuscany by the 1840s), boards were able to head off reforms until the mid-1840s by pointing precisely to the threat of such retaliatory quarantines, indicating their hands were tied by practices standardised by correspondence among like-minded

[37] The vast majority of ships had clean bills of health.

[38] Michel Morin, 'La loi du 3 mars 1822 relative à la police sanitaire: une loi essentiellement maritime en prologue au code de la santé publique' (2022) 39 *Annuaire de Droit Maritime et Océanique* 151.

professionals. The success of this argument can explain why procedures remained so robust until national governments coordinated to engage much more actively with quarantine practice and to insist on reform. Guardians were wiggling their arms in thousands of bales of cotton each month, and clothes were being fumigated (of perfectly healthy travellers proceeding from cities with no reports of disease) right up until quarantine essentially ceased to exist.

IV. Sanitary Extraterritoriality

In this way, during the early nineteenth century, when a sense of epidemic crisis and an increased level of trade and travel after the Napoleonic Wars meant that Mediterranean quarantine was at its peak, lazarettos operated according to dictates and customs shaped not by national laws, but rather by transnational understanding, itself shaped by local bureaucrats in different port cities. Indeed, the unique way in which health boards built up contacts with each other was occasionally explicitly cited as a reason for their power. We could consider the Napoleonic-era law, in which the Government of the short-lived Republic of Liguria granted powers to the Magistrato di Sanità of Genoa, in which one of the 'whereas' clauses justifying this preeminent role specifically invoked the *Magistrato's* 'expected correspondence with boards of health in foreign states' as a reason for its status.[39] In this way, part of the very rationale by which such boards were licensed by national governments was an acknowledgment that they had built up a distinct sanitary world in common with each other, and were thus the only ones able to regulate the sanitary border.

In the words of different travellers who experienced quarantine, Malta's lazaretto represented 'a gate for the whole Continent', or 'the chain of the European world'.[40] But though it was the largest such gate, it was only one of many. Another traveller found the much smaller lazaretto at Galatz (in the principality of Wallachia) to represent 'the stars that herald in the dawn of European civilization, in the form of custom-house officers, sanitary officers, police officers, &c'.[41] In this way, lazarettos crystallised elements of border crossing that would make administrative frontiers visible at a time when other border establishments were lacking.

Each of these travellers clearly perceived a single institution of quarantine as one part of a continent-wide frontier. This is partly attributable to the fact that having ventured outside the zone of protection, past the boundaries of the '*droit sanitaire*', quarantine *somewhere* was always necessary for a European traveller to return home. But more fundamentally, travellers were reacting to the way

[39] *Raccolta delle leggi, ed atti del corpo legislative della Repubblica Ligure*, Vol III (Genoa, G Franchelli, 1799) 191.

[40] The sources are, respectively, John Henry Newman, quoted in Paul Cassar, *A Medical History of Malta* (London, Wellcome Institute, 1964) 303 and Griffith (n 26) 81.

[41] Edmund Spencer, *Travels in the Western Caucasus*, Vol II (London, Henry Colburn, 1838) 197.

lazarettos as institutions assembled a formidable repertoire of border signifiers. Once quarantine had been performed, such a border would not usually be met with again on the same journey.

I do not intend to suggest that quarantine authorities operated seamlessly in one grand Foucauldian display of state power alongside all other sorts of authorities. In fact, though they mingled every day in the quarantine harbour, the relationship between Customs officials and lazaretto employees was often acrimonious.[42] In extreme cases, lazaretto workers even participated in smuggling activities that contravened the quarantine laws out of a desire to share in the profits of skirting customs. In Malta, for example, the venerable Pulis family had members serve as Captain of the Lazaretto well back into the era of rule by the Knights of St John (prior to 1798), but in 1831 the then Captain Pulis was suspended from his role after he was caught smuggling wheat. This incident was seriously embarrassing for Sir Hector Greig, Malta's Superintendent of Quarantine and later Chief Secretary to the Government, who had vouched for Pulis on multiple occasions when such allegations had surfaced in the past, and who continued to advocate for leniency on the grounds that the smuggling only occurred after quarantine was over.[43]

From Pulis's willingness to participate in a smuggling operation only *after* quarantine had expired to Greig's request for lenience, it can be inferred that lazaretto employees saw their institutions as centred solely on public health, with the other administrative functions appended to them (like customs) as incidental. But Pulis *did* end up permanently suspended, and customs inspection and sanitary inspection continued to occur together almost everywhere. This shows how governments continued to make use of lazaretto complexes as sites for border paraphernalia of all kinds. In Malta, for example, after the abolition of slavery in the British Empire in 1833, regulations imposed by the Board of Health mandated that all servants in travelling parties should be inspected for signs that they were in fact enslaved, in which case they were to be immediately liberated.[44] It is unclear how often or how willing quarantine officials were to do this in practice, and there is good reason to assume that such gestures were more symbolic than practical.[45] But it is precisely *as a symbol* that such a rule shows the importance of the lazaretto as the clearest sign of a political border.

Lazarettos were always cosmopolitan. At Malta, favoured by ships as a quarantine port in the 1830s and 1840s for a variety of reasons, lazaretto records from those decades show that those who stayed there were, on average, roughly 30 per cent

[42] Malta's Superintendents of Quarantine developed a longstanding institutional antagonism towards the Department of Marine Police. See numerous letters in National Archives of Malta, Rabat (NAM) CUST-04-01 and CUST-04-02.

[43] Hector Greig to Sir Frederick Hankey. 19 December 1831. NAM CUST-04-01.

[44] Cassar (n 40) 292.

[45] On the ambivalent way with which Britons confronted slavery in the Mediterranean, see Alison Frank, 'Children of the Desert and the Laws of the Sea' (2012) 117 *American Historical Review* 410.

Maltese, 5 to 10 per cent British, and 60 per cent 'foreign'.[46] Almost all lazarettos were dominated by those proceeding somewhere other than the city in which they were located. They were waypoints into a shared zone, nodal points of travel, but rarely a sign that a journey was ending. Travellers compared them to both prisons and zoos, noting (usually by way of complaining about the difficulties of communication) the varieties of languages spoken inside.

Even in their official forms, health boards and lazaretto staff members needed to be able to operate in a large number of different languages. Bills of health might be in English, French, German, or Italian. When consuls from newly independent Greece began (at the end of the 1820s) to issue bills of health in modern Greek, by contrast, health boards found they needed to employ translators. A Maltese quarantine administrator sniffed that Greek captains should bear the cost of this, as the language was one 'that no one in this office understands' and 'cannot be considered to be one of the generally known languages of Europe'.[47] Still, at most lazarettos, this cost came to be borne by boards of health and could be relatively substantial. The international ambit of health boards was thus limited by an understanding of Western and Central European norms – outsiders (such as the British, Dutch, Scandinavians, Ottomans, and Russians) were implicitly pressured to adapt to the norms and tended to compose bills of health in French or Italian.

The fusion of a grand continental network, operating according to shared norms, and the bureaucratic grandeur associated with a border institution combining different political and sanitary functions, served to create lazaretto extraterritoriality. Situated precisely at the boundary between health and disease, domestic and foreign, lazarettos held their inhabitants in a literal border space, separated from those on either side of the boundary (and from each other), and simultaneously bound by the inherent grandeur granted to the project of protecting a continent's health.

This extraterritoriality conceded a level of expertise and independence toward lazaretto affairs that was shockingly durable. In Britain, for example, not only did eighteenth-century legislation (as explored above) unilaterally outsource British prophylaxis to Mediterranean bureaucrats, but even after the development of a domestic foul bill quarantine regime and after the passage of the reformist Quarantine Act 1825, foreign certification on sanitary matters played an outsized role. The efforts of MPs to exempt more goods from quarantine in the 1825 Act, for example, resulted in an onerous regulation to include some sort of documentation (presumably often composed and signed by foreign diplomats and sanitary authorities) that the goods in question were 'not the produce of Turkey or Barbary'.[48] Further, bills of health remained important well into the late nineteenth century, since the removal of the need to quarantine ships with clean bills of health

[46] This is based on a calculation of various representative months in 1831, 1835, 1840, and 1845. I relied on the numbers in the National Library of Malta, LIBR 810/I and 810/II.

[47] Hector Greig to the Lieutenant Governor. 23 December 1831. NAM CUS/04/1.

[48] On the onerousness of this particular rule (section 38 of the 1825 Act), see Booker (n 6) 442–43.

(after the 1847 order-in-council in Britain and across most of the Mediterranean world by the early 1850s) clearly only accentuated the importance of carrying … a bill of health.

In such ways, it is revealing to consider the final decade of regular quarantining to see the ways the extraterritoriality of lazarettos continued to shape the development of global health. The tight coordination among boards of health created a clear sense, even for advocates of reform, that unilateral action was impossible; intra-European trade was too important to all of the major powers in the quarantine system to face every ship from domestic ports being held up for weeks in foreign harbours. For this reason, from the early 1830s, attempts were made to host a general Europe-wide conference that would (presumably) have resulted in the reduction of quarantine across the board.[49] That it took until 1851 to host such a conference shows how strongly the traditions among boards of health created a belief that abrogating quarantine was subjecting the Continent to unacceptable risk. That it took place at all is a testament to the fact that impinging on the world of the lazaretto could be seen as a violation of *ius gentium*; possible only for national governments to achieve in concert at an extraordinary conference that, itself, established a new pattern.

V. Conclusion

This chapter has argued that 'lazaretto extraterritoriality', the legal independence of boards of health, and the international practices and considerations that guided their work created an assumption that epidemic policy naturally occupies a transnational sphere. The idea of non-nationally specific and relatively abstract 'quarantine laws' underlay this understanding, as did the cosmopolitan world of lazarettos. The border status of these institutions and the way quarantine proved impossible to reform in one national context alone created a clear sense by the 1830s that the system could change only if France, Britain, and Austria acted together (with the latter power ostensibly able to pressure its Italian client states like Tuscany to follow suit). The 1851 International Sanitary Conference was created to address this concern and was the inaugural event in a series of such sanitary conferences (that the WHO cites as its own origin story).[50]

These conferences ended the quarantine system explored here, primarily because they limited its use to ships coming from areas infected with plague (in an era when that disease was retreating). But conference participants nevertheless helped to make permanent many of the innovations of the lower-level bureaucrats

[49] See FJ Martinez, 'International or French? The Early International Sanitary Conferences and France's Struggle for Hegemony in the Mid-Nineteenth Century Mediterranean' (2016) 30 *French History* 77.

[50] See Norman Howard-Jones, *The Scientific Background of the International Sanitary Conferences, 1851–1938* (Geneva, WHO, 1975).

whose health boards they had made redundant. Future practice clearly drew from the earlier era discussed here, marked by the vague, yet powerful, position of boards of health and the enduring link between diplomats and international sanitary problems. In the end, the sense that the needs of epidemic prevention transcended national particularities, that being a participant in international health institutions in good stead *requires* adherence to best practices, can be seen to derive substantially from the Mediterranean in the late eighteenth and early nineteenth centuries and from the fight against a very old antagonist: bubonic plague.

4

Frontline Powers and the Uses of the Law: Official Authority, Public Trust, and Public Health in England, c 1850–1910

TOM CROOK

I. Introduction

Of what use was the law in preventing infectious diseases during the Victorian period? In some obvious respects it was central. Statute law in particular – and more especially, 'general' or 'public' statute law – was crucial to enabling the great battery of institutions, policies, personnel, and technologies that developed from the 1830s, amid rampant urbanisation and industrialisation and their devastating epidemiological consequences. The powers granted via general public health statutes were vast, from the power to raise local taxes and build large-scale sewerage systems to imposing fines on property owners and compelling the hospitalisation of the sick. One annotated guide to the great Public Health Act of 1875, which sought to consolidate the multiple statutes passed in previous decades, extended to just under 600 pages.[1] References to general statute laws litter the existing historiography, old and new, and with good reason.

In other respects, however, the law was entirely peripheral: at best a kind of bystander. For what mattered in practice, as Foucauldian scholars are wont to emphasise, was not the agency of judges, lawmakers, or even ministers, but the agency of councillors, engineers, medical officers, inspectors, doctors, and chemists, among others: all those who, in one way or another, operated the many administrative and infrastructural systems which made up the complex field

[1] William Cunningham Glen and Alexander Glen, *The Public Health Act, 1875; and the Law Relating to Public Health, Local Government, and Urban and Rural Sanitary Authorities* (London, Knight & Co, 1876).

of public health as a day-to-day enterprise.[2] Joseph Bazalgette's Main Drainage Scheme for London serves to illustrate the point. Built under the authority of the Metropolitan Board of Works (MBW, 1855–89), the project began in 1859 and was largely complete by the late 1860s.[3] It was the largest civil engineering project of the nineteenth century and mobilised scores of surveyors and more than 20 private engineering firms. The system eventually comprised four steam-powered pumping stations and over 1,300 miles of main sewers. One might regard this as a monument to the law which established the MBW, the Metropolis Management Act 1855. But no law or set of lawmakers or judges prescribed the design or drew up the contracts, still less built, operated, or maintained it. Bazalgette's system was and remains, first and foremost, a monument to sanitary engineering and the agency of infrastructure.

This chapter argues for what we might think of as the space in between these two perspectives: the way in which the law, and the higher and lower courts of the legal system, were, at times and for some purposes, central, at others only peripheral, if still present. We need not choose. The law functioned as both an active and a latent form of authority, and one aim of what follows is to examine how, why, and where the law moved back and forth between these two forms – between active judicial intervention and deliberation on the one hand, and its latent, if still vital, presence as a form of authority that facilitated official action through the *possibility* of legal sanction on the other. To develop this argument the chapter examines three key administrative areas where the need for official authority was especially acute on account of their frontline status and the very intimate interference they entailed with the homes, bodies, and private interests of the population at large: the notification and isolation of cases of sickness and infection; the sanitary inspection of dwellings and small businesses; and the vaccination of the young.[4]

The intricacies are immense in each case, but examining them together suggests these areas shared at least two features which determined how the law was used and the forms it assumed. The first is that the effectiveness of the law was constrained by the relative autonomy granted to local authorities and the variable quality and quantity of resources in which its application was embedded, not least manpower. The law, in other words, was only as good as the *non*-legal resources that gave it any kind of purchase. The second is the importance of what might be thought of as the social element of these systems: public trust and co-operation. It was the presence or not of this crucial ingredient that did most to determine

[2] For a review of recent approaches to the Victorian state, including those of a Foucauldian sort, see Philip Harling, 'The State' in David Brown, Gordon Pentland and Robert Crowcroft (eds), *The Oxford Handbook of Modern British Political History, 1800–2000* (Oxford, Oxford University Press, 2018).

[3] Stephen Halliday, *The Great Stink of London: Sir Joseph Bazalgette and the Cleansing of the Victorian Metropolis* (Stroud, Sutton Publishing, 1999).

[4] Other areas, notably the Contagious Diseases Acts regime, might have been used. See Miles Ogborn, 'Law and Discipline in Nineteenth-century English State Formation: The Contagious Diseases Acts 1864, 1866 and 1869' (1993) 14 *Journal of Historical Sociology* 28.

the shifting forms of the law and quite how it participated in their functioning – and certainly, where public trust was low or absent, the law might have to assume an active form and intervene in ways that were straightforwardly punitive and disciplinary.

Crucially, both of these features reflect the way the three areas partook of a broader transformation that occurred in the legal culture of public health during the nineteenth century, and the tensions this incorporated – which we might call 'liberal' – between central and local authorities, and the need to balance the urgency of intervention with the rights of property and person. We begin with an overview of this culture, before turning to the three areas.

II. Statute Law and its Limits

The centrality of general statute laws to the development of Victorian public health is often seen as a symptom of an increasingly interventionist, bureaucratic, expert-driven state.[5] There is no question that it was. These laws eventually helped to displace an earlier culture of administration that was principally rooted in the authority of propertied civic elites and a complex landscape of administrative elements that included local common law courts (eg sewer courts, manorial courts, petty sessions), chartered municipal corporations, and urban improvement commissions, plus, in times of epidemic emergency, the Privy Council, which would issue nationwide 'orders'.[6] Though much of this would be condemned as inadequate by the 1840s, which in many ways it was, certainly in cities, the common law of 'nuisances' and associated legal procedures provided at least a modicum of administrative coherence. Surveyed and analysed by Blackstone in the 1760s, when he distinguished between 'private' nuisances (affecting individuals only) and 'public' nuisances (affecting small groups of people and communities), the term encompassed a variety of civil and criminal infringements and it was concerned, above all, with the enjoyment of property.[7] Pig-keeping, chemical manufacture, heaps of dung, projecting street signs: all might be designated a 'nuisance'; and as historians have suggested, in the decades prior to the ascendancy of statute law at mid-century, the common law was routinely drawn upon by civic authorities to

[5] See, eg, Derek Fraser, *The Evolution of the British Welfare State: A History of Social Policy since the Industrial Revolution*, 4th edn (Basingstoke, Palgrave Macmillan, 2009).

[6] Bryan Keith-Lucas, *The Unreformed Local Government System* (London, Croom Helm, 1980); Joanna Innes and Nicholas Rogers, 'Politics and Government, 1700–1840' in Peter Clark (ed), *The Cambridge Urban History of Britain, Volume II: 1540–1840* (Cambridge, Cambridge University Press, 2000); Stuart Anderson, 'Local Government' in William Cornish et al (eds), *The Oxford History of the Laws of England, Volume XI, Part II: 1820–1914: English Legal System* (Oxford, Oxford University Press, 2010).

[7] William Blackstone, *Commentaries on the Laws of England* (Oxford, Oxford University Press, 1765–69; Chicago, IL, University of Chicago Press, 1979) Vol 3, 216–22. These infringements were civil in the case of private nuisances, but could be both civil and criminal in the case of public nuisances.

secure more salubrious waterways, markets, streets, and homes, and by wealthy landowners in the higher courts (eg the King's Bench and the Court of Chancery) in private actions against industrial polluters.[8]

Crudely, the 60 or so general public health acts that emerged during the 1840s–70s made two decisive interventions. One is institutional: the creation of new central and local authorities. The Public Health Act 1848 marks a key threshold in this respect, placing England and Wales under the authority of the first dedicated official home for public health policy in Whitehall, the General Board of Health (GBH, 1848–58). While London was dealt with separately, eventually coming under the authority of the MBW, the Act also empowered the creation of local boards of health outside of the recently reformed municipal corporations. Other central offices created by statute would follow, notably the Local Government Board (LGB) in 1871, which remained until 1919 and brought together the central administration of the poor laws (previously under the Poor Law Board) and the public health responsibilities of the two bodies which had replaced the GBH in 1858, the Local Government Act Office (LGAO) and the Medical Department of the Privy Council (MDPC). Following a further public statute in 1872, the existing map of centre-local relations was redrawn again, and existing local authorities rationalised into a new structure of 'rural' and 'urban' sanitary districts which covered the entirety of England and Wales.

The other is more epistemological: enabling the employment of new forms of official authority. The central offices noted above were home to small bureaucracies composed of secretaries and roving inspectors. Still more important was the introduction of new kinds of expertise and officialdom at the local level. Edwin Chadwick's signal contribution during his six years as the chief official at the GBH was to place water-borne sewerage systems and civic drainage at the heart of public health and thereby empower engineers and surveyors as key agents. At the same time, a number of general statutes – the 1848 Act just mentioned; a series of Nuisances Removal Acts (1846–55); and the Sanitary Act 1866 – enabled the appointment of local medical officers of health (MOsH) and nuisance inspectors. Their appointment by local authorities was made compulsory by the same act of 1872 which created rural and urban sanitary districts; and both MOsH and nuisance inspectors gradually self-organised professionally, becoming more assertive of their expertise in the process.

These same officials were also legally equipped with remarkable powers of intervention over people's bodies and homes, as we shall see in our three frontline areas. Yet, whatever statist, technocratic impulses were secured by general statutes,

[8] Christopher Hamlin, 'Public Sphere to Public Health: The Transformation of "Nuisance"' in Steve Sturdy (ed), *Medicine, Health, and the Public Sphere in Britain, 1600–2000* (London, Routledge, 2002); Ben Pontin, 'The Common Law Clean Up of the "Workshop of the World": More Realism about Nuisance Law's Historic Environmental Achievements' (2013) 40 *Journal of Law and Society* 173; James G Hanley, 'Parliament, Physicians, and Nuisances: The Demedicalization of Nuisance Law, 1831–1855' (2006) 80 *Bulletin of the History of Medicine* 702, 704–11.

the legal culture of public health remained: (a) profoundly composite, in that it continued to comprise multiple forms of law, of which general statutes were only one; and (b) multi-functional, in that these various forms of law served multiple purposes, from empowering officials and local authorities to protecting the rights of the public and property holders. Ultimately, one legal-administrative patchwork was only replaced by another, while property owners continued to enjoy considerable authority, even if this now mixed with that of a new breed of officials and experts, and the demands of a more inclusive (though certainly not democratic) public realm.

The sheer complexity and scale of what developed, its fitful gestation, and the contestation that accompanied its application and refinement, preclude speaking of any conscious design. What we might say, however, is that it was in keeping with an emergent ethos of what might be called liberal pragmatism on the part of ministers, officials, and the majority of MPs, composed of a measured deference to local authorities and the plurality of 'possessive interests' – relating to land, property, businesses, ratepayers, and so on – which they represented.[9] As was so often suggested, reform was not meant to override the agency of local communities, but to augment, clarify, and stimulate the powers and rights they already enjoyed. Anything else would be counterproductive and costly, as well as antithetical to what was now seen as a distinctly English tradition of 'local self-government' and a limited process of democratisation through the empowerment of propertied councillors and ratepayers, something begun with the Municipal Corporations Act 1835. This broad liberal ethos was far from hegemonic, but it can be accurately characterised as dominant and was eventually institutionalised in the working culture of the LGB, as Christine Bellamy's much neglected study of the Board long ago argued.[10]

We see this liberalism in the very form and function of the general statutes that otherwise empowered experts and officials. One of their functions was to 'model' clauses that either had been, or might be, incorporated into *private* statutory acts, of the sort that had earlier been used to establish bespoke urban improvement commissions in the late eighteenth century.[11] Far from diminishing in the nineteenth century, the use of private statutes by local authorities grew enormously, not least among the larger towns and cities. In the case of public health, they were especially used for purposes of capital formation (eg securing funding for water and sewerage works, and later hospitals) and obtaining powers not yet available elsewhere. Some 270 acts were passed by municipal authorities during the

[9] This liberal reading is advanced in a variety of accounts, old and new, though different understandings of 'liberal' are used: see Tom Crook, *Governing Systems: Modernity and the Making of Public Health in England, 1830–1910* (Berkeley, CA, California University Press, 2016) ch 1.

[10] Christine Bellamy, *Administering Central-Local Relations, 1871–1919: The Local Government Board in its Fiscal and Cultural Context* (Manchester, Manchester University Press, 1988).

[11] John Prest, *Liberty and Locality: Parliament, Permissive Legislation, and Ratepayers' Democracies in the Nineteenth Century* (Oxford, Clarendon, 1990) chs 1–5.

period 1858–72 alone.[12] Hundreds more would follow under the reign of the LGB. Passing a private bill through special parliamentary committees was an expensive, adversarial, and often messy business, and the process was significantly streamlined and rendered more accountable to central officials and local publics from the 1870s; but it enabled local authorities (which were considered for these purposes private, rather than public, bodies) to exercise considerable initiative nonetheless.[13] The use of private bills would diminish markedly in the twentieth century, but their number and variety at this juncture stands as testament to the authority that local authorities enjoyed.

Above all, the liberal, pragmatic nature of reform was reflected in the incremental, inconsistent, and routinely tortuous nature of the general statutes themselves. No uniform network of local authorities emerged. After 1872, boards of guardians generally formed the all-purpose sanitary authorities in outlying rural districts. In urban areas, by contrast, they might be municipal corporations, improvement commissions, or local boards of health, save that vaccination and access to medical relief remained in the hands of poor law officials. London was different again. Already home to the distinctively structured MBW, the Metropolitan Asylums Board (MAB) was set up in 1867 to provide an analogous form of integrated management regarding the poor law and associated institutions (workhouses, asylums, and isolation hospitals).

At the same time, the multiple sections and clauses of general statutes pulled in multiple directions. Just as they empowered local officials and experts, so too did they empower and protect the public (through instituting mechanisms of public audit, initiation, appeal, compensation, and arbitration), while also equipping central officials with quasi-judicial powers of inspection, sanction, and adjudication. Much was left to local discretion. Even where certain measures were prescribed – which in theory extended to providing sewerage systems after 1866 – the pace and nature of their implementation and the resources dedicated to them was in the hands of elected councillors and poor law guardians. The variations of provision that resulted were immense, as we shall see. Equally, central officials found themselves entangled in all sorts of local disputes regarding, among other things, the adoption of new administrative responsibilities and the compulsory purchase of land.[14] The most common course of resolution was via 'provisional' and 'departmental orders' issued from Whitehall. The former type of order was subject to parliamentary approval, however, while the latter could be contested in the higher courts. The default position of central officials was to avoid such scenarios through negotiation and compromise in the hope of avoiding the costs and delays that invariably accompanied formal litigation. But even the studious patience of Whitehall officials was exhausted on occasions and there was some

[12] RJB Morris, *Local Government, Local Legislation: Municipal Initiative in Parliament from 1858–1872* (London, Routledge, 2016) 1–2.

[13] Bellamy (n 10) 200–08.

[14] ibid chs 4–6.

resort to mobilising the law against defaulting authorities in cases of entrenched recalcitrance. In 1874, the LGB began applying to the Queen's Bench for a mandamus to compel an authority to do its statutory duties: some 16 orders were made in this way between 1875 and 1905.[15]

The courts maintained an active presence in the public health system in other ways, too, and certainly some of this was concerned with matters of statutory enforcement. We shall see in a moment the role played by the lower courts – and magistrates' courts in particular – in facilitating the application of statutory powers at the local level. Common law, however, retained a crucial role, not least in relation to the amorphous category of 'nuisances' and protecting property holders and their rights to amenity. For all that 'public' nuisances had been subject to a kind of statutory takeover in the name of public health, private actions pursued by individuals through the higher and lower courts remained a lively area of litigation – and formed another manifestation of the pluralistic liberalism of the legal culture. To be sure, civil actions seeking compensation or an injunction remained extortionately expensive, much beyond the reach of the working classes. Judgments also remained unpredictable and were intrinsically particular, condemning action in one place that elsewhere might be allowed simply because it did not offend someone.[16] But there is no question that it was of significant consequence, or that it formed, for the wealthy at least, a vital tool for protecting their property interests.

Some of these actions worked with the grain of the growing mass of public health statutes, in that they helped to prevent large-scale industries (eg, chemical manufactories) from contaminating rivers, and smaller urban trades (eg, brickmakers) from polluting their neighbourhoods.[17] But they also pulled in the other direction, in that civil actions under the common law of nuisances were also used to prevent or modify the development of novel forms of public health infrastructure. By far the most affected were those associated with water-borne sewerage systems, and more especially outfall works, where the sewage was supposed to be managed in some fashion – the practices were many – before allowing the water back into nearby rivers.[18] Such actions were not without good reason. Prior to the development of sewage treatment works at the end of the century (of the kind still used today), managing sewage was beset by multiple technical problems, with the result that sewage was often effectively dumped into rivers.[19] The most notorious case at mid-century was launched by the Conservative MP and local landowner, Charles Adderley, later Lord Norton. In 1858, he obtained an injunction from the Court of

[15] ibid 217–18.

[16] Jamie Benidickson, *The Culture of Flushing: A Social and Legal History of Sewage* (Vancouver, UBC Press, 2007) 138–39.

[17] For a reassessment of the efficacy of these actions, see Ben Pontin, 'Nuisance Law and the Industrial Revolution: A Reinterpretation of Doctrine and Institutional Competence' (2012) 75 *MLR* 101.

[18] Leslie Rosenthal, *The River Pollution Dilemma in Victorian England: Nuisance Law versus Economic Efficiency* (Farnham, Ashgate Publishing, 2014).

[19] For an overview of the multiple sewage utilisation schemes that were tried, generally without success, see Crook (n 9) ch 4.

Chancery preventing Birmingham corporation from developing its nascent outfall works at Saltley, where they drained into the river Tame and thence into the waterways that flowed through his estate. Modifications were made; further injunctions secured; only in 1875 was the 270-acre Saltley Farm works fully operational (and only in 1895 was the dispute finally settled).[20] Statute law in the shape of the Rivers Pollution Prevention Act 1876 provided the principal basis for later actions; but resort to common law continued, especially on the part of smallholders. In one typical case, heard before the Warwickshire Assizes in 1897, a farmer successfully sued Coventry corporation on account of the nuisance created by the discharge of the city's sewage into the river Sowe. He was awarded the handsome sum of £300 in damages.[21]

III. Frontline Powers

The law was thus a protean resource, multiple in form and uses. Liberal remains the most useful political quality we might attach to this complexity, though this is not because it served a liberal agenda per se. Rather, it is because we might see this complexity as forged in a series of overlapping liberal tensions that the governing elites, both Conservative and Whig-Liberal, were, by and large, content to work with and through, gradually and pragmatically – tensions, for instance, between centre and locality, the rights and duties of citizens, and more broadly between the interests of private individuals and property holders on the one hand, and the interventionist demands of public health acting on behalf of the community on the other. Crucially, however, this was not without resort to compulsion in the last instance, and active, judicial forms of intervention had a crucial role to play. In short, when and where there was dispute, and all other means of resolution had been exhausted, judges, or else Whitehall officials acting with quasi-judicial powers, intervened, mobilising powers of enforcement that were otherwise latent and activating a whole chain of events in the process: voluminous correspondence; court appearances; meetings with lawyers. It is no surprise that all the central offices established by public statute – the GBH, LGAO, MDPC, LGB – contained legal expertise, the LGB especially. Its first permanent secretary, John Lambert, was a qualified solicitor. The three secretaries that succeeded him – Hugh Owen, Samuel Provis, and Horace Munro – were all barristers.[22] Legal literacy mattered.

Fashioned out of parliamentary statutes, general and private, the frontline of public health was necessarily implicated in these broader liberal dynamics. Legal literacy mattered here, too. Digests of legal cases litter the professional press: the

[20] ibid 173; Rosenthal (n 18) ch 5; Bill Luckin, 'Pollution in the City' in Martin Daunton (ed), *The Cambridge Urban History of Britain, Volume III: 1840–1950* (Cambridge, Cambridge University Press, 2001) 217–19.

[21] JB Reignier Conder, *A Handbook of Sewer and Drains Cases* (London, St Bride's Press, 1904) 31.

[22] Bellamy (n 10) 133–34.

British Medical Journal, the *Sanitary Record*, the *Sanitary Inspectors' Journal*, among others. No less than at the centre, too, the exercise of powers on the frontline was hampered by insufficient staffing and variable resources. But as the place where public health in human form, as it were (eg, as MOsH and inspectors), directly confronted the public in whose name it operated (eg householders and parents), the frontline also possessed peculiar social dynamics of its own. Above all, it was the place where public co-operation and trust, and all that might secure this, however subtly or otherwise, mattered. Clearly, the latent threat of legal action was a crucial resource, but it was by no means the only one, and it might be insufficient in any case. We turn first to a bundle of mechanisms designed to control infectious diseases.

A. Stamping Out

Victorian public health is best remembered for the assembling of vast, subterranean systems of water supply and sewerage. Just as crucial, as historians have come to realise, was the building of localised systems above ground designed to manage the threat and incidence of a range of infectious diseases, chief among them cholera, smallpox, scarlet fever, typhoid, typhus, and diphtheria.[23] The key elements were notification, isolation, and disinfection. Combined, they came to be thought of as systems for 'stamping out' infectious diseases and waging war against pathogenic forces. They first began to emerge in the 1870s and by the early 1900s all towns and cities had in place systems led by MOsH for overseeing the compulsory notification of infectious diseases, the compulsory isolation of the infected persons at home or at ratepayer-funded hospitals, and the cleansing of dwellings by specialist disinfection teams. The figures are striking. Whereas there was only a handful of bespoke facilities at mid-century, by 1914 there were some 755 borough- and county-based isolation hospitals, providing roughly 35,000 beds, as well as a further 363 hospitals dedicated to caring for those with smallpox.[24] Of course, the bureaucracy it entailed ebbed and flowed according to the incidence of local and national outbreaks of infection, but there is no question of its novelty or extent. In London, during the 10 years between 1889–99, almost 410,000 cases of infectious diseases were officially notified, most relating to children suffering from scarlet fever (206,000) and diphtheria (99,000).[25]

This remarkable transformation was wrought in the same way as the remarkable transformation in subterranean networks: locally, in a piecemeal fashion,

[23] Graham Mooney, *Intrusive Interventions: Public Health, Domestic Space and Infectious Disease Surveillance, 1840–1910* (Rochester, NY, University of Rochester Press, 2015); Matthew L Newsom Kerr, *Contagion, Isolation and Biopolitics in Victorian London* (Basingstoke, Palgrave Macmillan, 2018).

[24] *Local Government Board: Forty-fourth Report: Part III–(a) Public Health and Local Administration*, PP 1916 [Cd 8197] Vol XII, 26–27.

[25] T Orme Dudfield, 'Address: Conference of Medical Officers of Health' (1899) 20 *Journal of the Sanitary Institute* 410.

via public and private statutes, and with no little experimentation and contestation along the way. The first towns to embrace compulsory notification did so via private local improvement acts – over 20 during the late 1870s and early 1880s, beginning with Huddersfield in 1876 and Bolton in 1877 – before a general statute in 1889 imposed it on London and made it optional elsewhere. By the time another general statute in 1899 imposed the responsibility on all local authorities, the vast majority (upwards of 80 per cent) had already embraced it. Providing isolation facilities was the necessary counterpart to notification and various private acts and general statutes (in 1866, 1875, and 1893) provided the necessary empowerment to do so. The problem was building the facilities and deciding where to locate them, given the epidemiological risks they posed to nearby householders (and thus property values). The problem was especially acute for urban authorities. They not only required larger facilities, but also faced greater constraints in terms of available land; and any hospital could not be too far away from the population it sought to serve. Ratepayers everywhere, it seems, were restive and occasionally launched legal actions.

To be sure, such cases only added to the tortuous bureaucratic circuits these systems had to negotiate and a broader set of frustrations. Hospital plans and loan agreements had to be vetted by the LGB, while MOsH consistently bemoaned the inadequacy of facilities and the slowness with which they were erected, as plans passed through the hands of councillors and local authority clerks. But such cases were not without consequence, and they were one place where the higher judiciary was pressed into active service. Fierce ratepayer opposition in London, for instance, played a role in the MAB's decision to supplement its existing four hospitals with shipping hulks moored on the Thames. Among other metropolitan cases, two suits were launched in 1878 and 1879 claiming that the MAB's smallpox facilities in Hampstead constituted a 'nuisance' under common law. Further actions followed, some of which passed through the Court of Appeal and the House of Lords, before the case was settled out of court in 1883 (see also the cases analysed in chapter nine by Jonathan Garton and Charles Mitchell in this volume).[26] Three ships, which between them provided an additional 300 beds, were still being used at the turn of the century: the *Atlas* (opened in 1881), the *Endymion* (1881), and the *Castalia* (1884).

The more pervasive challenge was the lowly operational one of administering notifications and the legal provisions relating to the fate of infected persons, which included powers to compel them to enter a hospital, as well as to prevent them from mixing in public – powers indeed which had previously only been applied to itinerant 'dossers' and prostitutes. As we might expect, debates were had regarding the very principle of compulsion.[27] Doctors, for instance, objected to compulsory notification, citing their sacred Hippocratic obligations to their clients' privacy.

[26] Gwendoline M Ayers, *England's First State Hospitals and the Metropolitan Asylums Board, 1867–1930* (Berkeley, CA, University of California Press, 1971) 58–59, 72–74.

[27] Mooney (n 23) ch 2.

There was thus some experimentation with different systems of notification prior to statute law prescribing the 'dual' system, whereby both doctors and householders were obliged to notify the local sanitary authority. Ultimately, powers to compel were judged necessary in both cases: failure to notify was made punishable by fines; magistrates could order the removal of an infected person to a hospital. It was, however, entirely in keeping with the liberal scruples of the time that advocates of compulsion felt the need to use the language of their opponents and defend it as a crucial bulwark of 'liberty', as well they might of course – which is to say, in terms of the (positive) freedom to enjoy good health and the (negative) freedom from the threat of infected others. 'To take precautions against the spread of smallpox or cholera is surely as legitimate and justifiable as against felony', argued Bolton's pro-compulsion medical officer of health (MOH), John Livy, in the pages of the *British Medical Journal* in 1882. 'There is not much individual liberty left to a man laid prostrate from typhus … To restore him to health is to restore his lapsed liberty', to which he added: 'we must not permit free trade in disease.'[28]

Of the two components – notification and isolation – the former was the most compromised. Doctors were almost entirely compliant: in Derby, which introduced a dual system in 1879 via a private act, only three fines were paid by doctors in eight years; in 1898, one MOH described prosecutions against his fellow professionals as 'rare'.[29] The problem was the lack of compliance among members of the public and especially the poor. Judging by the comments of frustrated MOsH, it seems this was less a product of wilful resistance and more the product of diagnostic ignorance and even the hope that any symptoms would pass without any significant infection; and both were difficult to prosecute. Here, too, it seems fines were rare.[30] Despite efforts to publicise measures using handbills and posters, it seems that this half of the dual system – the public half, as it were – was generally unreliable.

By contrast, isolation operated much more smoothly. To be sure, notification did not necessarily entail dispatch to a specialist local facility following a subsequent visit by a MOH or sanitary inspector (or poor law officer in London). Statute was quite clear that only when an infected person was 'without proper lodging or accommodation, or lodged in a room with more than one family or being on board a ship or vessel' was removal necessary, in which case a magistrate's order could be applied for. The result was that removal from home was largely sought in the case of the working classes, simply on account of their generally more crowded dwellings. The middle classes, by contrast, were usually able to isolate at home, perhaps in a special 'sick room'.[31] Still, this left the largest section of the population

[28] 'The Notification of Infectious Diseases' *British Medical Journal* (*BMJ*) (12 August, 1882) 291–92.

[29] 'Compulsory Notification of Infectious Diseases' *BMJ* (5 November 1887) 1021; Arthur Newsholme, 'The Notification of Infectious Disease' (1897–98) 10 *Public Health* 228.

[30] Crook (n 9) 215–16.

[31] Shirley F Murphy (ed), *Our Homes and How to Make them Healthy* (London, Cassel & Co, 1883) chs 88–90.

vulnerable to enforced institutional isolation and what is striking is just how little resort there was to magistrates' orders, even in London where admission to a MAB (poor law) hospital carried with it the taint of pauperisation. Anecdotal commentary from MOsH suggests a general culture of compliance; and though general surveys conducted at the time are few, they too suggest that most parents were essentially co-operative, despite the obvious emotional difficulties of releasing a loved one (normally a child) into institutional care. In his substantial national inquiry into existing practices in England and Wales conducted during the early 1880s, the LGB medical inspector, Richard Thorne Thorne, happily reported that he had come across no more than 'three dozen' cases where resort to a magistrate's order was necessary.[32]

This is not to suggest there was no organised opposition, of the sort that frustrated vaccination (see below). In 1891, some 16,000 people signed a petition co-ordinated by Nottingham's 'Rights and Liberties Defence League' objecting to the city council's recent adoption of notification and isolation measures.[33] Nor is it the case that magistrates always endorsed an isolation order; and judgments might be contested in the higher courts. In 1899 in Cumberland, two county magistrates refused to endorse an order on the grounds that an infected person did in fact have access to 'proper' accommodation at home: a decision that was later ruled incorrect by the Court of Appeal.[34] Yet these scenarios were entirely exceptional and the challenge is to explain why non-domestic isolation commanded such public compliance and there was so little resort to legal compulsion. We should not overlook the importance of local peculiarities. In Leicester, compliance was high precisely because of intense local opposition to vaccination and the appeal of hospital isolation as an alternative solution, at least to outbreaks of smallpox (the so-called 'Leicester method').[35] But we can also point to some general factors. It seems from what MOsH reported that the growing use of isolation facilities among communities helped matters enormously, breeding confidence and trust through familiarity.[36] Some MOsH even reported receiving letters of thanks from parents after their child had returned home, fully recovered. And, to put it baldly, hospitals *were* effective, as the statistical studies of the time suggest. Some hospitals were certainly more stringent than others and there was some anxiety about the dangers of cross-infection during the Edwardian period; but all hospitals partook of a culture of risk management that was unprecedented in its attention to

[32] *Local Government Board: Tenth Report: Supplement Containing Report and Papers Submitted by the Board's Medical Officer on the Use and Influence of Hospitals for Infectious Diseases*, PP 1882 [C 3290] Vol LXXIX, 28.

[33] Mooney (n 23) 44.

[34] HH Copnall, *The Law Relating to Infectious Diseases and Hospitals* (London, Hadden, Best, 1899) 258.

[35] Alderman T Windley, 'Leicester and Small-pox–Thirty years' Experience' (1903) 11 *Journal of State Medicine* 21.

[36] Lucinda McCray Beier, *For Their Own Good: The Transformation of English Working-Class Health Culture, 1880–1970* (Columbus, OH, Ohio State University Press, 2008) 174–80.

detail regarding the movement and management of bodies, the classification and separation of patients, and the use of different types of disinfectant solutions and technologies.[37]

Another significant part of the answer is surely the lurking presence of the *possibility* of legal action – its latency as a resource – which all officials carried with them, if only because this helped to constitute their official authority in the first place. It is difficult to know quite how explicitly this was wielded by sanitary officials on-site. We know that in some places, including Nottingham, Leicester and London, mention was also made of the possibility of notifying a householder's employer that they were harbouring an infected person, thereby raising the prospect of diminished earnings.[38] Likewise, mention was sometimes made that shopkeepers might be forced to close their premises; but whether loss of earnings was raised in conjunction with the possibility of compelled isolation, or as an alternative, is hard to tell – though both scenarios speak of what Graham Mooney has called the 'subtle form of coercion' that animated stamping-out systems.[39] What is clear is that the advice to MOsH and sanitary inspectors was always to use 'tact and discretion', as one leading guide to the law put it in 1894. The ideal, as the same text went on, was that hospital treatment should be 'regarded as a privilege, to which the ratepayer is entitled, [rather] than a penance, to which he is compelled to undergo by legal proceedings in the event of contumacy'.[40] Skills of persuasion and negotiation were evidently crucial; and certainly, no MOH or sanitary inspector relished legal action, given the time and expense it entailed. Equally, of course, the fact that MOsH felt the need to remind colleagues of the importance of discretion and diplomacy suggests that at least some officers were not averse to foregrounding their powers – to verbalising them in the form of a threat, rather than leaving them lingering in the background.

B. Sanitary Inspection

Another crucial arena of frontline action was the work of nuisance inspectors, or sanitary inspectors as they came to be known from the 1870s.[41] They played a crucial role in administering stamping-out systems and were often the first on the scene following the receipt of a notification certificate. Their principal role, however, was to identify an array of environmental nuisances and sanitary dangers and to initiate remedial action. As noted above, a variety of mid-century statutes enabled and eventually (in 1872) compelled their appointment by local authorities. The

[37] Crook (n 9) 223–36.

[38] Mooney (n 23) 80; Kerr (n 23) 143.

[39] Mooney (n 23) 80.

[40] Thomas Stevenson and Shirley F Murphy (eds), *A Treatise on Hygiene and Public Health, Volume III: Sanitary Law* (London, Churchill, 1894) 165.

[41] Crook (n 9) ch 4; Christopher Hamlin, 'Nuisances and Community in mid-Victorian England: The Attractions of Inspection' (2013) 38 *Social History* 346.

cumulative result was another remarkable expansion in public health bureaucracy. By the 1880s rural sanitary authorities (generally boards of guardians) commonly employed two inspectors. Major towns and cities such as London and Liverpool had begun appointing inspectors in the late 1840s, but by the end of the century all urban centres boasted expansive teams, often comprising a chief inspector and a variety of subordinate, specialist roles. By the mid-1890s Manchester corporation was employing 28 residential nuisance inspectors, four smoke inspectors, two food and meat inspectors, and six factory and workshop inspectors. Figures for April 1895 to April 1896 give an indication of their industry: some 46,270 dwelling houses, 2,480 workshops, 451 slaughter-houses, and 29,984 'miscellaneous' sites were inspected in total.[42] The biggest employer was London County Council (LCC). In 1900, there were some 260 sanitary inspectors, of all descriptions, working in the metropolis.[43]

Crucially, inspectors enjoyed considerable powers. By the late 1860s, following the Sanitary Act 1866, there were seven types of statutory nuisance altogether, including insanitary premises, overcrowded dwellings, and noxious chimneys and furnaces. These were confirmed in later statutes while existing powers to condemn meat and to seize suspected food stuffs from retailers were formalised in the Public Health Act 1875 and Sale of Food and Drugs Act 1875. Meanwhile, statute law equipped inspectors with extensive powers of entry and abatement. Between 6am and 9pm in London, and 9am and 6pm elsewhere, inspectors could gain access to any premises they saw fit. The exceptions were common lodging houses ('doss houses') and 'infected premises', which could be entered at any time. Should entry be refused, an inspector could lay a complaint before a magistrate and obtain a warrant. Just as importantly, an inspector could act in a summary fashion when it came to seizing suspected food items (which, after 1875, were then sent to a public analyst), condemning unsound meat, and identifying nuisances. In the case of the latter, once convinced of an infringement, the next step was to issue a preliminary notice of abatement and then, should the former have been ignored, a legally binding formal notice; and if this, too, was ignored, an inspector could proceed by court summons and seek a magistrate's order.

It is little wonder that inspectors were denounced as meddlesome agents of 'red-tapism'. After the 1870s it seems that dispatching abatement notices was, if not a daily occurrence, then at least a weekly one for inspectors. In 1877, the four inspectors who patrolled Kensington, London, visited some 4,559 homes and businesses and issued 1,259 formal notices.[44] In rural Romford, where two part-time inspectors oversaw a population of 17,000, some 333 formal notices were issued

[42] James Niven, *Health Officer Report: 1896* (Manchester, 1897) 148–49.

[43] WH Greg, 'The Status and Duties of a Sanitary Inspector in England' (1900) 21 *Journal of the Sanitary Institute* 505.

[44] T Orme Dudfield, *Annual Report on the Health and Sanitary Condition of the Parish of St Mary Abbotts, Kensington, for the year 1877* (Kensington, J Wakeham, 1877) table VI, appendix.

in 1897.[45] In large cities thousands of items of food would be seized every year, and tens of tonnes of meat condemned. The law, however, was both a help and a hindrance. On the one hand, besides affording summary powers to condemn meat and seize foodstuffs, statutes also provided a suitably pliant, capacious rationale with which to identify environmental offences. To be sure, a growing mass of housing byelaws helped sharpen a sense of what constituted an acceptable environment (eg drainage arrangements); but it was of the essence of sanitary inspection to act in a proactive, risk-averse fashion and to target all that *might* undermine good health. Statute provided room for just this kind of loose, probabilistic reasoning by explicitly stating, in the case of six of the seven environmental nuisances, that they might be considered as such if they were either a 'nuisance *or* injurious to health'. In other words, it explicitly legitimised the kind of reasoning intrinsic to the common law tradition, which foregrounded considerations of sensory comfort and amenity. In practice, this meant that inspectors were agents of civility just as much as health, but it also made their jobs easier. Ultimately, as Christopher Hamlin has argued, they did not have to satisfy themselves (or a magistrate) that a given nuisance would cause ill-health, only that it caused sensory distress and physical annoyance – a much lower bar of significance.[46]

On the other hand, however – and in keeping with the overall liberal settlement of centre-local relations – statute law left inspectors at the mercy of their local authority employers. The law was clear that inspectors were accountable to the elected councillors and guardians that appointed them and who oversaw their work and agreed their formal notices. Many were clearly supportive; but as inspectors complained, the fact that statute failed to prescribe terms of employment, with the result that the vast majority were employed only on short-term contracts, left them especially vulnerable to any councillors or guardians who wished to obstruct their work and who might oppose their re-appointment.[47] Still more crucial was the discretion left to local authorities in terms of the manpower allocated to inspection. Some places were better staffed than others, perhaps; but a pervasive commitment to municipal economy meant that complaints of unwieldly workloads appeared frequently in the professional press. In 1897, the MOH for Coventry lamented that just one inspector, an assistant, and a clerk dealt with over 12,000 houses on some 40 miles of road.[48] Even in bustling London, which was relatively well resourced, each inspector on average had to contend with a population of roughly 20,000.[49]

Nonetheless, inspectors were at least spared widespread public opposition to their work. As with isolation, resistance of the sort that required the use of court

[45] *Romford Rural District Council: Annual Report of the Medical Officer of Health, 1897* (Romford, Essex Times, 1898) 25.

[46] Hamlin (2002) (n 8) 198–99.

[47] Crook (n 9) 135–36.

[48] 'Sanitary Inspection' *BMJ* (21 January 1899) 172.

[49] Anthony S Wohl, *Endangered Lives: Public Health in Victorian Britain* (Cambridge, MA, Harvard University Press, 1983) 195.

proceedings was extremely rare. The only comprehensive account we have covering all of England (and Wales) is a parliamentary survey ordered in 1873, and this suggests that only one per cent of nuisance abatement orders were legally contested – a miniscule amount.[50] Snapshots from later decades suggest much the same. In 1902, the inspector of suburban Wood Green, London, issued 243 formal notices, of which only three ended in court summonses.[51] In 1904, Blackburn's nuisance inspector reported no recourse to legal proceedings at all, not even in relation to common lodging houses, which were notoriously troublesome.[52] At least three caveats are in order. First, in relation to some aspects of inspection – notably food inspection, where adulteration was determined by a public analyst in a laboratory setting – courts were used simply to administer fines for proven infringements. Second, in the case of nuisances, as with isolation orders, if matters did go to court, it was by no means guaranteed that a magistrate would side with an inspector. In 1906, among hundreds of other instances, a magistrate found against an inspector, disputing the latter's argument that the law entitled him to inspect a faulty drain while it was in the process of being fixed by the owner.[53] It was also possible, as it was with isolation orders, to appeal a magistrate's decision and seek redress in a higher court, such as the Queen's Bench Division or the Court of Appeal. There were dozens of such cases around the turn of the century alone.[54] Finally, judging by their handbooks, it seems most inspectors regularly experienced verbal abuse. Some were even physically assaulted: in 1891, an inspector in Workington exchanged blows with a butcher, who then turned a knife on him, demanding that he leave the premises.[55] Put another way, we should be wary of equating low levels of legal action as a sign of near universal public willingness to co-operate: grudging acceptance was clearly part of the equation.

Still, it remains striking just how little resort there was to court proceedings, especially in relation to their biggest task, searching out environmental offences, the consequences of which could be incredibly costly to property and business owners. Once more, the explanation surely resides in a confluence of factors, one of which was again the latent possibility of legal action, with all the hassle that this promised, if activated. Both preliminary and formal notices made clear the consequences of non-compliance. Equally, and just as crucially, there must have been some trust placed in inspectors; or more accurately, some sense of the legitimacy of their status and task, and the efficacy of their actions. We can

[50] *Return from the Urban and Rural Sanitary Authorities in England and Wales of Nuisances Reported and Dealt with, and Estimated Cost of Sanitary Structural Works, 1874*, PP 1875 (434) Vol LXIV.

[51] *Urban District Council of Wood Green: Report of the Medical Officer of Health for the Year 1902* (London, Haylar & Cole, 1903) 21.

[52] *Annual Report upon the Health of Blackburn for the Year 1904* (Blackburn, Times Printing, 1905) 258.

[53] 'The Rights of Sanitary Inspectors' *Sanitary Record* (14 June 1906) 520.

[54] Conder (n 21) 110–47.

[55] 'An Inspector of Nuisances Threatened with Assault' (1891–92) 4 *Public Health* 251.

infer that at least some members of the public were invested in the process and recognised its efficacy, simply because, every year, in both urban and rural areas, a small section of them would exercise their statutory right to report nuisances. In 1882, just over 2,500 nuisances were reported by the public in Liverpool, about three per cent of the overall total identified that year.[56] In Witney, Oxfordshire, the inspector received 98 complaints in 1893, compared to 352 identified on his own rounds.[57]

At the same time, inspectors did all they could to build trust and foster a spirit of co-operation, or at least the best of them did. Time and again, in handbooks, in the professional press, and at conferences, they were reminded of the importance of cultivating good relations with the public.[58] In a typical example, Croydon's MOH, Alfred Carpenter, speaking at a national gathering of inspectors in 1890, criticised those officers who 'went with the threat of legal proceedings in their mouth, and did not attempt to explain why certain work had to be done'. This invariably 'set up the backs of people', rendering them less likely to undertake work either quickly or properly, or even at all. 'It was far better', he went on, 'for them [the public] to do the work willingly, and look upon the sanitary inspector as their friend rather than as a prying, intolerant autocrat'.[59] At its most refined it was a pastoral art and inspectors were often encouraged to see themselves as 'advisers' and 'friends' of the public – and this, too, must surely have played some role.

Finally, if more prosaically, we should remember that the process of resolving a nuisance was, as statute specified, a *staggered* affair, involving a series of orders in its most elongated instances. What did this mean in practice? In 1895, a metropolitan inspector detailed the worst-case scenario.[60] Even once it had been determined that a preliminary notice had not been complied with, it could still take up to 49 days for a local sanitary committee to sanction the issue of a formal notice (as again statute required); and if this was not complied with, up to 70 days to proceed by court summons; and then a further four weeks for the police to enforce the order, should a magistrate have decided that this was appropriate. This was a source of frustration for inspectors, but we might also infer that this was another reason why court cases were rare: simply that those served with a notice had considerable time to reconcile themselves to the consequences and costs of complying with a notice.

[56] J Stopford Taylor, *Report of the Health of Liverpool during the Year 1882* (Liverpool, Henry Greenwood, 1883) 58.

[57] *Witney Rural Sanitary Authority, Annual Report of W. Dyson Wood, Medical Officer of Health, for the Year 1892* (Oxford, 24 June 1893) 4.

[58] Tom Crook, 'Sanitary Inspection and the Public Sphere in Late Victorian and Edwardian Britain: A Case Study in Liberal Governance' (2007) 32 *Social History* 369, 384–89.

[59] Alfred Carpenter, 'Presidential Address: Sanitary Inspectors' Conference' (1890–91) 13 *Public Health* 144.

[60] JM Jones, 'The Public Health Acts: Difficulties in Administration and Suggestions for Amendment' (1895) 1 *Sanitary Inspectors Journal* 250.

C. Vaccination

Smallpox vaccination constitutes a further arena of remarkable statute-sponsored incursion into the lives of the English population. In contrast to systems of stamping out and sanitary inspection, vaccination evolved solely within the framework of the poor law, where it remained until the interwar period.[61] Its emergence as a facet of local poor law administration began in 1840, with the passage of a general statute which provided free access to all those who wanted it. Following more years of high levels of smallpox mortality, another general statute was passed in 1853 which made vaccination compulsory for all infants under four months of age and which enabled magistrates to inflict fines on parents who refused. Further acts in 1867 and 1871 significantly tightened the statutory framework, among other things by extending the provisions to all children under the age of 14, compelling Boards of Guardians to appoint paid public vaccinators, and enabling magistrates to impose continuous penalties on repeat defaulters – an unprecedented cat-and-mouse provision for general health legislation.

The result was another expansive system of public health bureaucracy which relied on a mass of paperwork – registers of newborn children, certificates of vaccination, and so on – as well as infrastructure in the shape of lancets, stores of lymph, and 'stations' where the procedure could take place, as distributed according to 'vaccination districts'. By the late 1870s there were some 3,125 public vaccinators working in England and Wales across almost 650 poor law unions.[62] Up to the 1890s, moreover, the developing legal and administrative framework had its desired effect. Although the statistics should be treated with caution, they point to a cumulative increase in vaccination take-up.[63] Whereas in the years before 1853 about 30 per cent of children under the age of one were vaccinated, this had increased to over 60 per cent by 1854, the vast majority of which were publicly vaccinated (private vaccinations, however, still had to be accompanied by a certificate).[64] Further improvements were to come after the reforms of 1867 and 1871. Figures for the years 1875 to 1885 suggest that over 80 per cent of children under the age of one were vaccinated every year in England and Wales, again most of them at public expense.[65]

Of course, other factors surely helped, among them the increasingly assertive promotional efforts of poor law authorities and registrars of births. There are even instances of employers threatening their adult workforce with dismissal were

[61] Nadja Durbach, *Bodily Matters: The Anti-Vaccination Movement in England, 1853–1907* (Durham, NC, Duke University Press, 2005); Deborah Brunton, *The Politics of Vaccination: Practice and Policy in England, Wales, Ireland, and Scotland, 1800–1874* (Rochester, NY, University of Rochester Press, 2008).

[62] *Local Government Board: Tenth Report, 1880–81*, PP 1881 [C 2982] Vol XLVI, 411.

[63] These figures include those vaccinated privately, which might be more than 30% of the total.

[64] *Memorial presented to the President of the Board of Health, by the President and Council of the Epidemiological Society, on a Proper State Provision for the Prevention of Small Pox and the Extension of Vaccination*, PP 1854–5 (88) vol XLV.

[65] *Royal Commission to Inquire into Vaccination: Sixth Report*, PP 1896 [C 7993] Vol XLVII, 77.

they to remain unvaccinated (as in Sheffield in 1887 and Gloucester in 1895).[66] Parental minds were also focused by the proximity of smallpox itself: vaccination rates always improved during years of epidemic distress, sometimes markedly, as in 1871–72. We should remember, too, that not all appearances before a magistrate resulted in fines and that the legislation was sometimes tested in the higher courts. In 1864, for instance, in a much-publicised case heard in the Court of Queen's Bench, it was determined that the existing legislation allowed for only one fine to be inflicted on a defaulting parent and no more (something remedied in later legislation, as noted above).[67] Even so, clearly another significant factor was the increasingly punitive statutory framework that developed from mid-century, together with the provision of more numerous and better organised facilities. Here, as elsewhere, the very threat of legal action and fines – and even imprisonment in the event of nonpayment – was a hugely important administrative resource.

Nonetheless, the case of smallpox brings into relief the high levels of compliance enjoyed in relation to the two frontline areas examined above. This is simply because vaccination is the one practice which *did* arouse considerable public hostility and where public trust and co-operation were most lacking – and where, accordingly, the limits of statute law were most keenly exposed. To be sure, opposition was localised and the areas where it was most concentrated were generally towns characterised by high levels of non-conformity and radical activism.[68] But there is no question that it was highly organised and that for some it was part of a principled commitment to a heterodox lifestyle, which might encompass vegetarianism, antivivisectionism, and an interest in alternative medicine. The movement was served by a variety of organisations (the first of which was the Anti-Compulsory Vaccination League set up in 1866), and several publications, among them the *Anti-Vaccinator* (1869–74) and *Vaccination Inquirer* (1879–1971). All the tactics of a modern mass protest movement were employed: exuberant rallies were held; MPs were lobbied; solidarity was practised in the form of establishing collective funds to pay fines. The cause even generated its own pantheon of 'martyrs' composed of those who remained steadfast in their refusal, despite spending time in prison.[69] There is no question, too, that opposition proved effective. In 1886, the rates of 'default' in Keighley and Leicester, two hotspots of anti-vaccination sentiment, were roughly 70 per cent. Dewsbury (38 per cent) and Luton (30 per cent) were next, followed by Oldham (28 per cent) and Banbury (24 per cent).[70]

[66] Durbach (n 61) 93.

[67] 'Compulsory Vaccination' *Justice of the Peace* (14 February 1864) 99–100; Algernon C Bauke, *The Vaccination Act, 1867, and the Vaccination Act, 1871* (London, Shaw & Sons, 1871) iv–v.

[68] Dorothy Porter and Roy Porter, 'The Politics of Prevention: Anti-vaccinationism and Public Health in Nineteenth-century England' (1988) 32 *Medical History* 231; Durbach (n 61).

[69] One of the early 'martyrs' was Charles Washington Nye, who was imprisoned at least five times for short periods. *The Anti-Vaccinator and Public Health Journal* (15 April 1872) 12.

[70] *Local Government Board: Eighteenth Report, 1888–89*, PP 1889 [C 5813] Vol XXXV, clvii. Equally, it was not unknown for places to record entirely negligible levels, as in Bolton and Newcastle, which in the same year registered under 2%.

Crucially, this opposition eventually took its toll on national rates. Official LGB returns show that by the late 1880s overall levels of vaccination were beginning to drop and by 1895 national coverage had sunk to just under 68 per cent (though this did rise again afterwards, hitting 75 per cent in 1903).[71]

How can we explain such intense opposition? Principle played a part and many objected on straightforward libertarian grounds: that it interfered with their rights as persons and parents, or as 'freeborn' English men and women. This, however, was a moot point. The counterargument, which advocates routinely made, echoing the defence of compulsory hospital isolation, was that vaccination protected the liberty of all to enjoy good health. Of more importance were two interrelated factors, both of which undermined trust. The first was the visceral reality of vaccination as it was then practised, which generally involved boldly scoring an arm with a lancet and then inserting lymph cultivated from either a calf or a human vaccine vesicle. The former was preferred by middle-class patients who could afford the services of private doctors; but even here there was no guarantee of the purity of calf lymph (eg it might contain blood) and it was of course derived from an animal. The latter, which entailed the so-called 'arm-to-arm' method, was preferred by local authorities, largely on the grounds of cost and convenience. Yet, besides the problem of assembling a suitable chain of children and the dangers of doing so, the risk of contamination (eg with blood and dirt) was high and it entailed, by design, directly transferring putrid matter from one body to another. And both methods involved inducing symptoms: that was how it worked. It was, in short, an operation at once intimate, invasive, and thoroughly unpleasant, and this inspired, as well it might, all sorts of fears.[72] The anti-vaccination propaganda brimmed with the emotive language of 'poison' and 'corruption'. Gothic imagery of bodily degeneration and vampiric doctors abounded. The most potent charge was that in some cases it had been responsible for transmitting syphilis.[73] The macabre sensationalist fantasies were many, but all were born of the uniquely invasive, grubby reality of vaccination.

Matters were not helped by the variable resources that were allocated to the practice in its public forms – another product of the liberal settlement of centre-local relations.[74] Public vaccinators routinely complained of the lack of any permanent facilities: 'stations' might be local libraries, coffee houses, chapel vestries, workhouse infirmaries, or pubs. At the same time, variable support was offered by the poor law guardians to whom vaccinators were responsible. Some guardians indeed were actively hostile to vaccination and might even

[71] *Local Government Board: Twenty-seventh Report, 1897–98*, PP 1898 [C 8978] Vol XXXIX, 452; *Local Government Board: Thirty-fifth Report, 1905–06*, PP 1906 [Cd 3105] Vol XXXV, cvii.

[72] Durbach (n 61) chs 5 and 6.

[73] This seems to have been the most damaging claim, at least judging by the efforts dedicated by one doctor to refuting it: Edward Seaton, *A Handbook of Vaccination* (London, Macmillan, 1868) 328–76.

[74] Logie Barrow, 'In the Beginning was the Lymph: The Hollowing of Stational Vaccination in England and Wales, 1840–98' in Sturdy (n 8).

have been elected on just this basis. Famously, in 1876, seven members of the Board of Guardians in Keighley were imprisoned in York Castle for their refusal to enforce the 1871 Vaccination Act.[75] The more significant problem, however, was evidential and overcoming what in places was pronounced public scepticism as to what passed for the science of vaccination. The most useful tool to hand in terms of offering proof of its success was statistics and those in favour certainly pressed their case as best they could in statistical terms (there could be no resort, of course, to virology or immunology, which were pioneered later). Yet sections of the anti-vaccinationist lobby were incredibly adept at contesting the same statistics and showing that any decline in smallpox mortality may have derived from other causes; and most anti-vaccinators, it should be emphasised, were not opposed to public health measures per se – quite the contrary, many were fulsome in their recommendation of alternative sanitary measures.[76] The result was that the efficacy of the practice was steeped in confusing, contradictory assessments and it was much too easy to place one's trust elsewhere, in other practices.

Ultimately, following a mammoth royal commission inquiry which took place between 1889 and 1896, it was decided that the law should accommodate such resistance and in 1898 a statute was passed that ended stational, arm-to-arm vaccination and allowed for exemption on the grounds of 'conscientious objection'. It was swiftly heralded as a victory for the anti-vaccination lobby and exemption certificates were soon issued. Roughly three per cent of all births were granted certificates in 1898, rising to four per cent in 1903.[77] Significant grievances remained, however.[78] Not only did objectors have to pay for an exemption certificate and obtain one within four months of a child's birth; they also had to appear before two magistrates whose job it was to judge the conscientiousness of an objector's opposition – a difficult, and arguably bizarre, situation, and one made all the worse by the failure of the Act to specify how this might be assessed. The result was highly variable rates of success among those who applied, prompting many anti-vaccinators to boycott the system entirely. The situation was only resolved with the passage of a further statute in 1907, which simply required the completion of a statutory declaration form and its dispatch to a vaccination officer. The impact was immediate and highlights just how relatively effective the earlier regime of unadulterated legal compulsion had been. In the first four years of the 1907 Act only 56 per cent of births were vaccinated, while the proportion of exemptions on the grounds of conscientious objection rose to 25 per cent.[79]

[75] Durbach (n 61) 1.

[76] For accounts which contested the statistics, see George Gibbs, *A Brief Statistical Answer to the Speech of the Rt. Hon. Robert Lowe, … Delivered in the House of Commons, on Compulsory Vaccination* (Darlington, 1861); Alfred R Wallace, *Vaccination Proved Useless and Dangerous: Forty-five Years of Registration Statistics* (London, EW Allen, 1889).

[77] *Local Government Board: Thirty-fifth Report* (n 71) cvii.

[78] Durbach (n 61) ch 7.

[79] ibid 196.

Although not formally repealed in statute until 1948, the era of compulsion was effectively over. (Fortunately, it might be added, by this point – and for reasons that remain unclear – smallpox was in rapid decline as a significant epidemiological threat.)

IV. Conclusion

One of the core arguments of the above account is that we need to think in plural terms about the law and public health during the Victorian period. This extends not just to its various sources and the use that was made of public and private statutes and common law proceedings. The law also played multiple roles, empowering various agents and processes, all of which reflected a broadly liberal culture of governing, attentive to the rights of property holders, local authorities, and the public, but also to the need to enforce measures to uphold the health of the public. This is amply apparent in the three frontline areas examined above; but what these areas also suggest is that we need to recognise the utility of what has been termed the latent authority of the law – the lurking, background threat of legal action, which all officials carried with them, though it was often made explicit (through a verbal or written communication). This is not to diminish the importance of the law in its more active judicial forms. Court-based actions, however, were important, not because they were numerically significant (which they were not, in the bigger scheme of things), but because of what they promised somewhere down the administrative line, should co-operation not be forthcoming: hassle, costs, fines, even imprisonment. Put another way, powers of legal compulsion were no less useful for not being used.

This latent authority was especially crucial given the liberal scruples of the time, even if compulsion was eminently defensible on the grounds that JS Mill famously outlined in his 1859 work *On Liberty*, namely preventing harm to others (the so-called 'harm principle') – and this was essentially the line taken by those who defended compulsion in the realms of public health. Yet, as the case of vaccination suggests, there were also limits to this. Ultimately, in this area, the Government had to give way to decades of popular hostility and allow for exemptions, thereby creating a form of legal subjectivity at the very margins of liberalism: the 'conscientious objector'. This is one reason why vaccination has attracted so much scholarly attention; but for our purposes it is more interesting for what it reveals about the importance of trust, suggesting, as it does, that legal resources, no matter how draconian, will still come undone in the absence of at least some sense of the legitimacy of a particular measure. The contrast with hospital isolation and nuisance removal is instructive. It is reasonable to infer that most people complied with some degree of reluctance in the case of both courses of action, wary of the legal consequences of acting otherwise. Yet, comply they did and this seems to have been because the efficacy of both was also readily demonstrable and their rationale easy to grasp. They had, in short, a basic kind of functional legitimacy: a logic most could trust. Just this was absent in the case of smallpox vaccination, hence the pockets of localised resistance which even recourse to extensive legal action could not diminish. To be sure, the evidence suggests that in general, across England as a whole, the threat of legal action helped to drive up vaccination rates; but ultimately the regime of compulsory vaccination was not something that could be sustained in the absence of widespread public confidence. Though few, the 'martyrs' who endured multiple prison sentences usefully dramatise the point and illustrate how, in the absence of a modicum of trust, substantive legal powers can serve only to provoke what might be regarded as their definitive limit – militant, absolute resistance.

5

Revisiting Disease in Immigration Law: Colonial and Commonwealth Histories

ALISON BASHFORD

I. Introduction

It is plain, if complex, that infectious diseases spread with the movement of humans and other animals, as well as via inanimate materials. Analysis of different comprehensions of precisely how or why this takes place, and of the nature of disease and contagion itself, has engaged and fascinated medical historians for generations. This has typically involved analysis of the history of the *regulation* of human movement as well; often, but not always, a common sense response. The long history of quarantine sites and procedures is explained by just this, historical work that shows the extent to which goods and materials as much as animals and humans were targets for multiple processes of segregation, fumigation, or isolation, and in the case of materials and non-human animals, sometimes elimination.[1]

Certainly, in British colonial and Commonwealth histories, powers, laws, and authority to regulate human movement have often been twinned with public health measures. This is so especially with regard to various quarantine acts, which early (at least from the 1830s) included powers to restrict embarkation at point of departure, disembarkation at point of arrival, and to enforce deportation. Multiple immigration statutes across many jurisdictions routinely included disease clauses, referring typically to 'loathsome and contagious diseases' that would render a would-be immigrant 'prohibited' or 'undesirable'. Under changing regulations, specific loathsome and contagious diseases were nominated: often cholera, plague and smallpox in the nineteenth century, while perhaps surprisingly, tuberculosis was the most commonly nominated disease, over the twentieth century.[2]

[1] Mark Harrison, *Contagion: How Commerce has Spread Disease* (New Haven, CT, Yale University Press, 2013); Alison Bashford (ed), *Quarantine: Local and Global Histories* (London, Palgrave, 2016).

[2] John Welshman and Alison Bashford, 'Tuberculosis, Migration, and Medical Examination: Lessons from History' (2006) 60 *Journal of Epidemiology and Community Health* 282.

Yet the United Kingdom (UK) differed from its own colonies (and later Commonwealth) in this regard. On the whole, British political and economic policy traditions supported freedom of international movement (alongside free trade), not *restriction* of movement, and so the UK was a reluctant latecomer to the normalisation of medico-legal border control that came to characterise the nineteenth, and especially the twentieth century world.[3]

This broad exceptionality of the UK on the one hand, and the striking similarity between many colonial and postcolonial statutes on the other, became apparent in scholarly terms less in the light of the COVID-19 pandemic, than in the light of SARS in 2003, when the history of medico-legal borders was freshly investigated. After COVID-19, the whole question of measures through which the regulation of human movement become measures of public health and biosecurity needs another assessment. It was only during COVID-19 that the UK instituted medico-legal border controls that approached those that had been implemented in colonial/Commonwealth countries (especially Australia) for a century and more. And even then, a long history of British reluctance to close borders (Brexit notwithstanding) was repeated, as was other nations' familiarity with more restricted, if not closed borders. How does this comparative history of medico-legal border control look after COVID-19, 20 years on from its initial investigation after SARS?

II. Health and Disease Clauses in Colonial Immigration Statutes

For the first half of the nineteenth century, restriction of movement between polities was unusual and was often limited to emergency periods and circumstances: in war time, for example, when temporary limitation on 'alien' entry was established, and occasionally when large-scale epidemics of infectious diseases threatened economy and security of various orders. In the UK, this remained the default policy throughout the century: domestic borders were minimally regulated until the Aliens Act 1905, of which more below.

In other hemispheres and continents, however, experiments in more standard, or even permanent border controls were underway from the middle of the nineteenth century. By 1900 regulated entry at national borders was globally more usual than unusual, approaching the system and agreements with which we are familiar today. The growing normalisation of regulation of movement over international borders was prompted by two phenomena: first, quarantine laws and procedures; and second, a suite of labour-based immigration restriction acts, focused often but not solely on the movement of Chinese people across nations and between

[3] For the globalisation of borders, see Adam M McKeown, *Melancholy Order: Asian Migration and the Globalization of Borders* (New York, NY, Columbia University Press, 2008).

continents. This was not exclusive to the nineteenth century 'British world', but certainly was widespread and significant within it.[4]

In the 1850s, various forms of Chinese exclusion acts emerged in California and in the British colonies of Victoria and New South Wales, just then transitioning to self-government. This was primarily as a response to Chinese people working on gold fields.[5] It is important to note that at this point statutes were often titled 'Chinese' acts, but this explicit nomination later diminished. And while their short titles sometimes included the term 'exclusion', and at other times 'restriction', in fact these were rarely, if ever, total bars on entry. The exchanges of trade and commerce needed protection and facilitation by freer entry and movement of the agents of trade. For example, the US Chinese Exclusion Act 1882 exempted merchants, teachers, students, travellers, and diplomats.[6] We should remember also that entry *into* China had for centuries itself been highly regulated, and for many (including traders) was impossible. By the middle of the nineteenth century, and after the Opium Wars, the late Qing dynasty gradually relaxed its own exclusion, for American merchants beginning with the Treaty of Wanghia 1844, 'the treaty of peace, amity and commerce'.[7]

These kinds of statutes escalated over the 1880s, with various immigration acts in southern Africa (Natal, the Cape Colony), in New Zealand, across the Australian colonies (Victoria, New South Wales, Queensland), and in British Columbia. In 1901 the newly federated Commonwealth of Australia (a federation of six self-governing colonies) passed an Immigration Restriction Act 1901 as its first piece of independent legislation. As Marilyn Lake and Henry Reynolds explored, this was together the gradual accretion of a 'global colour line'.[8]

Over time (that is, by about 1900), immigration statutes in the British colonies and dominions moved away from the specification of national or racial or ethnic groups to be excluded. As a rule, they were no longer 'Chinese' exclusion/restriction acts or 'Indian' exclusion acts. The impetus for this trend lay not with the various self-governing colonies or dominions, but with the Colonial Office in

[4] For the 'British world', see Carl Bridge and Kent Fedorowich (eds), *The British World: Diaspora, Culture and Identity* (London and Portland, OR, Frank Cass, 2003); Phillip Buckner and R Douglas Francis (eds), *Rediscovering the British World* (Calgary, Calgary University Press, 2005).

[5] Mae Ngai, *The Chinese Question: The Gold Rushes and Global Politics* (New York, NY, WW Norton, 2021).

[6] Chinese Exclusion Act 1882 (US).

[7] Treaty of Peace, Amity and Commerce between the United States of America and the Chinese Empire, Concluded at Wánghiá, 3 July 1844, in *Treaties between the United States of America and China, Japan, Lewchew and Siam, Acts of Congress, And the Attorney-General's Opinion, With the Decrees and Regulations Issued for the Guidance of U.S. Consular Courts in China* (Hong Kong, United States Legation to China, 1862) 9–21.

[8] Marilyn Lake and Henry Reynolds, *Drawing the Global Colour Line. White Men's Countries and the Question of Racial Equality* (Cambridge, Cambridge University Press, 2008); see also Robert A Huttenback, 'The British Empire as a "White Man's Country" – Racial Attitudes and Immigration Legislation in the Colonies of White Settlement' (1973) 13 *Journal of British Studies* 108; Charles Price, *The Great White Walls are Built: Restrictive Immigration to North America and Australasia, 1836–1888* (Canberra, Australian National University Press, 1974).

London. Many historians have investigated this, but it remains extraordinary and important that the disinclination to specify populations (or nations or races) for special restriction or even exclusion from British colonies, stemmed directly from the metropole, from British policy, and (over this key period) from the influence of Joseph Chamberlain personally, as Secretary of State for the Colonies.[9] At the same time as recognising this British government resistance to the specification of particular 'races' or 'nationalities', it is clear that on the ground, at coastal and territorial borders across the world, individuals were nonetheless discriminated one from another, according to a visual code of 'race': a 'colour line' endured, notwithstanding nominally race-neutral laws. In Australia, for example, other measures were introduced to enable targeted responses by immigration and customs officers at borders. A 'dictation test' borrowed from Natal was designed more or less to guarantee failure, thus enabling an officer to lawfully refuse entry.[10]

What is less well known – partly because of the great historiographical emphasis on, and interest in race, ethnicity, and the nomination (or not) of 'Chinese' or 'Indian' restriction – are the health and disease clauses and powers in late-nineteenth and early-twentieth century immigration statutes. Almost every colonial statute specified the presence of contagious or infectious disease as constituting a prohibited entrant or prohibited immigrant. Versions of this clause were very similar across jurisdictions and across time. They endure into the present.

In general, there were two versions of 'health' clauses. The first dealt with the likelihood of an individual becoming a public charge. He or she might be deemed a prohibited or undesirable entrant if a chronic illness was declared, or was evident, or if an infirmity or disability was apparent that would likely require public care, and so government expense, in a hospital, a tuberculosis sanatorium, or an asylum, for example. The second related to disease risk; bringing in an infectious disease that would likely spread. It is useful to recall that across British self-governing colonies, as in the UK itself, it was not yet deemed a responsibility of government to deliver primary health care (or welfare) for most subjects or citizens. Three specific health care domains (and populations) *were* already deemed to be a responsibility of government, however, and this was common across British self-governing colonies, even if implementation was inadequate. First, governments had long assumed responsibility for measures to manage infectious or contagious disease that would likely become widespread, or epidemic. Second, it was conventional that a government would take responsibility for acute and chronic hospital or institutional medical and nursing care for the indigent or poor, unable to provide for their own care. And the same was true, thirdly, of institutional care for the

[9] David C Atkinson, *The Burden of White Supremacy: Containing Asian Migration in the British Empire and the United States* (Chapel Hill, NC, University of North Carolina Press, 2016); Freddy Foks, 'Emigration State: Race, Citizenship and Settler Imperialism in Modern British History, c 1850–1972' (2022) 35 *Journal of Historical Sociology* 170; Lake and Reynolds (n 8).

[10] Jeremy C Martens, *Empire and Asian Migration: Sovereignty, Immigration Restriction and Protest in the British Settler Colonies, 1888–1907* (Crawley, UWA Publishing, 2018).

mentally ill, who were also indigent or poor. For example: New Zealand passed the Imbecile Passengers Act in 1873 which penalised shipping lines for landing anyone who was 'lunatic, idiotic, deaf, dumb, blind or infirm and likely to become a public charge'.[11] To take another example, outside the British Empire and so to show how similar and widespread such health clauses were, the United States' (US) Immigration Act of 1891 denied admission to 'certain classes of alien' including 'all idiots, insane persons, paupers or persons likely to become a public charge'.[12] The same clause in the 1891 Act went on to describe prohibited immigrants also as 'persons suffering from a loathsome or a dangerous contagious disease'.[13] The Australian Immigration Act of 1901 separated the two kinds of health powers, with different clauses; first for those likely to become a charge on the public or on charity, any idiot or insane person; and second for 'any person suffering from an infectious or contagious disease of a loathsome or dangerous character'.[14]

On occasion, statutes *did* continue to conflate race, health and disease in their nomination of prohibited immigrants. For example, the Canadian Chinese Immigration Act 1903 excluded 'paupers, idiots, the insane, and any Chinese person suffering any loathsome, infectious, or contagious disease'. The non-raced 1906 amendment, however, simply prohibited any person with 'loathsome, contagious or infectious disease'.[15]

All of these immigration laws dovetailed with quarantine laws which had proliferated earlier in the nineteenth century, and had become part of the standard regulation of vessels: in New South Wales in 1832, in Hong Kong in the 1850s, in Canada, Queensland and the Straits Settlements in the 1860s, in Ceylon, Natal and Tasmania in the 1880s. I have argued elsewhere that taken together such quarantine laws were not a prelude to immigration restriction, they *were* immigration restriction. Powers to restrict movement in quarantine and immigration statutes were effectively interchangeable, the former enabling the deportation and return of people as well as their compulsory isolation or segregation, the latter almost universally including infectious disease as a justification for the limitation of movement.[16]

It is also important to recognise that the rationale for some colonial immigration law-making was not always exclusion, or the limitation of free movement, but sometimes to secure satisfactory minimal conditions of passage, and of labour conditions, for emigrants on various kinds of work contracts, including indentured labour contracts. These were protection acts, of sorts. For example, the Indian Immigration Act 1882 passed by the province of South Australia, was, in its own terms 'An Act to encourage the introduction of Indian Native Immigrants

[11] Imbecile Passengers Act 1873 (New Zealand, no 70).

[12] Immigration Act 1891 (US chap 551).

[13] ibid.

[14] Immigration Restriction Act 1901 (Commonwealth of Australia), s 3 (b), (c), (d).

[15] Chinese Immigration Act 1903 (Canada, chap 8); Immigration Act 1906 (Canada, chap 19), s 27.

[16] Alison Bashford, 'Immigration Restriction: Rethinking Period and place from Settler Colonies to Postcolonial Nations' (2014) 9 *Journal of Global History* 26.

into the Northern Territory of the Province of South Australia'.[17] It set the conditions of employment for emigration agents in Calcutta, Madras and Bombay, and empowered an Immigration Agent-General in the Northern Territory of Australia

> to visit every plantation upon which there may be immigrants under indenture, to receive and take cognizance of the complaints of immigrants, and thereupon to give advice, to conduct investigations, and institute prosecutions, as the circumstances may require.[18]

That Immigration Agent-General was empowered to enter any plantation, inspect the state of houses, and of hospital accommodation, and to investigate any complaint that might be brought by a medical officer. It enabled the appointment of medical officers to hospitals on plantations, responsible to the Immigration Agent-General, not the plantation owner or manager. Indeed, since such medical officers were salaried by the Government, not by plantation owners or those who paid for the indentured labourers' passage and work, we might see this as another early foray into state responsibility for health. A medical officer was charged to inspect ships on arrival (and on departure, those returning Indians after indenture periods ended, or after their having obtained exemption from indenture and the required passport to return), examine the sick, 'if any', and arrange for hospitalisation if required.[19] Part IX of the statute governed minimal standards for hospitals. They were required to be physically on the plantation itself, and not shared with any other plantation. One of the medical officer's duties was certification of hospital building plans (especially for ventilation and drainage) and to monitor the hospital's standing regulations, its dietary, medical and surgical supplies. Plantation employers were required to pay for dispensers and 'sick nurses' themselves, of which one at least must be female, if there were any female indentured labourers. On any plantation in which five or more immigrants were employed, a hospital was required to be built, large enough to accommodate at least 10 beds for every 50 labourers (the statute says 'immigrants'). It held plantation owners to account for the health of their labourers. If a medical officer determined that a labourer-patient in a plantation hospital required transfer to, and treatment in, a public or government hospital in Port Darwin, the expense was to be covered by the plantation owner, one shilling for each day for the hospitalisation of 'their' labourer. Should that labourer/immigrant die, the expense of burial was also the responsibility of the plantation owner.[20]

The extent to which immigration law was, historically, labour law, needs far more scholarship. And the extent to which immigration law across the British world, including 'British India', was passed to *facilitate* movement of indentured labourers under minimally satisfactory conditions, as much as to *restrict*

[17] An Act to encourage the introduction of Indian Native Immigrants into the Northern Territory of the Province of South Australia 1882 (South Australia, no 240).

[18] ibid, part I, s 10.

[19] ibid, part III, s 33.

[20] ibid, part IX.

movement, or to totally exclude entry, requires far more attention and recognition. This is so, both through legal history methods that track aspirations and optimal standards, and through social history methods that track implementation and, inevitably, the failure in practice of such 'protection'. In the British world, this suite of laws to *facilitate* immigration was entirely shaped by post-abolition politics, by mid- and late-nineteenth century 'indenture' that replaced enslaved labour systems. Politicians, new generations of planters, and company investors needed indenture to be clearly differentiated (at least in law, and on paper), from both slave-ship conditions and 'plantation' treatment that had been associated with the prior legal world in which chattel enslavement was lawful. For our purposes here, it is notable how fully and deliberately those conditions and standards concerned health, medicine and disease.

III. Free Trade and Free Movement in the UK

In the UK, both the quarantine laws, policies and practices, and immigration or entry regulations that were becoming increasingly standard elsewhere in the world, were still unusual or emergency measures.[21] Put even more strongly (and more interestingly), the very principle of immigration restriction was *actively resisted* in the decades either side of 1900, especially by liberal MPs amongst the Whigs, by some Conservatives, but also by some Labour MPs, which was perhaps most unexpected given the labour rationale for so much immigration restriction law.

The suite of colonial and US immigration statutes, including their 'loathsome disease' clauses, were understood to counter British policy on freedom of trade and movement, as well as a British tradition of asylum, or at least its perceived historical tradition. This was stated in nationalist terms. Labour MP John Burns, for example, declared in 1904 that 'it was because this was the only civilized nation that did not possess this kind of legislation that he was proud of being a Briton'.[22] Liberal-Radical Sir Charles Dilke rejected such state intervention, upholding principles of individual liberty and freedom of movement, in a defence of classical liberalism. He also defended a long tradition of free movement into England for purposes of asylum.[23] It was the historical case of Protestant Huguenot refuge which was mainly being referenced. Winston Churchill, to take a third example, then an economically liberal member of the Conservative Party, also opposed immigration restriction, in part because it may set up a system or a precedent for the refusal of those seeking asylum from persecution. This would challenge

[21] For the minimisation in quarantine at coastal territorial borders in Britain itself, see Krista Maglen, *The English System: Quarantine, Immigration and the Making of a Port Sanitary Zone* (Manchester, Manchester University Press, 2014).

[22] HC Deb (25 April 1904) vol 133, cols 1149–59.

[23] Quoted in Bernard Gainer, *The Alien Invasion: The Origins of the Aliens Act of 1905* (London, Heinemann Educational, 1972) 144–65.

> the old tolerant and generous practice of free entry and asylum to which this country has so long adhered and from which it has so greatly gained … those ancient traditions of freedom and hospitality for which Britain has been so long renowned.[24]

Over the 1890s, such pronouncement was prompted by English responses to the increasing numbers of East European Jews arriving in the UK, many *en route* to North America. The entire question of immigration restriction *and* the surprising resistance to it, was debated and entertained in this context. A suite of immigration or 'aliens' bills were presented over the 1890s, but the interesting point – often ignored by historians – is that they were defeated repeatedly, up until the 1904 bill that became the Aliens Act 1905.

This disinclination for many British members of Parliament, across parties, to bring in new and unfamiliar measures for border control, should be analysed alongside the more common historical interpretation that emphasises British anti-Semitism in the passing of early Aliens Acts. Both are apparent in historical records, but in general the latter is a far more common focus of scholarship. And yet, as a matter of fact, not interpretation, British parliamentary *resistance* to immigration restriction was exceptional for its time and global context. Arguments presented in Westminster *against* immigration restriction – successful in many cases – was completely different to parliamentary debate in the colonies, where hardly anyone spoke against the idea, and bills were passed quickly. There, as we have seen, laws equivalent to the various Aliens bills in the UK, were often already decades old. Indeed, with various amendments (because border control was seen to be so important) they were in their second and third generation of refinement in powers and expansion in scope. Accordingly, there were large customs, immigration, and quarantine infrastructures in self-governing colonies like New South Wales, British Columbia and New Zealand. Meanwhile, in the UK, MPs and civil servants had some difficulty even imagining let alone implementing a structure and personnel to implement what we would now call a 'border policy'.

This British reluctance on the part of some went *against* the trend in Britain's own Empire and *against* the trend in various ocean-facing US states and in Washington, DC. This is why I have argued elsewhere that the debate around and leading up to the UK Aliens Act 1905 is especially telling and important in world history terms.[25] In so many ways, British liberalism held out longest and strongest in the global normalisation of border control. And as Jane McAdam and I have analysed, while a bill *was* finally passed, and became the Aliens Act 1905, in fact it included one of the first clauses that guaranteed the safe entry of anyone who declared themselves to have been 'politically or religiously persecuted'.[26] Its significance has long been overlooked.

[24] Winston Churchill to Mr N Laski *The Times* (31 May 1904) 10; see Alison Bashford and Jane McAdam, 'The Right to Asylum: The 1905 Aliens Act and the Evolution of Refugee Law' (2014) 32 *Law and History Review* 309.

[25] Alison Bashford and Cate Gilchrist, 'The Colonial History of the 1905 Aliens Act' (2012) 40 *Journal of Imperial and Commonwealth History* 409; Bashford and McAdam (n 24).

[26] NW Sibley and Alfred Elias, *The Aliens Act and the Right of Asylum* (London, William Clowes and Sons, 1906).

Where was health and disease in the Aliens Act? In its assent in 1905 the final legislation ended up with a health clause, like all its colonial and US models, combining the two versions of health clauses explained above. Powers were granted to prevent an undesirable immigrant from landing if: 'he is a lunatic or an idiot, or owing to any disease or infirmity appears likely to become a charge upon the rates or otherwise a detriment to the public'.[27] If anything, this was weaker than in comparable clauses in immigration statutes elsewhere at the time, with the emphasis on public charge rather than health risk to the domestic population. In fact, in a (UK) Royal Commission on Alien Immigration, 1903, it had been recommended that all alien immigrants should be medically inspected upon arrival and (as was typical for immigration laws elsewhere), those found to have an infectious disease or mental incapacity be prevented from landing, the shipowner penalised and be required to return the passenger at their company's expense. This recommendation was directly drawn from the Commission's examination of pre-existing US, Natal, New Zealand, Australian and Canadian laws.[28]

IV. Disease in Immigration Statutes of Postcolonial Polities

One of the more interesting aspects of the ongoing history of disease clauses in immigration statutes is the process by which they became standard, and even standardised, so similar were they to one another. Many historians of the British world have tracked race-based immigration restriction laws and policies through the nineteenth century to a mid-twentieth century period, especially to the post-war moment when principles of human equality, including racial equality, were declared by the United Nations:

> Everyone is entitled to all the rights and freedoms set forth in this Declaration, without distinction of any kind, such as race, colour, sex, language, religion, political or other opinion, national or social origin, property, birth or other status.[29]

[27] Aliens Act 1905, s 3 (b).

[28] Great Britain. Royal Commission on Alien Immigration (1903), *Report*, Cd 1742, vol 1, part 2, *Measures Adopted for the Restriction and Control of Alien Immigration in Foreign Countries and in British Colonies, Recommendations no 267, 42* (London, 1903); see also *House of Commons Select Committee on Emigration and Immigration (Foreigners), Report, Proceedings, Minutes of Evidence, and Appendix I*, 27 July 1888; David Feldman, 'Was the Nineteenth Century a Golden Age for Immigrants? The Changing Articulation of National, Local and Voluntary Controls' in Andreas Fahrmeir, Olivier Faron and Patrick Weil (eds), *Migration Control in the North Atlantic World. The Evolution of State Practices in Europa and the United States from the French Revolution to the Inter-War Period* (New York, NY, Berghahn Books, 2003).

[29] United Nations Declaration of Human Rights, 1948, Article 2. Note also Article 13: 'Everyone has the right to freedom of movement and residence within the borders of each state. Everyone has the right to leave any country, including his own, and to return to his country'. This period is the end point, for example, of Lake and Reynolds (n 8).

Historians of Britain itself tend to track the history of immigration acts and their powers (rarely their health/disease powers, however), to a slightly later period, beyond the arrival of *Windrush* (also 1948) to the Commonwealth immigration acts of 1962 and 1968. There was certainly a racial politics to those statutes that was similar to the Australian Immigration Act passed 50 years earlier: a racial intent, and racialised context, without explicit racial content in the statutes themselves.[30] And yet if we consider the disease clauses more closely, beyond this period and into the last half of the twentieth century, we can begin to see just how continuous immigration acts have been, into the present.

The United Nations' Declaration of Human Rights in 1948 appeared on the cusp of major post-war decolonisation, and the establishment of new and independent states. Accordingly, over the 1950s, 1960s and 1970s, all manner and any number of newly independent polities established versions of immigration acts, often (like Australia) as their first order of business, the first bill passed of new legislatures. The irony is that almost all of those postcolonial immigration statutes were based directly – in their structure, wording, clauses, powers – on the older generation of immigration acts that had defined the settler colonial world (read: the so-called 'white dominions'). That is, they had a legal genealogy that lay with the nineteenth-century exclusion acts that were implicitly, and sometimes explicitly, race-based.

In Fiji, to take one example, prohibited persons were defined in a list and with wording that was entirely familiar, indeed drawn from, earlier Australian and New Zealand Acts. A prohibited person was anyone unable to show that 'he has the means of supporting himself and his family and dependents (if any) or that he has a permit to work in Fiji or who is likely to become a pauper or a charge on the public'. The following clause prohibited any person refusing to submit to medical examination, who was suffering from a contagious or infectious disease, or from 'mental disorder or is a mental defective'. This was followed by standard clauses on prostitution, on living off earnings of prostitution, and on criminal offences.[31]

Another example is the Singaporean Immigration Act 1970 which specified the following prohibited classes: 'any person who is unable to show that he has the means of supporting himself or who is likely to become a pauper or a charge on the public'; 'any person suffering from mental disorder or being a mental defective, or suffering from a contagious or infectious disease which makes his presence in Singapore dangerous to the community'; 'any person who refuses to submit to a medical examination'.[32] In such ways, new polities like Singapore or Brunei, Fiji or Malaysia, Ceylon or Nauru, declared their postcolonial independence through a capacity to determine who came into their territorial nation-state, but in one of

[30] Kennetta Hammond Perry, *London is the Place for Me: Black Britons, Citizenship and the Politics of Race* (Oxford, Oxford University Press, 2015) esp ch 5: 'Exposing the Racial Politics of Immigration Controls'.

[31] Act to consolidate and amend the law relating to immigration 1971 (Fiji, chap 88) s 11(2).

[32] Immigration Act 1970 (Republic of Singapore) s 8 (2)(a)–(g).

the great ironies of modern world history, the authorising legal documents had colonial origins. The disease rationales for exclusion, quarantine or deportation were directly repeated in these postcolonial acts, perhaps the key turn that effected a world in which border control (including for health reasons) started to become routine.

V. Disease, Movement and Law after SARS and COVID-19

Disease clauses in immigration and alien laws came to be so common as to be unremarkable over the last half of the twentieth century. Yet they were suddenly visible again in the SARS outbreak in 2003, when some border zones and border crossings – mainly at international airports – were newly and strongly regulated and constrained. The phenomenon of temperature checks as part of incoming processing of travellers raised alarm and concern, as well as widespread critique on illiberal compulsion. During and immediately after SARS, international travellers were subject to unfamiliar medical surveillance, asked to declare prescribed symptoms. Airport paraphernalia that checked temperatures of incoming passengers then seemed outrageous, but of course paled into nothing, compared to the measures implemented 20 years later, in COVID-19 times. The phenomenon energised scholars across history, law, geography, and anthropology as well as public health, to look again at medico-legal border control, and its history.[33]

One line of inquiry was geographical. In the light of SARS, Convery, Welshman and Bashford asked: 'where is the border'?[34] In a comparative study on disease management (mainly of tuberculosis) and migration between the UK and Australia, 1950–2000, we showed how polities continued to have different sites for the implementation of medico-legal border control. In such processes, borders were and are a function as much as a place, but we were interested in how the border could literally be located offshore as well as onshore.[35] It might be at a territorial edge (in a maritime world) or at an airport 'sterile zone' in a world of air traffic and mobility. But effectively, a 'border' that facilitates or restricts movement might not be within

[33] Elim Chan and Andreas Schloenhardt, 'The 2003 SARS Outbreak in Hong Kong: A Review of Legislative and Border Control Measures' (2004) 24 *Singapore Journal of Legal Studies* 484; Alison Bashford (ed), *Medicine at the Border: Disease, Globalisation and Security, 1850 to the Present* (Basingstoke, Palgrave Macmillan, 2006); Lung-Sang Chan et al, 'Screening for Fever by Remote-Sensing Infrared Thermographic Camera' (2004) 11 *Journal of Travel Medicine* 273; Alvin Y So and Ngai Pun, 'Introduction: Globalization and Anti-Globalization of SARS in Chinese Societies' (2004) 28 *Asian Perspective* 5.

[34] Ian Convery, John Welshman and Alison Bashford, 'Where is the Border? Screening for Tuberculosis in the United Kingdom and Australia, 1950–2000' in Bashford (2006) (n 33).

[35] Donna Hastings and Thomas W Wilson, *Borders: Frontiers of Identity, Nation and State* (Oxford, Berg, 1999); Sharon Pickering and Leanne Weber (eds), *Borders, Mobility and Technologies of Control* (Dordrecht, Springer, 2006).

the territorial jurisdiction of a nation-state at all. It might be on another continent entirely, in a medical officer's rooms, or a custom or immigration officer's desk in the country of departure, where an application for visa might be granted or denied on health grounds; where an X-ray, evidence of previous mental ill-health, or a physical examination, might render a would-be entrant ineligible.

Over much of the nineteenth century, and into the twentieth, Australia was globally atypical in implementing the latter; offshore practices defined by its island status in a maritime era. Key health borders had long been located outside its own territory, at the point of departure – often London or Portsmouth or Liverpool – at a time when most polities operationalised such borders (if they had them) at the point and place of entry. Health screening came to be managed through an increasingly complex visa system, now globally familiar but early implemented in the Australian case. Except for a few categories (for example, diplomatic visas and certain emergency humanitarian visas) various health criteria, declarations, and diagnostic tests, typically applied. These varied – then as now – according to the length of stay in Australia, the category of visa sought, and especially the risk status of the country from which the visa is applied, which came to be determined over time by prevalence of particular infectious diseases. Some entrants, from some countries, may simply 'declare' their health and infectious disease status – usually on forms distributed *en route*. Applicants from countries deemed to be 'very high risk', and who intended to stay over three months must fulfil the health criteria. Any applicant from any country who wished to stay over 12 months – intending migrants, asylum claimants, international students, and those seeking long term residency – must likewise undertake a compulsory health screening process. In other words, the compulsory health criteria were (and are) common reasons why visas are not issued.

Until recently, medico-legal border control has been very different in the UK. Regulations did not operate at the point of departure or at the point of entry, but actually *within* its own territorial borders: at-risk travellers and immigrants would be referred by various border authorities to the local health authority of the traveller or immigrants' final destination. This was increasingly understood to be out of step, and for different reasons. Some research in the 1950s was concerned with tuberculosis among Irish, Pakistani, and Indian migrants in London, Birmingham, Bradford, and Wolverhampton. These studies seemed to show that most tuberculosis was imported, and control might be supported by early detection of disease through medical examinations at the ports of entry.[36] From the late 1950s, the British Medical Association also exerted pressure on the Ministry of Health that all migrants should have medical examinations at the ports of entry, a policy endorsed by Enoch Powell as Minister of Health in March 1962.[37] Some proponents of medical examinations at the national border pointed to the action routinely taken by

[36] VH Springett et al, 'Tuberculosis in Immigrants in Birmingham, 1956–57' (1958) 12 *British Journal of Preventive and Social Medicine* 139.

[37] National Archives (UK). MH 55/2632: JE Powell to Secretary, 20 March 1962.

other countries, most obviously Australia. But even then, this pressure was only mildly successful. Under the Immigration Act 1971, there were powers to require medical examination after entry if immigration officers are of the opinion that 'a further medical test or examination may be required in the interests of public health'.[38] But that would still happen *within* the country, *after* arrival, and within the NHS system, not at the port of departure, as part of the visa process.

It was this port of arrival system of health inspection that was still current in the next century in the UK, when SARS became a threat. British epidemiologists and health policymakers recommended change, again, to what had come to be called 'the Australian model': the 'point of departure' system. This pushed the health border back to the point of departure, so as to make it part of the (offshore, so to say) visa application process itself.[39] In February 2005, the UK Government announced proposals to implement existing powers by screening visa applicants for tuberculosis on 'high risk' routes, and requiring those diagnosed to seek treatment before they would be permitted entry to the UK.[40] The Conservative party also announced that visas would be denied to prospective migrants in whom tuberculosis was detected. Michael Howard then stated that

> the British people deserve the best standards of public health. We need to control who is coming to Britain to ensure that they are not a public health risk and to protect access to the NHS. It's plain common sense. And it's exactly what they do in New Zealand, Canada and Australia.[41]

Ironically and tellingly, when I organised the international conference that became the edited book *Medicine at the Border*, an initially wide geographic and national distribution of participants narrowed, as visas were either not granted or became too complex and expensive to pursue. There was a geographic pattern to this that seemed like an inversion of, or a twist on, the UK Commonwealth Immigrants Act. Speakers arriving from the UK (as UK subjects) simply had to tick 'no', indicating they had never had tuberculosis, on an in-flight declaration form (still the single most problematised, and specifically nominated infectious disease) and deliver this to a customs and immigration officer on arrival. Speakers (and would-be speakers, since not a few withdrew because the process itself was prohibitive) arriving from Pakistan or Sri Lanka or Indonesia had already been through a

[38] Immigration Act 1971 (chap 77).

[39] Richard Coker and Alan Ingram, 'Passports and Pestilence: Migration, Security and Contemporary Border Control of Infectious Diseases' in Bashford (2006) (n 33).

[40] HM Government, Home Office, *Controlling our Borders: Making Migration Work for Britain: Five Year Strategy for Asylum and Immigration*. Cm 6472 (London, The Stationery Office, 2005) 26 (para 52).

[41] B Russell and N Morris, 'Test Migrants for HIV and TB, say Tories' *The Independent* (15 February 2005); Richard Coker, 'Compulsory Screening of Immigrants for Tuberculosis and HIV: Is Not Based on Adequate Evidence, and Has Practical and Ethical Problems' (2004) 328 *British Medical Journal* 298; Richard Coker, *Migration, Public Health and Compulsory Screening for TB and HIV* (London, Institute for Public Policy Research, 2003); John Welshman, 'Compulsion, Localism, and Pragmatism: The Micro-Politics of Tuberculosis Screening in the United Kingdom, 1950–1965' (2006) 19 *Social History of Medicine* 295.

multi-step visa process, which may have required a chest X-ray, undertaken by an authorised radiologist. This was based on a risk status yielded by epidemiological data, in particular the prevalence of multi-drug resistant tuberculosis. While our meeting was SARS-inspired, aiming to consider medico-legal border control in an extraordinary moment of threatened global pandemic, in fact it was the everyday and longstanding health criteria for certain visas that emerged as a major topic for enquiry and that differently shaped the constituents' capacity to travel internationally. Medicine at the border was playing out before us.

It was neither SARS, however, nor chronic tuberculosis, but the recent COVID-19 pandemic which seems finally to have pressed UK policy towards the kind of hard health borders long drawn around other polities in the Commonwealth. Political scientists have suggested that

> widespread travel and immigration restrictions instigated the largest and fastest decline in global human mobility in modern history, and COVID-19 may fundamentally change immigration over the longer term.[42]

Yet as I have set out here, there was considerable divergence in this overall global pattern, with British systems still an outlier, for better or worse. In the UK and Australia, policy response to COVID-19, insofar as international movement was concerned, diverged, recapitulating versions of their historic policies on national borders as health borders. The UK was still inclined toward open borders (despite Brexit). The Australian Government, by contrast, almost immediately closed its borders entirely.

On the one hand, the UK doubled down on lessons learned from SARS, and put into place new powers to contain or slow the virus through restriction of movement. On the other hand, this geography was still operationalised at 'port of arrival'. 'Protecting the border is a fundamental duty of government', a 2020 Department of Health response to proposed bills stated,[43] adding that:

> In the event that Border Force resources are depleted due to Covid-19 to such an extent that there is a real and significant risk that there are or will be insufficient border force officers to maintain adequate border security, a power is needed to ensure that we can direct arrivals to ports of arrival in the UK where there will be sufficient Border Force officers to carry out the necessary border security checks.

This was then elaborated:

> The proposed powers will allow the Secretary of State to direct a port operator (i.e. a person concerned in the management of a port) to suspend relevant operations, partially or wholly, in the event that there is a real and significant risk there are or will be insufficient resources to maintain adequate border security.

[42] Ann Boucher et al, 'Covid-19: A Crisis of Borders' (2021) 54 *Political Science & Politics* 617.

[43] UK Department of Health & Social Care, *Impact Assessment. Coronavirus Bill: Summary of Impacts*, 23 March 2020, available at www.gov.uk/government/publications/coronavirus-bill-summary-of-impacts/coronavirus-bill-summary-of-impacts.

And further, detailing legitimate implementation at the point of arrival:

> The proposals will also ensure that immigration officers and constables can support the wider public health effort where they encounter a person who is, or may be, infectious during the course of their normal functions at the border or while exercising immigration enforcement functions in country. The proposed powers will allow an immigration officer to direct or remove such a person to a suitable place for the purpose of screening and assessment or to keep that person there or at another suitable place for a time-limited period to be handed over to a relevant health official for the same purpose.

During COVID-19, and after Brexit, the island status of Britain was bought to the fore in the way that it had been in Australia for generations.[44] Even so, and even still, the UK did not shut borders with anything like the vigilance that characterised the Australian response.[45] There, almost immediately, travellers from China were denied entry, a nationality-based bar with an infectious disease rationale, that was far more all-encompassing than any of the historic Chinese restriction acts. Indeed, the response was so strong that the Commonwealth of Australia barred entry even to its own citizens, some legal scholars have argued, unlawfully. Extraordinarily, citizens' 'right to return' was momentarily denied.[46]

VI. Conclusion

In the light of the global COVID-19 pandemic, it is germane to ask what impact this long history of the legal regulation of human movement for health reasons has had. We know that responses to COVID-19 across the world were crudely spatial in the first instance. The management of sometimes highly local intra-state borders came strongly to govern conduct and to serve as the key preventive strategy before vaccinations were rolled out. Indeed, the prominence and governance of *internal* borders has challenged the previous historiography of disease management which had long problematised *international* borders, including the focus of my own scholarship.[47] Yet we also know that disease clauses in national immigration, aliens, and quarantine acts continued to govern movement. Typically, historians

[44] Des Fitzgerald, 'Normal Island: COVID-19, Border Control, and Viral Nationalism in UK Public Health Discourse' (2021) 28 *Sociological Research Online* 596.

[45] Lorenzo Piccoli et al, 'Restricting Human Movement During the COVID-19 Pandemic: New Research Avenues in the Study of Mobility, Migration, and Citizenship' (2022) 57 *International Migration Review* 505.

[46] Regina Jefferies, Jane McAdam and Sangeetha Pillai, 'Can We Still Call Australia Home? The Right to Return and the Legality of Australia's COVID-19 Travel Restrictions' (2021) 27 *Australian Journal of Human Rights* 211; Regina Jefferies and Jane McAdam, 'Locked In: Australia's COVID-19 Border Closures and the Right to Leave' (2023) 41 *Australian Year Book of International Law Online* 185.

[47] For example, Alan M Kraut, *Silent Travelers: Germs, Genes, and the "Immigrant Menace"* (Baltimore, MD, and London, John Hopkins University Press, 1995); Amy L Fairchild, *Science at the Borders: Immigrant Medical Inspection and the Shaping of the Modern Industrial Labor Force* (Baltimore, MD, and London, John Hopkins University Press, 2003); Adam M McKeown, *Melancholy Order: Asian Migration and the Globalization of Borders* (New York, NY, Columbia University Press, 2011). But see

have assessed this as a history of race-based laws. This certainly characterised the response to SARS. One of the key scholarly interventions was to problematise the racialisation of policy, procedures, and popular discourse vis-à-vis China. It was the 'Chinatowns' in various cities, for example, which were shut down.[48] The response to the more recent COVID-19 pandemic also started this way, in early 2020.[49] The long history of race, immigration and disease prevention was mobilised by critics, and for good reason.[50] The need for a critique stands, but the race-immigration-biosecurity triad is now well-known and strongly researched. In many ways, COVID-19 became so genuinely globalised that to some extent it escaped the grip of facile anti-Asian sentiment and policy derived from it.

My own initial response to COVID-19 was to think 'beyond quarantine critique'.[51] As a historian, I was struck less by the racialised repetitions than by different national legal and political cultures or tolerances, we might say, around the possibility of hard or soft borders. Of course, those cultures as well as precedents have been historically constituted: in law, in popular understanding, in political feasibility. The long Australian history of border closure was immediately re-operationalised, disease prevention trumping even the right of citizens to return to their own country. Simultaneously, the long British history of more open borders – we might see this as a deeper liberalism, unfashionable though that claim is – mitigated its national border closedown, comparatively speaking. The very proximity of the Brexit decision, on the cusp of COVID-19, *might have* authorised a stricter British policy and legal response rather more along the Australian model. Yet that it did not, underscores the argument that the UK's long and general disinclination to border closures endured, even through that unprecedented emergency period when all kinds of other extreme measures were tolerated.

British law, in so many ways historically definitive of colonial and Commonwealth polities, has been tested again and again by biosecurity imperatives, acute and chronic. Over the long term, responses have unsurprisingly differed, for geopolitical, geographic, epidemiological, and political reasons. There is a pattern to those trends, however, that the COVID-19 emergency revealed. While the Australian Government's all-but total border closure was flagged as a global exception, in fact this was more akin to an intensification of its own longstanding domestic policy and practice of strong medico-legal border control, the history of which contributed to the normalisation of disease clauses in immigration acts across the world

Tiarne Barratt and Alison Bashford, 'Lines of Hygiene: Pandemic Border Control in Australia, 1919' (2022) 53 *Australian Historical Studies* 284.

[48] Carolyn Strange, 'Postcard from Plaguetown: SARS and the Exoticization of Toronto' in Bashford (2006) (n 33).

[49] JT Huang et al, 'The Cost of Anti-Asian Racism During the COVID-19 Pandemic' (2023) 7 *Nature Human Behaviour* 682.

[50] Yao Li and Harvey L Nicholson Jr, 'When "Model Minorities" Become "Yellow Peril" – Othering and the Racialization of Asian Americans in the COVID-19 Pandemic' (2021) 15 *Sociology* e12849.

[51] Alison Bashford, 'Beyond Quarantine Critique' (*Somatosphere*, 6 March 2020), available at http://somatosphere.net/forumpost/beyond-quarantine-critique/.

over the twentieth century. This is not to excuse it, so to say, but to explain it. Meanwhile, traces of a long British modern history of relative *reluctance* to control borders for biosecurity and other reasons, and even politicians' little-recognised active *resistance* to the restriction of free movement, historically speaking, can still be discerned in COVID-19 responses; in the discussion about what was politically tolerable and legally possible, into 2020 and 2021. It has been disease events – the threatened global pandemic of SARS, and then the actual global pandemic of COVID-19 – that have brought the UK's border policies closer to, but still not as uncompromising as, those of its own historic Empire. It was that early colonial and then Commonwealth lawmaking that spearheaded, and then over time disseminated and normalised, some of the very statutes that made restriction of international movement lawful in recent years.

6

Old Laws, New Logics: Medical Management at Britain's Borders 1962–1988

ROBERTA BIVINS*

I. Introduction

The deployment of medical interventions and medical professionals in efforts to prevent the international spread and importation of epidemic disease is in many ways a familiar practice. As other chapters in this volume detail, quarantine and exclusion have been well-established local, regional and national responses to epidemics since the middle ages. In the modern period, these strategies have persisted and globalised, as we saw during the COVID-19 pandemic that began in 2020. However, both quarantine and medical exclusion operate in tension with wider social, legal and economic demands for freedoms of movement, association, bodily integrity, and trade. Britain's specific history as a free-trading, colonising, and (neo)imperial nation profoundly shaped its response to COVID-19, just as these traits shaped responses to cholera in the nineteenth century, importations of smallpox in the interwar years, and the threat of AIDS in the 1980s and 1990s.[1] This history, alongside the United Kingdom's (UK) international treaty commitments

* All webpages cited in this chapter were last accessed on 15 April 2025.

[1] On the historical relationship between free trade and British attitudes to quarantine, see Sarah Green, 'Locating Disease: On the Coexistence of Diverse Concepts of Territory and the Spread of Disease' in Sevasti Trubeta et al (eds), *Medicalising Borders: Selection, Containment, and Quarantine since 1800* (Manchester, Manchester University Press, 2021) 187–89; Mark Harrison, 'Disease, Diplomacy and International Commerce: The Origins of International Sanitary Regulation in the Nineteenth Century' (2006) 1 *Journal of Global History* 197; for comparison, see Miriam Ticktin, *Casualties of Care: Immigration and the Politics of Humanitarianism in France* (Berkeley, CA, University of California Press, 2011); Richard Coker and Alan Ingram, 'Passports and Pestilence: Migration, Security and Contemporary Border Control of Infectious Diseases' in Alison Bashford (ed), *Medicine at the Border: Disease, Globalization and Security, 1850 to the Present* (Basingstoke, Palgrave Macmillan, 2006); to explore some of the modern tensions between public health and human rights law, see Lawrence O Gostin and Zita Lazzarini, *Human Rights and Public Health in the AIDS Pandemic* (Oxford, Oxford University Press, 1997).

and existing legal doctrine about privacy, confidentiality, and citizenship, have also informed the persistent reshaping and repurposing of biomedical management at and beyond Britain's borders. Together, nineteenth century programmes of quarantine, coercive hygiene, and selective medical examination; subsequent border sanitary regimes instituted to prevent the spread of contagious and epidemic disease; and the (global) normalisation of medicalised practices of identification have all rendered migrant bodies uniquely vulnerable to the state, entitled only to Agamben's 'bare life' – and sometimes not even that.[2]

The legal framework of modern British responses to global epidemics originated in the International Sanitary Conferences of the late nineteenth century. The Conferences and the regulations they defined and promoted reified the perceived threat of imported 'exotic' disease. They coded such threats as 'foreign' to the ostensibly hygienic and healthy states of Western Europe, North America, and the Antipodes, but 'native' to the indigenous populations of their tropical colonies and trading spheres as well as mobile individuals from other geographies. States culturally coded these pathologised groups as 'alien' regardless of their legal statuses.[3] Simultaneously, the self-declared 'civilised' nations developed increasingly (but never completely) standardised and medicalised responses to epidemic importations. States empowered medical inspectors and other scientific and medical experts to assess the perceived risks posed by global epidemics to the health of national publics. However, medical assessments were only ever informative rather than determinative either of policy or of the fates of individual migrants.[4] Governments, politicians, and their advisors weighed such medical threat assessments against potential risks to national and individual wealth that would be caused by interruptions to trade caused by quarantines, port inspections, and port closures. As technologies of travel and medical understandings of disease changed, so too did the exact tools of the medical inspectorate's trade and the precise locations of medical inspection. From lazarettos in ports and quarantines at geographical borders to shipboard inspections of goods and people alike, to port sanitary regimes,[5] and later to medical testing in countries of origin, the reach of medical controls lengthened, and became tentacular. The 'medical gaze'

[2] Paul Weindling, 'Sealing Borders and Containing Prisoners: From Free Movement of Migrants to Containment in Concentration Camps' in Trubeta et al (n 1); Vincenzo Binetti and Cesare Casarino (trans), Giorgio Agamben, *Means without End: Notes on Politics* (Minneapolis, MN, University of Minnesota Press, 2000) 16.

[3] Harrison (n 1); Krista Maglen, '"The First Line of Defence": British Quarantine and the Port Sanitary Authorities in the Nineteenth Century' (2002) 15 *Social History of Medicine* 413.

[4] Becky Taylor, 'Immigration, Statecraft and Public Health: The 1920 Aliens Order, Medical Examinations and the Limitations of the State in England' (2016) 29 *Social History of Medicine* 512.

[5] So much has been written on these subjects in the North American and Western European contexts that here I will point to work from less familiar geographies: Sabine Jesner, 'Hapsburg Border Quarantines until 1837: An Epidemiological "Iron Curtain"?'; Christian Promitzer, 'Uses of Quarantine in the Nineteenth Century until the Crimean War: Examples from South-east Europe' and John Chircop, 'Lazarettos as Border Filters: Expurgating Bodies, Commodities and Ideas, 1800-1870s' 129–54, all in Trubeta et al (n 1).

was repeatedly re-imagined, evolving from direct visual examination to incorporate bacteriological, radiological and even genetic scrutiny.[6] However, I will argue here that until the late twentieth century, its exclusionary visions were consistently framed as protective of individual and public health. Latterly, they were also intended to protect the UK's much prized but always economically fragile National Health Service (NHS) (legally established in 1948 as three separate systems and since devolution operating as four interconnected but distinct entities, but treated collectively here as the NHS).

Building on the framework established by earlier laws and further defined by the International Sanitary Regulations of 1951 (ISR 1951), post-war Britain balanced its deeply embedded (and during post-war reconstruction economically essential) commitments to free trade and free intra-imperial movement with a net of Port Sanitary and public health inspections and laws. These mandated the quarantine, vaccination, or exclusion of 'suspect' travellers and migrants who might threaten the British population with any of six transmissible diseases: plague, cholera, yellow fever, smallpox, typhoid, and relapsing fever. These regulated conditions shared a number of features: all could trigger epidemic outbreaks; all were in sharp decline or no longer endemic in the British Isles; all could (in theory) be distinguished by the medical gaze either alone or in conjunction with simple and fast acting clinical tests; and none required intimate, invasive, or specialist investigation. They were, in short, highly tractable to identification under the specific and limiting circumstances of port health. So too were mental illnesses, learning disabilities, and non-heteronormative pregnancy, all of which might see a traveller turned back at the border. None of these conditions were among the most significant epidemiological threats to British public health. Indeed, ISR 1951 covered neither the most common imported conditions of the UK's post-war era; nor, with the partial exception of smallpox, the conditions which most commonly affected perceptions of and relationships between migrants and members of the UK host communities.[7]

In thinking about the role of medicine at the ever-mobile epidemiological frontiers between states and between incoming and established populations, it is important to recognise the enduring disjuncture between conditions that *could* and *can* be detected and regulated, and those that remain medically or legally

[6] On the evolving 'medical gaze', see Amy Fairchild, *Science at the Borders: Immigrant Medical Inspection and the Shaping of the Modern Industrial Labor Force* (Baltimore, MD, Johns Hopkins University Press, 2003); Evan Smith and Marinella Marmo, *Race, Gender and the Body in British Immigration Control: Subject to Examination* (Basingstoke, Palgrave Macmillan, 2014); Roberta Bivins, 'Pilot Programs and Postcolonial Pivots: Pioneering "DNA Fingerprinting" on Britain's Borders' (2023) 65 *Comparative Studies in Society and History* 346.

[7] I have written in detail about smallpox in Roberta Bivins, *Contagious Communities: Medicine, Migration and the NHS in Post War Britain* (Oxford, Oxford University Press, 2015) 115–67. There were also occasional 'typhoid scares' during which fingers were sometimes pointed at migrants, but the causes of these were usually quickly identified as tainted imported meat; see Lesley Diack, Hugh Pennington, and David Smith, *Food Poisoning, Policy and Politics: Corned Beef and Typhoid in Britain in the 1960s* (Martlesham, Boydell & Brewer, 2005).

intractable despite posing significant health risks. It is also important to address the degree to which biopolitical bordering conflates perceptible or presumed medical risks with a range of other 'threats' that are only tangentially related to the physical entities that are on the move. Health has long featured in debates over immigration control, and the 'foreignness' of germs is perhaps their most stable cultural feature.[8] But 'germs' travel in bodies that can be perceived as dangerous for other reasons too. In the nineteenth century, some migrants to the UK were seen to pose not just health threats to individual bodies, but social, cultural and economic threats to the body politic. For instance, Irish migrants to Liverpool during and after the potato famine were variously linked to cholera and Catholicism, insanity and insolvency, filth and Fenianism. They were racialised and then positioned as a cause of racial degeneration and a eugenic menace.[9] In other words, some politicians and some publics assumed that Irish incomers burdened the host society not only through their communicable diseases, but also through their communicable beliefs, behaviours and impecuniousness. Medical screening at and beyond the ports sought to protect both citizens' bodies and their incomes by excluding the direct threat of disease and the indirect threat of economic dependency caused by disability, pregnancy, madness, old age or alcoholism.

Britain's epidemiological transition was accompanied by a step change in health provision, as the nation gradually left behind the punitive terms of 1834's reform of the Poor Law. In 1848, when Parliament passed the first Public Health Act, Britain was ravaged by epidemic infections. A century later, as the 1948 National Assistance and National Health Service Acts were approved, it was already becoming a nation blighted by chronic morbidity. This coincidence, I argue, prompted an important shift in the tenor of public and legal responses to the threat of imported health risks, not least because tax-funded NHS care was available to all, including travellers, visitors and legal migrants upon arrival. As epidemic and endemic infectious diseases became less familiar and more tractable, they were coded as 'consigned to history' among local populations. Simultaneously, their disappearance became a talisman of modernity and a tribute to the NHS and the British public's lauded compliance with the 'rules of health'.[10] Consequently, any instances of these diseases were reflexively linked to 'strangers' and 'incomers' on one hand, and to social degeneration on the other.

Yet as Britain's post-war reconstruction and new welfare state drove a global labour recruitment boom, familiar medical threats like smallpox and madness were joined at the border by new or newly problematised ones. These included

[8] Howard Markel and Alexandra Minna Stern, 'The Foreignness of Germs: The Persistent Association of Immigrants and Disease in American Society' (2002) 80 *Milbank Quarterly* 757.

[9] Catherine Cox, Hilary Marland and Sarah York, 'Emaciated, Exhausted and Excited: The Bodies and Minds of the Irish in Nineteenth-Century Lancashire Asylums' (2012) 46 *Journal of Social History* 500; Catherine Cox and Hilary Marland, '"A Burden on the County": Madness, Institutions of Confinement and the Irish Patient in Victorian Lancashire' (2015) 28 *Social History of Medicine* 263.

[10] Alex Mold et al, 'The Public and Public Health' in Alex Mold et al (eds), *Placing the Public in Public Health in Post-War Britain, 1948–2012* (London, Palgrave Pivot, 2019).

less readily detected infectious conditions like venereal disease and tuberculosis (TB), both of which had been excluded from the ISRs on the grounds that they could not be readily screened out at the border (and were, in any case, endemic even in 'civilised' Europe). With the rise of genetic understandings, undetectable and non-infectious genetic conditions like sickle cell anaemia and thalassaemia also attracted public and political concerns.[11] So too did highly visible cultural and racialised differences that were *perceived* as 'threats' to the imagined homogeneity and well-being of the host society and its members. In this contentious context, the increasingly mobile populations of Britain's tropical colonies and New Commonwealth were transmogrified. Once a vital source of military and material strength, they were swiftly reconfigured by racial prejudice, economic anxiety, and a national identity crisis into a threat to both public health and population identity.[12]

What effect did this reconfiguration have on the medicalised borders on which Britain relied to protect its population from epidemic risk? Did the laws that enabled medical inspections, quarantine, and exclusion for legal aliens change when they became applicable to a new class of people, British subjects no longer entitled to move to the self-proclaimed 'mother country of a multiracial Commonwealth'? In the remainder of this chapter, I will look first at interactions between the border public health controls and procedures established by the ISRs (and related legislation) and the perceived 'danger' of racialised mass migration from Britain's former and remaining colonies. These two phenomena intersected in late 1961, when the

[11] Bivins (2015) (n 7) 304–67; Grace Redhead, '"A British Problem Affecting British People": Sickle Cell Anaemia, Medical Activism and Race in the National Health Service, 1975–1993' (2021) 32 *20th Century British History* 189.

[12] This transition has attracted considerable attention from scholars, though fewer have examined it though medical or health optics. Exemplary (if often starkly contrasting) political, legal, social and cultural studies include Jordana Bailkin, *The Afterlife of Empire* (Berkeley, CA, University of California Press, 2012); Nicholas Deakin et al, *Colour, Citizenship and British Society: Based on the Institute of Race Relations Report* (London, Panther, 1970); Stuart Hall with Bill Schwarz, *Familiar Stranger: A Life between Two Islands* (Durham, NC, Duke University Press, 2017); Randall Hansen, *Citizenship and Immigration in Post-War Britain: The Institutional Origins of a Multicultural Nation* (Oxford, Oxford University Press, 2000); Marjory Harper and Stephen Constantine, *Migration and Empire* (Oxford, Oxford University Press, 2010); Tariq Modood and Runnymede Trust, *Not Easy being British: Colour, Culture and Citizenship* (Stoke-on-Trent, Runnymede Trust, 1992); Kathleen Paul, *Whitewashing Britain: Race and Citizenship in the Postwar Era* (Ithaca, NY, Cornell University Press, 2018); Bill Schwarz, *The White Man's World*, Vol 1 (Oxford, Oxford University Press, 2011); Ambalavaner Sivanandan and Colin Prescod, *Catching History on the Wing: Race, Culture and Globalisation*, Vol 3 (London, Pluto Press, 2008); Vicki Squire, *The Exclusionary Politics of Asylum* (Basingstoke, Palgrave Macmillan, 2009); Martin Thomas and Andrew Thompson (eds), *The Oxford Handbook of the Ends of Empire* (Oxford, Oxford University Press, 2017); Wendy Webster, *Englishness and Empire, 1939*-1965 (Oxford, Oxford University Press, 2005). Historical studies attending to questions of health and disease include Bashford (2006) (n 1); Bivins (2015) (n 7); Joanna Herbert, *Negotiating Boundaries in the City: Migration, Ethnicity, and Gender in Britain* (London, Routledge, 2016); Julian Simpson, *Migrant Architects of the NHS: South Asian Doctors and the Reinvention of British General Practice (1940s-1980s)* (Manchester, Manchester University Press, 2018); Smith and Marmo (n 6); Ticktin (n 1); John Welshman, 'Tuberculosis and Ethnicity in England and Wales, 1950–70' (2000) 22 6 *Sociology of Health & Illness* 858; John Welshman and Alison Bashford, 'Tuberculosis, Migration, and Medical Examination: Lessons from History' (2006) 60 *Journal of Epidemiology and Community Health* 282.

threat of new exclusionary legislation to control Commonwealth migration triggered a wave of migration to Britain through one node of a smallpox epidemic, the Pakistani city of Karachi. Here, a traditional epidemic disease importation covered by existing legal frameworks nonetheless facilitated a radical constriction of established rights of movement and abode.

Next, I will examine responses to the perceived and actual importation of TB by migrants from Ireland, Cold War Europe, and Britain's former and remaining tropical colonies in the 1960s. In this case, TB, a once-common and still endemic UK disease, was transformed into an anachronistic threat to the new NHS and its local beneficiaries. Invisible to and uncontrollable under the existing ISR provisions, new fears and new technologies of inspection both drove the creation of new legal powers – but TB still evaded border and medical control, as it continues to do today.

Finally, I will turn to a new, DNA-based form of medical control, one that no longer even pretended to protect the physical health of the British public. Instead, 'DNA fingerprinting' was imagined by the UK's powerful Home Office as a tool to protect the ideological (and always imaginary) whiteness of the British population from a deceptive Asian 'other'. Here, politicians and civil servants seized upon novel medical technology as a weapon to control the uncontrollable: the legal but unwelcome migration of 'entitled families' to join a settled parent, child or spouse.[13] Adopting the use of DNA profiling for border control necessitated an atypically swift reinterpretation and expansion of existing legal parameters both for medical inspection and for migration control. Yet in this case, the migrants posed no epidemic or even clinical risk. The perceived 'threat' that they represented was demographic and political, not medical.

Across and through these case studies, I will suggest that international recognition of *epidemic* risks – whether to bodies or to economies – and the legal responses intended to mitigate those risks opened the door to a border biopolitics that coded otherness as pathological, and population diversity itself as a risk to the health of the national body politic.

II. Excluding Health 'Risks': From Smallpox to TB

After 1961, the archives of UK government ministries, including the Home and Foreign and Commonwealth Offices, but also the Lord Chancellor's Office and the Ministry of Health and its successors, are full of claims asserting or assuming the end of primary migration. The frequency of such claims is only matched by that

[13] 'Entitled families' comprised classes of family members (defined and repeatedly re-defined in successive immigration Acts) who were related to primary migrants who themselves legally entered and settled in the UK between 1962 and 1973, under a legislative regime that specifically granted them an absolute right to reunite their families in Britain.

of public promises to 'control' the inward flow of migrants to the UK, whether those individuals are labelled 'economic migrants', 'asylum seekers' (a term all too frequently modified with the adjective 'bogus'), refugees, or 'illegal immigrants'.[14] Time and again, such claims and promises become political millstones. Britain's legal corpus and structure, imbued as it is with notions of individual rights and liberalism; its long-standing international humanitarian commitments; and its historical geopolitical sensitivities all constrain the practices of arbitrary exclusion and deportation that would be necessary to 'end immigration'.[15] Similarly, Britain's international legal commitments have operated against efforts to effectively limit inward migration to numerical targets in a world shaped by violent conflict, deep economic inequality, environmental destruction, and increasing access to both legal and illegal tools of mobility. Hostile as the domestic political climate has become to human mobility, migrants' rights of entry and appeal and the existing humanitarian protections of British law (particularly those rooted in the Universal Declaration of Human Rights of 1948 and the European Convention on Human Rights) are still enforced by the UK courts.

It is therefore no coincidence that Britain and its international counterparts adopted the United Nation's 1951 International Convention Relating to the Status of Refugees in the same year that they accepted the new ISRs. If migrants could not be excluded arbitrarily, at least they could be sifted to exclude disease. Like the sanitary regimes which preceded it, the 1951 Convention allowed the exclusion or detention of individuals for 'the prevention of the spreading of infectious diseases', or for being 'of unsound mind', or for alcoholism, addiction or criminality – a linkage that holds intriguing parallels with the contemporary discourse of the 'crimmigrant'.[16] Indeed, for post-war Britain, measures that could be construed as 'health controls' became almost the only politically palatable and uncontroversial tools with which governments could navigate the troubled intersection between a national self-image saturated with mythologised acts of humanitarianism towards refugees and high levels of political, ideological and (perceived) popular

[14] Lisa Hassan, 'Deterrence Measures and the Preservation of Asylum in the United Kingdom and United States' (2000) 13 *Journal of Refugee Studies* 184.

[15] Gareth Mulvey, 'When Policy Creates Politics: the Problematizing of Immigration and the Consequences for Refugee Integration in the UK' (2010) 23 *Journal of Refugee Studies* 437; Tony Kushner, 'Truly, Madly, Deeply … Nostalgically? Britain's On–Off Love Affair With Refugees, Past and Present' (2018) 52 *Patterns of Prejudice* 172; Panikos Panayi, 'Refugees and the End of Empire' in Thomas and Thompson (n 12); Jordana Bailkin, *Unsettled: Refugee Camps and the Making of Multicultural Britain* (Oxford, Oxford University Press, 2018) 453–76; AJ Sherman, *Island Refuge: Britain and Refugees from the Third Reich, 1933–1939* (London, Frank Cass, 1995). For a concise critical summary of this national myth, see Becky Taylor, 'Where Should We Look to Find Britain's "Tradition of Welcome" for Refugees?' (*Refugee History Blog*), available at https://refugeehistory.org/blog/2017/6/19/where-should-we-look-to-find-britains-tradition-of-welcome-of-refugees; and on the ineffectiveness of the UK's immigration restrictions, see Taylor (2016) (n 4); David Feldman, 'History of Immigration and Border Controls', History and Policy: Home Office Seminar Series, 12 November 2014, available at www.historyandpolicy.org/img/news/uploads/dfeldman_immigration_border_control.pdf.

[16] Katja Franko Aas, '"Crimmigrant" Bodies and Bona Fide Travellers: Surveillance, Citizenship and Global Governance' (2011) 15 *Theoretical Criminology* 331.

anti-immigrationism.[17] Given this situation, the retooling of biomedical inspections, legally introduced to address public health concerns, to serve other agendas was always highly likely. However, for Britain, the process was facilitated by one of the nation's last significant outbreaks of smallpox.

In the winter of 1961, the House of Commons was already debating the Commonwealth Immigrants Bill. This legislation would, for the first time, explicitly limit the rights of British subjects to enter and reside in the UK, long promoted across the Empire as 'Home'.[18] The Bill was by this point well on its way to becoming the Commonwealth Immigrants Act 1962, despite fierce debate and opposition. An extensive literature analysing the emergence of immigration restrictions in post-war Britain concurs that by 1961 the era of the Open Door was itself closing.[19] Successive UK governments had been exploring the impacts of post-war migration, particularly from the Commonwealth and colonies since at least 1948. The goal of such investigations was evident: civil servants and their ministers sought internationally palatable justifications to restrict the rights of British subjects of colour to enter and reside in the UK, while allowing their white counterparts to retain those rights. To explicitly racialise Britain's migration laws would stain not just the nation's self-image, but the image of the West; this was intolerable as the Cold War came increasingly to dominate geopolitics. Yet to limit the movements of Australians, New Zealanders, Canadians, and White British subjects returning from empire would place unacceptable strain on economic and affective ties and sources of geopolitical soft power that Britain could not yet afford to loosen.[20] Among the potential avenues of legitimation examined by the state were the possibilities that the unwanted migrant groups were particularly prone to criminality, to dependency or, crucially for the purposes of this chapter, to disease or ill health. Repeated surveys found that the migrants produced no such risks – but in 1961 the Conservative Government chose to introduce the Commonwealth Immigrants Bill nonetheless, accepting that it would face significant political resistance while expecting high levels of public support. What they did not expect was that the Bill would be debated in the shadow of a series of imported smallpox outbreaks across England and Wales, seeded by migrants predictably seeking to 'beat the ban' on free movement that all sides anticipated.[21]

Britain had long been subject to episodic importations of smallpox by British officials and service personnel returning from duties in the empire; such importations were normally detected and swiftly quashed by the UK's well-developed public health system.[22] Moreover, as noted above, importations of smallpox had been covered by international sanitary agreements since the late nineteenth

[17] Bailkin (2018) (n 15); Becky Taylor, 'Their Only Words of English Were 'Thank You": Rights, Gratitude and "Deserving" Hungarian Refugees to Britain in 1956' (2018) 55 *Journal of British Studies* 120.

[18] Webster (n 7).

[19] For scholars who agree on little else, compare Hansen (n 12) with Paul (n 12).

[20] Hansen (n 12).

[21] Bivins (2015) (n 7) 115–67.

[22] ibid 265–66.

century. New legislation was by no means required to enable continued protection of the nation's health from this particular epidemic disease. Admittedly, the rise of mass travel by air had rendered the disease more difficult to detect reliably: with a 14-day incubation period, smallpox's tell-tale high fevers and skin lesions might not erupt before travellers passed through port controls. But even this was not novel; previous outbreaks, too, had produced fatalities before the disease was recognised, but were swiftly controlled by standard public health measures: quarantine, ring-fence vaccination, and where necessary mass vaccination. Members of the British public were encouraged and trusted to come forward if they had been exposed or experienced symptoms, and the press routinely cooperated with public health officials to either announce or silence outbreaks depending on what was deemed most expedient by health officials.[23] Medically, the 1961–1962 outbreak differed from preceding outbreaks more in degree than in kind. News of the Commonwealth Immigrants Bill triggered a surge in migration from across the Commonwealth, and particularly from Pakistan. Since Karachi, the site of Pakistan's international airport, was in the midst of a smallpox epidemic (of which UK officials in the Ministry of Health had, as usual, been notified by the World Health Organization (WHO)), UK public health authorities faced multiple importations, and much higher numbers of potentially exposed newcomers than usual. Many of these newcomers were not coming to established addresses, were less than fluent in English, and were unfamiliar with the UK's health system. These complicating factors were acknowledged and discussed in public health circles with typical pragmatism, and certainly without panic – though one Medical Officer of Health did note that migrants' often-circuitous pathways to their eventual destinations within Britain reminded him of 'war-time escapes'.[24]

In the media, in Parliament, and in affected localities, however, these real but manageable amplifications of a well-known disease threat attracted far less attention than the visible differences of the migrants themselves. Journalists, MPs and communities focused not on the familiarity of the outbreaks, nor on avoidable domestic mistakes in responding to it, but on the 'foreignness' of the germs and their importers. As with COVID-19, almost 60 years later, first reactions included lurid tales of exotic customs and behaviours that were presented as endangering 'everyday British people'.[25] Moreover, the fact that almost all of the Pakistani migrants who were later identified as smallpox carriers were also smallpox vaccination certificate holders played into well-established imperial 'deception anxiety' which had already undermined the authority of official documents and personal testimonies produced by South Asian migrants.[26] As sociologist Eric Butterworth

[23] See for previous importations, the National Archives [TNA], MH55/1907; MH55/2525.

[24] TNA MH55/2520 Hugh Bryant to AT Roden, 8 January 1962.

[25] See, eg, Michael Jacobson, 'The Tribesmen who Died of Shame' *Daily Mail* (16 January 1962).

[26] Christopher Hamlin, 'Forensic Facts: The Guts of Rights' in Ian Burney and Christopher Hamlin (eds), *Global Forensic Cultures: Making Facts and Justice in the Modern Era* (Baltimore, MD, Johns Hopkins University Press, 2019) 20.

noted as early as 1966, media coverage of the smallpox importations drew public attention to this issue, exacerbating public suspicion: 'Pakistani Smallpox Papers "Can Be Forged"' read one local paper's headline.[27] Only later (again foreshadowing the UK's COVID-19 discourse) would journalists and commentators critique the Ministry of Health's failure to respond speedily and effectively to WHO warnings about the Karachi outbreak, before finally reporting on the generally low levels of public vaccination, failures in vaccine supply, the patchiness of public health coverage and staffing, and other endogenous factors that prolonged and worsened the outbreak.

By the time such inwardly directed critiques surfaced, the 1961–62 smallpox outbreak had already shaped far-reaching changes in the UK's immigration law. 'Imported' smallpox provided political cover for restrictive actions that had been impossible to justify based on the generally robust health of the new migrants in the UK. In particular, it became the seemingly irresistible justification for the insertion of a new health inspection clause into the Commonwealth Immigrants Bill. From the inception date of the legislation, Commonwealth citizens and most foreign-born British subjects, as well as legal aliens, could be refused admission to the UK 'if … suffering from mental disorder' or if 'it is otherwise undesirable for medical reasons that he [sic] should be admitted'.[28] Moreover, medically qualified staff were specifically empowered to deploy 'any test or examination required' to assess the health of a migrating passenger.[29] This very sweeping provision was in fact targeted at one specific disease that was not covered by the ISRs: TB; and one specific technology that was at the time unavailable at UK airports: the chest X-ray. While the smallpox outbreak provided the justification for this extension of medical controls, the tests that legislators and their medical advisors had in mind would in no way have aided detection and exclusion of smallpox.

As well as legitimating a critical change in the laws to significantly and permanently expand the applicability and capacity of border medical inspection, the increased focus on imported illness prompted by the 1961–62 smallpox outbreak raised the profile of the medical impacts of mass migration. Alongside the wider debates on immigration provoked by the legislation, the outbreaks brought into the public domain heated discussions about imported TB that had previously been conducted primarily in professional journals and behind closed doors in Whitehall. The British Medical Association (BMA) and other professional bodies had been unsuccessfully demanding radiological health controls for would-be migrants since the 1950s. However, only in the final years of that decade did a clinical consensus emerge that specific groups of migrants imported TB, while others

[27] Eric Butterworth, 'The 1962 Smallpox Outbreak and the British Press' (1966) 7 *Race* 354.

[28] Commonwealth Immigrants Act 1962, s 2(4) a.

[29] Commonwealth Immigrants Act 1962, sch 1, para 1. Any tests that took longer than 24 hours from arrival to produce results would require written notification to the affected migrants, and by convention, to their nation's High Commission, of further detention.

arrived immunologically naïve, only to acquire it from an endemically infected British public or their fellow migrants under deplorable living conditions.[30]

On 7 December 1961, well before the smallpox importations were detected but while ferocious parliamentary debates over the Commonwealth Immigrants Bill 1961 featured across the UK press, the BMA's concerns became fodder for the national and regional newspapers.[31] The coverage was ostensibly driven by a strongly worded statement from the BMA's Council. They sharply criticised the Government for a 'steep rise' in TB cases, raised fears that migrants might import antibiotic resistant strains of the disease, and demanded that the compulsory X-ray examination of all migrants be inserted into the Commonwealth Immigrants Bill as it passed through Parliament. This was, of course, a message far too marketable for the press to resist, and newspapers across the country amplified its clarion call. Headlines shouted about 'Health Danger', demanded X-rays for all migrants, and focused particularly on implementing checks to bar entry at least for those who refused treatment.[32] Coverage continued to flourish, amplified by angry headlines about government incompetence that will sound familiar to all of us who lived through COVID-19: 'Unnecessarily Exposed'; 'The Killer that Slipped through the Net'; 'Keep Out the Germs'; 'MPs Want Smallpox Report Published', etc.[33]

In part the furore around TB responded to the fact that it was almost the only illness for which evidence existed of higher rates among migrants than among the indigenous population, and for which there was a body of medical evidence indicating importation. But anti-immigrationists in Parliament and members of the public in destination communities had been demanding tighter health controls without success since the mid 1950s.[34] E Smitherman from Birmingham's Women's Co-Operative Guild, for instance, wrote to the Ministry in 1955, complaining that:

> we are spending thousands of pounds fighting this disease yet these people are bringing TB … into the country. … Where is it going to end and what of our standard of Health? Are we going to watch this being undermined without at least trying to uphold it?[35]

[30] Bivins (2015) (n 7) 62–113. Those who are immunologically naïve have no previous exposure or learned immunity to a given infectious condition, and are therefore especially susceptible to infection.

[31] ibid 106.

[32] TNA MH53/246 Clippings: 'BMA Warning on Health Danger' *Birmingham Post* (7 December 1961); 'X-Ray Immigrants and Doctors Urge: Send Home the TB Cases Who Refuse Treatment' *Daily Express* (7 December 1961); 'Check All Migrants for TB Demand Doctors' *Daily Mail* (7 December 1961); 'Doctors: X-Ray All Immigrants' *Daily Sketch* (7 December 1961); 'BMA Suggests X-Ray of All Immigrants: Expulsion of TB not Treated' *Daily Telegraph* (7 December 1961); 'BMA Urges Compulsory X-Ray for Immigrants: Dangers of "Importing" TB' *The Guardian* (7 December 1961); X-Ray Check Urged for Immigrants' *The Times* (7 December 1961).

[33] 'Unnecessarily Exposed' *The Times* (17 Jan 1962) 11; 'The Killer that Slipped Through the Net' *The Observer* (21 January 1962) 40; 'MPs Want Smallpox Report Published' *The Guardian* (29 September 1962) 9; 'Comment: KEEP OUT THE GERMS' *Daily Mail* (3 January 1962) 1.

[34] See, eg, repeated parliamentary outbursts from Cyril Osbourne MP, eg, Cyril Osborne, 'Queen's Speech: Debate on the Address', HC Deb (28 October 1958) vol 594, col 199.

[35] TNA MH55/2275, E Smitherman to the Minister of Health, 29 November 1955.

As Smitherman's letter suggests, the 'return of the white plague' was seen as spoiling British (and indeed Australian) modernity and burdening the NHS just as the nation was poised to reap the benefits from the near eradication of TB among the local population.[36] The weaponisation of this particular condition, always imagined as simultaneously anachronistic and newly threatening, can be judged by the persistence of TB importations as a focus for anti-migrant headlines in Britain's media ever since the 1960s.[37]

The Ministry of Health, on the other hand, was lukewarm at best about the new powers bestowed on them. Radiographically examining migrants required resources and expertise – machines, technicians and experts required to read the X-ray films produced – that were in short supply not just in the home nations of the 'suspect' migrants, but in the UK itself. As England's Chief Medical Officer grumbled, the deployment of X-ray machines at Britain's geographical boundaries was 'extravagant' in terms of costs and staff, and 'quite impractical'.[38] His bureaucratic counterpart in the Ministry agreed, but noted that the public would certainly see any resistance to radiographic controls, no matter how fiscally or epidemiologically sensible, as mere 'disingenuousness'.[39] In the end, the intense association drawn between Pakistani migrants and the deadly risks of imported disease (over-)exposed by the 1961–62 outbreaks – the very association that drove the initial insertion of the X-ray enabling clauses in CIA 1962 – also forced a reluctant Ministry of Health to implement what many experts saw as costly, wasteful and clinically ineffective border TB screening. As one civil servant explained:

> We have, of course, for years been living with the situation in which people get infected with TB by immigrants … The situation, though unsatisfactory, has not been found to place an intolerable burden on the country's Health Services, nor to lead to great public outcry. It was the great increase in immigrants from countries like Pakistan (where TB is rife) which led us to feel that some action should be taken.[40]

The specific reference to Pakistan here confirms the importance of the smallpox outbreaks in shaping policy around TB control at the border: it moulded the Pakistani migrants and to a greater or lesser degree all new racialised migrants,

[36] Alison Bashford, 'The Great White Plague Turns Alien: Tuberculosis and Immigration in Australia, 1901–2001' in Flurin Condrau and Michael Worboys, *Tuberculosis Then and Now: Perspectives on the History of an Infectious Disease* (Montreal, McGill-Queens University Press, 2010) 111.

[37] ibid. Eg, Anat Arkin, 'Quiet Return of the "White Plague"' *Times Educational Supplement* (25 May 2001) 29; Rosie Waterhouse, 'Return of the White Plague' *Sunday Times* (9 April 2000) 13; 'Return of the White Plague; It was one of History's Great Plagues, Virtually Eradicated Here 20 Years Ago. Now TB … is Back with a Vengeance. Could Political Correctness be to Blame?' *Daily Mail* (23 October 2004) 16; Jessica Potter, 'NHS Urged to Share Data so Patients Can Be Deported' The Conversation (6 February 2017) https://theconversation.com/nhs-urged-to-share-data-so-patients-can-be-deported-72380; Storm Newton, 'UK Could Lose Low TB Status Amid Rising Cases, Officials Warn' *The Standard* (25 March 2025) www.standard.co.uk/news/health/england-countries-jenny-harries-world-health-organisation-dame-b1218725.html.

[38] TNA MH55/2632 Memo, George Godber to Bruce Fraser, 7 February 1962.

[39] TNA MH55/2632 Memo, Fraser to Godber, 14 March 1962.

[40] TNA MH148/27 Bruce D Fraser to Enoch Powell, 15 May 1963.

despite their enormous diversity, into the archetypal infectious foreigners. Starting with a 'pilot' trial of chest X-ray screening for primary migrants at Heathrow (and later in their countries of origin), radiographic testing was gradually expanded to secondary familial migrants. This group, also described as 'entitled' migrants, could not initially be refused entry even on medical grounds. However, the new testing regime, while it could not exclude settled migrants' dependants, could and did render them available for medical surveillance after arrival through what John Welshman has described as the 'port of arrival system'.[41] Still later, such legal migrants would become excludable on medical grounds, at least until they had been satisfactorily treated. Ill health, almost alone among the growing panoply of exclusionary factors generated by successive UK governments, remained relatively uncontroversial even among migrant-sending Commonwealth nations (which often had their own, even stricter, health controls).[42]

Together, these two examples demonstrate that the insertion of health controls into the Commonwealth Immigrants Act 1962 was powered by the coincidence, of the 1961–62 smallpox outbreak with debates over the legislation, not their epidemiology. That overlap made it impossible for the Ministry of Health to resist changes to the Bill which required the border medical screening of British subjects. However, it is revealing that the specific medical examination imposed after the Act was not selected to control (already excludable) smallpox. Instead, enabled by the Act, the new screening tool was designed to extend border health controls to a still endemic condition both as a way to reduce unwanted racialised migration, and to 'protect' the NHS. It was anxiey about TB, the reliable detection of which required surface-penetrating X-rays, that drove the insertion of an open-ended. medical screening-enabling clause in the Commonwealth Immigrants Act 1962. In turn, this opened the door to the use of other clinical and biological investigations as part of the general process of screening and excluding British subjects seeking to exercise the rights of entry and abode in the UK confirmed by the 1948 British Nationality Act and retained (albeit in ever more limited forms) under subsequent immigration legislation.

These changes significantly expanded the epidemiological and political remit of the ISRs. The reach of the medical gaze was then further extended to encompass those migrants who could not legally be excluded on the grounds of health. The Commonwealth Immigration Act 1968 and the Immigration Act 1971 introduced the requirement for pre-departure Entry Certificates with a health inspection component even for entitled dependants of legal migrants, settled residents and naturalised citizens. The former introduced and the latter reinforced the importance, too, of 'patriality': a blood tie to the UK.

[41] John Welshman, 'Compulsion, Localism, and Pragmatism: The Micro-Politics of Tuberculosis Screening in the United Kingdom, 1950-1965' (2006) 19 *Social History of Medicine* 295.

[42] Commonwealth attitudes towards the use of health controls in particular was specifically assessed by British civil servants in 1965. See TNA H154/103, LET Storar to JT Dodds, 16 March 1965.

III. Excluding 'Dis-Ease' to Exclude Disruption? Medicalising Racism

Together, the Commonwealth Immigrants and Immigration Acts marked a crucial turning point in the process of converting 'health checks' into 'identity checks'. The formal introduction of *jus sanguinis* elements into immigration law through privileging 'patriality' also naturalised what would be a growing desire on the part of the state to assess migrants through their bodies, rather than their documents or testimony. They therefore also act as milestones in the mapping of legal responses to 'epidemics' in the modern period, manifesting the political shift from worries about the physical, epidemiological threats of imported disease and disability to concerns about the perceived moral and cultural threats posed by the social 'dis-ease' and 'dis-abilities' constituted by racism and xenophobia. These 'threats' to the body politic were, of course, propagated by the majority community but experienced by the migrants (not unlike the many cases of TB contracted by migrants on arrival in the UK). Nevertheless, the racialised migrants whom the Acts sought to exclude were still to shoulder the social costs of their prevention.

This is particularly evident in discourses surrounding racism and race relations in the UK from the 1960s to the 1980s. As the Ghanaian Robert Gardiner, then Executive of the United Nations' Economic Commission for Africa, commented in 1965, 'race prejudice' acted in societies as 'a *pathological state of mind*, as a form of irrationalism, and *as an epidemic*' (emphasis added). Had these qualities been formally recognised by international law, 'racism' might have become the newest candidate for inspection and exclusion under the ISRs. Explaining the incurability of racial prejudice and its resistance to 'social therapies', Gardiner referred specifically to the use of TB statistics by racists, whom he categorised as 'mentally ill':

> Presenting facts in the hope of removing prejudices is a form of social therapy. But, as with most mentally ill people, success in refuting one false notion only makes room for another. Take the familiar allegation that one particular racial group is more prone to tuberculosis … Health statistics may disprove this. But if they do, the statistical evidence will be ignored or the figures will be challenged. If statistical evidence supports the allegation, racists will ignore the fact that any group living in similar conditions would be prone to the same disease.[43]

The very language of related debates around the UK's Race Relations Acts of 1965, 1968 and 1976 evidences the seamlessness of the discursive shift from concerns about transmissible diseases to concerns about pathologised 'threats' to social cohesion. In the House of Lords, for example, speakers like Henry Walston, then

[43] Robert Gardiner, 'A World of Peoples: on Racism' (*Listener* 11 November 1965). A recording of the lecture is available at www.bbc.co.uk/programmes/p00hbcc5.

the Chairman of the Institute of Race Relations, likened racism to a social disease, and migration to the X-rays which exposed this pathology of Britain's social body:

> My Lords, I think we all agree that racial discrimination is, in fact, *a disease of society* … forms of racial discrimination as we see them in this country to-day are, in fact, a disease, they must then be treated as a disease and, what is more, as *a disease which affects not solely the patient but society as a whole* (emphasis added).

Like Gardiner, Walston drew specifically on TB, a disease most commonly spread by airborne bacteria, in making his case for racism as a threat to the nation. Moreover, like TB and smallpox, he positioned it as anachronistic, and as undermining Britain's modernity:

> In the past we have suffered from many such diseases … More recently we have had epidemic typhoid fever and tuberculosis as an endemic disease of society. These diseases have now been largely conquered … by laws which enforce public health, by laws of hygiene … What are needed now are laws against defiling our society with the excrement of diseased minds as well as bodies and laws against *spitting foul words in the atmosphere as well as against spitting germ-laden sputum into the atmosphere to infect other people* with those horrible diseases (emphasis added).[44]

In fact, the use of radiography at the border that had been enabled by the Commonwealth Immigrants Act 1962 proved ineffective in eliminating importations of TB or other conditions, and was similarly unable to achieve the true exclusionary aims of many of the politicians who supported its introduction.[45] While migration briefly declined after 1962, by the end of the decade it had rebounded. It would continue to expand as Commonwealth migrants, no longer able to move readily back and forth across the UK's borders, instead brought their families to join them in settlement. Moreover, as Gardiner had expected, the new evidence generated by border radiography, evidence which indicated that most migrants contracted TB in Britain,[46] did little to stamp out the pathology of racism.

Instead of easing British anxieties about immigration 'risks', the implementation of border radiography amply demonstrates the easy slippage from laws and practices intended to limit the movement of contagious diseases to those intended to foreclose the mobility of human beings. The radiological examinations that initially symbolised an extension of the familiar medicalisation of border control amid heightened fears about imported disease rapidly became a new tool in battle to reduce – by any available means – the rate of inward migration to the UK. Operating outside the remit and expertise of the Department of Health and Social Services (DHSS), X-rays were adopted by the Home and Foreign and Commonwealth Offices (FCO) (the two arms of government responsible for operating UK immigration controls at home and abroad). The Home Office and

[44] Henry Walston, 'Race Relations Bill' HL Deb (15 July 1968), vol 295, cols 32–159, 62–63.
[45] Bivins (2015) (n 7) 168–226.
[46] See, eg, M Khogali, 'Tuberculosis among Immigrants in the United Kingdom: The Role of Occupational Health Services' (1979) 33 *Journal of Epidemiology and Community Health* 13.

FCO eagerly repurposed the radiographic scrutiny enabled specifically for *health* screening under the Commonwealth Immigrants Act 1962 to perform a political task: to enable the exclusion of apparently legal family migrants from South Asia (and to a lesser extent, the rest of the 'New' Commonwealth).

Much like an earlier generation of imperial bureaucrats, civil servants of post-colonial Britain suffered from what Hamlin has termed 'deception anxiety' when it came to the documentary regimes of identification in place in the new nations of the former Raj.[47] Under intense pressure to reduce migration from those nations to the UK, the Home Office implemented a series of new regulations intended to supplement the 1962, 1968 and 1971 legislation ending primary migration, by limiting the secondary migration those laws had enabled on humanitarian grounds. Among other things, the new rules re-defined who could be considered a legally entitled 'dependant' of settled and naturalised migrants based on age. Yet the suspect family migrants targeted by these Regulations often either lacked or were not trusted to produce reliable documentation of birth dates or age.[48]

On Whitehall, at least, radiographic age estimation looked like an efficient solution. In the hands of the Home Office and FCO, skeletal X-rays were operated as a purportedly objective tool for age identification intended to limit the number of working-age family migrants entering the UK. Despite protests from medical professional groups that this technique was neither ethical nor accurate,[49] radiographic scrutiny has remained popular with officials in the Home Office and FCO. Indeed, since the late 1960s, radiographic age estimation has persistently reappeared at Britain's borders across episodes of 'crisis' – that is, during any publicly debated spikes in inward migration numbers. Most recently it was deployed in the Nationality and Borders Act 2022 (NBA 2022) and Illegal Migration Act 2023 as a 'solution' to the supposed problem of small boats 'flooding' Britain with purportedly fraudulent, over-age 'child migrants'. The former provided for the use of any 'imaging technology' or other 'scientific method' in age assessment, and the latter adopted the use of such assessments as tools in fighting 'illegal' immigration.[50]

This medicalisation of identity has been opposed by professional organisations since the 1970s as inaccurate, inhumane, and unethical on two grounds, rooted in the Nuremberg Code for medical experimentation: first, because of X-rays' potential to cause harm without commensurate benefit to the exposed individual; and second, because affected migrants are not in a position to give genuine consent under border conditions. Yet despite expert opposition, the pathologisation of immigration as a threat to a body politic continues to legitimate this retooling

[47] Hamlin (n 26) 20.

[48] Smith and Marmo (n 6) 117–27.

[49] Ahmed Iqbal Ullah Race Relations Resource Centre, Manchester, Commission for Racial Equality Pamphlet, *Immigration Control Procedures: Report of a Formal Investigation* (Commission for Racial Equality, 1985).

[50] 'Illegal Migration Bill', HL Deb (12 June 2023) vol 830, cols 1804–13 for discussion. This language appears in the Nationality and Borders Act 2022, ss 50–52.

of border inspection regimes. Once, at least presentationally, intended to exclude diseases, they are now designed to exclude classes of people.

IV. From Health Checks to Identity Checks: Families and 'Fingerprints' in the Age of AIDS

While the use of X-rays at the border has consistently provoked controversy without producing certainty, a newer, more powerful, and ultimately far more disruptive biomedical technology came onto the scene in 1985. Named 'DNA fingerprinting' by its inventor, geneticist Alec Jeffreys, this new tool seemed to answer the most heartfelt wishes of Home Office mandarins. By enabling the clear and comprehensive mapping of biological relationships between kinfolk, DNA fingerprinting was expected to cut the Gordian knot of entangled and competing values that ensnarled Britain's borders, at least in the then pressing matter of family reunification migration. Officials in the Home Office and FCO envisioned enacting an objective and yet firmly exclusionary immigration regime to end the wave of 'bogus' family migrants they believed were flooding the nation. DNA profiling, as the technique is now known, promised to provide statistical certainty as to whether children were 'related as claimed' to the settled or citizen parent upon whose status their own rights of entry and abode relied. At the same time, the patterns revealed by their DNA would implicitly serve to test the claims of spouses to be in enduring marital relationships with those sponsoring individuals when neither their own testimony, nor their state's documentation were to be trusted.[51]

Notably, the DNA profiling procedures that were established in response to the needs of the Home Office served no medical or public health purposes. Unlike chest X-rays, they had no medical benefits either for their subjects or for the communities into which their subjects would move if allowed to enter. Instead, the ever-deepening penetration of medical inspections and assays into the abject bodies even of legal migrants was motivated by desires to protect Britain's international reputation and its self-identification with ideals of liberal 'tolerance' on one hand and 'whiteness' on the other. In fact, the DNA profiling of family reunification migrants proved to be a double edged sword. A pilot trial of the technique was enthusiastically sponsored by the Home Office in the expectation that it would expose large numbers of 'bogus' family migrants in fact showed that most of those tested were related as they had claimed. The Home Office swiftly dropped plans to

[51] Alec Jeffreys Collection, University of Leicester, UK (Jeffreys-Leicester), unnumbered box, folder heading 'First Immigration Case and Summary of Results from Initial Immigration and Paternity Cases Processed in Lab 1985–6', 'Background Note: The Possible Use of DNA Fingerprinting in Immigration Work', 16 August 1985.

require or fund DNA testing for migrants, and imposed new economic conditions on would-be sponsoring relatives to reduce the flow of family members.[52]

In fact, the UK's capacity and willingness to perform health rather than identity checks at its own borders has been noticeably limited. Although mooted since the 1960s, and strongly supported not only by anti-immigrationists but also by medical professional organisations including the BMA, the primary legislation required to enable exclusionary health screening in migrants' home countries or regions of origin only came into effect in 2005. In part this represents the persistence of what had seemed in the 1960s to be a stable truth: with a well-established public health surveillance system and a NHS free at the point of need for all dwelling in the UK, the benefits produced by border health screening simply were not worth their costs in terms of specialist time and equipment. It identified few cases, produced even fewer exclusions on health grounds, and caused significant disruption and delay at ports and airports.[53] The goal of limiting 'none-too-desirable' migration clearly superseded public health aims both in politics and in practice even in the 1960s. Its dominance only grew stronger in proportion to the demonstrable ability of modern medicine to combat infectious disease.[54]

By the early 1980s, when Jeffreys' DNA profiling technology became available, acute epidemic disease was not the spectre it once had been. It no longer offered the powerful leverage to override medical ethics or moral scruples that it had in the wake of the 1961–62 smallpox outbreaks. Indeed, even when AIDS emerged as a potential imported health threat, the fear and stigma it produced were insufficient to generate exclusionary legislation mandating border testing or barring HIV-positive migrants from entering the UK. This was not for want of trying by the Home Office and the 'New Right', which strongly favoured exclusionary screening for HIV. As the examples of radiographic age estimation and DNA profiling suggest, the Home Office rather uncritically welcomed many forms of border medicalisation across the period between 1971 and 1986 (and beyond) if they proffered leverage in reducing inward migration flows. However, just as with tuberculosis in the 1960s and 1970s, the practicalities and polemics around instituting port and airport HIV/AIDS screening forced a stalemate. Testing all entrants to Britain for the disease was too slow and complicated to meet legal requirements to facilitate travel and trade. Targeting gay or drug-injecting travellers – groups in any case hard to identify at the border – would drive these groups underground

[52] Roberta Bivins, 'Pilot Programs and Postcolonial Pivots: Pioneering "DNA Fingerprinting" on Britain's Borders' (2023) 65 *Comparative Studies in Society and History* 346.

[53] This underpinning assumption is made in UK Border Agency Central Policy Unit, *Screening for Tuberculosis And the Immigration Control: UK Border Agency Review of Current Screening Activity 2011*, available at https://assets.publishing.service.gov.uk/media/5a7b5c7de5274a34770eb2c6/tb-screening-review.pdf. It can be followed across the UK's health ministries since 1962: TNA, MH55/2632, Memo, George Godber to Bruce Fraser, 7 February 1962. Follow the persistence of this view via MH148/30; MH154/1510.

[54] A label applied to racialised migrants as early as the 1950s: TNA MH58/670 Letter, C Waterhouse to William Deedes, 13 November 1956.

and hamper efforts to promote voluntary screening, whilst also harming perceptions of Britain abroad. Testing only travellers from epidemiologically high-risk nations might have gratified the Home Office, eager to exclude African migrants – but testing the 3.5 million American visitors who would also have fallen into that category was unthinkable as well as impractical.[55] In the end, despite public and Parliamentary rhetoric equating the threat of AIDS to that of nuclear war, border medical screening to protect the UK public from importations of this epidemic was deemed impractical and globally unpolitic. Border medical inspectors were coyly instructed to protect the NHS and Welfare State from the burdensome costs of would-be migrants' treatment by notifying immigration officers of those costs as part of their medical recommendations, but even these instructions were an insiders' secret.[56]

Later, in 2003–04, new rules were put forward to exclude HIV treatment from the list of contagious diseases for which testing and routine treatment was made free for all (including recent and irregular migrants) on the grounds of public health.[57] This, in theory, protected the 'struggling' NHS from the costs of treating failed asylum seekers, described by then Health Secretary John Reid as 'effectively stealing treatment from the people of this country'.[58] The rules certainly did nothing to protect the public from the perceived health risks of unidentified and untreated entrants to the UK. However, by this point the UK had publicly condemned HIV-based immigration restrictions enacted elsewhere in the world, and had little freedom to shift from that position.[59] Thus when Tory MPs and then Home Secretary Theresa May sought to insert a requirement that migrants should prove their HIV- status before entering the UK into 2014's immigration legislation, their amendment provoked scandal and insufficient support was mustered even to enable debate on the provision.

HIV/AIDS was recognised as a global health threat by the late 1980s, but a range of medical and non-medical factors ensured that it could not be resolved by exclusionary health screening. Initially, HIV was too hard to detect; its early identification with an increasingly visible and vocal sexual minority and later with 'innocent victims' made harsh restrictions too morally fraught for a 'liberal and tolerant nation'. More pragmatically, HIV/AIDS was also too common amongst populations either entitled or desired to enter the UK – European citizens and tourists from the United States in particular. In many ways HIV/AIDS acted as a

[55] Virginia Berridge, *AIDS in the UK: The Making of Policy 1981-1994* (Oxford, Oxford University Press, 1996) 101–08.

[56] Phyllida Brown, 'Britain's Back Door Ban on HIV Immigration' (*New Scientist*, 6 July 1991), available at www.newscientist.com/article/mg13117762-500-britains-back-door-ban-on-hiv-immigration/.

[57] Phillip Cole, 'Migration and the Human Right to Health' (2009) 18 *Cambridge Quarterly of Healthcare Ethics* 70.

[58] See Stephen Ladyman, 'HIV/AIDS Adjournment Debate' HC Deb (12 November 2023) vol 413, cols 126–34 WH, 130–131 WH; BBC News, '"Health Tourism" Rules Unveiled' (30 December 2003), available at http://news.bbc.co.uk/1/hi/health/3355751.stm.

[59] Berridge (n 55).

red herring, distracting officials and politicians from the steady erosion of the UK's epidemiological defences and prompting little investment in the resources necessary to identify and respond to the epidemics which were yet to come.

Ironically, then, just as medical screening technologies were re-invented to solve the perceived crisis of 'crimmigration', public health spending was diminished and re-targeted to address home grown threats like obesity and the diseases of old age.[60] Under these circumstances, new acute threats proved intractable to the conventional practices of either legal or medical border-making. In Britain, at least, the new pandemics would not be stopped by exclusionary testing, quarantine, or the cash-strapped and enfeebled tools of domestic health surveillance.

V. Conclusions

Following Alan Ingram, among others, I suggest that the shift from medical gaze to biotechnologies of identification, and corresponding shifts from the legalisation of health borders to the medicalisation of identity borders reflects the rise of securitisation. In the period covered by this chapter, Britain experienced a reconfiguration of risk that positioned communicable disease as just one among many security risks to western states. Crimmigrants, in this model, sowed the seeds of disease, but far more dangerously of disruption, distrust, and disaffection from the state.

Notable as a sign of this transition is the fact that in the 1962 law and all of the health-related legislation and regulation that followed, while the medical inspectorate had the legal power and duty to inspect eligible migrants, and to advise immigration officers of any health concerns, they did not take final decisions on whether to admit or refuse entry to the UK. They could advise that entry be allowed, denied or made conditional on further health checks, testaments, or registration with suitable authorities. However, even if a migrant was found to be suffering from an excludable condition, their advice could be overruled, and often was. The primacy of the border immigration officer to overturn medical advice (as well as any decisions made outside of the UK, even by the official entry clearance officers of the Foreign and Commonwealth Office) reveals the fundamentally secondary role of public health protection at the border. Health protection was theoretically positioned as the justification for intrusive and exclusionary screening, but in the post-war period, public health was rarely the primary consideration in border decision-making. This tension between a discourse of borders as tools to protect the health of citizens from the threat of imported disease, and the pragmatic use of

[60] On public health spending, see Luna Dolezal and Tanisha Spratt, 'Fat Shaming under Neoliberalism and COVID-19: Examining the UK's Tackling Obesity Campaign' (2022) 45 *Sociology of Health and Illness* 3; on increasing media and public concern, see Shona Hilton, Chris Paterson and Alison Teyhan, 'Escalating Coverage of Obesity in UK Newspapers: The Evolution and Framing of the "Obesity Epidemic" from 1996-2010' (2012) 20 *Obesity* 168n.

borders as tools to facilitate trade and the movements of goods and capital, while hindering – ideally preventing – the movement of people and any immigration-led changes to the imagined homogenous and White British population would become a significant problem during the COVID-19 pandemic.

After generations of rhetoric describing UK border restrictions as, in part, a means to protect the public health and the economically fragile NHS, the UK Government faced high expectations that the spread of COVID-19 to the UK could be prevented through strict border control and intensive quarantine practices. But the UK's medical borders were not – and indeed in the post-war period had never been – designed to exclude disease. Even the ISRs were intended to promote trade, and the global mobility required to facilitate it. As contagious and epidemic disease declined as a cause of UK mortality and morbidity, health border controls were repurposed to prevent more symbolic and ideological 'harms' and 'dis-eases': the pathogens of such social threats as racism and intercommunal violence.

7

Values and Infectious Disease Regulation in 20th Century England and Wales: The Cases of Tuberculosis and HIV/AIDS

JANET WESTON

I. Introduction

In this chapter, I examine the values that shaped infectious disease regulations in twentieth-century England and Wales. By 'values', I mean the standards that were commonly used for evaluating the various legal options on the table, such as their effectiveness in reducing the spread of infection, or their interaction with patient confidentiality.[1] In order to identify these values, and to examine if or how they changed and what this might tell us about legal responses to infectious disease, I take a close look at two case studies: tuberculosis in the first few decades of the twentieth century, and HIV/AIDS towards the century's end.[2]

Tuberculosis and HIV/AIDS often appear side-by-side in contemporary epidemiological and sociological literature,[3] but the pairing is less common in historical research. HIV/AIDS has usually been treated as a sexually transmitted infection

[1] Elizabeth Anderson, *Value in Ethics and Economics*, 2nd edn (Cambridge, MA, Harvard University Press, 1995).

[2] Although 'HIV/AIDS' is no longer the preferred terminology because it can promote confusion between the virus (HIV) and the clinical syndrome (AIDS), much of my discussion relates to a period when this distinction was poorly understood and the two were frequently muddled. I therefore use 'HIV/AIDS' to reflect this conceptual confusion, but also use 'HIV' or 'AIDS' where specificity is needed.

[3] For eg, Kevin M De Cock and Nicola Low, 'HIV and AIDS, Other Sexually Transmitted Diseases, and Tuberculosis in Ethnic Minorities in United Kingdom: Is Surveillance Serving Its Purpose?' (1997) 314 *British Medical Journal* 1747; World Health Organization/Joint United Nations Programme on HIV/AIDS, 'HIV/AIDS, Sexually Transmitted Diseases and Tuberculosis in Prisons: Joint Consensus Statement' (1998); Penelope Scott, Hella von Unger, and Dennis Odukoya, 'A Tale of Two Diseases: Discourses on TB, HIV/AIDS and Im/Migrants and Ethnic Minorities in the United Kingdom' (2017) 15 *Social Theory & Health* 261.

for the purposes of historical analysis and comparison,[4] but in its early days it shared a number of striking features with tuberculosis at the start of the twentieth century. Both were at those times incurable and poorly understood, causing much public and policy concern. In both cases, people affected could live for many years after diagnosis, rendering the disease a chronic condition to be managed alongside everyday life. Policy responses were therefore organised around the need to educate those affected to live as well as possible and to reduce the chances of contagion spreading to others. Both diseases were highly stigmatised, albeit in different ways, and both were framed as exceptional, leading to special measures that placed them in unique regulatory positions.

Here, I focus on two interconnected regulations that were debated for both tuberculosis and HIV/AIDS during the periods in question: regulations requiring doctors to notify local health officials of all known cases of these diseases (compulsory notification), and regulations empowering local authorities to remove people so diagnosed and perceived as contagious to hospital, or to detain them there (compulsory removal or detention). These were part of the 'key triad' of infectious disease surveillance measures that had been gradually introduced in the second half of the nineteenth century and formalised in the Infectious Disease (Notification) Act 1889 and its extending Act of 1899: notification, disinfection, and isolation.[5] These Acts marked the start of a gradual move within public health in England and Wales towards interventions that targeted individual people and the 'germs' that harmed them, rather than the physical environment around them.[6] Notification aimed to facilitate data collection about the prevalence of specific serious infectious diseases such as cholera and smallpox, and to enable local authorities to take action quickly to interrupt their spread. Upon receipt of a certificate of notification, local health officials were empowered to disinfect buildings and belongings that might harbour contagion, to interview infectious individuals about their movements to identify other possible cases or sources of disease, and to require contagious people to isolate themselves, whether at home or in hospital.[7]

Notification and its corollaries could therefore involve intrusion into domestic and business spaces; close scrutiny of individuals, families, and their networks; and restrictions upon movement and association. Unlike the controversial

[4] For eg, Frank Mort, *Dangerous Sexualities: Medico-Moral Politics in England since 1830*, 2nd edn (London and New York, NY, Routledge, 2000); Allan M Brandt, *No Magic Bullet: A Social History of Venereal Disease in the United States since 1880*, expanded ed (New York, NY, Oxford University Press, 1987).

[5] Graham Mooney, *Intrusive Interventions: Public Health, Domestic Space, and Infectious Disease Surveillance in England, 1840–1914* (Rochester, NY, University of Rochester Press, 2015) 19.

[6] Dorothy Porter and Roy Porter, 'The Enforcement of Health: The British Debate' in Elizabeth Fee and Daniel M Fox (eds), *AIDS: The Burdens of History* (Berkeley, CA, University of California Press, 1988); Christopher Hamlin, 'State Medicine in Great Britain' in Dorothy Porter (ed), *The History of Public Health and the Modern State* (Amsterdam, Rodopi, 1994).

[7] For a more detailed account of statutory notification, see Mooney (2015) (n 5).

Contagious Diseases Acts or the Vaccination Act 1853, though, these measures did not prompt much public protest – except from doctors.[8] For some doctors, as Graham Mooney and John Eyler have discussed, notification demanded an unacceptable breach of doctor-patient confidentiality, while the follow-up action that it prompted was of doubtful worth. However, opinion was divided, and by the early twentieth century the medical naysayers increasingly found themselves shouted down as infectious disease notification and its corollaries achieved acceptance as the status quo.[9] Against this backdrop, compulsory notification for tuberculosis was introduced in England and Wales in stages between 1908 and 1912. Powers of compulsory removal to hospital of people with tuberculosis who were unable to isolate at home followed soon thereafter, initially as a regional initiative through local Corporation Acts, and then nationally in the Public Health Act 1925. Some 60 years later, compulsory notification of HIV/AIDS was debated and decisively rejected, but in 1985 compulsory hospital detention of persons with AIDS was very readily adopted.

Throughout this chapter, I make several arguments. Firstly, drawing on concepts from valuation studies, I suggest that it is useful to think about values as numerous fluid and interacting themes, rather than fixed points.[10] This approach teases apart that which is commonly understood as the 'distinctive core of public health ethics', namely, the need to strike a balance between two specific values: individual freedom and the collective good.[11] The initial introduction of infectious disease notification in the nineteenth century has been seen in these terms, as an example of the emerging willingness in late Victorian Britain to sometimes prioritise the health needs of the population over personal freedom from interference.[12] It has also been treated as evidence of changes to the very concept of personal freedom, with Tom Crook arguing that individual liberty came to encompass 'freedom from the danger of other people' (such as carriers of contagion), rather than simply freedom from state-imposed restrictions and requirements.[13] Building on this insight, I argue here that when historical actors weighed up legal responses to tuberculosis and HIV/AIDS, the views that they expressed about what was good or bad in relation to a particular value were indeed prone to change. Values were

[8] Porter and Porter (n 6) 108; Graham Mooney, 'Public Health versus Private Practice: The Contested Development of Compulsory Infectious Disease Notification in Late-Nineteenth-Century Britain' (1999) 73 *Bulletin of the History of Medicine* 238.

[9] John M Eyler, 'Scarlet Fever and Confinement: The Edwardian Debate over Isolation Hospitals' (1987) 61 *Bulletin of the History of Medicine* 1, 7; Mooney (1999) (n 8).

[10] Although I prefer not to use their term 'registers of valuing', this draws on Frank Heuts and Annemarie Mol, 'What Is a Good Tomato? A Case of Valuing in Practice' (2013) 1 *Valuation Studies* 125.

[11] Stephen Holland, *Public Health Ethics*, 2nd edn (Cambridge, Polity Press, 2015) 4.

[12] Porter and Porter (n 6); Angus H Ferguson, *Should a Doctor Tell? The Evolution of Medical Confidentiality in Britain* (Farnham, Ashgate, 2013).

[13] Tom Crook, *Governing Systems: Modernity and the Making of Public Health in England, 1830–1910* (Oakland, CA,University of California Press, 2016) 198 and 218. This could also be framed as a recognition of that which Isaiah Berlin later described as positive freedom as well as negative freedom.

numerous and interacted with one another in complex ways; they sometimes even contained internal contradictions or tensions. A narrow focus on individual freedom versus collective good cannot fully capture this complexity.

Secondly, I organise the values identified in the case studies into six themes, all of which can be found, to a greater or lesser extent, across both of the examples under examination: confidentiality, effectiveness, usefulness, protection, responsibility, and public reaction. I argue that these reflect a degree of consistency in terms of the standards that commentators applied to infectious disease regulations, although each theme was open to different interpretations at different times. Such changes were shaped to a large extent by views of who, exactly, was expected to be directly affected by the regulations in question. These perspectives shifted over time in relation to the disease, its prevalence and reputation, and the state of knowledge about it.

Relatedly and finally, the most pronounced shift between the two case studies was not greater attention to rights, as might be expected in the rise of human rights, health rights, and bioethics after World War II,[14] but an increased effort to second-guess public responses to regulatory change. This, as well as other shifts across the themes, reflects trends across health policy towards positioning the public as consumers making choices and taking charge of their own health.[15] Scrutiny of these themes also indicates that existing accounts of a 'British approach' to infectious disease that relies largely on voluntary rather than compulsory actions should be adjusted to make space for a consistent element of that which Pamela Cox has called 'hidden coercion'.[16] What's more, the example of HIV/AIDS indicates that when this 'hidden coercion' fails, criminalisation may be enlisted to fill the perceived gap in controlling those seen as the most dangerously contagious – something that would have been unthinkable in relation to tuberculosis at the start of the century.

[14] On this rise in relation to health, see Anne-Emanuelle Birn, 'Special Section: Health and Human Rights: Historical Perspectives and Political Challenges' (2008) 29 *Journal of Public Health Policy* 32; Elizabeth Fee and Manon Parry, 'Jonathan Mann, HIV/AIDS, and Human Rights' (2008) 29 *Journal of Public Health Policy* 54; Daniel Fox and Rudolf Klein, 'Ethics and Health Policy in the United Kingdom and the United States: Legislation and Regulation' in Laurence B McCullough and Robert B Baker (eds), *The Cambridge World History of Medical Ethics* (Cambridge, Cambridge University Press, 2008); Duncan Wilson, *The Making of British Bioethics* (Manchester, Manchester University Press, 2014). For a review of histories of the rise of human rights more generally, see Kenneth Cmiel, 'The Recent History of Human Rights' (2004) 109 *American Historical Review* 117.

[15] Alex Mold, *Making the Patient-Consumer: Patient Organisations and Health Consumerism in Britain* (Manchester, Manchester University Press, 2015); Peder Clark, '"Problems of Today and Tomorrow": Prevention and the National Health Service in the 1970s' (2019) 33 *Social History of Medicine* 981.

[16] Pamela Cox, 'Compulsion, Voluntarism, and Venereal Disease: Governing Sexual Health in England after the Contagious Diseases Acts' (2007) 46 *Journal of British Studies* 91. On the voluntaristic 'British approach', see Peter Baldwin, *Contagion and the State in Europe, 1830–1930* (Cambridge, Cambridge University Press, 1999); Peter Baldwin, *Disease and Democracy: The Industrialized World Faces AIDS* (Berkeley, CA, University of California Press, 2005).

II. Tuberculosis

In the early twentieth century, discussion arose amongst doctors about whether tuberculosis should be made compulsorily notifiable. It had previously been expressly excluded from the list of notifiable diseases, as Richard Coker has described.[17] However, evidence was mounting that tuberculosis was indeed infectious, not hereditary, while anxiety about 'national efficiency' and 'degeneration' was raising the profile of problems including poor health that appeared to affect the working classes in particular. Tuberculosis, along with issues like alcoholism and mental 'deficiency', became an urgent social problem that threatened the future of the country.[18] Under a new Liberal government, social reform to address urban poverty and deprivation was very much on the agenda in the 1900s, with innovations such as state-funded school meals indicating that greater state engagement with matters of health and welfare was becoming acceptable.

The argument in favour of compulsory notification of tuberculosis drew on the theme of effectiveness. Notification was presented as effective in terms of lessening the harmful impact of the disease on those already affected, and also eventually reducing the number of cases overall. This would be achieved because, as one memorandum enthusiastically recorded, after the notification was made the person with tuberculosis

> gets visitation and instruction from the Medical Officer of Health and his assistants, and, in some cases, he may receive sanatorium treatment and be provided with spit bottles at the cost of the Sanitary Authority.[19]

Advice, education, and sometimes also state-funded treatment and services would therefore be provided as a direct result of compulsory notification, enabling people to improve and maintain their health while reducing the chances of passing the disease to others. The greatest benefit, so it was said, would accrue to the poorest people who would be otherwise unable to acquire these services.

Those who were not wholly in favour of compulsory notification frequently raised concerns about confidentiality. This echoed objections in the previous century, which had characterised compulsory notification as an unacceptable breach of the patient-doctor relationship. Here, though, concern about confidentiality largely took a different form. Many people had tuberculosis, and many continued to work after diagnosis, sometimes for years – a point specifically made in the instructive notes accompanying the tuberculosis regulations, and by

[17] Richard Coker, 'Civil Liberties and Public Good: Detention of Tuberculous Patients and the Public Health Act 1984' (2001) 45 *Medical History* 341, 344.

[18] RA Soloway, *Demography and Degeneration: Eugenics and the Declining Birthrate in Twentieth-Century Britain* (Chapel Hill, NC, University of North Carolina Press, 1995) especially ch 1; Daniel Pick, *Faces of Degeneration: A European Disorder, c.1848–c.1918* (Cambridge, Cambridge University Press, 1989); Mathew Thomson, *The Problem of Mental Deficiency: Eugenics, Democracy and Social Policy in Britain, c.1870-1959* (Oxford, Clarendon Press, 1998).

[19] Memorandum dated 25 May 1910 in The National Archives (London) (hereafter TNA) MH 55/525.

commentators elsewhere.[20] If strict confidentiality were not maintained, and if it became common knowledge that local health officials were visiting a household because of tuberculosis, these large numbers of working patients might be labelled 'a leper to be shunned' by employers and landlords.[21] Arthur Newsholme, the Chief Medical Officer of the Local Government Board (LGB) and the driving force behind the regulations, frequently found himself responding to complaints that compulsory notification would lead to people losing their jobs and homes, if and when their diagnosis became widely known. He consistently maintained that confidentiality could and would be maintained within processes of compulsory notification, avoiding any such adverse effects.[22]

Here, a need for confidentiality was not presented as a right, nor as a desirable feature of the clinical encounter, but as a prerequisite for fulfilling social responsibilities. As has been argued elsewhere, tuberculosis was frequently understood at this time in relation to labour.[23] In 1908, Newsholme himself estimated the national value of working days lost to tuberculosis at £400 million, and this kind of profiling of the disease helped to justify considerable forays into state-funded health care decades before the National Health Service.[24] Such a strong connection between tuberculosis and work brought the themes of confidentiality and responsibility into harmony: any crusade against tuberculosis could not prevent the tubercular working classes from working.[25] Those affected were, after all, usually of an age 'when the responsibilities of the person attacked are greatest, and his value both to the State and to the home is at the maximum'.[26] As a result, the usual corollaries of compulsory notification, such as disinfection and isolation, were under scrutiny. Would they not reveal the identities of those with tuberculosis to the community, and – given the chronic nature of the disease – keep workers out of employment or away from their families for excessive periods of time? Richard Powell, President of the Royal College of Physicians, maintained that it was 'impossible' to require breadwinners and parents with tuberculosis to abandon their duties for treatment

[20] TNA MH 55/521; Henry Kenwood and others, 'A Discussion On The Action Which Can Be Taken By Local Authorities For The Prevention Of Tuberculous Disease, Apart From The Control Of Milk And Meat Supplies' (1900) 2 *British Medical Journal* 411, 414. See also Nathan Raw, 'The Compulsory Notification of Tuberculosis' (1907) 170 *The Lancet* 1150.

[21] W Bruce, 'The Compulsory Notification of Tuberculosis' (1906) 167 *The Lancet* 1279; 'The Prevention of Tuberculosis in Ireland' (1907) 170 *The Lancet* 1095.

[22] TNA MH 55/525.

[23] Alison Bashford, 'Tuberculosis & Economy: Public Health & Labour in the Early Welfare State' (2002) 4 *Health and History* 19–40. See also Linda Bryder, *Below the Magic Mountain: A Social History of Tuberculosis in Twentieth-Century Britain* (Oxford, Clarendon Press, 1988) on tuberculosis and 'national efficiency'.

[24] Arthur Newsholme, *The Prevention of Tuberculosis* (London, Methuen & Co, 1908) 15; Bashford (n 23) 32; Bryder (n 23) 36–37.

[25] On these kinds of values within other social legislation of this period, see John Brown, 'Social Control and the Modernisation of Social Policy, 1890–1929' in Pat Thane (ed), *The Origins of British Social Policy*, 2nd edn (Abingdon, Routledge, 2019).

[26] Report prepared by William J Howarth, in TNA MH 48/74.

or isolation. There were, in his view, 'much higher considerations of national life' that precluded such demands.[27]

These objections were sufficiently weighty to ensure that tuberculosis was not simply added to the list of diseases to which the existing Acts applied, as was done for plague in 1900 and poliomyelitis in 1912. Instead, the LGB introduced a series of tuberculosis-specific regulations which acknowledged that tuberculosis differed from other notifiable diseases by virtue of being endemic, chronic, and stigmatised. 'Tuberculosis', explained Dr Nathan Raw, poor law hospital superintendent and rising tuberculosis expert, 'must be considered in a class by itself'.[28] The LGB regulations delivered this separate consideration by expressly disallowing the steps that would usually be permitted following receipt of a notification, including disinfection and isolation.

Compulsory notification of tuberculosis quickly lost much sense of controversy, although there were persistent concerns in subsequent decades that doctors failed to notify all cases and that local officials failed to keep adequate records.[29] More pressing, for some local authorities, was the issue of compulsory removal to hospital. This was prompted by situations where domestic overcrowding made it impossible for advice about isolation at home to be followed, but offers of isolation in hospital were declined.[30] A small number of local authorities took the initiative during the 1910s and granted themselves powers in their local Corporation Acts to remove a person with tuberculosis in such a situation to hospital.[31] This mimicked the powers available for other notifiable diseases, and met with limited objections despite obviously flying in the face of calls to treat tuberculosis entirely differently and in absolute confidence. The Public Health Act 1925 then gave all local authorities in England and Wales power to remove to and detain in hospital anyone with pulmonary tuberculosis who presented a risk to others.[32] These powers were presented (and accepted) in Parliament as uncontentious. The only equivocation in parliamentary debate touched on the theme of responsibility, highlighting that local authorities would bear the cost of enforced hospitalisation and arguing that this encroached in an undesirable way upon citizens' duties to provide for their own needs.[33]

In support of these powers of removal, a new vision of effectiveness was overshadowing earlier concerns about confidentiality and the responsibilities of working-aged people. Doctors and local health officials began to insist that tuberculosis would never be conquered without such powers. The goal of regulation

[27] Richard Powell, 'Discussion: The Care and Control of the Consumptive Poor in England and Wales' (1907) 1 *British Journal of Tuberculosis* 20, 25.

[28] Raw (n 20) 1151. See also, eg, Herbert de Carle Woodcock, *The Doctor and the People* (London, Methuen, 1912) 160.

[29] Bryder (n 23).

[30] See the correspondence from various local authorities in TNA MH 55/520.

[31] Joseph Cates, 'Compulsory Isolation of Cases of Pulmonary Tuberculosis' (1922) 43 *Journal of the Royal Sanitary Institute* 106.

[32] 'The Public Health Act, 1925' (1925) 2 *British Medical Journal* 535, 535.

[33] 'Public Health Bill', HL Deb (23 July 1925) vol 62, col 365.

was no longer to benefit the person with tuberculosis, but to reduce the number of cases of tuberculosis, even to 'conquer' or eradicate it entirely. This was simply impossible if those who were infectious remained in overcrowded homes. The Medical Officer of Health (MOH) for Nottingham complained in cold terms about the 'fatal homing tendency' of those soon to die from tuberculosis: until the local authority could 'insist' on their removal from the home, he wrote, 'infection will certainly be allowed to remain and to spread there'.[34] Newsholme, who so emphatically maintained that his regulations must cause no detriment to persons with tuberculosis, nonetheless felt that compulsory hospital removal or detention should be permitted for two cohorts: workhouse patients, and those who lacked the space to isolate at home.[35] These were, of course, the very poorest.

The goal of eradication was accompanied by a different cohort of beneficiaries in the minds of commentators and policymakers: future generations. The theme of protection, and specifically protecting children and the citizens of the future, therefore emerged as a value against which regulations should be considered. Many were in favour of removing children from parents with tuberculosis, and overcrowded homes with children were a particular concern.[36] Calls to go further still, and to require *everyone* who was infectious to take up residence in a dedicated sanatorium or colony, whether or not they could isolate at home, looked boldly to the future: John Esselmont, the superintendent of a Bournemouth sanatorium who was himself to die of tuberculosis, argued that a 'drastic policy of segregation' would finally 'give security from infection' to the people of the future. 'Surely it is better to face once and for all the expense and hardship of a heroic cure', he proposed, 'than to allow this disease to go on, generation after generation, sapping the life of the nation'.[37] In equally stirring terms, the MOH for Croydon held that all objections to complete segregation were flawed because they adhered to a cowardly kind of soft-heartedness instead of favouring the efficient protection of the people of the future. 'For the sake of sentiment', he complained,

> we are to allow infective cases of a fatal and prevalent disease to wander at will amongst the population, to infect the coming generation, and to cause huge loss in life and treasure. This is a policy of inefficiency engendered by a lack of courage. It is a short-sighted policy, and above all it is, to my mind, an unrighteous policy.[38]

[34] 'Notes of the Week: The Homing Tendency of Advanced Consumptives' (1920) 24 *The Medical Officer* 113. See also the Medical Officer of Bedfordshire in 'Tuberculosis Notes' (1921) 25 *The Medical Officer* 138.

[35] Arthur Newsholme, 'Notification of Tuberculosis In Great Britain: A Historical Note' (1934) 2 *The British Medical Journal* 75. See also Raw (n 20) 1152.

[36] Raw (n 20) 1152; W Bolton Tomson, *The Grancher System for the Prophylaxis of Tuberculosis in Poor Delicate Children* (London, Balliere, Tindall & Cox, 1927). See also John Esselmont's letters in TNA MH 55/520.

[37] Clipping of JE Esselmont, 'Tuberculosis: Its Eradication. The One Thing Needful', under cover of letter dated 16 October 1913, in TNA MH 55/520.

[38] Oscar M Holden, 'Housing in Relation to Tuberculosis' (1920) 24 *The Medical Officer* 15.

Compulsory removal to hospital met with a degree of criticism on the basis of its usefulness. Many regions lacked sufficient hospital or sanatoria beds for all those who wanted admission, let alone those who did not. Newsholme was also very doubtful about the benefits of compulsory removal to hospital when the only hospital available was the poorly equipped (and stigmatised) workhouse infirmary.[39] Without adequate hospital facilities – and, as some pointed out, adequate food and fresh air to boost general health – the power to remove a few recalcitrant isolators to hospital might deliver precious little.[40] There was also some hesitation within the medical profession for the hospital 'to become the gaol, and the doctor the gaoler'.[41] This was addressed in terms of the overall effectiveness of the regulations: the MOH of Birmingham, for one, felt that 'rigorous and compulsory segregation of all infective cases would in many instances be a harsh procedure, and might defeat the end in view'.[42] His implication was that if compulsion was widely practised and also highly unpopular, people might simply avoid diagnosis and treatment in the first place, with the result that infection would spread unchecked.

This reflection was a rare example of explicit attention to the theme of public reaction, in relation to tuberculosis regulations. It had not been entirely absent from deliberations about compulsory notification, with various commentators wondering whether those with worrying symptoms might be prompted to stay away from medical services if their diagnosis would be shared, but this seemed to carry little weight.[43] In relation to compulsory hospitalisation, though, concern that overly heavy-handed approaches might be poorly received and result in concealment of illness ensured that special safeguards were in place, unique to tuberculosis.[44] This represented a firm connection between the themes of effectiveness and public reaction, also in evidence in even more pronounced ways in relation to sexually transmitted infection.[45] As Salim al-Gailani observes in relation to claims about public reaction to proposals to make pregnancy notifiable at around the same time, debates reveal more about 'perceptions of working-class sensibilities, and the ways in which these were mobilised in professional disputes', than about actual public reaction.[46] The muted attention to 'working class

[39] Bryder (n 23); see also TNA MH 55/520.

[40] For discussion of nutrition and space as ways of addressing tuberculosis, see extracts from MOH reports from 1909 in TNA MH 55/525.

[41] 'The Compulsory Segregation Of Tuberculous Persons' (1917) 1 *British Medical Journal*, 433.

[42] GB Dixon, 'Pulmonary Tuberculosis In Childhood' (1931) 1 *British Medical Journal* 694, 697.

[43] Some examples are in the responses from hospital administration in TNA MH 55/525.

[44] Coker (2001) (n 17).

[45] There is an extensive literature on this, such as Susan Lemar, '"The Liberty to Spread Disaster": Campaigning for Compulsion in the Control of Venereal Diseases in Edinburgh in the 1920s' (2006) 19 *Social History of Medicine* 73; Lesley A Hall, 'Venereal Diseases and Society in Britain, from the Contagious Diseases Acts to the National Health Service' in Roger Davidson and Lesley Hall (eds), *Sex, Sin and Suffering: Venereal Disease and European Society since 1870* (London, Routledge, 2001).

[46] Salim Al-Gailani, '"The Mothers of England Object": Public Health, Privacy and Professional Ethics in the Early Twentieth-Century Debate over the Notification of Pregnancy' (202)) 33 *Social History of Medicine* 18, 38–39.

sensibilities' in debate over tuberculosis notification and hospitalisation suggests that there was little rhetorical mileage in highlighting the wishes and feelings of the tubercular. This was, after all, a disease that generated considerable popular fear – including some willingness for drastic action.[47] Implicitly, the majority of the public were perceived as supportive, even compliant.

Compulsory hospital removal was, however, also evaluated as extremely useful for those instances when compliance was lacking. This was not because many court orders and involuntary removals would be enacted – and historians have agreed that probably very few court orders were ever obtained.[48] These powers were characterised as useful simply because they existed, adding legal weight to that which was officially just advice. This was public health in 'the shadow of the law',[49] with regulations shaping informal negotiations between health officials and people with tuberculosis in settings far beyond the court room. Ministry of Health officials were reassured in 1920 that, where compulsory removal had been introduced, it rarely came to magistrates because the threat of doing so was generally enough to elicit cooperation.[50] Editorial comment elsewhere confirmed that 'the knowledge that such powers exist is of considerable effect when arranging for the removal of late cases to hospital'.[51] In blunter terms, in its 1931 edition, a leading manual for MOHs advised in some detail on the deployment of threats. People who were reluctant to take themselves to hospital should be warned that any failure at all to isolate perfectly at home would mean that 'a *justice's warrant* directing removal will be obtained and will have to be obeyed'. Officers were advised to mention that 'those of the household who are employed may lose their employment', in stark contrast to the earlier emphasis on protecting work. The textbook confirmed that it was very rarely necessary to go through with actually obtaining a court order, since these threats were usually enough to generate co-operation and 'voluntary' removal to hospital.[52]

Such widespread agreement that powers of compulsory removal to hospital were useful as a means to cajole and threaten suggests that 'hidden coercion' was welcome. 'Hidden coercion' has been described by Pamela Cox in relation to venereal disease treatment over the same period. In her account, it was deployed towards those who were seen as the most troublesome in terms of spreading infection, and used existing power imbalances to leave people with little or no meaningful choice when it came to hospitalisation or treatment. As Cox argues, it enabled

[47] For eg, 'Fighting Tuberculosis' *The Western Times* (25 October 1929) 10; 'National Association For The Prevention Of Tuberculosis' (1923) 2 *British Medical Journal* 112.

[48] Bryder (n 23); Coker (2001) (n 17).

[49] Robert H Mnookin and Lewis Kornhauser, 'Bargaining in the Shadow of the Law: The Case of Divorce' (1979) 88 *Yale Law Journal* 950.

[50] 'Administration of Sanatorium Benefit: Bradford' (1920) 23 *The Medical Officer* 138.

[51] Norman Lorraine, 'Correspondence: Compulsory Detention of Consumptives in Hospital' (1921) 25 *The Medical Officer* 181.

[52] W Robertson and Charles Porter, *Sanitary Law and Practice*, 7th edn (London, The Sanitary Publishing Co Ltd, 1931) 352.

a more genuinely voluntary approach to persist for the rest of the community, whose behaviour caused less concern.[53] A very similar framework of 'constrained choice' has been described in relation to the uses of contemporary mental health law, but whereas this has been described as a bad use of a good law,[54] the ability to threaten was very much part of the stated usefulness of tuberculosis regulations in the early twentieth century. This is suggestive of a moral culture, or 'regime of normativity',[55] in which an ability to enforce compliance by constraining choice was valued. The values surrounding these regulations revealed tensions between the impracticality and potential loss of effectiveness that might result from widespread compulsory hospitalisation, on the one hand, and the protection of future generations from the scourge of tuberculosis on the other: 'hidden coercion' represented a satisfactory compromise.

III. HIV/AIDS

HIV and AIDS emerged in the early 1980s, just as the broad goals for health and welfare under a newly elected Conservative government were being reoriented towards a reduction of state involvement and expenditure. Contagious disease was no longer the priority that it had been 70 years earlier, and public health activity since the 1960s had increasingly focused on individual behaviours such as smoking that incurred health risks, and ways of influencing them through education.[56] Increasingly, the public were conceptualised as 'consumers' with choices and rights, and the role of public health activity was to provide information about health 'risks' to inform those choices.[57] The authority of the medical profession had also been weakened to some degree in the decades after World War II, by revelations of harms enacted in the name of medicine and public health and the rise of movements including anti-psychiatry and bioethics.[58]

In this context, the values expressed in relation to regulations for HIV/AIDS fell within the six themes of confidentiality, effectiveness, usefulness, protection, responsibility, and public reaction, but were interpreted differently. As with tuberculosis, compulsory notification of HIV/AIDS would require doctors to notify

[53] Cox (n 16) 92 and 94.

[54] Sarah-Jane Fenton, Sarah Carr, and Louise Isham, '"Anyone Can Make Bad Use of a Good Law": Exploring How Constrained Choice Can Result in Moral Injury' (2024) 22 *Clinics in Integrated Care* 100190, available at https://doi.org/10.1016/j.intcar.2023.100190.

[55] Martyn Pickersgill, 'The Co-Production of Science, Ethics, and Emotion' (2012) 37 *Science, Technology, & Human Values* 579.

[56] Virginia Berridge, 'Medicine and the Public: The 1962 Report of the Royal College of Physicians and the New Public Health' (2007) 81 *Bulletin of the History of Medicine* 286; Alex Mold et al, *Placing the Public in Public Health in Post-War Britain, 1948–2012* (Cham, Palgrave Macmillan, 2019).

[57] Mold et al, ibid.

[58] On anti-psychiatry: Oisín Wall, *The British Anti-Psychiatrists: From Institutional Psychiatry to the Counter-Culture, 1960–1971* (London, Routledge, 2019). On bioethics: Ruth Chadwick and Duncan Wilson, 'The Emergence and Development of Bioethics in the UK' (2018) 26 *Medical Law Review* 183.

local authorities of known cases, which would then permit various actions to prevent the spread of infection. Such actions for notifiable diseases in the 1980s still included the removal to hospital of 'infectious individuals' believed to be a danger to others, or their detention in hospital. AIDS nearly became notifiable in England and Wales in late 1984 without debate, as Virginia Berridge has recounted. A man diagnosed with AIDS, in a hospital in the south of England, 'threatened to leave and was assessed as a public health hazard'.[59] The press later reported that the patient had 'attempted to discharge himself with a fixed catheter in a vein that could have put others at risk from infected blood if it had leaked', but that he was eventually 'persuaded to remain in hospital'.[60] The Health Minister Kenneth Clarke initially indicated that AIDS should be added to the list of notifiable diseases to allow the detention of this individual to take place, but in the event, this step was not needed or taken.[61]

The situation nevertheless prompted further discussion. In short order, following the advice of its new Expert Advisory Group on AIDS (EAGA), the Government determined that AIDS would not be made notifiable.[62] Although there were calls in subsequent years to reverse this decision, the official position remained unchanged.[63] At the same time, in 1985, powers of compulsory detention in hospital were quickly delivered by means of regulations under the Public Health (Control of Disease) Act 1984. These regulations made AIDS a notifiable disease but only in relation to provisions concerning compulsory medical examination, removal to hospital, detention in hospital, and the removal and isolation of the dead. Somewhat confusingly, therefore, AIDS was in the unique position of being technically notifiable but without any requirement for doctors to carry out notification itself.

A significant theme within these debates, especially in the 1980s, was the protection of human health in a global sense. Some argued that the exceptional scale of the threat posed by AIDS was such that compulsory notification was one amongst many measures that should be taken. The Association of the British Pharmaceutical Industry proposed that various steps such as the compulsory screening of 'heterosexual and homosexual prostitutes' as well as compulsory notification might be needed, given the 'major threat to human health right across the globe' that HIV and AIDS presented.[64] Legal scholar Matthew Weait reminds us that initial demands for coercive laws were 'premised on the catastrophic

[59] Virginia Berridge, *AIDS in the UK: The Making of Policy, 1981–1994* (Oxford, Oxford University Press, 1996) 65.

[60] 'Aids May Be Made Notifiable Disease' *The Times* (11 February 1985) 3.

[61] ibid. See also Berridge (1996) (n 59) 65.

[62] 'Aids', HC Deb (20 February 1985) vol 73, col 499.

[63] See, eg, the response drafted to calls in the media for notification in 1986 and briefing for the Secretary of State's oral evidence to the Select Committee Enquiry on AIDS in 1987, both in TNA JA 628/202.

[64] Thomas Prentice, 'Drug Firms Suggest Curbs on Aids Victims to Stop Spread of Disease – Recommendation of the Association of the British Pharmaceutical Industry' *The Times* (12 August 1985).

consequences of HIV infection' at that time,[65] and compulsory notification was understood as an effective mode of disease control that would help to stop infection in its tracks. Drastic measures – likely to impact marginalised groups such as gay men or sex workers in particular – were presented as justifiable when HIV/AIDS was understood as an urgent threat to everyone.

Many argued that compulsory notification and its corollaries would convey a message to the public. This theme of public reaction became extremely important, far more so than had been the case earlier in the century. For some, notification was its own kind of health education, conveying a sense of urgency and a call for people to take seriously the potential for infection. It would help 'to secure standards of behaviour', Birmingham's chief medical officer argued in the *British Medical Journal*, by 'mak[ing] an honest attempt to codify rules to harness our value judgements' about how to respond to risk. It would also restore 'public confidence' by presenting solutions to this much-feared new disease through the 'recognised institutions' of public health law.[66] Here, attention to likely public reactions overlapped with responsibility, reflecting trends in public health that emphasised the public as consumers who should exercise informed choice, and the role of the state as the gatherer and provider of information. Whereas the early twentieth century saw some concern that regulations might encourage less personal responsibility for health when the state stepped in to give instruction and resources, by the 1980s the same regulations could be seen as an inducement to greater personal responsibility, by authoritatively indicating that HIV/AIDS was a real and present danger to all and that everyone should heed expert advice in terms of personal behaviour.

The idea that compulsory notification would send a strong message to the public was one with which many could agree. A major concern was to anticipate how different publics might interpret this message. Members of the EAGA felt that compulsory notification would stoke fears and widespread misconceptions by implying that HIV could spread just as easily as other notifiable diseases, in the air or through casual contact.[67] Amidst heated public debate about involuntary HIV testing, immigration restrictions, and banning people with HIV or AIDS from certain jobs, the EAGA was persuaded that anything associated with compulsion risked alienating important cohorts of the public. This implicitly recognised the powerful stigma surrounding HIV/AIDS, and that not everyone would be reassured by the involvement of the 'recognised institutions' of public health, and particularly not members of '"at risk" groups' who had already experienced discrimination and marginalisation from state institutions of various kinds.[68]

[65] Matthew Weait, 'Unsafe Law: Health, Rights and the Legal Response to HIV' (2013) 9 *International Journal of Law in Context* 535, 536.

[66] Surinderjit Bakhshi, 'History Says No to The Policeman's Response To AIDS' (1987) 294 *British Medical Journal (Clinical Research Edition)* 245.

[67] See EAGA discussion in TNA JA 398/68.

[68] Note of meeting on Tuesday 29 January 1985 in TNA JA 398/68.

Concern about public reactions to compulsory notification was therefore considered in connection with the theme of effectiveness. The EAGA concluded that those affected by or at particularly high risk of HIV/AIDS, and the voluntary or community groups that supported them, may well be alienated and alarmed by regulations promising compulsion of any kind, including compulsory notification. Such regulations could as a result be damaging to the goal of reducing the spread of HIV, by driving people away from testing and treatment. Furthermore, the EAGA insisted that compulsory notification offered no advantages in terms of data collection and precious little in terms of contact tracing or counselling.[69] In its view, this was not the best way of obtaining or sharing the information that was, at this stage, a most important tool. In short, compulsory notification would not help to achieve the goal of reducing the spread of infection.

Confidentiality was also a prominent theme, if not quite so decisive as it was for American HIV/AIDS policy.[70] Attention to confidentiality in relation to compulsory notification looped back again to effectiveness. The specific point of concern was spelled out in EAGA discussion: certificates of notification had to be confidential but 'problems' could arise within the local authority with names and addresses discovered or shared inappropriately. There were already 'special arrangements' in place for leprosy, with notifications sent to the Director of the Communicable Disease Surveillance Centre personally and not to the local authority, but there was no enthusiasm for associating AIDS with leprosy.[71] As with tuberculosis, the unwelcome idea of turning people with AIDS into 'lepers' was expressed: leprosy still served as shorthand for diagnoses that provoked extraordinary public fear and ostracisation.[72]

Concern about confidentiality did not dwell on the potential for people affected to lose their jobs and homes, as had been the case for tuberculosis notification, although campaigners were certainly alive to the realities of discrimination against those known or suspected to have AIDS or HIV.[73] Instead, attention focused back on public reaction, and specifically public fears that confidentiality could be breached. This might 'make those at risk reluctant to come forward for treatment' or testing, the Government's representatives frequently explained,

[69] 'Aids (Control) Bill', HC Deb (27 March 1987) vol 113, cols 678–79; 'Aids' HC Written Answers, Social Services (20 February 1985) vol 73, col 499; 'Community Medicine Conference: Community Physicians' Important Place In Management' (1986) 293 *British Medical Journal (Clinical Research Edition)* 217.

[70] Dennis Altman, *AIDS and the New Puritanism* (London, Pluto Press, 1986) 80; Ronald Bayer and Amy L Fairchild, 'The Genesis of Public Health Ethics' (2004) 18 *Bioethics* 473, 481–82; LJ Moran, 'Illness: A More Onerous Citizenship?' (1988) 51 *MLR* 343, 348.

[71] Department for Health and Social Security and Communicable Disease Surveillance Centre discussion papers; notes of first EAGA meeting, in TNA JA 398/68.

[72] 'Aids', HL Deb (13 February 1985) vol 460, col 182; 'Aids: Prevention and Control', HL Deb (18 March 1985) vol 461, col 360.

[73] Jonathan Grimshaw, 'AIDS and Human Rights in the United Kingdom' in Martin Breum and Aart Hendriks (eds), *AIDS and Human Rights: An International Perspective* (Copenhagen, Akad Forlag, 1988) 143.

and would therefore be wholly counterproductive.[74] This argument echoed the same points made decades earlier in relation to tuberculosis, but took on much greater weight in the 1980s. Public support became an important (and explicit) consideration, and particularly the support of those most directly affected. As one report from the parliamentary Social Services Committee noted, the 'alienation of any sub-group from the rest of society … will undermine the public health' and so the reactions of 'sub-groups' to any campaigns or interventions should always be considered.[75] Public trust in medical expertise and compliance with official advice could no longer be taken for granted, and commentators were aware that some 'sub-groups' were at particular risk of being marginalised or 'alienated'.

Although compulsory notification of HIV/AIDS was rejected, the picture surrounding compulsory removal to or detention in hospital was more complex. The EAGA agreed that if 'patients with AIDS could present a serious public health hazard to close contacts' then there should be legal provision in 'an emergency situation to allow the detention of an AIDS patient in hospital'.[76] The regulations that were introduced in 1985 followed this expert advice closely, reiterating that detention was for rare and exceptional situations only. This became a common refrain, alongside efforts to distinguish between 'the overwhelming majority of AIDS patients' who presented no threat to the public, and the exceptional case who became dangerous.[77] The theme of usefulness was present but very different, compared to tuberculosis: these legal powers were certainly portrayed as useful in an emergency, but only because they might provide immediate protection to a generalised public, not because they would enable threats or coercion. It is certainly very possible, if not likely, that regulations were sometimes used to induce co-operation, but the official line remained that 'they are useful fall back provisions' for 'very rare, extreme cases'.[78]

Predictions that this power would rarely be used were correct: a court order was sought and obtained only once, in Manchester in September 1985. On appeal, the order was found to have been issued correctly but by then it was no longer needed.[79] This case prompted a degree of public protest and some debate over whether the regulations were fit for purpose.[80] There are signs that their use was contemplated in other instances – for example, when a man in Leeds was

[74] 'Aids: Prevention and Control', HL Deb (18 March 1985) vol 461, col 383; 'Aids (Control) Bill', HC Deb (27 March 1987) vol 113, col 679.

[75] Extract from the Third Report of the Social Services Committee in TNA JA 628/202, 100.

[76] Note of first meeting of the EAGA on 29 January 1985, in TNA JA 398/68.

[77] 'Aids', HC Written Answers, Social Services (20 February 1985) vol 73, col 499. See also 'British Association: Aids victims "should not lose their jobs" *The Times* (28 August 1985) 4; John Oates, APM Coxon, and SS Bakhshi, 'Need for Urgent Action over Aids' *The Times* (20 August 1985) 13.

[78] Briefing for Secretary of State's evidence to Select Committee Enquiry on Aids in May 1987, in TNA JA 628/202.

[79] 'Detaining Patients With AIDS' (1985) 291 *British Medical Journal (Clinical Research Edition)* 1102; 'Judge Lifts Detention Order on Aids Man' *The Times* (25 September 1985) 3.

[80] Berridge (1996) (n 59) 71.

discovered in 1987 to have given blood on several occasions despite knowing that he was HIV positive – but not pursued for largely practical reasons.[81]

Increasingly, powers of compulsory removal or detention were criticised. Such criticism returned to the theme of protection, but the focus of protection was not humanity at large (or future generations), but those already affected by HIV/AIDS. Activists and academics drew on this theme and the language of civil liberties to criticise compulsory removal to hospital,[82] and parliamentarians and their advisory bodies were not blind to this: the parliamentary Social Services Committee reflected that 'the implications [the regulations] raise for civil liberties make us doubt if they should ever be used again', while internal Department of Health memoranda acknowledged the need for any revised regulations to include 'some kind of appeal mechanism as a safeguard for civil rights'.[83] Nevertheless, this theme was perhaps surprisingly faint, given wider attention to protecting rights in relation to HIV/AIDS.[84] It was largely absent from EAGA discussions and carefully avoided by policymakers. As with limited discussion decades earlier of public reactions to tuberculosis regulations, commentators perhaps perceived limited traction in this line of argument.

Stronger criticisms drew on the theme of usefulness. Increasingly, the consensus amongst experts was that powers of compulsory detention were simply of no use. The Association of District Councils (whose members could be involved in invoking these powers) described them as 'draconian and unnecessary', while those in the Government's AIDS Unit pointed out in 1990 that these powers were 'of little, or no, practical value'.[85] This was partly because of the specific wording of the powers, but mainly because they referred only to AIDS, and not HIV. Knowledge and treatment had improved since 1985, and the most dangerous person was no longer someone with AIDS who was bleeding, but someone with HIV who appeared perfectly well. This came to the fore in 1992, when a Birmingham newspaper reported that a local man with HIV had deliberately infected four female sexual partners, one of whom had since died. Health officials were meeting 'to discuss the case and whether there is anything they can do to stop the man claiming more victims', the article ran, but their options were limited. Quoting experts in both criminal law and public health, the article described 'a nightmare for the medical and legal professions', with no legal recourse – except, perhaps, to detain the individual under the Mental Health Act 1983 since he must be 'so mentally

[81] Correspondence in TNA JA 628/203/2.

[82] Grimshaw (n 73); Jonathan Montgomery, 'Victims or Threats? The Framing of HIV' (1990) 7 *Liverpool Law Review* 25, 41.

[83] Extract from the Third Report of the Social Services Committee in TNA JA 628/202; minute dated 23 June 1992 in TNA JA634/91.

[84] Jonathan M Mann et al, 'Health and Human Rights' (1994) 1 *Health and Human Rights*; Grimshaw (n 73).

[85] Minute from AB Barton, 17 August 1990, in TNA JA 634/90.

unbalanced [that] he is unfit to wander at will in the community'.[86] Professional debate over whether doctors could legitimately disclose confidential patient information to sexual partners or families had largely been resolved in favour of prioritising confidentiality.[87] There were grave doubts as to whether compulsory detention would be possible, since it was highly debatable as to whether the regulations encompassed HIV as well as AIDS. 'As it involves infringing personal liberty, it is likely to be the subject of strict interpretation', pondered the note from one meeting.[88] Perhaps the case could be made, but it was far less certain in 1992 than had been assumed just a few years earlier.[89]

Although media interest died down almost as quickly as it had flared up,[90] this case raised the question of using criminal instead of public health measures. The role of the criminal law in responding to HIV/AIDS had already been contemplated in legal journals, in evidence to the Social Services Select Committee, and in an unsuccessful proposal to include a clause making the deliberate transmission of HIV a criminal offence in the Criminal Justice Bill 1990.[91] The Crown Prosecution Service had also considered 'the policy implications of AIDS and its impact on the criminal law' towards the end of that year, concluding that the legal position was unclear.[92] In 1993 the Law Commission recommended that this uncertainty should be eradicated in order to ensure that a conviction for the intentional or reckless inflicting of disease, including HIV, would be achievable.

According to the Commission, this would allow 'a serious sanction for a serious form of irresponsible behaviour'.[93] This was a new value, of punishment, albeit one that overlapped with the theme of responsibility. Successive governments throughout the 1980s and 1990s had resisted calls to clarify the criminal law or to introduce a new offence concerning HIV transmission. The option was also avoided when applying elements of the Public Health Act 1984

[86] Mason Lewis, 'Aids Maniac on Loose with a Mission to Kill' *Birmingham Post* (22 June 1992) 1. See also Hansard Early Day Motion 429, 'TV Rewards for Mr Roy Cornes,' tabled 6 July 1992, and John Mullin and Paul Myers, 'Scotland has "Legal Power to Act on Deliberate Spreaders of Aids"' *The Guardian* (25 June 1992) 2.

[87] Alex McCall-Smith, 'When Should Doctors Break Their Silence?' *The Times* (19 June 1987) 16.

[88] Note on meeting on 24 June 1992, in TNA JA 634/91.

[89] Montgomery argued in 1990 that an expansive definition of AIDS to include HIV was likely: Montgomery (1990) (n 82) 42.

[90] The case prompted much media debate about the risks of heterosexual transmission, while later accounts indicate that the man – who denied any intentional wrongdoing – and his family suffered significant persecution for some time: Simon Garfield, *The End of Innocence: Britain in the Time of AIDS* (London, Faber & Faber, 1995). 'Contaminated Blood Inquiry: "My Four Brothers Died"' (*BBC News*, 11 June 2019), available at www.bbc.co.uk/news/uk-england-leeds-48597421.

[91] Alistair Orr, 'Legal AIDS: Implications of AIDS and HIV for British and American Law' (1989) 15 *Journal of Medical Ethics* 61; Helen Power, 'Consensual Sex, Disease and the Criminal Law' (1996) 60 *Journal of Criminal Law* 412. Evidence from Professor Kennedy and Tony Whitehead in the Third Report of the Social Services Committee, available in TNA JA 628/202.

[92] Letter from Crown Prosecution Service to AIDS Unit, 13 December 1990, in TNA 634/90.

[93] Law Commission, *Legislating the Criminal Code: Offences against the Person and General Principles*, Law Com No 218 (London, HMSO, 1993) 33.

to AIDS in 1985.[94] Criminalisation would have contradicted the tenor of the Government's health education strategy, which tried to signal that responsibility for limiting the spread of HIV lay with everyone, and not only with those already affected.[95] This idea of universal risk and universal responsibility had underpinned the UK Government's large-scale health education campaign in 1987, with its infamous icebergs and tombstones.[96] Criminalisation proposed a new status quo in which the burden of responsibility shifted to those with HIV,[97] made possible in the 1990s thanks to changing attitudes towards HIV/AIDS, changing education strategies – and, I argue, the very limited usefulness of powers of compulsory removal to hospital. Without scope for 'hidden coercion', alternative routes for controlling those perceived as the most dangerous became highly desirable.

The criminalisation of HIV transmission evolved, as James Chalmers has argued, out of 'judicial rationalisation of the criminal law'.[98] The Offences Against the Person Act 1861 was used successfully to prosecute a man in 2001 of recklessly transmitting HIV to two female sexual partners.[99] There were some 30 similar prosecutions by 2018, and as has been noted elsewhere, these cases were pursued against men racialised as non-white and 'foreign', who were positioned as malicious corruptors of innocent women and girls.[100]

IV. Conclusions

There are elements of both continuity and change across the two case studies. I argue that six themes of value – confidentiality, effectiveness, usefulness, protection, responsibility, and public reaction – can be traced across both examples under scrutiny here, but that interpretations of these themes was prone to change. Confidentiality, for example, was frequently raised within debates about compulsory notification and reflected consistent recognition of the implications of stigma, but in very different ways. Breaches of confidentiality for people with tuberculosis

[94] For a useful discussion and analysis, see James Chalmers, *Legal Responses to HIV and AIDS* (Oxford, Hart Publishing, 2008) ch 5.

[95] Montgomery (1990) (82) 44.

[96] Available from the British Film Institute online at https://player.bfi.org.uk/free/film/watch-aids-monolith-1987-online and https://player.bfi.org.uk/free/film/watch-aids-iceberg-1987-online.

[97] Jonathan Montgomery, 'Medicalizing Crime – Criminalizing Health? The Role of Law' in Charles A Erin and Suzanne Ost (eds), *The Criminal Justice System and Health Care* (Oxford, Oxford University Press, 2007) 265.

[98] Chalmers (n 94) 9.

[99] Matthew Weait, 'Criminal Law and the Sexual Transmission of HIV: *R v Dica*' (2005) 68 *MLR* 121, 129–30.

[100] AIDS Action Europe, European HIV Legal Forum (EHLF), *HIV Criminalisation in the EU/EEA: A Comparative 10 Country Report*, November 2019, 39; https://www.aidsactioneurope.org/en/publication/hiv-criminalisation-eueea-comparative-10-country-report. Montgomery (2007) (n 97); Weait (2005) (n 99).

in the early twentieth century were presented as a threat to their ability to work and support their families, overlapping with ideas of responsibility, and the solution was to ensure that local health officials did nothing to alert the community to the presence of tuberculosis in their midst. In contrast, the problem of confidentiality in relation to HIV/AIDS in the 1980s was associated with public reaction: the primary concern was that the public might suspect or worry that their confidentiality would not be protected. This had implications for effectiveness as well, since any such suspicions could reduce engagement with testing, treatment, and official advice, thereby impeding efforts to prevent the spread of infection.

The clearest example of changing views of what was good or bad in relation to a particular value emerges from close attention to discussion about usefulness. In dealing with tuberculosis, powers of compulsory removal to hospital were seen as both useless and useful: useless where adequate hospital facilities were lacking, but extremely useful in delivering 'hidden coercion'. The value of these powers was described explicitly and consistently in terms of their capacity to cajole, persuade, or threaten people with tuberculosis to achieve compliance. The fact these threats would, in all likelihood, only be issued to the poorest people in overcrowded homes was probably relevant to the confidence with which they were expressed. In contrast, the same powers in the 1980s were never described in such terms. Coercion, by this point, was not endorsed so baldly. This can be attributed to increased attention to civil liberties and patients' rights alongside the repositioning of the public as consumers. Emerging consensus that powers of compulsory detention for AIDS were, in fact, useless reflected the changing state of knowledge about HIV/AIDS, as it became apparent that people who were infectious might be entirely asymptomatic. The kind of person who was perceived as dangerous and the potential target of compulsory detention was no longer someone with AIDS, actually or soon likely to be bleeding, but rather the malicious man with HIV spreading infection through (heterosexual) sex. Without any clear route to deliver 'hidden coercion', criminal prosecutions were eventually pursued – an option that had been unthinkable decades earlier in relation to the transmission of tuberculosis.

This adds nuance to the idea that England and Wales has historically pursued a primarily voluntary approach to public health. As Pamela Cox argued in relation to responses to sexually transmitted infection in the early-to-mid-twentieth century, it is very possible that the hidden coercion of those seen as the most dangerous – for tuberculosis, the poorest families in overcrowded homes – enabled the maintenance of a broadly voluntary approach for others. Towards the end of the century, as the usefulness of regulations could no longer easily encompass hidden coercion, the criminal law was eventually enlisted to fill the gap. Although it is certainly true that regulation concerning HIV/AIDS in England and Wales was inspired by history to rely less on compulsion, compared to elsewhere,[101] this history

[101] Roy Porter, 'History Says No to the Policeman's Response to AIDS' (1986) 293 *British Medical Journal* 1589; Chalmers (n 94) 123.

nonetheless includes elements of compulsion which have been highly valued. As a further chapter to this story, the advent of drug resistant strains of tuberculosis at the end of the century coincided with a greater willingness in England and Wales to use the powers of compulsion that public health regulations can provide.[102]

Perhaps surprisingly, despite the second half of the twentieth century being the era of human rights, patients' rights, and the rise of bioethics,[103] explicit attention to protection in terms of the rights of people affected by HIV/AIDS was not especially pronounced when these regulations were considered. This echoes arguments elsewhere that human rights laws and concepts played a minimal role in responding to HIV/AIDS in the UK.[104] Instead, the dominant theme was that of public reaction: how would regulations be received by various publics? This was frequently deployed alongside attention to effectiveness: would those reactions help or hinder the goal of regulation? Commentators recognised to an increasing extent the rhetorical value of associating all other values with that of effectiveness. After all, if it could be argued that a particular regulation might work against the end in view, then what possible purpose could it serve? More focused attention to public reaction reflects trends towards framing the public as consumers, and the growing role of the media and advertising expertise within health policy.

Last but not least, this chapter proposes that the idea of two primary and opposing values within public health – individual freedom and collective benefit – tends to conceal from view the full range of values at work. Although many dilemmas could be boiled down to a tension between these two priorities, in practice, commentators reflected widely and applied many and varied standards, which interacted in complex ways. These values drew on practical considerations just as much (if not more) than questions of fiercely held principle, and reflected broader social goals and trends as well as shifting medical knowledge and perceptions of the populations most directly concerned. Values expressed in public debate and policymaking are only a part of the picture, but an important part nonetheless. By thinking about values in terms of fluid themes that collide, overlap, and are imbued with different meanings according to context, it is possible to recognise a fuller account of the ways that legal responses to infectious disease have been interpreted and justified.

[102] Coker (2001) (n 17); Richard Coker, 'For Debate. The Law, Human Rights, and the Detention of Individuals with Tuberculosis in England and Wales' (2000) 22 *Journal of Public Health* 263.

[103] On patients' rights: Alex Mold, 'Patients' Rights and the National Health Service in Britain, 1960s–1980s' (2012) 102 *American Journal of Public Health* 2030; Alex Mold, 'Repositioning the Patient: Patient Organizations, Consumerism, and Autonomy in Britain during the 1960s and 1970s' (2013) 87 *Bulletin of the History of Medicine* 225.

[104] Chalmers (n 94); Janet Weston, 'Sites of Sickness, Sites of Rights? HIV/AIDS and the Limits of Human Rights in British Prisons' (2019) 16 *Cultural and Social History* 225.

PART III

Longer-term Legal and Social Consequences of Infectious Disease

8

Centralisation of Labour Regulation in Response to the Black Death: The Statute of Labourers and Contract Law

LORREN ELDRIDGE

I. Introduction

The Black Death killed an estimated third to a half of the English population in 1348–49, causing a shortage of agricultural labour.[1] Survivors were more mobile and less willing to take on poor quality work. The Ordinance (1349)[2] and Statute (1351)[3] of Labourers attempted to combat the consequent inflation and wage rises.[4] Further outbreaks in 1361, 1368–69, and 1375 also triggered legal responses: more legislation in 1361, case law developments in the 1370s, petitions presented to the House of Commons seeking legislative change in response to particular grievances and, eventually, the Statute of Cambridge in 1388. Their effectiveness in controlling the labour market was limited by, inter alia, a lack of enforcement infrastructure.

It was once believed that the labour legislation was part of a 'seigneurial reaction': a reinforcement of existing villeinage powers at common law focused on unfree tenants.[5] This led scholarship to focus on social or economic history,[6] in

[1] The percentage is subject to debate: Ole J Benedictow, *The Complete History of the Black Death* (Woodbridge, Boydell 2021) estimates 60%, whilst the consensus is closer to 50%.

[2] *Statutes of the Realm*, vol 1, 307.

[3] *Statutes of the Realm*, vol 1, 311.

[4] Dyer notes that wages were already rising in the 1330s/40s, and so the phenomenon was not solely caused by the plague mortality, but was exacerbated by it: Christopher Dyer, 'Work Ethics in the Fourteenth Century' in James Bothwell et al (eds), *The Problem of Labour in Fourteenth-Century England* (York, York Medieval Press, 2000) 25.

[5] See discussion and citations in Mark Bailey, *After the Black Death: Economy, Society, and the Law in Fourteenth Century England* (Oxford, Oxford University Press, 2021) 10–13 for a summary of views. Maitland told Putnam informally that he saw little enforcement of master-servant contracts in manor or hundred courts, but this is difficult to substantiate – then and now – because research has tended to focus on other institutions: Bertha Haven Putnam, *The Enforcement of the Statute of Labourers: During the First Decade After the Black Death 1349–1359* (New York, NY, Colombia University Press, 1908) 160; Elaine Clark, 'Medieval Labour Law' (1983) 27 *American Journal of Legal History* 330, 331.

[6] As noted by Lawrence Poos, 'The Social Context of the Statute of Labourers Enforcement' (1983) 1 *Law and History Review* 27.

relation to the end of villeinage and a 'more economic' society.[7] However, the idea that workers demanding more led to improved living conditions and the decline of villeinage is too simple. Firstly, it ignores high inflation: some were unable to pay fines under the labour legislation because higher wages were spent on higher costs – although this did not prevent employers accusing labourers of malice or greed.[8] Nor do a handful of heavily-cited examples from the work of Warren Ault, who thought the labour legislation was based on local custom, fit the wider evidence – as Mark Bailey has now shown.[9]

Instead, the Ordinance and Statute of Labourers can be seen as a development in the common law of contract, and in how legislation was used to regulate the limits of private law agreements in respect of waged labour. Like most legislation at the time it was more incremental than dramatic, but it was adapted and used in ways not predicted by the drafters. Ultimately, it provided a new route for the development of common law thinking about contract enforcement, and procedural avenues in which to explore those ideas.

Master-servant contracts were a noted exception to the general rule that informal covenants were not enforceable at common law.[10] The action of 'covenant' – which focused on promises and could award only damages[11] – was also circumscribed from the beginning of the fourteenth century by an increasingly strict insistence on writing under seal (the requirement of 'specialty').[12] Enforcement of oral contracts, including actions for non-performance, remained routine in local courts, but the royal courts' need for formalities made them exceptional there.[13] Agreements to serve were usually oral, and as such fell outside these royal court actions in both covenant and debt. There was no general sense that the common law could be used to compel performance of a promise, and certainly not without a formal written agreement.

The Ordinance and Statute of Labourers, however, created an exceptional category of contract which was enforceable in common law courts without the need

[7] Robert C Palmer, *English Law in the Age of the Black Death, 1348–1381* (Chapel Hill, NC, University of North Carolina Press 1993) 11–12 and 17–20.

[8] Bailey (2021) (n 5) 74–76.

[9] Warren Ault, 'Some Early Village By-Laws' (1930) 178 *English Historical Review* 210; Warren Ault, *Open-field Farming* (London, Allen and Unwin, 1972) esp 81–93; Mark Bailey, 'The Regulation of the Rural Market in Waged Labour in Fourteenth-Century England' (2023) 38 *Continuity and Change* 127; Bailey (2021) (n 5) 36–37.

[10] See, eg, AWB Simpson, *A History of the Common Law of Contract: The Rise of the Action of Assumpsit* (Oxford, Oxford University Press, 1987) 47.

[11] David Ibbetson, *A Historical Introduction to the Law of Obligations* (Oxford, Oxford University Press, 2001) 21–22.

[12] ibid 24. The rule was firmly settled in 1346: YB 20 Edw III (Rolls) Vol 2, 263; Simpson (n 10) 10–13. In practice, many contracts valuable enough to be worth royal court enforcement were already made under seal.

[13] Putnam (1908) (n 5) 158; Bailey (2021) (n 5) 38; Ibbetson (n 11) 49. Contemporary actions in debt were also of limited use because of a writing requirement: Ibbetson (n 11) 28; Palmer (n 7) 66–69 and 86; Morris S Arnold, 'Towards an Ideology of the Early English Law of Obligations' (1987) 5 *Law and History Review* 509. Arnold thought this 'disguised' the substantive enforcement of promises: Morris Arnold, 'Fourteenth-Century Promises' (1976) 35 *Cambridge Law Journal* 321.

for writing, and which had regulated content.[14] Whereas it had become routine for royal courts to intervene to resolve private law disputes and provide for formalities, particularly in respect of rights in land, it was innovative for central government to attempt to regulate social life.[15] A moral economy where social pressure governed economic relationships was the norm, especially in rural communities where agricultural co-operation was essential.[16] This meant the legislation was created and refined in a context where expectations about service and status shaped both the availability and terms of labour contracts[17] alongside ideas about a 'common good'.[18] Palmer analysed what ensued as a development in how government operated, from limited social regulation to an expanding range of regulatory and state-mandated activity in the attempt to preserve the pre-plague status quo.[19] That the labour legislation did so by providing set terms for labourer contracts is both a remarkable social shift, and the product of gradual changes at work before the arrival of the Black Death. This chapter analyses that development specifically in respect of the common law of contract. Whilst Palmer's claim is that the development of new actions in private law was the result of deliberate government action in response to the Black Death, the focus here is on the incidental possibilities created by those deliberate responses, and the impact on law.

II. Legislation in 1349–1351

A. Introduction

An emergency ordinance[20] was issued by the council of Edward III on 18 June 1349 in response to rising labourers' wages.[21] Loss of life due to the pestilence had created a 'scarcity of servants' which many were taking advantage of to demand 'excessive wages' or by refusing to work. The Ordinance attempted to restrain the resulting rise in labour costs and 'idleness'. It had retroactive effect: agreements for labour at higher wages entered before the Ordinance were void and unenforceable.

[14] Clark (n 5) 334. I am grateful to Mark Bailey, Ryan Rowberry, John Baker, and the editors of this volume for their comments on this idea, and on earlier versions of this chapter.

[15] Palmer (n 7) 5.

[16] For a discussion of 'moral economy' see Rosamond Faith, *The Moral Economy of the English Countryside: Anglo-Saxon to Anglo-Normal England* (Cambridge, Cambridge University Press, 2019).

[17] See generally J Whittle and T Lambrecht (eds), *Labour Laws in Preindustrial Europe* (Woodbridge, Boydell, 2023).

[18] Robert Braid, 'Behind the Ordinance of Labourers: Economic Regulation and Market Control in London before the Black Death' (2013) 34 *Journal of Legal History* 3, 22.

[19] See generally Palmer (n 7).

[20] The practical and theoretical distinctions between ordinances and statutes developed in the course of the 14th century: Geoffrey Barraclough, 'Law and Legislation in Medieval England' (1940) 58 *Law Quarterly Review* 75. The Ordinance was treated as authoritative even though it was not made statute until 1378 (2 Ric II, st 1, c 8).

[21] References to the text of the legislation use the Latin and English printed versions in *Statutes of the Realm*, vol 1, 23 Edw III, 307–10; 25 Edw III, 311–16.

Government regulation of economic activity was routine in some spheres: there were assizes of bread, ale, and wine from the late twelfth century.[22] Braid has noted, however, that older rules tended to pursue a free and fair market for goods by prescribing the time and place of sale, prohibiting stockpiling, and regulating their quality.[23] Price caps were unusual, although the assize of wine did use royal writs to control retail and wholesale prices.[24] Regulating sellers of 'victuals' was therefore less innovative than other provisions.[25] The labour legislation did not, however, make reference to existing royal regulation of commodities, suggesting it was not thought of in the same vein.[26]

Bailey has challenged accounts finding the origins of the labour legislation in earlier customary practice, partly because those rules themselves were uncertain.[27] Such accounts usually rely on evidence that comes from Ault,[28] but Bailey's larger survey and revisiting of sources reveals problems.[29] The Ordinance and Statute do, however, appear to borrow from the local custom of London.[30] The particular trades targeted beyond agricultural labourers correspond to those regulated in London prior to the Black Death.[31] The term '*operarii*' is present in older London ordinances concerning urban labour, as Braid notes, but was also used as a general term for agricultural work or services – and was perhaps more likely to indicate free labour than the terms '*consuetudinarii*' or '*customarii*'.[32]

There are also conceptual problems with an explanation based on local custom: Levett thought that by-laws would have been hard to enforce – especially between two tenants of one lord, and so the labour legislation offered an easier machinery.[33] However, extending an already imprecise and easily abused custom enforced by local officials to institutions which were part of the common law would have

[22] Bailey (2021) (n 5) 42; Braid (n 18) 8–13; Gwen Seabourne, *Royal Regulation of Loans and Sales* (Woodbridge, Boydell, 2003).

[23] Braid (n 18) 5.

[24] ibid 12–13; Seabourne (n 22) 76–79.

[25] *Statutes of the Realm*, vol 1, 51 Henry III, 199–200. See generally Seabourne (n 22); Braid (n 18) 8.

[26] Braid (n 18) 26.

[27] Bailey (2023) (n 9). See for instance, Clark (n 5) 331. It was noted in the 1980s that there was a lack of evidence for, for instance, specific occupational liability for shepherds in local courts prior to the Black Death: Palmer (n 7) 201.

[28] See, eg, Clark (n 5) 332, citing Ault (1972) (n 9) 29; Poos (n 6) 36.

[29] Bailey (2021) (n 5); Bailey (2023) (n 9).

[30] This is explored in detail in Braid (n 18), although Braid's goal is not to consider the legislation from the perspective of existing agricultural customs, focusing primarily on urban and royal provision. See also Bothwell et al (n 4). The legislation shares features with the text of the Norwegian Code of 1274, which also sought to control labour and vagrancy. I am grateful to Jørn Øyrehagen Sunde, Brage Thunestvedt Hatløy, and Jòhanna Katrin Friðriksdóttir for discussions on this subject.

[31] Braid (n 18) 26. Braid's evidence that two trustworthy men were used rather than a standard 12-man jury is less persuasive because jury practices varied so much: ibid 27; John S Beckerman, 'Procedural Innovation and Institutional Change in Medieval English Manorial Courts' (1992) 10 *Law & History Review* 197.

[32] For a summary of terminology used in manorial courts concerning labourers before the Black Death, see 'A Note on Terminology' in Lorren Eldridge, *Law and the Medieval Village Community* (London, Routledge, 2023).

[33] Ada Levett, 'Note on the Statutes of Labourers' (1932) 4 *Economic History Review* 77, 80.

been impractical,[34] even if it had some advantages over covenant actions. A more limited conclusion is justified: there were some attempts to set rules concerning labour during the harvest period on the manors Ault studied, but the lack of presentments suggests there was limited formal enforcement even if such rules were present.[35] Reference to older practices do not fully explain the origins of the labour legislation – even given similarities with London custom. Instead, the legislation combined a number of existing ideas and put them into a new shape in order to respond to the crisis of the Black Death.

B. The Ordinance of 1349

The Ordinance provided for a general mobilisation of the work force via a compulsory service clause,[36] regardless of gender or legal status, if able in body and under the age of 60. Those who had their own means of subsistence were excluded, including some craftspeople, or those with 'proper' land to tend for themselves. This would have included many unfree villeins with larger plots of manorial land, but not 'cottagers' or others lacking land in village fields.[37] The latter already provided waged labour in local communities, but it was unusual for the common law to recognise this: royal courts had paid limited attention to the services provided by the unfree, and interference was restricted generally to recognition of a lord/villein relationship. The ongoing existence of villeinage and lordship was acknowledged in the legislative provision that preferred lords as employers for both unfree and free tenants – subject to not retaining more labour than was 'necessary' – a provision similar to the limit on seigneurial appropriation of waste land in the Statute of Merton 1235.[38] Giving alms to able-bodied beggars who ought to be working was also prohibited in an attempt to discourage idleness.

In return for work, labourers were to take only what payment – in money or kind – had been customary in 1340–46. As well as agricultural workers, various key crafts were singled out, including tailors, smiths, carpenters, and masons. They were not to depart from service before the end of the contractual term – even if they were personally free – without 'reasonable cause'[39] or permission. Reapers

[34] Bailey (2021) (n 5) 207.

[35] ibid 36–37. This has significant impact for the argument in Anthony Musson, 'New Labour Laws, New Remedies? Legal Reaction to the Black Death Crisis' in Nigel Saul (ed), *Fourteenth Century England*, vol 1 (Woodbridge, Boydell, 2000), which seems to rest primarily on Ault's evidence in its departure from Palmer's thesis.

[36] Judith Bennett has emphasised the significance of this clause over the following centuries in 'Compulsory Service in Late Medieval England' (2010) 209 *Past & Present* 7.

[37] Some Year Book cases consider whether a worker had sufficient land to be outside the legislation, for example (1366) Mich 40 Edw III, f 39a–39b, pl 16. For debate over whether a person had sufficient land to be an employer – an extension of the logic of the legislation, see (1364) Trin 38 Edw III, f 12b, pl [1] where the plaintiff argued a rival employer did not have sufficient land to employ a servant.

[38] *Statutes of the Realm*, vol 1, 20 Hen III, 1: '… that they have as much pasture as sufficeth to their tenements …'.

[39] For instance, 'immoderate correction' or not being paid: Morris S Arnold, *Select Cases of Trespass from the King's Courts (1307–1399), vol 1* (1984) 100 SS xl and citations therein, and section D below.

and mowers were identified as either particularly valuable, or particularly liable to offend. These remedies extended only to a limited range of scenarios and kinds of work: for instance, if an agreement was not for the 'usual term' (often a year) the legislation did not apply and there was unlikely to be a remedy for worker non-performance or early departure.[40] To disincentivise leaving one employer for a better opportunity elsewhere, or poaching labour, employers were not to retain workers who had left service in these conditions. Again, this represents at least an attempted shift in practice for agricultural labour: regulation of poaching servants and apprentices was more usual in urban settings under guild jurisdiction.[41]

At first, the enforcement process was decentralised and local. Two 'true men' swearing before the sheriff or constables[42] of the neighbourhood[43] could imprison the offending worker. There were also financial consequences: if an agreement was made for 'excessive' wages, the Ordinance imposed a fine of double that amount. Enforcement initially relied on the community in the local court, harnessing the presentment jury routinely already managing agricultural and public matters.[44] There was nominally also provision to fine lords who ignored the Ordinance using the county and hundred courts, with a fine of triple the promised amount. As will be discussed below, this had limited impact.

The Ordinance was promulgated by secular and ecclesiastical authorities, with church officials from archbishops to local parishes instructed to publish it and exhort the populace to comply, which they did via fairs and marketplaces. That the churches were also reminded not to raise the salaries of their chaplains gives some indication of the general inflationary pressures at the time.[45] However, it quickly became evident that the lack of a specific enforcement mechanism hindered the effectiveness of the legislation in controlling the labour market, prompting further interventions.

C. Revision in Late 1349

A 'conclusion'[46] to the Ordinance explains how the enforcement mechanism was changed in November 1349. It had been realised – probably by Justice Shareshull – that the taxation machinery was highly effective in using local officials to appropriate resources to the centre, and this could be used to enforce the labour legislation.[47]

[40] Ibbetson (n 11) 38. For example in (1371) Mich 45 Edw III, f 13b–14a, pl 11 it was disputed whether the legislation applied given the alleged term of service was six years, not one; similarly (1383) Hil 6 Ric II, Ames 205, pl 23 the writ was not good where the alleged term was two years.

[41] Braid (n 18) 20–21.

[42] Some printed copies also refer to the bailiff of the local lord.

[43] 'Ville' has been translated as 'town', but could also mean village, neighbourhood, etc.

[44] See generally Eldridge (n 32).

[45] A clerical equivalent of the Ordinance of Labourers, with very similar provisions, was enacted in 1350: Bertha Haven Putnam, 'Maximum Wage-Laws for Priests after the Black Death, 1348–1381' (1915) 21 *American Historical Review* 12.

[46] Putnam argued this was better described as a second ordinance, not a 'conclusion', as it changed the enforcement mechanism – or at least how the proceeds of enforcement were used: Putnam (1908) (n 5) 101.

[47] Mark Bailey, *The Decline of Serfdom in Late Medieval England* (Woodbridge, Boydell, 2014) 164; Bertha Haven Putnam, *The Place in Legal History of Sir William Shareshull, Chief Justice of the King's*

Local tax collectors already existed and had detailed local knowledge about individuals' economic arrangements, without the need for new infrastructure. Individuals and juries were still able to bring local actions for their own profit, too, maximising the probability that somebody would pursue offenders.

This plan was effected in relation to the 'disme' and 'quinzime' – tenth and fifteenth. These were taxes levied in blocks on communities and granted by Parliament from 1349–1352. The fines under the labour legislation were to be offset against this tax after an amendment issued on 18 August 1350.[48] This incentivised enforcement: for every labour fine, the community had a lower tax burden, shifting the cost to individual offenders. An assize case from 1353 suggests local communities quickly realised this: two tax collectors were presented for levying 'a great sum of money' from labourers which ought to have been used to discharge the royal tax.[49] Dyer notes that the older tenth and fifteenth system had effectively placed the tax burden on those with more capital by taxing goods and livestock, whereas this tax and the poll tax introduced in 1377 accessed the new wealth of labourers and servants. The changes in population would have also meant that even unchanged tax amounts were distributed amongst fewer people in 1349, increasing individual burdens and incentivising communities to collect taxes from a wider cohort.[50]

Putnam perceived the fines from the legislation as ensuring the tax burden was shared by those who had benefitted economically from the plague, where employers had suffered,[51] and local employers did make extensive use of the offsets.[52] When the tax breaks were removed after the second wave of plague in 1361, enforcement of the labour legislation also declined.[53] However, the taxation of poorer people continued: it had become clear after the labour legislation that taxes which disproportionately burdened the poor were an option, and Commons proved more willing to agree to them, at more regular intervals, than when the burden fell primarily on the wealthier groups from which Commons membership was drawn.[54] Whilst the tax offset appears to have been introduced as an ad hoc response to enforcement difficulties, it became an established feature of the labour legislation in 1351–1352.

D. The Statute of 1351

When Parliament next met in February 1351, complaints about rising wages continued, and the labour shortage was one reason for summoning it.[55] Wealthier taxpayers complained they could not afford the tenth and fifteenth because they

Bench, 1350–1361 (Cambridge, Cambridge University Press, 1950).

48 Putnam (1950), ibid 256; *Calendar of Patent Rolls 1348–1350*, 594.

49 (1353) YB 27 Edw III, f 135a, Lib Ass 15.

50 Dyer (n 4) 28.

51 Putnam (1908) (n 5) 99.

52 ibid 129–30; Poos (n 6) 37.

53 Bailey (2021) (n 5) 79–80.

54 Chris Given-Wilson, 'The Problem of Labour in the Context of English Government, c. 1350–1450' in Bothwell et al (n 4) 95–96.

55 *Rotuli Parliamentorum*, vol 2, 225b.

were forced to pay labourers so much.[56] The Statute of Labourers was therefore enacted to refine and supplement – but not override or replace – the Ordinance.[57]

The tone differed from the Ordinance, which described the labour shortage as an 'incommodity': the Statute ascribed the idleness of labourers to 'malice'. This was gentler than the canon law equivalent from 1350, which described the 'unbridled covetousness of the human race' risking the loss of charity from the world.[58] The Statute referred to the Ordinance, but said labourers were still demanding double or treble wages out of laziness and covetousness, and were withdrawing themselves from one employer in order to serve another. The provisions of the Statute were more detailed as to particular types of agricultural labour than the Ordinance, expanding an earlier reference to ploughmen to a host of roles including carters, shepherds, and swineherds. That these were roles with lower economic value and importance than ploughmen, and therefore included workers who earned proportionately less, suggests the labour crisis had indeed worsened.

The Statute attempted to control the duration of labour contracts where the Ordinance had only prohibited leaving before the end of whatever the agreed term was. The 'usual term' – often a yearly contract – was to be preferred to daily work in agriculture, presumably to give employers certainty. Wages were set nationally, with specific rates in the Statute, but the discretion of justices was invoked for at least part of the year. A wider range of craftsmen were also included in the Statute than the Ordinance, their wages, like those of agricultural workers, now capped by reference to the period 1342–46. Judicial decisions would expand the scope of regulated work,[59] so that bailiffs, merchants, and even sometimes chaplains[60] were held to fall under the legislative jurisdiction. Skilled workers such as carpenters and masons were also prohibited from contracting for work by the day, but were not subject to detailed provisions.

Contracts for agricultural labour were to be concluded openly, in public marketplaces. Publicity requirements for important contracts were traditional from pre-Conquest England, where cattle sales – ie sales of the most valuable

[56] Putnam (1950) (n 47) 68.

[57] Until further legislation confirmed and amended the Ordinance and Statute during the reign of Richard II, the Year Books continued to refer to the 1349 legislation, often alongside a reference to the 1351 version: Putnam (n 5) 179; Theodore Plucknett, *Year Books of Richard II: 13 Richard II (1389–1390)* (London, Ames Foundation, 1929) 31, fn 1; 32, fn 2.

[58] Putnam (1915) (n 45) 20. The 1362 re-issue of the canon law effrenata after another wave of plague was even more aggressively worded.

[59] In (1373) Mich 47 Edw III, f 22b, pl 53 an embroiderer's attempt to argue that the legislation did not apply to him because he was a craftsman (artificer) was unsuccessful until it was added that the agreement was not for a year. (1376) Trin 50 Edw III, f 13a, pl 3 was content that the legislation applied to labourers and artificers, but not chaplains. See also n 64 below and discussion in John Baker and Stroud Francis Charles Milsom, *Sources of English Legal History*, 2nd edn (Oxford, Oxford University Press, 2019) 424, fn 11.

[60] Putnam (1915) (n 45) 27–28. The applicability of the secular legislation to chaplains or in respect of divine services was the subject of several Year Book cases in the 1370s: (1372) Pasch 46 Edw III, f 14b, pl 19; (1376) Trin 50 Edw III, f 13a, pl 3. It was settled that the legislation did not apply to a chaplain by 1383, as Belknap CJCP was able to say that it had often been ruled so: (1383) Hil 6 Ric II, Ames 205, pl 23.

capital assets – were of particular concern,[61] and this may have continued as local custom into the period where local courts depended on witnesses and presentment juries.[62] The requirement that certain labourers present themselves twice a year to swear before local officials that the Statute was being complied with, echoes the functioning of the hundred courts and frankpledge system, and again emphasised visibility.[63] Publicity requirements may have been designed to mitigate evidential difficulties,[64] but for a frequently made contract of relatively low value, it seems unlikely to have been practical.

Agricultural worker mobility was also controlled: if work was available where a person lived during the winter, they were prohibited from travelling for summer jobs. This kind of movement was probably common: the amount of waged labour needed on a manor was variable and depended on factors including the number of unfree tenants, the extent of commutation, and how actively the lord managed their demesne. Lords had always had significant powers over their unfree tenants, including the ability to retrieve them when they absconded, but they had rarely been willing or able to do so in practice in the earlier period.[65] The powers given here to control free labourers were more circumscribed, and it seems unlikely that this aspect of the labour legislation was ever going to be effective. It was also subject to recognition that agricultural practices varied, and that in places like the Marches of Wales and Scotland, more itinerant labour was routine – essential, even – for the transhumance that characterised upland areas.[66]

The punishments adopted for offences also changed between 1349 and 1351. The Statute favoured the stocks, presumably because imprisoning potential workers was not helpful during a labour shortage. Instead of gaol, the stocks were an unsubtle mechanism for persuading recalcitrant labourers that agreeing to serve was in their best interests. The Ordinance reference to sureties was also replaced in one part of the Statute by a requirement to 'justify themselves', suggesting less utilisation of local reputational networks and a greater focus on centralised judicial process. The Statute also made use of the common law procedure for attachment, and set particular periods of time for imprisonment: this was more detailed than the provisions of the Ordinance, and more closely integrated with other common law procedure.

One practical problem which remained was that the rates designed to function as caps on wages were not always explicitly stated or clear. That the 1349 Ordinance was less specific about wage maximums was probably no accident: local officials'

[61] Braid (n 18) 7.

[62] See Rosamond Faith, 'Markets and Marketing' in Faith (n 16).

[63] Helen Cam, 'Studies in the Hundred Rolls: Some Aspects of the Thirteenth-century Administration' in Paul Vinogradoff (ed), *Oxford Studies in Social and Legal History*, Vol 6 (Oxford, Oxford University Press, 1914).

[64] Bailey (2021) (n 5) 209.

[65] See generally John Ambrose Raftis, *Tenure and Mobility: Studies in the Social History of the Mediaeval English Village* (Toronto, Pontifical Institute of Mediaeval Studies, 1964).

[66] See, eg, Tom Williamson, *Shaping Medieval Landscapes: Settlement, Society, Environment* (Bollington, Windgather, 2003). The Assize of Ale also recognised economic differences between town and country in respect of goods: Seabourne (n 22) 82.

knowledge was utilised, but they were ill-equipped in this context. Bailey summarises the problem, writing that

> the legislation required constables and local presentment jurors to make clear-cut legal judgements in manifold cases where the original contract itself was likely to have been unclear, where standards of proof for breaches had been lowered, and the presumption was guilt.[67]

In the Statute, some detail was added in the form of maximum wages for specific tasks: at most a penny a day for haymaking, and five pence for mowing a meadow. However, Bailey notes vague terminology elsewhere: 'able bodied' was not defined, nor was the extent of 'appropriate' food to be provided. The concept of 'reasonable wage' might have been used previously to ensure a (minimum) subsistence wage was paid to workers recognising their skill and status. Now, however, 'common good' required workers to not demand too much.[68] A 'common good' was familiar from thirteenth-century theology, and it is not surprising that the 1350 canon law on the labour of chaplains was similar to the secular legislation.[69] Refusal to undertake poor quality work or take lower wages was thereby framed as a moral issue justifying employers' positions.[70] What 'reasonable' price meant was also unclear – although it was not identical with canon law 'just price'. The former would reflect historic rates, costs of production, and transportation, but deliberately allowed for flexibility within the plurality of jurisdictions in medieval England.[71]

Local officials were thus expected to enforce the Statute in accordance with new and uncertain standards and without detailed guidance, increasing the scope for abuse and the variability of royal justice.[72] Poos notes that the role of local officers made enforcement as much a matter of social control within communities as economic control from above.[73] The Statute attempted to resolve this by creating a new judicial commission: Justices of Labour.[74] The enquiries of itinerant justices into local enforcement activity four times a year would have been familiar from the eyre processions which ended at the turn of the fourteenth century. Palmer describes how the use of Keepers of the Peace as full justices to enforce the Statute of Labourers was also novel: prior to the Black Death, the king had resisted full felony jurisdiction for Keepers of the Peace, but in 1350 this policy was reversed to facilitate labour legislation enforcement.[75] At least some parties still used the Statute in manorial courts to strengthen their position as regarded villein labourers: in any case, manorial courts were a cheaper, closer, and less public forum to resolve disputes. They were also accessible to persons who were unfree or had doubtful

[67] Bailey (2021) (n 5) 207–10.
[68] ibid 35–36 and 77–79.
[69] Putnam (1915) (n 45) 12.
[70] Bailey (2021) (n 5) 77.
[71] Seabourne (n 22) 89.
[72] Bailey (2021) (n 5) 210.
[73] Poos (n 6) 28.
[74] Bailey (2014) (n 47) 72.
[75] Palmer (n 7) 23.

claims to free personal status, where common law actions and courts were supposedly unavailable.[76] Whereas royal justice was generally more standardised than local custom, this fused common law substance with local procedure to provide a royal justice administered inconsistently by local officials. The pros and cons of this were the same as ever: locals were well informed, but equally liable to self-interest and pursuit of personal goals. Here, they were asked to enforce supposedly standardised legislative provisions where their discretion (or failure to exercise it correctly) mattered for the common law and economy as a whole. This was also in a context where there may have been a limited supply of experienced officials due to plague mortality.[77]

As with the amended version of the Ordinance, the Statute used local tax collection mechanisms. Initially it seemed this would be superseded by the new Justices: the grant of the tenth and fifteenth would in any case end in 1352. However, when a new subsidy was granted in 1352, it was specifically on the condition that labour legislation penalties be put towards it.[78] If the labour fines exceeded the tax amount due, they were to be applied to neighbouring towns' liabilities, ensuring the income ultimately found its way back to the Crown. Initially, this mechanism had caused problems: it was difficult to segregate the labour fine 'excess' from other profits of jurisdiction. However, the 1351 Statute simplified collection as, under the terms of the new commissions, all such penalties were to be applied to the royal tax.[79] This corresponded with a shift of accountability: local officials had been answerable to the communities who elected them (whatever process that involved) but were now increasingly accountable to the Justices of the Peace.[80]

Once a person was accused of breaching the labour legislation, pragmatically accepting the accusation and paying the fine was usually a preferable response to attempting to challenge it in court. In 1352, around 15 per cent of adults in Essex were fined, up to 80 per cent in places.[81] This might suggest less that enforcement was strict or that a lot of wrongdoing occurred, and more that the fines under the statute were being treated as a fee for certain practices and a way of generating income. Such fines under the Assizes of Bread and Ale have been posed as routine costs of doing business, rather than actual deterrents.[82] The Statute of Labourers tends to be contrasted with this: it was not simply a mechanism for regulation or the shifting of economic incentives but a genuinely social response to the labour shortage.[83]

[76] Bailey (2014) (n 47) 181; M Bailey, 'The Implementation of National Labour Legislation in England after the Black Death, 1349–1400' (2024) 78(2) *Economic History Review* 529.

[77] Bailey (2021) (n 5) 211–18.

[78] Putnam (1950) (n 47) 53.

[79] ibid 70. This caused other problems in respect of the supposedly preserved claims of franchise holders.

[80] Bailey (2021) (n 5) 219.

[81] ibid 79.

[82] Braid (n 18) 8–11.

[83] Some have argued that high rates of fines indicate that the legislation was not working to control labour: Samuel Cohn, 'After the Black Death' (2007) 60 *Economic History Review (new series)* 457; Chris Given-Wilson, 'Service, Serfdom and English Labour Legislation' in Anne Curry and Elizabeth Matthew (eds), *Concepts and Patterns of Service in the Later Middle Ages* (Woodbridge,

However, as Seabourne has shown, assuming an opposition between a scheme of licensing and proper prosecution is to misunderstand medieval law: generating judicial income and changing social incentives were not mutually exclusive.[84]

The labour legislation was clearly used as a revenue raising tool from the first revision onwards. But it did not follow that the legislation only operated as a licensing scheme adding an extra cost as the price of working in certain trades or charging certain rates. If that had been intended, a focus on imprisonment, ie bodily control of offenders as opposed to just fines, seems unlikely – especially in the 1361[85] and 1364 iterations. If the statutory fines were double or triple the contract value, but not imposed in every single instance due to lack of enforcement apparatus, they may not have done much to deter the practices targeted. The fine under the 1351 statute, however, was the 'excess'. Unlike the double fine adopted by the Ordinance, the Statute focused on the difference between the actual, illegal, rate charged, and the acceptable, legal, value.[86] If the purpose was to licence certain activities, a set rate would have been more logical. The use of the concept of 'excess' suggests a genuine attempt at social control, as Palmer argued. This and the emphasis on imprisonment indicates that the Statute was genuinely intended to stop wage inflation and control labourers.[87] It did this by closely regulating the content of service contracts as well as capping wages.

III. Service under the Statute of Labourers

A. Introduction

Bailey argues that government intervention in markets after the Black Death was a milestone in the expansion of state power.[88] The Ordinance and Statute show that lords were concerned about the increasing mobility of villeins as well as the cost of labour.[89] The Statute of Cambridge (1388) emphasised this, and supports the view that the Statute of Labourers marked a significant change in how legislation was used. The 1388 Statute sought to control labourer movement (and beggars), and required the use of 'letters patent' with the seals of their locality to introduce a travelling labourer.[90] It may have also led to the innovation of lords requiring the payment of fees to pursue trades, and the increased importance of chevage in identifying the unfree.[91] A magnified concern for the mobility of workers generally

Boydell, 2000) 24; Edmund Fryde, 'Peasant Rebellion and Peasant Discontents' in Edward Miller (ed), *The Agrarian History of England and Wales*, Vol 3 (Cambridge, Cambridge University Press, 1991) 758, which argues that employers, at least, could afford to ignore the legislation.

[84] Seabourne (n 22) 17.

[85] 34 Edw III, 1360-4, CRR 262–63.

[86] Putnam (1908) (n 5) 81.

[87] Palmer (n 7) 21.

[88] Bailey (2021) (n 5).

[89] Bailey (2014) (n 47) 44.

[90] Tom Johnson, *Law in Common* (Oxford, Oxford University Press, 2019) 251.

[91] Bailey (2014) (n 47) 298.

is also evidenced in urban employers' new concern to track down and return departed servants and apprentices, where prior to the Black Death complaints of neglect from the apprentices were more likely.[92]

However, the older idea of a 'seigneurial reaction' to the Black Death intensifying existing villeinage powers rests on a misunderstanding of manorial relations. Perhaps half of the fourteenth-century rural labour force consisted of legally free peasants, with the other half unfree and subject to greater seigneurial control – but many unfree villeins also undertook waged labour.[93] Labour services had been utilised to their greatest extent during the second half of the thirteenth century, but had long been declining, with seasonal and harvest services surviving longer than most.[94] Extreme seigneurial powers existed only in the minds of theorists and custom had always regulated the relationship.[95] Any lords who did attempt to force labour using villeinage were exceptionally demanding or were doing something new. As Bailey has pointed out, if lords had been able to exploit the unfree before this legislation was enacted, government intervention would hardly have been necessary. Nor would it have made sense to regulate voluntary contracts for labour in general, rather than just tightening villeinage.[96] This was not a shift from status to contract, but a shift from local to central, as Palmer argued.[97]

The Ordinance and Statute of Labourers did represent a significant change in the common law approach: its previous emphasis on legal status in statements of the law like *Bracton*, a century before, was replaced by an emphasis on economic value.[98] It has been argued elsewhere that the common law courts previously lacked the infrastructure and information needed to look to detailed economic differences, or the desire to interfere in lord-tenant relations.[99] By 1349, however, the incentives had shifted, with the royal council and Parliament ready to innovate to cope with the impact of the Black Death. Because the legislation regulated all labour contracts – not just those of the free or the unfree, but anyone labouring for money, it cut across the distinction between personally free and unfree workers. Instead, it looked to substantively similar relationships as a matter of economics.[100]

By deprioritising the legal categories of free and unfree and focusing on economic weight – and looking to whether they farmed their own land or worked as waged labourers – this legislation had significant impact on the law of villeinage. Royal courts had not interfered generally in the relationship between lord and unfree tenant. Now, they would, in the interests of the wider economy and ensuring a supply of labour.

[92] Braid (n 18) 20. See also (1365) Mich 39 Edw III, f 22a–22b, pl [12], where it was made clear in a case concerning neglect of an apprentice's training that the writ under the labour legislation applied to servants, not apprentices.
[93] Dyer (n 4) 34–35.
[94] Bailey (2014) (n 47) 50–51.
[95] Bailey (2021) (n 5) 11–12 and 29; Eldridge (n 32).
[96] Bailey (2021) (n 5) 13.
[97] ibid 78; Palmer (n 7).
[98] GE Woodbine and SE Thorne (eds), *Bracton on the Laws and Customs of England* (Cambridge, MA, Selden Society and Harvard University Press, 1968) 4.
[99] Eldridge (n 32).
[100] Bailey (2014) (n 47) 332.

A Year Book case from soon after the legislation illustrates the shift: in 1352, a trespass writ was brought in the Common Pleas under the 'novel statute' alleging the defendant had beaten the plaintiff's wife.[101] The defendant said that, since the husband was his villein, they ought not to be able to use this writ against him. The attempt to argue that the wife herself was free failed, but towards the end of the entry, when the plaintiff insisted he was free, the discussion turned to the labour legislation:

> then the plaintiffs said that by the new statute a remedy was ordained to lords of their villeins … to aid them to take their villeins … The defendant said that of common right a villein was amenable to justice by his lord, and would be taken and put in the stocks; therefore the plaintiffs should not have such a writ. And the Court did not want to grant such a writ.

It appears that the Common Pleas were at least initially reluctant to use the labour legislation in a way that cut across villeinage. But their aversion was quickly overcome, as demonstrated in a 1355 case concerning eloigning a villein servant (ie tempting him away from another employer).[102] The servant agreed he was the villein of the defendant, who had coerced him home, removing him from the plaintiff's service. When the plaintiff tried to use the labour legislation to enforce the agreement to serve, he made two interesting points. Firstly, he said it was irrelevant that the servant was someone else's villein: it was the villein's own folly to agree to serve knowing he was not at liberty. Secondly, if an employer made an agreement to serve with a person who was at large, he ought not to lose the protection of the legislation just because that person happened to be a villein. Green JCP did not like the latter argument: if it were correct, a villein could make successive service agreements and end up staying away from the lord forever, which did not sit well with the concept of villeinage. Willoughby JCP, however, was less interested in preserving seigneurial rights: he thought villeinage irrelevant to the question of whether a person had been in service, which was what engaged the statute.[103] Within just a handful of years, the interpretation of the labour legislation in the Common Pleas seems to have shifted from preserving villeinage to regarding it as irrelevant to Statute of Labourers questions. By 1375, Belknap CJCP could tell plaintiffs that if they wanted to discuss the freedom of an individual, that was a distinct issue to the writ issued under the labour legislation:[104] that the opportunity was not taken to use the labour legislation to add an extra layer of enforcement for seigneurial lords is further undermines the conventional narrative of the labour legislation reinforcing villeinage. And, as Putnam noted, unless and until a case was referred to a higher common law court, where villeinage might be important, freedom and unfreedom were usually immaterial in labour cases.[105]

[101] (1352) YB Mich 26 Edw III, f 19b–20a, pl 19.

[102] (1355) YB Trin 29 Edw III, f 41a–41b, pl [29].

[103] Another case the following year similarly split the argument of villeinage into a separate point from the argument of service: (1356) Mich 30 Edw III, f 31a, pl [66].

[104] (1375) Hil 49 Edw III, f 2a, pl 3.

[105] Putnam (1908) (n 5) 77–78 and 95–96.

The legislation had made a reservation for the use of villein labour by their lords, and there is evidence of it being used. In 1356, when a plaintiff complained the defendant had eloigned his servant, the reply was that the servant was a villein and needed for work on the manor.[106] The plaintiff argued the defendant had enough workers already, and the entry ends. A similar case appears in 1373: a carter had been reclaimed as a villein to work on the manor, and the plaintiff complained this was contrary to the Statute of Labourers because the man was his servant, and in any case free.[107] But there might be very little practical difference between villeinage and waged labour by this point. In a trespass writ in 1376, a plaintiff complained that two of his villeins had been taken.[108] The plaintiff explained he had commanded them to serve him as carver and fowler respectively, and given them pay, food, and clothing. This sounds little like Bracton's villein serving at the will of the lord. Belknap CJCP's comments are interesting:

> if my villein was in flight from my lordship, or in another county, and there he was vagrant outside of every service, it was permissible to everyone to make him serve him, and before until he was apprised that he was servant to another, or the villein of another, he was not bound to make restitution of him to anyone, and although his first master or his lord took him out of his service without giving notice to him, that he was his master, to whom he had been his servant before, that it was a permissible thing to take him back, and the plaintiff had not alleged that he had given notice.

Whilst acknowledging that villeinage still gave the plaintiff power over the villein's labour, Belknap CJCP had added a qualification: it was not permissible to take a villein out of service to another if the employer was not given some kind of notice. This is quite different to a simple assertion that a person is a villein, and therefore not free to leave or work for others. The agreement to serve had significance at common law, even when made by a villein, and this quickly began to cut across the older principles of villeinage.

B. Contract Enforcement in Royal Courts

The labour legislation was primarily about contract law and the enforcement of private legal obligations flowing from public policy, rather than the direct coercion of labourers or villeinage.[109] Labour arrangements on manors had been in some sense 'contractual' in the thirteenth century, insofar as villeins knew what services were due from them as a matter of custom, and the lord could not vary this at will. This was especially so when customs were confirmed in custumals (written collections of local customs) and recorded incidentally in court rolls, which gave them extra evidential weight when challenged or asserted in legal settings in the way

[106] (1356) Mich 30 Edw III, f 31a, pl [66].
[107] (1373) Mich 47 Edw III, f 16a, pl 24.
[108] (1376) Mich 50 Edw III, f 21a, pl 2.
[109] Bailey (2021) (n 5) 112.

that specialty supported a common law covenant.[110] This legislation was, however, the first attempt at *national* regulation of employment relationships[111] in a context where freedom of contract and equality of bargaining power were not guiding principles. The labour legislation was particularly useful for employers in providing an action when a servant departed before the end of the contractual period, as well as non-performance in not appearing for work.[112]

As Bennett has noted, it also had a role in creating contracts which would not otherwise have existed through compulsory service which went beyond simply enforcing or modelling agreements.[113] At one extreme, this enforced labour in respect of vagrants could even result in landlords who ought to have had sufficient demesne labour via the usual application of villeinage complaining that the justices of labourers had taken their tenants to work elsewhere.[114] However, this had limits. For example, in 1365, a plaintiff brought a writ against two workers who he alleged were vagrants and had refused to serve him. His writ was abated because his argument did not work for a refusal, as opposed to a trespass in not serving when it had been agreed.[115] At the other end of the spectrum, there was no objection to imprisoning would-be servants in order to compel their agreement:[116] the regulation of the contract and actions for breach did not introduce ideas like vitiation for duress.

As Bailey notes, enforcement of a statute-mandated clause in contracts for labour required actually knowing what the terms of any given contract were.[117] In a culture where these contracts were primarily oral, and may have lacked detailed negotiated content, it is difficult to see how the terms could practically have been enforced. It is possible that the legislation, by virtue of its mere existence, encouraged employers and labourers to be more precise as to terms.[118] However, the legislation effectively provided for standard form contracts for the types of labour it regulated: there was no need to discuss detailed terms each time.[119] If the substance of the provisions for

[110] ibid 33.
[111] Clark (n 5) 330.
[112] Ibbetson (n 11) 38.
[113] Bennett (n 36).
[114] Putnam (1908) (n 5) 93.
[115] (1365) Pasch 39 Edw III, f 6b–7a, pl [2].
[116] For instance, (1355) YB Hil 29 Edw III, f 5b–6a, pl [16], where the plaintiff put the worker in prison until he swore to stay and work for him. The writ concerned the fact that the worker had nonetheless left to serve another, allegedly on the basis of an earlier contract. See also (1373) Mich 47 Edw III, f 18b–19a, pl 38 which was brought as a writ of false imprisonment in the King's Bench and argued on the basis of having 'proper land' under the legislation.
[117] Bailey (2021) (n 5) 209.
[118] ibid.
[119] Simpson (n 10) 23 described service contracts containing implied covenants 'by very right' in the 15th century. The practice of using standardised contract forms may have been familiar from merchant practice, for instance in relation to the development of insurance contracts and the form of bonds: William Mitchell, *An Essay on the History of the Law Merchant* (Cambridge, Cambridge University Press, 1904), which facilitated certainty and speedy dispute resolution: Richard A Epstein, 'Reflections on the Historical Origins and Economic Structure of the Law Merchant' (2004) 5 *Chicago Journal of International Law* 1, 7–14.

agricultural labourer were rephrased to resemble a modern standard form contract, it would look something like that set out in Figure 8.1:

Figure 8.1 A Model Fourteenth-Century Labour Contract

1. DURATION

For a period of not less than one year, [LABOURER] will work for [EMPLOYER] as a [PLOUGHMAN] and not demand or take liveries and wages above those prevailing in the period 1342–46.

2. PAYMENT

[LABOURER] shall be paid [AGREED SUM] in return for their service.

- *a. If liveries and wages for this labour had been customarily paid in kind, that payment may be converted into money value or taken in kind at the discretion of [EMPLOYER].*
- *b. If [AGREED SUM] exceeds the amounts in Clause 3 below in respect of Harvest Activities, Clause 3 is to be preferred.*

3. HARVEST ACTIVITIES

'Harvest Activities' include the following tasks, for which payment is capped as follows:

- *a. Sarcling and Hay-making for not more than 1 penny a day;*
- *b. Mowing meadows for not more than 5 pence a day, or 5 pence an acre, whichever is lower;*
- *c. Reaping corn*
    - *i. In the first week of August, not more than 2 pence a day;*

ii. In the other weeks of August, not more than 3 pence a day;

iii. Where clauses (i) and (ii) above apply only if no Local Custom provides for a lower rate without provision of Meat or Drink or other provision, in which case the Local Custom is to prevail.

d. Threshing

i. Wheat or rye for not more than 2 pence a day;

ii. Barley, beans, peas, and/or oats for not more than 1 penny a day;

iii. Where clauses (i) and (ii) above apply only if no Local Custom provides for payment in kind, in which case the Local Custom is to prevail up to a maximum value of that custom in the period 1342-6.

4. FORMALITIES

The Parties hereby certify this contract was concluded openly in a Merchant Town, [LABOURER] having presented their Instruments in a common place.

5. ENFORCEMENT

The Parties hereby agree that where [LABOURER] performs the Harvest Activities specified in Clause 2(d) above, [LABOURER] will appear twice per Calendar Year to swear before the Lords, Stewards, Bailiffs, and Constables of the neighbourhood in which this contract was concluded that:

a. they have complied with Terms; and

b. they have not travelled out of the neighbourhood in which they reside in winter to undertake Harvest Activities, unless

i. no opportunity to engage in Harvest Activities was available; or

ii. the Harvest Activities or other subject-matter of this contract are to take place in Special Economic Areas where that term describes the Counties of Stafford; Lancaster; Derby; the people of Craven; the Marches of Wales; the Marches of Scotland and other Places as shall be specified from time to time.

c. where Travel has occurred in accordance with Clause 4(b) above, they shall safely return to their neighbourhood of origin.

6. BREACH OF CONTRACT

The penalty for breach of Clause 4 above by [LABOURER] shall be:

a. three days imprisonment in the stocks of the local Lord, Steward, Bailiff or Constable; or

b. imprisonment in gaol pending adjudication by the Court,

in accordance with The Statute of Labourers 1351.

Many of the cases described in the Year Books look like covenant actions, notwithstanding a lack of specialty, insofar that they rely on precise rules from the legislation and specify exactly which clause was breached. Where the traditional historiography holds that the labour legislation helped to show common lawyers that it was possible to enforce contracts without specialty,[120] this is a slightly different point demonstrating how it succeeded in doing so. The labour actions could be treated as analogous to covenant without the need for specialty precisely because the legislation provided the certainty as to terms which was necessary in principle.

Plaintiffs and defendants in the Common Pleas clearly had a detailed understanding of those provisions: disputes might concern length of service, the legal capacity of the alleged servant (due to age or marriage),[121] and a lack of reciprocity (what might now be called consideration) in the form of unpaid wages or benefits. The cases concerning age suggest a process of working out how young was too young for contractual capacity: in a 1355 case, it was argued a two-year-old girl could have been bound to a covenant to serve, which Willoughby JCP did not find convincing in a context where her parents were accused of taking her out of service seven years later.[122] In 1364, a case concerning an alleged covenant with an eight-year-old boy was more confused on the subject of age: it was argued there was no covenant, but there was still service, and it seems the child was not imprisoned despite being outlawed, perhaps because of their age.[123] By 1367, the law seems more settled: Fyncheden JCP was confident that a five-year-old could not be bound.[124] Wychyngham JCP put the more philosophical point that the common law would not say a girl was of age until she was 21 years old, but clearly she could serve before then, so what age would be suitable for making covenants? Any answer given by the defendant or judges is not recorded. A case in 1388 was supposedly at common law and not under the labour legislation because the alleged servant was four years old and could not make a covenant to serve.[125] By 1389, Thirning JCP was positively bored by the question of age.[126]

However, the labour legislation concerned informal agreements, and so it was enforced using actions in debt rather than the writ of covenant. This seems odd at first: damages were a sum certain, fixed by reference to customary wage values before the Black Death, and this kind of agreement would have naturally fallen

[120] Sir John Baker, *An Introduction to English Legal History*, 5th edn (Oxford, Oxford University Press, 2019) 354.

[121] See (1385) Hil 8 Ric II, f Ames 196, pl 9 regarding a husband's liability for a wife's departure from service, but not vice versa; (1387) Hil 10 Ric II, f Ames 288, pl 5 where a husband could take a wife out of service in response to an employer beating her; and n 126 below.

[122] (1355) YB Pasch 29 Edw III, f 27a–27b, pl [29]. The possibility and consequence of a femme covert retaining a servant was also discussed. The same issue arose again in (1389) Hil 12 Ric II, f Ames 106–107, pl 4, where servants hired by a wife before her marriage were discharged by her death, so the husband could not bring a writ under the labour legislation.

[123] (1364) Hil 38 Edw III, f 5b, pl [18].

[124] (1367) Mich 41 Edw III, f 17a, pl 1.

[125] (1388) Trin 12 Ric II, f Ames 14–16, pl 8.

[126] (1389) Hil 12 Ric II, f Ames 108–110, pl 5. The alleged servant was 12 years old.

into the covenant action and required specialty. But the legislation needed to be widely effective if it was to have any impact on the labour market, and formalities rules would have impeded that. Ibbetson argues that the use of the writ of debt in contractual contexts did not seriously challenge prevailing common law conceptual structures, but also notes that there was an accepted fragmentation of contractual remedies at the time.[127] He describes actions under the labour legislation as trespassory (ie an action for a wrong), but notes they were sometimes referred to as an action in covenant (ie an action based on a promise): for instance in a case of 1371 where the form was the statutory trespass action, but it was described in the Year Book as 'a writ of covenant upon the Statute of Labourers', and as a 'covenant without specialty' by Wychyngham JCP.[128] Simpson similarly noted that although it was necessary to avoid the term 'covenant' in the writ and count to avoid the specialty rule, lawyers were happy to use the term in argument once they were in court.[129] The term 'covenant' was routine in quarter sessions and local manorial courts, where specialty was not a problem.[130] For Arnold, the reference to covenants rather than trespass in some of the Year Book actions signified that covenant was made moribund by the specialty rule – but this appears to confuse the ordinary word 'covenant' with the technical action of covenant.[131] By 1372, a Year Book writer could express astonishment that a dispute over service under the labour legislation did not address the covenant, ie the agreement, between the parties: 'which was a wonder' (*quod mirum fuit*).[132] However, it remains true that the form of action was debt and not covenant, however the substance was conceived.

Discussions about the appropriate county for a writ in two Year Book cases from 1367 are interesting on this point.[133] In the first case, the plaintiff alleged that a covenant for service had been made in London, but the defendant left for St Albans within the term.[134] When the defendant challenged the location, Fyncheden JCP was relaxed: he thought the plaintiff could bring the writ in either county, and had brought it where he said he retained the servant. The defendant argued, however, that since the complaint was regarding departure, it should be tried in the place the defendant had gone. Thorpe CJCP pointed out that the complaint could have just as well been that the defendant had been retained, and it was held that the writ was good. This could be reframed in somewhat anachronistic terms as a debate over whether the action was to be brought where the

[127] Ibbetson (n 11) 38. It was the influence of continental thinking and natural law theory which eventually led English writers to attempt systematisation in the eighteenth century, for instance in the work of Geoffrey Gilbert: Michael Lobban (ed), *Jeffrey Gilbert on Property and Contract* (2017) 134 SS *cliii*.

[128] *Mussenden* v *Thomas* (1371) Mich 45 Edw III, f 15a, pl 15; CP 40/443, m. 371; Ibbetson (n 11) 38. Reference to 'covenant' seems to be a particular trend in the Year Book cases of the 1370s.

[129] Simpson (n 10) 209.

[130] Putnam (1908) (n 5) 162–63.

[131] Arnold (1976) (n 13) 323.

[132] (1372) Hil 46 Edw III, f 4b, pl 10.

[133] I am grateful to Professor Sir John Baker for discussion relating to these cases.

[134] (1367) Hil 41 Edw III, f 49b (40 Edw III), pl 2.

agreement was made (in contract), or where it was broken (in tort/trespass). The judges' comments suggest it was not particularly significant to them.

However, in another Year Book entry for the same year,[135] a different conclusion emphasised formality in covenant actions.[136] In the latter, the emphasis was that if the action was brought where the covenant was made, it required specialty: ie the action on the promise required the formalities associated with covenant. If the action was brought where the departure occurred, ie the statutory action in trespass, those formalities were not required. If there had been specialty, the writ of covenant would have allowed for an action in either location. Cavendish Sjt's remark is particularly helpful here in demonstrating the relationship between promise and trespass: 'The covenant is triable in this case as well as in a writ of Covenant, because if the defendant had not made any covenant with the plaintiff, then he did not commit any tort.'[137] Whilst the form of action was trespass/tort, the reason there was a legal remedy was because of a promise.

Baker and Milsom note this case as demonstrating that a purely executory breach of covenant was actionable using trespass under the labour legislation, where it would otherwise have required specialty.[138] This line of thought seems to have been a very recent development at the time, however: a new discussion prompted by the statutory action. In 1373, the principle was doubted by a serjeant in their argument in relation to a case where there was an agreement to serve, but no service had been done, leading to Fyncheden CJCP to confirm it:[139] at common law before the labour legislation, there would have been a trespass writ where a servant who was actually in service was taken away by another employer. However, after the legislation, an action was available where a servant had only agreed to serve and never actually performed anything (for what would come to be called 'nonfeasance'). Availability of an action under the labour legislation also did not preclude other common law actions, such as trespass vi et armis.[140]

Enforcement remained uneven in practice: employers could be punished, but rarely were in the quarter sessions – only the most egregious tempting away of labour was likely to attract attention, and the wealthier employer-landlords were particularly immune.[141] The statute was not, after all, designed primarily to control employer behaviour: as Fyncheden JCP noted in 1366, it was 'made to the

[135] This may have been the same case, although one entry says the departure was in Hertfordshire, the other that the covenant was.
[136] (1367) Mich 41 Edw III, f 20a, pl 4.
[137] Note the difference between 'the covenant here' – ie the promise or agreement in the ordinary sense of the word, and 'the writ of Covenant' – ie the specific species of promise which fell under the common law writ requiring specialty.
[138] Baker and Milsom (n 59) 23, fn 6.
[139] (1373) Mich 47 Edw III, f 14a, pl 15. This case is also noted in Baker and Milsom, ibid.
[140] Ibbetson (n 11) 46; Arnold (1984) (n 39)100 SS xliv. There was debate on this point in 1365, where Mowbray JCP said that although there was an action under the labour legislation, it did not revoke other applicable common law actions: (1365) Mich 39 Edw III, f 37b, pl [50].
[141] Bailey (2021) (n 5) 214–15.

advantage of lords, that they would not have a lack of servants'.[142] Being able to sue another employer was nonetheless useful where the problem was eloigning, and actions of that sort were more common in the Common Pleas and Kings Bench.[143] In these cases, Seabourne notes the potential culpability of both sides sheds light on contemporary views: these agreements were treated as voluntary and bilateral, such that both parties could and should be punished.[144] However, this does not imply freedom of contract and relative bargaining power was not equal. It was also held in 1367 that there was no action against a rival employer if the action against the servant themselves was not good: it was an accessory liability where the servant was the one primarily in the wrong.[145]

Favouring employers might not have been only due to socio-economic bargaining power. In the context of usury and high prices for victuals, Seabourne has shown that people agreeing to higher prices were seen as victims, not complicit in the act. If this was the perception, punishing the person forced to pay more due to the malice or covetousness of the labourer would not make sense. The available actions were not, therefore, focused on compensation – although this was offered as an incidental incentive to bring actions – but on punishing the wrongdoer: hence, anybody could begin the action under the Ordinance.[146]

Whilst simple presentments of labourers for paying high wages or charging high prices were most common before Justices of Labourers and Justices of the Peace,[147] in the Common Pleas and Kings Bench, the terms of the agreement were closely analysed.[148] For instance, in a Year Book case from 1354, an employer made the common double complaint that two servants had left within the term, and another employer had wrongfully hired them.[149] One of the workers claimed the plaintiff had only hired him for the day, not the full year the legislation required. The other worker claimed he had been hired on the basis of a certain salary and allowance of grain and barley, leaving when the latter was not provided. Both workers were, therefore, relying on the specific terms of the agreement, as provided by the legislation, to dispute the plaintiff's claims.

Perhaps more interestingly, the second worker in the 1354 case resisted the claim under the statute on the basis that the contract of service contained mutual obligations, and the failure on the part of the employer to uphold their side of the contract entitled him to leave: in modern terms, a repudiatory breach by the employer entitled the worker to terminate the contract. This argument does not appear often in the fourteenth-century Year Book cases, but in 1389 it gave rise

[142] (1366) Mich 40 Edw III, f 39a–39b, pl 16.
[143] Putnam (1908) (n 5) 182.
[144] Seabourne (n 22) 39.
[145] (1367) Mich 41 Edw III, f 17a, pl 1.
[146] Seabourne (n 22) 104.
[147] Putnam (1908) (n 5) 77.
[148] ibid 174–176. Confirmed more recently by Mark Bailey's work on the subject: Bailey (2024) (n 76).
[149] (1354) YB Mich 28 Edw III, f 21b, pl 18.

to a statement of principle.[150] An employer had failed to pay the servant's salary as a saddler and so the servant departed. Brynchesley Sjt argued the salary had been a condition of the agreement: 'with a covenant … and that the moment our salary fell into arrears it should be lawful for us to depart'. However, it was held that the principle was actually a wider one: a servant could depart 'with reasonable cause' in circumstances like this, even if the covenant did not specify a condition to that effect.[151] The reciprocity developed in respect of the procedure available was reflected in new ideas about reciprocal obligations within the substance of the agreement: an idea closer to modern contract law than medieval covenant.

The idea had emerged in the 1330s that a debt action ought to be possible to obtain payment in respect of a performance had already been entered into: there would be no concern about one-sided enforcement in such cases because the party without an action had already received what they bargained for.[152] On the same logic, once the Ordinance gave employers an action for departure, it followed that the worker ought to have an action, too.[153] It was also rules concerning debt actions that led to exceptions excluding wager of law and prioritising jury trial in master and servant disputes, initially based on the compulsory service clause but soon extended to all agricultural workers.[154] Whilst these were incidental consequences from the attempt to control labour in response to the Black Death, they represented new ways of thinking about agreements between private parties developed in response to the crisis. By 1400, the assumpsit case of *Wootton* v *Brygeslay*[155] was able to consider analogous actions in covenant and the Statute of Labourers to argue that assumpsit lay for nonfeasance, as Baker noted. The availability of an action without specialty for this kind of scenario under the specialist area of the Statute of Labourers seems to have opened the minds of the lawyers and courts to the possibility of it working elsewhere.

IV. Conclusion

At a time when 'contract' was yet to develop as a comprehensive category of common law in the modern sense, and trespass was the primary action for the enforcement of obligations, the fourteenth century labour legislation introduced a substantively contractual action for specific scenarios which was relatively easy to act upon. It did so by providing a clear and specific scope for that agreement,

[150] (1389) Mich 13 Ric II, f Ames 31–32, pl 1; Plucknett, *13 Richard II* (n 57) 31–32.

[151] See also *Illard de Ousefleet v Roger Beauchamp* (1365) Mich CP 40/421, m428d, where a servant left one employer for another after being beaten and unpaid.

[152] Simpson (n 10) 148–49.

[153] The reciprocal nature of the action here was not entirely settled until the fifteenth century: (1460) Hil 38 Hen VI, f 22a–22b, pl 4, although it was suggested earlier: (1366) Pasch 40 Edw III, f 24b–25a, pl 27; Simpson (n 10) 149.

[154] Simpson (n 10) 140–42.

[155] (1400) B&M 422; YB Mich 2 Hen IV, f 3v, pl 9.

and special enforcement mechanisms which were refined over time. The primary constraint on the action of covenant – the need for certainty in the form of a written document – was overcome by providing certainty through legislative provisions. The impetus for making this exception was provided by the mortality of the Black Death, the existing inflationary pressures which were exacerbated by the plague, and the moral and social understanding of labour at the time.

Whilst the legislation was based on existing social norms, it went well beyond existing practices and prompted a very different approach to oral contracts and regulation of labour than that which had hitherto existed in the common law. This was not an adaptation of existing local custom, but a tailored and novel regime which adapted various elements of the existing common law and its administrative structures. It likely borrowed ideas from the custom of London, and utilised existing tax collection machinery alongside moral ideas about necessity and the common good. It also cut across the developed legal theory of villeinage in order to prioritise economic regulation. It would be anachronistic to see the emphasis on mutuality in both procedure and substance which emerged as an incidental effect of the labour legislation as a precursor of the modern law of contract. However, the labour legislation suggested new opportunities, and new ways of thinking, opening routes of argument which may have helped facilitate the rise of the action of assumpsit. It was an interesting and long-lasting example of thinking differently within the prevailing structure of the common law, prompted by a legal response to an infectious disease.

9

Property Disputes about Leper Houses, Pesthouses and Fever Hospitals

JONATHAN GARTON AND CHARLES MITCHELL*

I. Introduction

This chapter concerns institutions which housed the infectious sick. More particularly, it concerns disputes about control of these institutions and the property dedicated to funding their activities, and some of the effects which resolution of these disputes had on the development of English property law. The institutions were not all created for the same purposes. Medieval leper houses performed a spiritual function and at least initially there were no bars against social interaction between the lepers and the rest of society. Early modern pesthouses, in contrast, were designed to isolate the sick, as were eighteenth- and nineteenth-century fever hospitals, which also provided care and, once medical advances had made this possible, treatment to effect a cure. The institutions had some common features, however: their activities took place inside physical structures built on land and they were often intended to last for a long time. As a practical matter, property rights in the land were therefore needed, and additional property was often needed to provide an income to pay for the institutions' activities. Some recurring questions therefore arose: for what length of time could property be dedicated to the pursuit of an institution's purposes; who was responsible for ensuring that these were carried out; and what should happen if the property were misapplied, or if the purposes became redundant, or if pursuit of the purposes compromised other people's enjoyment of their own property?

In Part II we examine disputes about patronage and other property rights relating to leper houses, in Part III we consider the cy-près application of funds held on charitable trusts for pesthouses, and in Part IV we discuss nuisance actions triggered by the building of fever hospitals. In Part V we make some concluding observations.

* We thank Aruna Nair and Ian Williams for their comments on a draft of this chapter.

II. Disputes about Leper Houses

A. Leper Houses

In medieval times, many leper houses were funded by Church bodies and/or lay donors.[1] This began in the late 1000s and reached its peak in the late 1200s and early 1300s, when over 300 *leprosaria* are thought to have existed.[2] Leper houses were created for spiritual reasons and not out of public health concerns. The image of the leper as a marginal figure, shunned by society, is now generally accepted to be a misconception dating from the nineteenth century,[3] and the original purpose of leper houses was not physical isolation but spiritual intercession.[4] Lepers were believed to have a special relationship with God, for, while leprosy was associated with sin, the earthly suffering of lepers was thought to cleanse their souls and enable them to ascend directly to Heaven on death.[5] In return for the gifts of founders and later donors, the lepers in *leprosaria* were expected to lead lives of devotion and to pray for their benefactors' souls.[6] Leper houses were run on a quasi-monastic basis[7] and headed by an ordained master 'of sufficient learning and character'.[8] Mastership was a lifetime appointment made by a bishop upon receiving a suitable candidate presented by the patron of the leper house.

[1] Martin Huggon, *The Archaeology of the Medieval Hospitals of England and Wales, 1066-1546* (Sheffield University PhD thesis, 2018), esp pp 44–51, available at www.rb.gy/61c1dv.

[2] Sheila Sweetinburgh, *The Role of the Hospital in Medieval England* (Dublin, Four Courts Press, 2004) 22.

[3] The shift in the historiography of leprosy was largely a result of the work of Touati and Rawcliffe: François-Oliver Touati, *Maladie et société au Moyen âge: la lèpre, les lépreux et les léproseries dans la province ecclésiastique de Sens jusqu'au milieu du XIVe siècle* (Brussels, De Broeck, 1998); Carole Rawcliffe, *Leprosy in Medieval England* (Woodbridge, Boydell, 2006) esp ch 1; Carole Rawcliffe, 'Creating the Medieval Leper: Myths of Segregation in the Middle Ages' in Peregrine Horden (ed), *Freedom of Movement in the Middle Ages: Proceedings of the 2003 Harlaxton Symposium* (Donington, Shaun Tyas, 2007). See also Timothy S Miller and John W Nesbitt, *Walking Corpses: Leprosy in Byzantium and the Medieval West* (Ithaca, NY, Cornell University Press, 2014) 3–4; Alexandra Houston, '"Seiknes Incurabill": The Evolution of Literary Representations of Leprosy in Medieval and Early Modern English Narratives' (2016) 7 *Chicago Journal of History* 30. The myth of the leper as outcast still persists, however: see, eg, Robert I Moore, *The Formation of a Persecuting Society: Authority and Deviance in Western Europe, 950-1250*, 2nd edn (Malden, MA, Blackwell, 2008) 10–11.

[4] The brethren were kept apart from wider society to no greater extent than was needed for them to live a life of piety: they received visitors, were free to leave their leper house to beg for alms, and often paid for the privilege of joining: Rawcliffe (2006) (n 3) 28, 256, 258, 264, 291; and many other scholars.

[5] Lily Stewart, 'Leprosy, Chastity and Desire in Medieval Hagiography' (2021) 27 *Magistra* 49; Rawcliffe (2006) (n 3) ch 2; Simon Roffey and Phil Marter, 'Treating Leprosy: St Mary Magdalen, Winchester' (2012) 267 *Current Archaeology* 12.

[6] Rawcliffe (2006) (n 3) 225.

[7] ibid ch 7; Carole Rawcliffe, '"A Mighty Force in the Ranks of Christ's Army": Intercession and Integration in the Medieval English Leper Hospital' in Elma Brenner and François-Oliver Touati (eds), *Leprosy and Identity in the Middle Ages* (Manchester, Manchester University Press, 2021).

[8] 3 Conc Lat, c 3 (1179), COD 212 = X 1.6.7. See Joshua C Tate, *Power and Justice in Medieval England: The Law of Patronage and the Royal Courts* (New Haven, CT, Yale University Press, 2022) 16.

In the 1300s, particularly after the Black Death, fears of leprosy infection grew.[9] This is illustrated by the case of St Giles's Hospital, Holborn, where in 1354 the master was accused of evicting the lepers and replacing them with non-lepers; this was problematic not only because it was 'contrary to the will' of the founders but also because it created 'the great danger of healthy persons intermingling with said lepers'.[10] Despite increasing concerns of this kind,[11] however, leper houses remained primarily religious institutions. As late as 1500, Dame Joan Frowyk made a bequest to the lepers of St Giles's, 'for to pray for my soul',[12] although the incidence of leprosy had much diminished by then,[13] and most leper houses had either fallen derelict or been put to other uses.[14]

B. Patronage

For leper houses, as for other medieval Church institutions, the highest authority was the patron. The patron was the holder of the advowson – the right to present an individual for appointment to the mastership, or benefice – and could be an individual or another institution.[15] The patron would usually be one of the founders of the leper house,[16] or someone who acquired patronage from him through inheritance or *inter vivos* transfer (though the Crown also acquired many advowsons through a combination of escheat and confiscation).[17]

The advowson was particularly susceptible to ownership disputes owing to its nature as an incorporeal hereditament, ie a right which could be owned, assigned and inherited, but which did not entail possession or occupation of a physical thing or space.[18] Moreover, patronage was an asset that came with many benefits.

[9] Rawcliffe (2006) (n 3) 274; Rotha Mary Clay, *The Mediaeval Hospitals of England* (first published 1909; reprinted: Abingdon, Routledge, 2006) 53–56.

[10] *Cal Let Bk G*, fol xxiv. See also the 1346 statutes of the Hospital at Ilford, noted below in the text to n 15, which warned of the dangers of lepers and non-lepers mixing within the leper house: Dugdale, *Mon*, vol vii, 629.

[11] eg the 1344 'Customs of Bristol' ordained that if a leper came within the city gates he would be stripped naked and ejected, and his clothes burned: reproduced in Joshua Toulmin Smith, *English Gilds* (Oxford, Oxford University Press, 1870) 241; also the 1346 Proclamation of Edward III expelling lepers from the City of London: *Cal Let Bk F*, fol cxvi.

[12] TNA PROB 11/12/74. Wife of Sir Thomas Frowyk, Chief Justice of the Common Pleas.

[13] Huggon (n 1) 182.

[14] See further n 83 below.

[15] It could also be shared between individuals, as in the case of St Lawrence's Hospital, Nantwich, the advowson to which was held in unequal shares by the Audley and the Lovell families: *VCH Cheshire*, vol iii, 186; see also Sweetinburgh (n 2) 37.

[16] Though it was sometimes unclear who the founder of a leper house was, as 'a variety of individuals or groups might be implicated' in its creation, such as the donor of the land upon which it was built, other original benefactors, and the first master: Sweetinburgh (n 2) 35.

[17] Peter M Smith, 'The Advowson: The History and Development of a Most Peculiar Property' (2000) 5 *Ecclesiastical Law Journal* 320, 327–28.

[18] As noted in William Blackstone, *Commentaries on the Laws of England* (first published 1765–69; reprinted: Chicago, IL, University of Chicago Press, 1979) vol 2, 21–22.

The lepers' intercessory prayers would bring down God's grace upon the patron and his ancestors. There were also temporal rewards: most importantly, patrons could use the advowson to their political advantage by conferring the sinecure of a mastership on a retainer or associate. An egregious example occurred in 1292 following a dispute between Edward I and the Bishop of Carlisle over the patronage of St Nicholas's Hospital, Carlisle, which we discuss below. The matter went before the assizes and the judge, the future Lord Chief Justice Hugh de Cressingham, confirmed that the patronage lay with the Crown. When the incumbent master of the hospital, who had been appointed by the bishop, resigned after the verdict, Edward replaced him with de Cressingham himself.[19]

Patrons could also control admissions for the benefit of their supporters, and it was common for monastic patrons in particular to use their authority to fill leper houses with their own ailing brethren.[20] In some cases this went beyond mere influence, and the right to choose the lepers was made a condition of benefaction: for example, in 1278 Ralph Perot, a descendant of one of the founders of St Julian's Hospital, St Albans, brought an action against the master for refusing to recognise his 'perpetual right to place a leper in the hospital';[21] the dispute was settled out of court. Nearly 70 years later, a similar right was imposed by the patron of the hospital, the Abbot of St Albans, following a 1344 visitation when a new constitution provided that the lepers were all to be admitted by him, with preference to be given 'to the monks of St Albans or people born within the abbey's jurisdiction'.[22] Patrons of the larger *leprosaria* could also expect to receive hospitality for themselves and their visitors.[23] This could crystallise into a corrody, which gave its holder an enforceable right to maintenance and accommodation within the leper house on a permanent basis.[24]

There were limits, however. On paper, the canon law rules on simony prohibited patrons from directly benefiting financially from the institution's assets,[25] though the reality may have been different. In 1391 a dispute arose over the advowson of St Giles-in-the-Fields Hospital, Holborn, which was granted by Richard II to the Abbot of St Mary Graces, Tower Hill (an institution founded by his grandfather), thus usurping the rights of the previous patron, the Master of Burton Lazars Hospital. In the proceedings that ensued, the Master alleged that the Abbot had used his position to appropriate 'live stock, grain, carts, furniture, books, vestments, and ecclesiastical ornaments worth more than £1,000'.[26] In

[19] *VCH Cumberland*, vol 2, 199–203.

[20] Sweetinburgh (n 2) 38–39.

[21] *VCH Hertfordshire*, vol 4, 464–67.

[22] ibid. See also the Crown's patronage of St Giles's Hospital, Chester, which entitled the monarch to nominate all the brethren: *VCH Cheshire*, vol 3, 178–80.

[23] See Sweetinburgh (n 2) 37; Rawcliffe (2006) (n 3) 225.

[24] Rawcliffe (2006) (n 3) 297–98. See, generally, Richard Harper, 'A Note on Corrodies in the Fourteenth Century' (1983) 15 *Albion* 95.

[25] 2 Conc Lat, c 1–2 (1139), COD 197. See Tate (n 8) 112.

[26] *VCH Middlesex*, vol 1, 204–12.

another example, an earlier Abbot of St Albans was accused, during a visitation of St Julian's at some time during the reign of Edward II, of confiscating the personal assets of two of the brethren worth £60.[27]

The relationship between the patron and the bishop could also be a source of contention. Originally patrons were able to install masters directly, but by the late 1100s this was thought inappropriate by the ecclesiastical courts as it risked laymen being appointed to what was a spiritual office.[28] At least from the time of Bracton, the common law followed suit, and individuals were presented to the bishop by the holder of the advowson, who was alone responsible for their admission and institution if they were appropriately qualified: '[A] layman presents to the vacant church, as constructed of timber and stone, that his presentee rule it, and the bishop gives it, that is, admits the presentee to rule and institutes him.'[29]

However, the law continued to distinguish between 'presentative' and 'donative' advowsons, the latter enabling the holder to put his candidate into office by his gift alone, without any episcopal approval.[30] Following a 1564 dispute involving St Mary Magdalene's Hospital, Newcastle, the Bishop of Durham was prevented from admitting one Edmund Wiseman to the benefice upon presentation by Elizabeth I to the bishop, not only because the true patrons were found to be the mayor and alderman of the city, rather than the crown, but also because the leper hospital 'was a donative and not a benefice inductible by any bishop'.[31] The bishop's jurisdiction was also ousted if the leper house was established by the crown as a royal free chapel, in which case the king, or exceptionally a layman,[32] could appoint the master directly.[33] Attempts to ring-fence free chapels in general from papal authority were the cause of many disputes in the 1200s and 1300s, as church and state jostled to consolidate and expand their authority, and sought to gain the perquisites that came with patronage.[34]

This is nicely illustrated in the context of leper houses by the cases of St Giles-in-the-Fields Hospital, Holborn, and St Nicholas's Hospital, Carlisle. St Giles's was founded by Matilda in the early 1100s and confirmed as a royal free

[27] *VCH Hertfordshire*, vol 4, 464–67.

[28] Council of Winchester 1072, c 5; Council of Westminster 1125, c 4; Council of Westminster 1127, c 10; Council of Westminster 1138, c 5. See JW Gray, 'The "Ius Praesentandi" in England from the Constitutions of Clarendon to Bracton' (1952) 67 *English Historical Review* 481.

[29] Bracton, *Laws and Customs*, 2.160.

[30] Robert Phillimore, *The Ecclesiastical Law of the Church of England*, 2nd edn (London, Sweet and Maxwell, 1895) 252–53.

[31] Eneas Mackenzie, *A Descriptive and Historical Account of Newcastle-Upon-Tyne including the Borough of Gateshead* (Newcastle-upon-Tyne, Mackenzie and Dent, 1827) 145–49.

[32] Elizabeth Gemmill, *The Nobility and Ecclesiastical Patronage in Thirteenth-Century England* (Woodbridge, Boydell Press, 2013) 20.

[33] See generally William R Jones, 'Patronage and Administration: The King's Free Chapels in Medieval England' (1969) 9 *Journal of British Studies* 1; Jeffrey H Denton, *The English Royal Free Chapels 1100–1300: A Constitutional Study* (Manchester, Manchester University Press, 1970).

[34] The Free Chapel of St Mary Magdalene, Cambridge, for example, was granted its free status, albeit after it had ceased to house lepers, probably due to the value of its charter to hold the Stourbridge Fair, at one time the largest in Europe.

chapel by Henry II.[35] Its special status appears to have been accepted by the Church during the Papal Interdict of 1208, when Innocent III granted letters of protection to the lepers requiring that their land and rents 'be duly observed under pain of excommunication'.[36] As a result they were exempted from the enforced closure of English churches prompted by John's refusal to accept the authority of a new Archbishop of Canterbury who had been consecrated against the king's wishes.[37] In 1293, an inquisition was held after the Bishop of London attempted to carry out a visitation in response to concerns over the hospital's administration raised by one of the brethren, Richard de Kynbele, despite the objections of the warden and all but one of the other brethren and sisters.[38] The inquisition heard that this was not the first time, as a previous bishop had apparently made a successful visitation sometime during Henry II's reign in response to the 'weakness and impotence' of the warden. Both instances were declared by the jury to have been cases of visitation 'by usurpation … and not of right', and the status of the leper house as a royal free chapel was confirmed.[39] Nor was this the end of the matter. Ten years later, after the king had transferred control of St Giles's to Burton Lazars Hospital,[40] a commission of oyer and terminer was granted to the master after the Archbishop of Canterbury (in the absence of an incumbent Bishop of London) entered the leper house after 'malefactors broke the locks' and carried out a visitation which resulted in him misappropriating items of property, including 'papal letters, charters, writings and muniments, as well privileges as others touching the rights and possessions of the hospital'.[41]

A similar story may have unfolded in Carlisle, although less is known about this. There is no surviving evidence to confirm that St Nicholas's Hospital was founded as a free chapel; all we know is that a 1341 visitation accepted that it had been established 'long before time of memory, by some king of England' to support 13 lepers,[42] and not every church or hospital established by the Crown enjoyed free status. In 1292, Edward I disputed the Bishop of Carlisle's admission of a master presented to him by the brethren, claiming not only that the brethren themselves did not hold the advowson but also that the bishop had no jurisdiction over the hospital 'for any purpose whatsoever'.[43] The matter went before the assizes and the judge confirmed that the patronage lay with the crown, but it is unclear from the records whether this was on the basis of a presentative or donative advowson or because the hospital was a free chapel. The latter seems more likely, as a later

[35] *VCH Middlesex*, vol 2, 204–12.

[36] *Cal Let Bk G*, fol xxv.

[37] Christopher Cheney, 'King John and the Papal Interdict' (1948) 31 *Bulletin of the John Rylands Library* 295.

[38] *Cal Pat*, 1388–92, 458. The inquisition, though held in 1293, was not entered in the patent rolls until the time of Richard II.

[39] ibid.

[40] *Cal Pat*, 1292–1301, 404.

[41] *Cal Pat*, 1302–1307, m 28d.

[42] *Cal Pat*, 1340-1343, m 48, m 49.

[43] *VCH Cumberland*, vol 2, 199–203.

attempt by the bishop to carry out a visitation at some point in the first half of the fourteenth century, was successfully blocked by the Crown as 'irregular or inconvenient in institutions of royal foundation or patronage'.[44] Although the bishop would later act as visitor on at least two occasions, when concerns were raised over the management of the leper house's assets in 1340 and 1380, these were by royal commission and not by exercise of the bishop's independent authority.[45]

Disputes of this kind show that patronage was thought to be a sufficiently valuable commodity in high medieval society to merit protection in the royal courts. The law recognised that patrons treated the right of presentation not merely as a right personal to themselves but as a right capable of being transferred to others.[46] So the advowson came to acquire proprietary status. The extension of the royal courts' jurisdiction over patronage disputes also played a part in the history of conflict between Crown and Church generated when Henry II sought to consolidate and extend his authority, and rein in the jurisdiction of the ecclesiastical courts, after the chaotic reign of his predecessor, Stephen. In the Constitutions of Clarendon, Henry II decreed that all such disputes, whether they arose between laymen or clerics, should be 'treated and terminated in the court of the lord king' rather than the ecclesiastical court.[47] To achieve this, Chancery developed the writ of right of advowson, which enabled litigants to initiate actions for the recovery of lost title, and various writs preventing the matter from being disputed in the ecclesiastical courts[48] – although there is evidence that the ecclesiastical courts continued to hear patronage disputes over the following century, if not later still.[49] However, the writ of right of advowson was procedurally cumbersome, causing lengthy delays,[50] and this became a particular issue in 1179 when, prompted by Pope Innocent III's concerns over the number of vacant benefices, the Third Lateran Council ruled that if an ecclesiastical office remained vacant after six months it was to be filled by the bishop or, should he delay in appointing someone, by the cathedral chapter.[51] This led to the creation of two additional writs to

[44] ibid.

[45] *Cal Pat*, 1340–43, m 48, m 49; *Cal Pat*, 1377–81, m 20d. As to these visitations, see below text to n 59.

[46] Brian Simpson, *A History of the Land Law*, 2nd edn (Oxford, Clarendon Press, 1986) 104.

[47] Constitutions of Clarendon 1164, cl 1.

[48] *Glanvill*, iv, 13–14. See Norma Adams, 'The Judicial Conflict over Tithes' (1937) 52 *English Historical Review* 205. There was, however, an element of jurisdictional compromise: disputes between two would-be masters, each claiming the benefice from different patrons, were still dealt with by the church, though either patron could obtain a writ to stay the church proceedings until the common law had determined which patron held the advowson: *Glanvill*, iv, 12–13.

[49] Charles Donahue, 'Roman Canon Law in the Medieval English Church: Stubbs vs Maitland Re-Examined after 75 Years in the Light of Some Records from the Church Courts' (1974) 72 *Michigan Law Review* 659; *cf* David K Millon, 'Ecclesiastical Jurisdiction in Medieval England' [1984] *University of Illinois Law Review* 624.

[50] *Glanvil* i, 6, 12, 18, 25–27. See generally Joshua C Tate, 'The Third Lateran Council and the Ius Patronatus in England' in Peter Erdö and Szabolcs Anzelm Szuromi (eds), *Proceedings of the Thirteenth International Congress of Medieval Canon Law: Esztergom, 3-8 August 2008* (Vatican City, Biblioteca Apostolica Vaticana, 2010).

[51] Canon 8.

ensure that vacancies were dealt with by the common law: darrein presentment[52] and *quare impedit*,[53] the latter superseding the former in the 1300s.[54] These writs were based on right rather than possession, and provided a quick but only temporary solution to disputes by permitting whoever had seisin of the advowson at the previous presentation to present to the next vacancy, regardless of who held the actual title to the advowson.

C. Visitorial Powers

Patronage of a leper house meant more than simply holding the advowson. Patrons expected, and were expected by the Church, to maintain a supervisory relationship with the leper house, as with any other hospital or religious institution. In the words of Pope Innocent IV:

> The responsibility of the patron consists of two things, namely, that he be mindful as to the temporalities, lest they be squandered; in spiritualities, that he present such a minister who will be able to serve God fittingly. Now duties come about from the right of patronage, because he [the patron] is bound to defend the church from attack, and to nurture carefulness in respect of [its] ecclesiastical goods, lest they be embezzled.[55]

The supervisory role performed by patrons derived from a mixture of rights, duties and customs which varied from one institution to another,[56] but it was usual for patrons to hold visitations or inquiries if concerns were raised over the administration of *leprosaria*.[57] Unlike disputes about the ownership of patronage rights, disputes about the application of property dedicated to a leper house did not normally trigger a common law response as decisions about this were seen as falling within the purview of the founder and his successors. As Lord Hardwicke LC explained much later in *Green v Rutherforth*:

> The original and nature of visitorial power … is the property of donor, and the power every one has to dispose, direct, and regulate his own property … [T]herefore if [the donor] creates an eleemosynary foundation[,] since a contest might arise about the government of it, the law allows the founder or his heirs, or the person especially appointed by him to be visitor, to determine concerning his own creature. … [T]he nature of this power is *forum domesticum*, the private jurisdiction of the founder.[58]

[52] *Glanvill*, xiii, 18, 20.

[53] *Bracton*, vol 2, 229–30.

[54] Robert C Palmer, *Selling the Church: The English Parish in Law, Commerce, and Religion, 1350–1550* (Chapel Hill, NC, University of North Carolina Press, 2002) 20–22; and generally Joshua C Tate, 'The Origins of *Quare Impedit*' (2004) 25 *Journal of Legal History* 203.

[55] Pope Innocent IV, *Quinque Libros Decretalium Commentaria* (Venice, 1578) fol 181r; translation in Gemmill (n 32) 24.

[56] ibid 25.

[57] Sweetinburgh (n 2) 41.

[58] (1750) 1 Ves Sen 462, 472; 27 ER 1144, 1149. See also *Thomas v University of Bradford* [1987] AC 795, 814–15 (Lord Griffiths).

D. Misapplication of Funds

There were many ways in which the property of a leper house could be diverted away from the purpose laid down by the founder, to correct which visitorial intervention might be required. The most egregious, at least to modern eyes, involved the misappropriation of funds by the master or brethren for their personal use. The evidence suggests that this was not uncommon. Consider, for example, the events which unfolded at St Nicholas's Hospital, Carlisle, after Edward I won his patronage dispute with the bishop.[59] Cressingham's mastership was interrupted by the outbreak of war with Scotland in 1296 and when he died the following year the mastership lay vacant for three years, the leper house was partly destroyed and its assets were greatly diminished.[60] In 1300, Richard de Oriell was given temporary custody and prevented its demise by securing for each of the lepers a yearly sustenance of two skips each of oats, barley and flour; three strikes of wheat, bread and ale; and an allowance of 4 shillings, 'until the house should be relieved'.[61] The house was indeed relieved, although details of its new benefactors do not survive, and it went on to prosper for a quarter-century under the masterships of Henry de Craystok[62] and John de Crossby,[63] the latter rebuilding the *leprosarium*'s chapel (which had been destroyed).[64] In 1327, however, Thomas de Wederhale was appointed by Edward II, the first lay master and the first in a long line who treated the property of the leper house as their own. It was typical for the constitution of a *leprosarium* to provide that its common seal should be kept in the custody not only of the master but of some of the lepers as well, to prevent abuses of power, but Wederhale kept sole custody of the seal, admitted no lepers to the hospital (although it did maintain some who lived outside the grounds), sold corrodies to 'divers men … without the assent of the brethren and sisters because there were no brethren or sisters' and 'retained for himself moneys received for corrodies, making no use of them for the hospital'.[65] His three successors did exactly the same, and the hospital assets were so depleted that in 1336 letters close were sent to the county tax collectors prohibiting them from collecting:

> as the hospital was founded by the king's progenitors, of their alms, and is so slenderly endowed that the goods thereof hardly suffice for the maintenance of the master and brethren and of the poor and infirm who resort there and for other alms to be done according to the ordinance of the king's progenitors, and if the hospital is charged with the aids granted to the king by the community of the realm, it will behove the master and brethren to diminish the said alms.[66]

[59] See above text to n 43 and following.
[60] *Cal Pat*, 1340–43, m 49.
[61] ibid.
[62] *Cal Pat*, 1301–07, m 17.
[63] *Cal Pat*, 1307–13, m 17.
[64] *Cal Close*, 1318–23, m 21.
[65] *Cal Pat*, 1340–43, m 49.
[66] *Cal Close*, 1333–37, m 14.

Under pressure from the bishop, who had unsuccessfully attempted his own visitation but who had lacked authority to intervene, the king appointed the bishop, together with the Prior of Carlisle and a local cleric, to carry out a visitation in 1340. The corrodies were declared void as they had been granted by masters when the common seal had been in their sole custody, contrary to the constitution.[67] The visitors also found that the current master, Thomas de Goldyngton, had left the common seal in the custody of two corrody holders, and they ordered its confiscation and delivery to the prior 'under the seal of the said master, until the king by his council see fit to order otherwise'.[68] Matters apparently did not improve, however: a further visitation was carried out in 1380 in response to 'divers defects in respect of its houses, books, vestments and other ornaments, diminution of its chaplains, alienation and waste of its lands, quarrels among its ministers',[69] though no record of its findings survives.

Similar visitations were undertaken in the 1340s at St Giles's Hospital, Shrewsbury, and at St Laurence's Hospital, Bristol. The former, founded in the mid 1100s, was 'greatly decayed' by the time of a 1348 visitation as masters and brethren alike had 'wasted the goods and alienated the lands',[70] while the latter suffered 'misrule of wardens … and by alienation of its lands and possessions, and numberless grants of corrodies, pensions and rents made by them, and the withdrawal of its good and things' and could no longer afford to maintain the master, brethren and sisters.[71]

E. Inactivity

Patrons were also concerned to protect their spiritual investment, and a common focus of visitations was the failure of the masters and brethren to carry on the intercessory activities which the institutions had been founded to support. This was another of the misdeeds committed by successive masters of St Nicholas's Hospital, Carlisle, where 'divine worship and works of piety were wholly withdrawn',[72] and similar concerns were the prompt for visitations elsewhere.[73] For example, in 1355, Edward III, as patron of St Julian's Hospital, St Albans, ordered a visitation because

> the number of those lepers is greatly diminished for lack of sustenance, and prayers, alms and other works which used to be made for the [the king's] progenitors and others and ought to be made for the king and his heirs have been withdrawn for a long time.[74]

[67] *Cal Pat*, 1340–43, m 49.
[68] ibid.
[69] *Cal Pat*, 1377–81, m 20d.
[70] *Cal Pat*, 1348–50, 177.
[71] *Cal Pat*, 1374–77, 310.
[72] *Cal Pat*, 1340–43, m 49.
[73] See Sweetinburgh (n 2) 43.
[74] *Cal Pat*, 1354–58, 330.

In these cases, the visitation usually resulted in the imposition of a new constitution for the *leprosarium* under which strict rules of conduct for the lepers were laid down to reaffirm their quasi-monastic existence.[75] Failure to comply with these rules could result in expulsion, even in the later years of the leper houses when fear of infection had grown.[76] In the case of St Nicholas's Hospital, the 1340 visitation also ruled that the lepers in receipt of support despite living outside the leper house, being neither 'resident not attendant upon the divine prayers there as required by the rules and constitutions', were to have their allowances suspended until they resumed 'obedience and residence' in the house.[77]

F. Mission Drift

The perpetual nature of charitable institutions means that corruption and incompetence are not the only reasons why property is diverted from the founder's purposes: as society changes, these purposes may cease to be relevant. The leper houses were left behind when leprosy declined significantly in England from the middle of the 1300s. Many *leprosaria* then found themselves with property designated for the upkeep of lepers when few, if any, lepers remained. This was undoubtedly the prompt for some unscrupulous masters to engage in the abuses detailed above, but the more conscientious applied the assets to other charitable endeavours, typically by opening their doors to the non-leprous sick or poor. The extent to which patrons were prepared to tolerate this sort of mission drift varied. In 1354, the master of St Giles's Hospital, Holborn, was brought up for evicting the lepers and replacing them with brothers and sisters 'who were not diseased' from Burton Lazars Hospital, the mastership of which he also held.[78] The Lord Chancellor, as visitor on behalf of Edward III, recognised the problem of a declining leper population, but found another solution closer to the *leprosarium*'s original purpose: he ordered that 14 lepers from the city should be 'for ever maintained' and that if fewer than 14 could be found then the catchment area should be extended to the whole county.[79] He also ruled that if future benefactors supplemented the hospital's assets then the number of lepers should be increased proportionately.[80] In contrast, when the bishop carried out the 1340 visitation of St Nicholas's Hospital, Carlisle, he apparently considered it unremarkable that at some earlier time under a previous master the lepers' places 'were filled by poor impotent folk under the same rules' when 'the greater part of the lepers died',[81] nor

[75] See, eg, the rules of the Hospital of Ilford, drawn up following a visitation by the bishop in 1344: Dugdale, *Mon* vii, 629.

[76] This was the case at Ilford: ibid; also St Julian's Hospital, St Albans: Rawcliffe (2006) (n 3) 264–65.

[77] *Cal Pat*, 1340–43, m 49.

[78] *Cal Let Bk G*, fol xxiv.

[79] ibid.

[80] ibid.

[81] *Cal Pat*, 1340–43, m 49.

did he object to the fact that the leper house had accepted a gift conditional on the donor and his successors having the right to present 'three poor persons, lepers or others' in return.[82] Rearrangements of this kind became common and some led to the creation of hospitals for the relief of the aged, poor and impotent that would continue into the nineteenth century. Examples are the Magdalen Hospital in Newcastle-upon-Tyne and Christ's Hospital in Sherburn.[83]

The problem of mission drift was avoided altogether by one founder with the foresight to provide for what should happen to the leper house should its purpose fail: the statutes of St Leonard's Hospital, Sudbury, drawn up in the 1200s by the first master, John Colneys, and the Bishop of London, stipulated that the hospital should maintain three lepers in perpetuity but that if the statutes 'should not be duly kept after the founder's decease' then its income was to go to St Gregory's church in the same town, for the saying of masses for the souls of the first master, the parents of the bishop, and 'all the faithful departed'.[84]

III. Cy-près Application of Funds Held on Charitable Trusts for Pesthouses

A. Pesthouses

Pesthouses were buildings where sufferers from plague and other diseases were isolated from the rest of the community. At first, they were temporary structures, built and razed as needed,[85] but more permanent buildings were used from the late 1500s. They were typically situated on the outskirts of towns and villages; sometimes existing houses were used, sometimes they were purpose built; often they had a dedicated cemetery or 'plague pit'. From the late 1500s until the early 1800s, many charitable gifts were made for pesthouses as a response to plague,[86] while others

[82] ibid.

[83] By the mid-1800s, both hospitals had an income which far exceeded the needs of the master and brethren, prompting the Charity Commissioners to have the funds applied cy-près (under rules discussed below in Part III); the latter intervention was resisted by the Bishop of Durham who viewed it as an attack on his jurisdiction over the hospital's endowment. See *Second Report of the Royal Commission for Inquiring into Those Cases Which Were Investigated by, and Reported upon, by the Charity Commissioner, but not certified to the Attorney-General* PP 1851 (HC No 1371) 5–6; *Fifth Report of the Charity Commissioners for England and Wales* PP 1858 (HC No 2346) 27; *Supplemental Report of the Charity Commissioners for England and Wales* PP 1854–55 (HC No 1966) 4–18; *Copies of All Correspondence between the Bishop of Durham and the Charity Commissioners Concerning the Scheme for Sherburn Hospital* PP 1856 (HC No 134); *Third Report of the Charity Commissioners for England and Wales* PP 1856 (HC No 2060) 13–28; *Fourth Report of the Charity Commissioners for England and Wales* PP 1857 (HC No 2187) 5–6.

[84] *VCH Suffolk*, vol 2, 140–41.

[85] Paul Slack, *The Impact of Plague in Tudor and Stuart England* (Abingdon, Routledge, 1985) 277.

[86] eg *VCH Surrey*, vol 4, 78–83; *20th Report of Commissioners Concerning Charities* (HC Paper 19, 1829) 27; *11th Report of Commissioners Concerning Charities* (HL Paper 34, 1825) 705.

were founded by parish and town authorities and paid for out of local taxation,[87] particularly after they were ordered to do this by the Privy Council in 1666.[88] In the eighteenth century, pesthouses were also used in southern England as a measure against smallpox,[89] initially by isolating sufferers of varied social status, but latterly reserved for the parish poor.[90]

B. The Cy-près Doctrine

Charitable trusts were often created to operate pesthouses. These were not subject to the rules against perpetuities and their purposes were typically expected by the settlors to continue indefinitely, although in practice this often became impossible, either because the money ran out – in which case the trust ceased to exist – or because it became impossible or impracticable to carry out the trust's purposes due to changed social circumstances. In situations of the latter kind, the cy-près doctrine might be applied, and the court would order that the trust property be applied to some other legally charitable purpose which resembled the original purpose as nearly as possible (the word 'cy-près' derived from the French '*aussi près que possible*').

The content of the cy-près doctrine became settled in the late 1700s and early 1800s.[91] Two key questions often arose in practice. One was whether fulfilment of the trust's purposes had become impossible or impracticable. This might be held to have occurred, for example, because changed social circumstances had made the purposes redundant,[92] or because the trust income had become greater than the expenditure needed to carry out its purposes.[93] The other question was which new purpose was 'as near as possible' to the original purpose. It was said in

[87] Kira LS Newman, 'Bubonic Plague and Quarantine in Early Modern England' (2012) 45 *Journal of Social History* 809; Andrew Wells, 'Urban Governance, Economic Intervention, and the Plague in Bristol, England, 1665–66' in Mohammad Gharipour and Caitlin DeClercq (eds), *Epidemic Urbanism: Contagious Diseases in Global Cities* (Bristol, Intellect, 2021); Aaron Columbus, '"To Be Had for a Pesthouse for the Use of this Parish": Plague Pesthouses in Early Stuart London, c 1600–1650' (2024) 51 *Urban History* 125.

[88] See further text to n 103 below; also Slack (n 85) 223–25; A Beard (ed), *Documents Relating to the Great Plague of 1665-1666 in Bristol* (Bristol Record Society, September 2021), available at https://archive.org/details/beardplague.

[89] Romola J Davenport, 'Cultures of Contagion and Containment? The Geography of Smallpox in Britain in the Pre-vaccination Era' in Véronique Petit et al (eds), *The Anthropological Demography of Health* (Oxford, Oxford University Press, 2020) 66–67.

[90] John R Smith, *The Speckled Monster: Smallpox in England, 1670-1970, with Particular Reference to Essex* (Chelmsford, Essex Record Office, 1987) 149–50.

[91] H Gray, 'The History and Development in England of the Cy-Près Principle in Charities' (1953) 33 *Boston University Law Review* 30; G Jones, *History of the Law of Charity 1532–1827* (Cambridge, Cambridge University Press, 1969) 138–56.

[92] As in eg *AG v Mayor of City of London* (1790) 3 Bro. CC 171, 29 ER 472 (propagation of Christianity among 'infidels' of Virginia; none remained); *AG v Ironmongers' Co* (1834) 2 M & K 576, 39 ER 1064 (release of Christian prisoners in Turkey or Barbary; none remained).

[93] As in eg *AG v Haberdashers' Co* (1792) 4 Bro CC 103, 29 ER 800; *AG v Rochester Corp* (1854) 5 De G M & G 797, 43 ER 1079; *Re Campden Charities* (1881) 18 Ch D 310.

many cases that this had to be the practicable purpose that was the closest to the settlor's original purpose, and that the views of the court as to the best possible use of the property were irrelevant, as was the fact that the settlor might have chosen a different purpose, had he foreseen the social changes which had taken place since the trust was settled.[94] However, it was also said that social usefulness was a factor that could be taken into account when deciding how trust property should be applied,[95] and so the cases on this issue were rather inconsistent.[96]

C. Two Nineteenth Century Cases

Both questions arose in two nineteenth century cases concerning pesthouse trusts: *AG v Kell*[97] and *AG v Earl of Craven*.[98] *Kell* concerned a pesthouse in Lewes built on land bought for the purpose in 1742 with money subscribed by town inhabitants and local gentry. The property was held on a trust so that anyone in Lewes who should thereafter 'fall sick of the small-pox or any other infectious distemper' could be isolated in the pesthouse.[99] Some 50 years later the trustees were town officials who decided to sell the buildings to one of the parish vestries for use as a workhouse, and to lend the sale proceeds to newly created town improvement commissioners to be spent on lighting, paving and cleaning the streets. It was said that the buildings were no longer fit for use as a pesthouse and that this had also become dangerous because they adjoined the highway and were close to 'divers inhabited houses' which had been built in the meantime.[100] Twenty-five years after that, the Brougham Commissioners found that the loan to the town improvement commissioners had never been repaid and recommended that the Attorney General should bring proceedings to recover the money and apply it to purposes nearer to those of the original trust.[101]

The Attorney General brought an action against the town improvement commissioners who made several arguments in their defence: first, that the original subscribers had made a private arrangement between themselves that the subscription money should be used for their benefit, that they could vary this arrangement

[94] *AG v Coopers' Co* (1812) 19 Ves Jun 187, 189, 34 ER 488, 489; *AG v Boucherett* (1858) 25 Beav 116, 118–19, 53 ER 580, 581–82.

[95] *AG v Ironmongers' Co* (1844) 10 Cl & F 908, 922, 8 ER 983, 988.

[96] Compare *Re Prison Charities* (1873) LR 16 Eq 129 (gift for poor prisoners could not be used to fund a school for prisoners' children) and *AG v Ironmongers' Co* (1844) 10 Cl & F 908, 8 ER 983 (gift to redeem English sailors captured by Barbary pirates applied to educational purposes).

[97] *AG v Kell* (1840) 2 Beav 375, (1840) 9 LJ (NS) Ch 389.

[98] *AG v Earl of Craven* (1856) 25 LJ Rep (Ch) 291, 27 LT 23, 2 Jur (NS) pt 1 296, 21 Beav 392. See also FHW Sheppard (ed), *The Survey of London, vols 31 and 32, St James Westminster, Part 2* (London, London County Council, 1963) ch 12. For a fuller account of these cases, drawing on MS sources, see Charles Mitchell, '*Attorney General v Kell* (1840) and *Attorney General v Earl of Craven* (1856): Recovery of Misapplied Charitable Property and its Cy-près Application' in Rebecca Fry and John Picton (eds), *Landmark Cases in Charity Law* (Oxford, Hart Publishing, 2026).

[99] *30th Report of Commissioners Concerning Charities* (HC Paper 101, 1836) 706.

[100] ibid 708.

[101] ibid.

if they liked, and that the court had no jurisdiction to investigate any decision they made about this; and second, in the alternative, that if the money had been held on charitable trust over which the court had jurisdiction, the purposes of this trust had become impossible because there was no longer anyone in Lewes with smallpox thanks to a successful inoculation programme; also that the money had in fact been spent on purposes analogous to those of the original purposes because paving and cleaning the streets prevented the spread of disease in the town.

Lord Langdale MR rejected all these arguments. He found that the pesthouse had been held on trust for a legally charitable purpose over which the court had jurisdiction; that it could not have been justified to use the property for other purposes unless the trust's original purposes had become impossible; that this was unlikely as it was 'very difficult to think' that smallpox had been permanently eradicated in Lewes; that even if the purposes of the trust had become impossible the commissioners' expenditure had not been for sufficiently 'near' purposes for this to be justified; that they should therefore repay the money in 20 annual instalments (the money to come out of future rates levied on the town's ratepayers); and that a scheme be made to use these funds in some other way. This was done by a Chancery Master who ordered that the funds should be put towards a new charitable dispensary in Lewes for the deserving poor.[102]

Craven was decided later than *Kell* but concerned a series of events that began earlier. During the 1665 plague outbreak in London, the infected sick and their households were confined to their own homes or sent to such pesthouses as existed. These measures were partly paid for out of city and parish tax revenues but insufficient funds were available and some of the shortfall was made up by charitable gifts. One was made by the Earl of Craven, a wealthy courtier and official who had been appointed by Charles II to act with the Duke of Albemarle to enforce the Privy Council's plague orders in the City and the Westminster parishes. Craven used his own money to lease three acres of fields at the edge of modern-day Soho where 36 pesthouses and a plague pit were built, all enclosed by a brick wall. Many people were sent there at the height of the epidemic. In 1666, Craven recommended to the Privy Council that central government funds should be used to build and maintain more pesthouses throughout the country to guard against future plague outbreaks, but this was considered too expensive. The Privy Council issued new plague orders requiring the justices and town officials to 'provide some convenient place remote from the [city or town], where a pest-house, huts, or sheds may be erected, to be in readiness in case any Infection should break out'.[103] However, these orders did not specify the number and size of the facilities and paying for these was left to local authorities.[104]

[102] *The Attorney-General v. Kell. Lewes Dispensary, Sussex. Scheme Approved of by the Report of N. W. Senior, Esq. Dated 12th Day of February, 1847, and an Order Dated the 6th March 1847, for the Future Administration of the Pest-House Charity* (London, W Wilcockson, 1847) cl 10.

[103] TNA SP29/155 f102, order 10.

[104] A Lloyd Moote and Dorothy C Moote, *The Great Plague: The Story of London's Most Deadly Year* (Baltimore, MD, Johns Hopkins University Press, 2004) 254–55.

Dissatisfied by this, Craven took steps of his own to ensure that the Soho pesthouses would continue to be available for use by the Westminster parishes in the event of future outbreaks. In 1671–72, he bought the freehold of the land, and in 1687 he conveyed this to a cousin and his heirs on trust 'to maintain, support and keep, in good and tenantable repair, the houses and buildings' for the use of those poor inhabitants of the parishes as should 'be visited with the plague, as a pesthouse or a place set apart for their relief, and for severing them from the well and uninfected, for their use and relief, during their sickness'. As events turned out, there were no more plague epidemics and the land became more valuable as the city grew. Craven's heirs wished to build houses and shops on the site which they could lease to tenants and in 1734 the trustees and parishes agreed that the Soho land could be used for this purpose and that land in Bayswater should be held on a new trust for future use as a pesthouse if needed. Nearly a century later, the same happened again: in 1825, villas were built on the Bayswater land under leases granted by the trustees, Craven family members who were heirs of the first trustees. In 1854, on a referral from the Charity Commissioners, the Attorney General brought proceedings, seeking a declaration that the Bayswater land was held on charitable trust, an account of the income received by the Cravens, and an order that a scheme should be made under which administration of the property was taken forward in accordance with the trust terms or as close to these as was practicable.

For the Cravens, it was argued that the 1687 and 1734 deeds of settlement reserved an interest in the relevant land to Craven family members and their heirs, defeasible only if another plague epidemic broke out. As this had not happened, the Cravens had been and indeed were still entitled to beneficial enjoyment of the Bayswater land and hence also to the rents.[105] Sir John Romilly MR rejected this, holding that the trustees of both settlements had been charged with keeping the land in a state of preparedness for pesthouses to be run there and that this would be impossible if the land was allowed to be built over.[106] The Soho land and Bayswater land had been held on 'immediate', and not contingent, charitable trusts to keep the property ready for pesthouses if they were needed, this being a 'distinct charitable purpose capable of being carried into effect'.[107] An account should therefore be taken to determine the amount of income received by Craven family members; those sums should be repaid; and an enquiry should be undertaken to decide how these funds and the future income generated by the Bayswater land should be applied.

After long negotiations between the Attorney General and the management committees of several voluntary hospitals in London, a scheme was approved by orders of 1864 and 1868. It was directed that the charity income should be divided between King's College Hospital and Charing Cross Hospital, with a power given to new charity trustees (who were representatives of the Westminster parishes)

[105] *Craven* (n 98) 25 LJ Rep (Ch) 291, 295–96.
[106] ibid 297.
[107] ibid 298.

to appoint the parish sick to reserved in-patient beds at the hospitals and also to send them for treatment as out-patients.[108] Under the scheme, in-patients would be 'received indiscriminately whether suffering from contagious or infectious diseases or not (smallpox being excepted)'.[109] This represented a concession by the hospitals, since their constitutions forbade admission of the infectious sick, due to the risk of institutional contagion, but they gave way because they wanted the money (although they stuck at smallpox infection which was understandably seen as a particularly serious risk in the mid-1800s); the Attorney General's insistence on the point suggests a desire not to stray too far from the original trust terms. So the case illustrates the compromises which might have to be struck in cy-près cases when identifying new purposes which could be carried out and which were sufficiently close to the original purposes of a charitable trust.

Craven also shows that the question whether the purposes of a trust had become 'impossible' or 'impracticable' was not always an easy one to decide – as does *Kell*. The judge in *Kell* rejected the argument that smallpox had been eradicated in Lewes, and was therefore presumably swayed by the points, first, that the buildings had become unsuitable because of their poor condition and nearness to other houses, and, second, that there was no endowment on which the trustees could draw to effect repairs or build a new smallpox hospital elsewhere. In *Craven* the judge seems to have accepted that the non-appearance of another plague epidemic in England during the past 180 years meant that there was no longer a need to provide against the eventuality of another outbreak. However, neither judge can have felt confident about this issue given the medical uncertainty about the causes of plague and smallpox which existed at the time (and it should not be forgotten that plague outbreaks continued in other countries). Nevertheless, both judges believed that the funds of each trust should be redirected to new purposes and to achieve this took a flexible view of what 'impossibility' or 'impracticability' entailed – an approach that is still taken by modern judges.

IV. Nuisance Actions about Fever Hospitals

A. Fever Hospitals

The first fever hospitals, founded in the 1700s and 1800s, were charitable institutions in which sufferers from smallpox and other infectious diseases could be isolated, cared for and treated. In the late 1800s, fever hospitals were also built by

[108] *Amended Scheme for the Management and Regulation of the Pest House Charity Founded by William Earl Craven in 1687 and the Application of the Income Thereof* (London, C Roworth and Sons, 1868); *Return Comprising the Reports Made to the Charity Commissioners on Endowed Charities in the Administrative County of London*, vol 5 (HC Paper No 181, 1903) 167–70.

[109] ibid cl 4.

urban sanitary and health authorities empowered to raise the funds from tax revenues by the Sanitary Act 1866, Public Health Act 1875 and Diseases Prevention (Metropolis) Act 1883;[110] county councils were also given such powers by the Isolation Hospitals Act 1893. Little use was made of these statutory powers before the 1890s, however, and the main period of hospital building by public bodies ran from 1890 to 1914.[111] When the recession in epidemics reduced the need for isolation facilities, most fever hospitals were repurposed or demolished, and government funds went elsewhere.[112]

B. Nuisance

For centuries, public nuisance has been a criminal offence arising from an act which endangers the life, health, property, morals or comfort of the public or prevents the public from enjoying rights common to all; it has also been actionable in tort in cases where a claimant has suffered special damage over and above the damage suffered by the public. The tort of public nuisance is distinct from the tort of private nuisance which has only ever been a tort centred on land. Private nuisance is typically committed when a defendant's acts on his own land cause damage to the fabric of the claimant's land and/or interfere with the claimant's reasonable enjoyment of his land. There is some overlap between the torts as a defendant's acts on his land may not only interfere with a claimant's interests as landowner but may also harm the interests of the public. Tort actions in nuisance prompted by a defendant's use of land require the courts to strike a balance between the defendant's interest in doing what he likes with his land and the claimant's interest in doing the same (in cases of private nuisance) and/or in making other life choices free from interference (in cases of public nuisance). When striking this balance in cases about land use, the courts are therefore engaged in a process of resource allocation.

C. Nuisance Actions against Fever Hospitals

In the 1700s and 1800s, a series of tort actions for nuisance were brought by landowners wishing to stop fever hospitals from being built in their neighbourhoods, or to have limits placed on their operation (numbers of patients, geographical

[110] Gwendoline M Ayers, *England's First State Hospitals and the Metropolitan Asylums Board 1867-1930* (London, Wellcome Institute of the History of Medicine, 1971); Anthony S Wohl, *Endangered Lives: Public Health in Victorian Britain* (Cambridge, MA, Harvard University Press, 1983) 77–82 and 119–27.

[111] John V Pickstone, *Medicine and Industrial Society: A History of Hospital Development in Manchester and its Region 1752-1946* (Manchester, Manchester University Press, 1985) ch 8; Steven Cherry, *Medical Services and the Hospitals in Britain, 1860-1939* (Cambridge, Cambridge University Press, 1996) 41–78; Anne Hardy, *Health and Medicine in Britain since 1860* (Basingstoke, Palgrave, 2001) 9–39.

[112] Alysa Levene et al, 'Patterns of Municipal Health Expenditure in Interwar England and Wales' (2004) 78 *Bulletin of the History of Medicine* 635.

origin of patients, precautions against contagion).[113] Most of the cases concerned actions for public nuisance but some concerned actions for private nuisance as well. They raised complex issues, among other reasons because medical experts disagreed about the ways in which infectious diseases spread. The cases were mainly concerned with smallpox, a disease that is now known to have been caused by a virus which could pass through the air from one person to another if they were in close proximity or via physical contact between people or via physical handling of infected clothing, blankets, etc. In the late 1800s, medical knowledge had not reached this point: some experts believed that the disease was communicated by physical bodily contact, others that infection was caused by air convection, although opinions differed as to whether this was the result of small particles of matter being carried through the air or of some other mechanism; they also held differing views about the degree of risk entailed by bringing sufferers together to be treated in a single place, what measures would be effective to reduce this risk, and whether removing sufferers from crowded slum tenements into a hospital located elsewhere would produce benefits to other tenement-dwellers that outweighed the harm caused to people living near the hospital who were exposed to an increased risk of infection.

An early case was *Baines v Baker*,[114] decided in 1752. The plaintiff owned houses near Cold Bath Fields in London, which he let to tenants. They gave him notice to quit on learning that the defendant planned to build a smallpox hospital nearby, fearing that they would catch the disease. The plaintiff sought an injunction but this was refused by Lord Hardwicke LC. He considered that the action was one for public nuisance as it was not 'confined to the particular property of the plaintiffs, because it is in the nature of terror to diffuse itself in a very extensive manner'.[115] It followed that there was a procedural problem because in cases where an injunction was sought from a court of Equity to restrain a public nuisance, an information had to be laid by the Attorney General (although relator proceedings were possible).[116] It seems, though, that Lord Hardwicke would also have refused an injunction on the merits. His reasons are exiguously reported, but according to one reporter, he said that 'bills to restrain nuisances must extend to such only as are nuisances at law … [and] the fears of mankind, though they may be reasonable

[113] On these cases see also Ayers (n 110) passim; Anne Hardy, *The Epidemic Streets: Infectious Disease and the Rise of Preventive Medicine, 1856–1900* (Oxford, Clarendon Press, 1993) 137–42; Philip Mortimer, 'Ridding London of Smallpox: The Aerial Transmission Debate and the Evolution of a Precautionary Approach' (2008) 136 *Epidemiology and Infection* 1297; Matthew Newsom Kerr, 'Sites of Complaint and Complaining: Fever and Smallpox Hospitals in Late Victorian London' in Jonathan Reinarz and Rebecca Wynter (eds), *Complaints, Controversies and Grievances in Medicine: Historical and Social Science Perspectives* (London, Routledge, 2015).

[114] *Baines v Baker* (1752) Amb 158, 27 ER 105. Also reported as *Anonymous* (1752) 3 Atk 750, 26 ER 1230.

[115] ibid 3 Atk 751. See too Amb 159.

[116] ibid 3 Atk 751; Amb 159–60. Discussion in JR Spencer, 'Public Nuisance – A Critical Examination' [1989] *Cambridge Law Journal* 55, 66–76.

ones, will not create a nuisance'.[117] According to another reporter, the judge said that the hospital was

> a charity like to prove of great advantage to mankind; such an hospital must not be far from a town, because those that are attacked with that disorder in a natural way, may not be in a condition to be carried far.[118]

The main principle emerging from the decision, therefore, identified and applied in later cases, was that actions in public nuisance required proof of damage, and a plaintiff could not satisfy this requirement by showing only that he and other people feared that they would catch smallpox (or some other disease) as a result of the defendant's actions in bringing the infected sick into the locality. A plaintiff had to prove that the defendant's actions significantly increased the risk of infection, and he could do this only by leading expert medical evidence to this effect that was accepted by the court (where an injunction was sought in equitable proceedings) or by a jury (where damages were sought at common law). In *Fleet v Metropolitan Asylums Board* (which concerned a smallpox hospital in Darenth), Cotton LJ later held that 'the plaintiffs must make out that there was real danger, otherwise, however much they might feel the hospital to be an annoyance, they could not get an injunction'[119] – and on the expert evidence in that case it could not be said that the plaintiffs had done this.[120] In *AG v Manchester Corporation*,[121] again, Chitty J refused an injunction because he was not satisfied that the plaintiffs had discharged the burden of proving that the defendant's hospital would cause an appreciable danger to public health. Applying the same test, but reaching the opposite conclusion on the facts, Brett LJ held that the plaintiffs had succeeded in proving this in *Chambers v Metropolitan Asylums Board*,[122] a case to which we shall return.

In the *Manchester* case, Chitty J also looked back to the second passage of Lord Hardwicke's judgment in *Baines* that has been quoted, and noted the question whether

[117] ibid 3 Atk 751.

[118] ibid Amb 159.

[119] *Fleet v Metropolitan Asylums Board The Times*, 3 March 1886, 3.

[120] The medical experts flatly contradicted one another: some of the plaintiffs' experts said that smallpox infection could be carried through the air for two and a half miles, or at least half a mile; the defendant's experts said there was no danger at a distance of 50 yards, or the length of the courtroom. Furthermore, the witnesses all 'admitted that their opinions were theoretical and not the result of experiment or observation, nor had science settled how the disease came to an end or how infection was transmitted': ibid 3 (Cotton LJ). For the witnesses' testimony in the court below, see *The Times*, 19 November 1884, 7. See too *AG v Guildford, Godalming and Woking Joint Hospital Board*, *The Times*, 21 November 1895, 3.

[121] *AG v Manchester Corporation* [1893] 2 Ch 87, 93–95. See also *Saunders v Mayor, Aldermen, and Burgesses of New Windsor*, *The Times*, 13 September 1881, 3; *Matthews v Mayor and Corporation of Sheffield*, *The Times*, 6 October 1887, 4; *AG v Rathmines and Pembroke Joint Hospital Board* [1904] 1 IR 161; *AG v Nottingham Corporation* [1904] 1 Ch 673.

[122] *Chambers v Metropolitan Asylums Board*, *The Times*, 3 December 1881, 4. See also *Bendelow v Guardians of the Wortley Union*, *The Times*, 16 November 1887, 3.

> if the evidence shews that the maintenance of a small-pox hospital is on the whole, balancing the good against the evil, more beneficial to the health of the public at large, or to that portion of the public that inhabits or frequents the neighbourhood, than the leaving of the persons suffering from the disease scattered in their own homes, some weight might not be properly allowed to this circumstance.[123]

Chitty J found it unnecessary to answer this, but in *AG v Local Board for the Fulham District*,[124] Jessel MR thought that such evidence would be relevant to the question whether erecting a temporary smallpox hospital constituted a public nuisance. There was no such evidence in that case, however, because 'the medical men whose affidavits had been produced differed in the strongest and most direct way' and the judge could not say which expert evidence was correct. According to the defendant's witnesses,

> the effect of erecting such a hospital would be that poor people suffering from this dreadful and infectious disorder would be withdrawn from their crowded homes and the numerous inhabitants of small tenements would thereby be protected … [so that] the hospital would be, not a public nuisance, but a public benefit.

But on the other hand, the plaintiffs' witnesses testified that 'the collection of all these cases into one centre increased the source of infection'. Moreover, even if it had been possible to say that view taken by the defendant's witnesses was right, Jessel MR recognised that a further question would then have arisen, namely whether 'the plaintiffs were entitled to say that a public benefit should not be conferred at their cost', ie whether it was fair for the plaintiffs to be made to suffer physical harm so that the suffering of other people should be reduced?

Jessel MR did not enter into a full discussion of this question, but it seems likely that he would have found for the plaintiffs in such a case, and this was the conclusion drawn by Brett LJ in *Chambers v Metropolitan Asylums Board*.[125] There the defendant ran a fever hospital in Fulham to which it planned to admit smallpox patients not only from the immediate neighbourhood but also from further afield. The plaintiff owners of nearby properties won an injunction to prevent them from doing this, for reasons set out by Brett LJ:

> It must be a great benefit to poor people afflicted with the smallpox in small dwelling-houses that the sick should be taken away from their neighbourhood and put into an excellent hospital, where they would be treated with care and skill. On the other side, there was the injury to the poor, and to those who were not poor, from the bringing in [of] a large number of patients into the district in which the hospital was situated. … Speaking for himself, he was inclined to take this into consideration – *viz*, in the case that people had been afflicted by Providence with a terrible disease, which would have fallen upon them apart from the proximity of a hospital; whereas, as to the other case, the people would not have been afflicted but for the presence of the hospital, which

[123] *AG v Manchester Corporation* (n 121) 93.
[124] *AG v Local Board for the Fulham District, The Times*, 23 May 1881, 6.
[125] *Chambers* (n 122) 4.

> had brought the disease among them. … [This] consideration was strongly in favour of preventing this probability of a great affliction being brought by the hands of men to persons who would not otherwise have suffered from it.[126]

The same view was taken by Lord Blackburn in *Managers of the Metropolitan Asylums District v Hill (No 2)*,[127] which concerned a hospital in Hampstead for smallpox and other infectious diseases that was operated by officers of the Metropolitan Asylums Board ('MAB'), exercising powers conferred by the Metropolitan Poor Law Act 1867, and acting on directions of the Poor Law Board ('PLB', which by the time of the action had been superseded by the Local Government Board). Proceedings for public nuisance were brought by local landowners who sought damages and an injunction preventing the defendant from using the hospital for patients infected with smallpox, scarlet fever or other diseases. The case was heard by Pollock B sitting with a jury in the Queen's Bench Division.[128] The defendant's witnesses included the hospital managers, who testified that reasonable precautions had been taken to guard against the spread of infection into the neighbourhood, and medical experts, who testified that as a result of these precautions no serious risk of infection had been caused to the plaintiffs. The jury was unpersuaded by this testimony and found as a fact that the plaintiffs had been harmed by the defendant's actions. The defendants then made a further submission that even so, they had not committed a tortious nuisance because they had been directed by the PLB, and authorised by legislation, to run the hospital and doing this had accordingly been a lawful act that could not be a tort.

Pollock B rejected this submission. He held that on a proper reading of the legislation under which the MAB had been obliged to follow the PLB's directions, the statute had not given the MAB's officers an immunity from tort liability for acts done when following those directions.[129] Nor was it a defence that their actions had been authorised by statute. The Metropolitan Poor Act 1867 had given the MAB a general power to build and run fever hospitals, but had not empowered the MAB to run this particular hospital in the particular place where it had been sited and in the particular way in which it had been run. The statute was therefore unlike statutes under which canal and railway companies had been given powers of compulsory purchase to acquire particular land and authorised to operate canals and railways across this land. The companies were expressly or impliedly exempted by the legislation from tortious liability which they might otherwise have incurred, eg to neighbouring landowners whose enjoyment of their own land had thereby been prejudiced, but the same could not be said of the MAB.[130] Nor

[126] ibid 4.
[127] *Managers of the Metropolitan Asylums District v Hill (No 2)* (1881) 6 App Cas 193, 205–06.
[128] *Hill v Managers of the Metropolitan Asylum District* (1879) 4 QBD 433.
[129] ibid 439–41.
[130] ibid 441. At 444, he cited cases to this effect including *R v Pease* (1832) 4 B & Ad 30, 110 ER 366, for discussion of which see Charlotte Smith and Mark Wilde, '*R v Pease* (1832)' in Charles Mitchell and Paul Mitchell (eds), *Landmark Cases in the Law of Tort* (Oxford, Hart Publishing, 2010). Another important case was *Hammersmith and City Railway Co v Brand* (1869) LR 4 HL 171, where a majority

should the 1867 Act be given a purposive construction to give the MAB a defence of statutory authority by drawing an analogy with the canal and railway statutes because the 1867 Act had been passed with a view to 'obviating, or at least lessening, a great public danger … so as not unduly to place difficulties in the way of those to whom its execution [was] entrusted'. That would create a precedent with no obvious limit which might be invoked by anyone carrying out this kind of public work.[131]

Following a procedural dispute between the parties,[132] the defendants unsuccessfully appealed to the House of Lords from Pollock B's findings about the defence of statutory authority. The Court held that the defence would have been available if the 1867 Act had not merely permitted, but had positively required officers of the MAB to interfere with

> private rights of property, within local limits which it might have thought fit to define, for the purpose of establishing this asylum … and had provided for compensation to those who might thereby be injuriously affected. … But the case is different, when (as here) no interference at all with any private rights is authorized, and no place, or limit of space, is defined within which the establishment of such an asylum is made lawful.[133]

The House of Lords considered that landowners had a right to enjoy their property which the common law would protect by giving them a nuisance action against any defendant who harmed them by increasing their risk of infection. Landowners might be exposed to an increased risk of infection if their neighbours contracted infectious diseases through natural agency for which no one was responsible, in which case tort law would give them no remedy; but they were entitled to object if a defendant harmed them by increasing their risk of infection by bringing contagious patients into the locality. Parliament might decide that the harm they would then suffer was a price worth paying for the benefits to other members of society and encode that decision into legislation providing public bodies such as the defendant with a defence to a nuisance action. But in that case one would expect Parliament to make this explicit in the statute and to provide affected property-owners with a statutory right to compensation – yet no such immunity was expressly given in the 1867 Act, nor did it provide for compensation, suggesting that Parliament had not intended to deprive property-owners such as the plaintiffs of the rights to compensation which they had at common law.[134]

of the common law judges advised that a nuisance action should be available to a person suffering from the noise and dirt of a railway running past his premises, but the House of Lords rejected this advice and held the opposite.

[131] ibid 441–42.

[132] The House of Lords' disposal of this dispute was reported as *Metropolitan Asylum District Managers v Hill (No 1)* (1880) 5 App Cas 582.

[133] (1881) 6 App Cas 193, 201 (Lord Selborne LC). See also 212–15 (Lord Watson), distinguishing 'imperative' from 'permissive' powers.

[134] ibid 203 and 208–09 (Lord Blackburn). Modern courts still regard these dicta as authority for interpreting legislation and its effect on private nuisance actions in this way: *Manchester Ship Canal Co Ltd v United Utilities Water Ltd (No 2)* [2024] UKSC 22, [2025] AC 761 [20]–[21].

D. The Royal Commission on Smallpox and Fever Hospitals

Following *Hill*, a Royal Commission was appointed to investigate the effects of London smallpox and fever hospitals.[135] They concluded 'that the increase of small-pox near these hospitals which has been so uniformly subsequent to their being brought into full working, has also been consequent on it',[136] that although 'personal communication' of the disease from patients to attendants to local residents was a possible cause, especially in poorly run hospitals, 'atmospheric dissemination' could not be ruled out as another cause, and so measures should be taken to guard against both.[137] It recommended, therefore, that some small hospitals should be maintained in London to treat the severest cases, and that various measures should be taken to prevent the spread of smallpox infection from these, but that less severe cases who could be moved should be sent to hospital ships on the Thames.[138] This recommendation was implemented: the MAB set up hospital ships in distant Dartford, where it also built a larger hospital, to which the infected sick of central London were transported by ambulance. Meanwhile, the MAB reached an agreement with the Hampstead residents that no more than 40 patients would be treated there, and that smallpox patients would no longer be admitted – thereafter the hospital cared mainly for patients with scarlet fever and diphtheria.

The Royal Commission also made some observations about powers of compulsory purchase.[139] It denied that the case for making hospital authorities pay for land acquired to build fever hospitals was weaker than it was for railway and canal companies, because they acted for the public good rather than private gain. In the Commission's view, the 'interest of a multitude is no doubt greater than that of two or three individuals; but so also is their power to bear the sacrifice by which that interest of theirs is secured'. Regarding the question whether a public body should be liable in nuisance for operating a fever hospital on land acquired by compulsory purchase, the Commission thought that they should be liable for damages because

> when a public authority takes statutory power not only to acquire land … but to use it in a manner which inflicts on the neighbours an injury against which the ordinary law would guarantee them, it appears to us that this abolition of the legal protection on which those persons have a right to rely, and on the faith of which they may, have built houses and invested money, gives in equity a strong right to compensation …

However, the Commission also thought that

> The power of arresting the operations of the hospital authorities by injunction should … be taken away. It is incompatible with the public safety that individuals

[135] *Report of the Royal Commission upon Small-pox and Fever Hospitals* (C 3314, 1882).
[136] ibid xx.
[137] ibid xxvi–xxvii.
[138] ibid xxvii.
[139] ibid xxxiii–xxxiv.

> should possess the power of suddenly paralysing institutions which furnish for the time the only machinery for controlling an epidemic.

No legislation was enacted to implement this last recommendation, although the courts have always recognised that the public interest is a factor to be considered when deciding whether to grant an injunction. Prior to the House of Lords decision in *Hill*, the MAB had itself unsuccessfully asked for stronger statutory powers of compulsory purchase of exactly the kind which the court said were needed if they were to build fever hospitals near the loci of infection. After publication of the Commission's report, the MAB went on asking for these, but with limited success:[140] the Diseases Prevention (Metropolis) Act 1883, s 6 gave them compulsory purchase powers to buy landing places for hospital ships on the Thames; and the Poor Law Act 1889, s 5 gave them compulsory purchase powers to buy land adjoining existing hospital sites.

V. Closing Thoughts

Some themes emerge from the case studies undertaken here. One that goes to the very nature of ownership is the extent to which an owner's dominion can be subordinated to the public interest. Our discussion suggests a shift in attitude across the centuries, as the importance of secure property rights increasingly came to be recognised as a pre-requisite for social order and economic growth. The medieval leper house cases show that the Crown's goals of consolidating the jurisdiction of the nascent common law, and of resisting the encroachment of the Church into what had come to be seen as a secular matter, were achieved at the expense of individual holders of advowsons when presentation to the mastership came to be accepted on the basis of possession rather than right. In contrast, the Victorian fever hospital cases were decided on the basis that the public interest in moving the infected sick from high density to low density neighbourhoods did not justify depriving property owners in the target localities of their private rights to beneficial enjoyment of their property.

Another theme is that when property-holding structures are created to support social activities for a prolonged period, it is all but inevitable that disparities will emerge over time between the attitudes and wishes of the original property owners, their successors, the current custodians of the property, and society at large. In the case of leper houses, the visitorial power of the patron ensured that the dominion of the founder's heirs took precedence: the *leprosaria* were their private jurisdiction, and they were free either to compel the master's compliance with their forebear's rules, or to overlook non-compliance, at their discretion. The charitable pesthouse trust cases show that when heirs or institutional successors

[140] Ayers (n 110) 58, 78, 80–81, 87, 90.

failed to establish that they had an exclusive right to decide the uses to which property should be put, the courts might override their opinions (as current trustees of the property or as interested parties) as to what should be done with the trust fund when the original mission could no longer sensibly be carried out. The courts might instead impose a solution with nearness to the founder's original purpose in mind. Both in the deference they paid to visitorial jurisdictions and in their applications of the cy-près doctrine, therefore, we see a commitment on the part of the courts to prioritise the choices made by settlors about the future use of their property over other social interests. One might find in this a desire to incentivise charitable gift-making. More significantly, it also reflects a commitment to the ideas that property ownership means the right to choose what happens to the property and that once such choices have been made they will be upheld, even after the owners' deaths, unless there are strong reasons not to do so.

10

The Taxation of Proprietary Medicines and the Regulation of Poisons in Nineteenth-Century Britain

CHANTAL STEBBINGS

I. Introduction

Proprietary, or 'quack' medicines were used extensively in nineteenth-century Britain, when infectious diseases were endemic and frequently epidemic and constituted the leading cause of death. Varying in their periods of intensity, cholera, smallpox, typhus, typhoid fever, influenza and tuberculosis ravaged the general population, while diphtheria, whooping cough, measles and scarlet fever particularly targeted the young. Many of these diseases, notably cholera, were exacerbated by poverty, but influenza, typhoid and scarlet fever, for example, affected both wealthy and poor alike. The diseases were all infectious and understood to be life-threatening. Before the causes of the principal infectious diseases were discovered, from the 1880s onwards, few effective therapeutic remedies existed. Treatment during most of the nineteenth century was necessarily speculative and empirical. The most common remedies for cholera and typhoid, for example, were brandy and calomel, but laudanum, a tincture of opium, was widely administered by medical practitioners. Bleeding, hot baths, saline solution, turpentine and quinine were also employed.[1] Some diseases, such as whooping cough, measles, diphtheria and scarlet fever responded to high quality nursing care, but it was widely understood that there were no effective medicines to treat the principal infectious diseases of the age. The Medical Officer of the Privy Council in 1866 spoke 'with despair of the medical treatment of developed cholera', observing it remained 'an almost hopeless task for the practitioner'.[2] With medical science insufficiently advanced

[1] James Barr, 'An Address on the Treatment of Typhoid Fever' (1900) 156 *The Lancet* 919.

[2] 'Ninth Report of the Medical Officer of the Privy Council', *House of Commons Parliamentary Papers* (hereafter *HCPP*) (1867) (3949) xxxvii 1, 32. See too George Johnson, 'The Pathology and Treatment of Cholera' (1865) 2 *British Medical Journal* (hereafter *BMJ*), 545, 545.

to address many of these diseases effectively, conjectural and largely futile medical treatment, and an outcome which was all too often fatal, the high level of public anxiety was understandable. Cholera outbreaks caused public panic,[3] tuberculosis was feared throughout the century, scarlet fever was a particularly dreaded disease in Victorian families, and because diphtheria was regarded as a new disease in the 1850s, it caused real terror.[4]

In this context, the public inevitably turned to the purchase of commercially prepared remedies, advertised and sold in a wide range of retail outlets, from chemists and druggists to general stores, grocers, booksellers and stationers. These medicines were invented and marketed to the general public by entrepreneurs, who were usually not medically qualified. Exaggerated claims were made for the medicines' effectiveness, their secret composition was stressed, and their sellers claimed proprietary rights in them, hence their description in this chapter as 'proprietary medicines'. There was an immensely strong and old tradition of such self-medication in England which continued in its full vigour in the nineteenth century.[5] This was inevitable where diseases were rife and often fatal, where people were fearful and, in times of epidemic, desperate, lacking confidence in regular medical treatments and often unable to afford them. Ever alert to a commercial opportunity, proprietors of these medicines flooded the market with their products in the nineteenth century, with their sales increasing substantially in that period. These remedies were certainly unproven, sometimes useless, but in many instances both dangerous and addictive.

The thriving market in proprietary medicines presented the Government with an opportunity to raise revenue, and from 1783 proprietary medicines, including toxic medicines, were subject to a tax – the medicine stamp duty. The overall aim in this chapter is to explore the role of tax in the legal regulation of poisons in the latter years of the nineteenth century and to assess the legal response to the problems to which this gave rise. In examining the place of toxic proprietary medicines in the first general legislative regulation of the sale of poisons to the public in 1868, it addresses specifically its unexpected, unusual and yet significant intersection with the stamp duty imposed on proprietary medicines. It demonstrates that a number of factors combined to evade the poisons legislation and undermine the safety of the public for over 25 years at the end of the nineteenth century. These were the presence and profound misunderstanding of the medicine duty stamp on proprietary medicines containing poisons, the widespread acceptance of informal and inaccurate nomenclature, intense commercial pressures and the deliberate misinterpretation of statutory provisions. The chapter explores tensions between cultural perceptions of safety and efficacy, scientific and medical knowledge, vested interests, financial imperatives and a growing

[3] 'Cholera', *The Times* (18 June 1831) 5.

[4] WH Ranking, 'Lecture on Diphtheria' (1859) 73 *The Lancet* 27.

[5] See generally Roy Porter, *Health for Sale, Quackery in England 1650–1850* (Manchester, Manchester University Press, 1989).

realisation that the legal control of poisons was essential. It assesses the extent to which the prevalence of self-medication in the second half of the nineteenth century acted as an engine for legal changes in the law of tax and of the regulation of poisons.

II. The Taxation of Poisonous Proprietary Medicines

A tax on proprietary medicines in the form of a stamp duty was first imposed in 1783,[6] when the practice of self-medication was already well established in Britain. It adopted its modern form in 1785,[7] and was abolished some 150 years later in 1941.[8] By the middle of the nineteenth century, when the market in proprietary medicines, responding to endemic and intractable disease and promoted by the growth in advertising, was reaching its zenith, the tax constituted a regular and secure, albeit relatively small, source of public revenue. The tax was imposed on every enclosure of chargeable medicine, namely the bottle or package, at a rate which depended on the value of the medicine, generally ranging between 10 per cent and 20 per cent.[9] The tax applied to all

> drugs, oils, waters, essences, tinctures, powders, or other preparation or composition whatsoever, used or applied, or to be used or applied, externally or internally, as medicines or medicaments for the prevention, cure, or relief of any disorder or complaint incident to, or in anywise affecting, the human body, which shall be uttered or vended in Great Britain.[10]

The Act refined this general charge, and in a more precise explanation of the remedies to be taxed it specified that the charge was to apply if the medicine was sold under letters patent, or the maker claimed a secret art in it, or an exclusive right to it, or recommended it to the public as an effective remedy, or, finally, if it was expressly named in the extensive schedule to the Act.[11]

The tax was paid by the maker of the medicine, and the evidence that the tax had been paid was a medicine duty stamp. The stamp itself was an elaborately engraved oblong red paper bearing an image of a crown.[12] It was purchased from the Inland Revenue or its distributors, and affixed by the maker to the bottle or package in such a way that the enclosure could not be opened without tearing

[6] Medicine Stamp Duty Act 1783 (23 Geo III c 62).
[7] Medicine Stamp Duty Act 1785 (25 Geo III c 79).
[8] See generally Chantal Stebbings, *Tax, Medicines and the Law: From Quackery to Pharmacy* (Cambridge, Cambridge University Press, 2018).
[9] During the nineteenth century, a medicine of the value not exceeding 1s paid a duty of 1½d (12.5%) and 3d for one not exceeding 2s 6d (10%).
[10] Medicine Stamp Duty Act 1785 (n 7) s 2.
[11] ibid s 16.
[12] See generally Michael Tanner, *Great Britain Medicine Stamp Duty: A Philatelic History* (Great Britain, The Revenue Society, 2013) 25.

the stamp. The final aspect of the medicine stamp duty was that in order to sell chargeable medicines, all vendors had to obtain a licence.[13] The licence originally cost £2 in London and 10 shillings elsewhere, but was reduced in 1875 to five shillings uniformly throughout England. The charge to tax, its evidencing stamp, and the requirement for a vendor's licence, applied to all proprietary medicines falling within the very general description in the Act. Their quality or effectiveness was immaterial. Whether a medicine was made of high-quality ingredients and known to be effective, or simply useless, or even actively dangerous, it remained subject to the tax if it came within the charge.

Proprietary medicines containing poisons were widely used. With no disclosure of their ingredients, they made comprehensive claims for their efficacy in alleviating a range of named symptoms, usually fevers, coughs, headaches, sore throat, rashes and diarrhoea. While all these could be symptoms of relatively mild disease, they could equally be indications of far more serious illness. In the absence of an expert diagnosis from a regular medical practitioner, patients or their families used their own judgement and resorted to self-medication of the symptoms. Many cough cures contained morphine, and laudanum, which was a highly addictive opium tincture and potent narcotic, and one of the most commonly abused medicines used as an analgesic and sedative in a wide range of remedies.[14] One proprietary medicine, chlorodyne, stood out above all others in this context. It was a celebrated and widely used preparation, produced to deal with epidemic cholera when regular medicine offered no treatment, but recommended for a further range of symptoms. It was advertised 'for the relief of coughs, colds, consumption, asthma, bronchitis, diarrhoea, dysentery, cholera, spasms, cramp and sea-sickness', and in relation to cholera 'it has proved itself a most valuable Specific, quickly relieving the pain and spasms, and seldom failing to check the disease …'.[15] It had been invented by Dr John Collis Browne when he served as an army surgeon in India and gained experience of the disease,[16] but had never been formally patented. It contained principally morphine, which was the active element of opium, and chloroform.[17] A witness to a departmental committee considering the statutory schedule of poisons in 1903 agreed that it contained more poison than any other proprietary medicine he knew.[18] Nevertheless it was 'highly extolled' in the mid

[13] Medicine Stamp Duty Act 1785 (n 7) s 5.

[14] See generally Virginia Berridge, *Opium and the People: Opiate Use and Drug Control Policy in Nineteenth and Early Twentieth Century England* (London, Free Association Books, 1999).

[15] See the advertisement at The National Archives, London (hereafter TNA), IR 40/2008. See too Augustin Pritchard, 'Chlorodyne' (1862) 1 *BMJ* 556.

[16] Henri C Silberman, 'The Many Aspects of Chlorodyne' (2006) 36 *Pharmaceutical Historian* 27; Peter G Homan, Briony Hudson, and Raymond C Rowe, *Popular Medicines* (London, Pharmaceutical Press, 2008) 53–60.

[17] TNA IR 40/2008 (n 15), 'Towle's Chlorodyne'.

[18] 'Minutes of Evidence before the Departmental Committee to consider Schedule A to the Pharmacy Act 1868' (hereafter 'DC on Poisons, Minutes, 1903'), *HCPP* (1903) (Cd 1443) xxxiii 17, q 3866 (WJ Leggett, honorary secretary of the Patent Medicines Vendors' Defence Association).

nineteenth century as a remedy for cholera,[19] and its popularity remained unabated throughout the century and into the next, as its high opiate content undoubtedly relieved pain and acted as a sedative.

Many of these proprietary medicines were specifically directed to infants, and were widely used to treat both mild and serious diseases. *Godfrey's Cordial* and *Dalby's Carminative*, both marketed as soothing draughts for children, contained opium, while *Winslow's Syrup* and *Kay's Compound Essence of Linseed* contained a large quantity of morphine. *Dr James's Fever Powders*, the most famous of the raft of remedies sold to relieve 'fever', contained antimony and ammonia in amounts which were undoubtedly toxic. *Holt's Specific for Whooping Cough* too contained antimony. *Hunter's Solution of Chloral* contained a very strong amount of chloral. *Burroughs and Wellcome's Tabloids*, *Fellows' Syrup* and *Bateman's Drops* all contained poisons,[20] while a number, such as *Daffy's Elixir*, contained mainly alcohol. In a select committee of the House of Lords on the sale of poisons in 1857, AS Taylor, Professor of Chemistry and Medical Jurisprudence at Guy's Hospital, said he made a list of the 26 principal proprietary medicines and found that 10 of them contained opium, three contained arsenic, four contained tartar emetic, seven contained corrosive sublimate, one contained Spanish flies, and one contained salt of sorrel.[21]

The medicine stamp duty thus applied to the large number of proprietary medicines consumed during the latter part of the nineteenth century containing substances that were toxic or addictive. Individual consumers were unaware of the constituents of the medicines they purchased commercially, or even of the main ingredients, because one of the principal characteristics of such medicines was that their composition was kept secret. That added to their allure and so secrecy constituted part of their commercial success, but they were indubitably dangerous. Furthermore, being sold by unqualified individuals in trade, no expert advice was available on purchase, and neither was there any indication on the bottle that the medicine contained poison. Customers relied on advertisements and personal recommendation, and consumed these medicines in prodigious quantities.

III. The Legal Regulation of Poisons

The sale to the public of proprietary medicines containing poisons was entirely unregulated for most of the nineteenth century, and yet the deaths from their use

[19] Edward McInall, Jr, 'Chlorodyne' (1868) 40 *American Journal of Pharmacy* 209 (3rd series vol 16) 211. See too Projit Bihari Mukharji, *Nationalizing the Body: The Medical Market, Print and Daktari Medicine* (London, Anthem Press, 2009) 199.

[20] DC on Poisons, Minutes, 1903 (n 18) qq 2375, 2420–21, 3751–52, 3807–11.

[21] 'Report and Minutes of Evidence, Select Committee of the House of Lords on the Sale of Poisons Bill', *HCPP* (1857 session 2) (294) xii 551, q 911.

were well known and received increasing publicity.[22] Despite an obvious need to protect the public, the first general control on the sale of poisons did not occur until the Pharmacy Act 1868,[23] a measure promoted by the professional body of pharmacists, the Pharmaceutical Society. The Act aimed to prevent the sale of poisons to the general public in open shop, on the underlying principle that poisonous substances could be sold by retail only by qualified chemists.[24] By no means were all poisons regarded as poisons for the purposes of the Act. Only those listed in Schedule A to the Act were subject to the new legislative control, though the Pharmaceutical Society was empowered to request the Privy Council to add other substances to it.[25]

While all scheduled poisons could be sold only by a qualified chemist, different regulations applied to the poisons in each of the two parts of the Schedule. Part 1 included the more active poisons, notably arsenic, prussic acid, morphine, cyanide and strychnine, being the deadliest poisons which tended to be used for improper purposes. These had to be clearly labelled 'poison' with the name and address of the chemist, but they could only be sold to individuals if they were known to the chemist, or had been introduced by someone the chemist knew, and their name and address recorded. Furthermore, details of the transaction had to be entered in the 'Poison Book'.[26] The poisons in the second part were not as dangerous as those in the first part, and included chloroform, belladonna and opium, being poisons which were commonly used in medicines for a range of often minor complaints. Again they could only be purchased from a qualified chemist, but the only other requirements were that the bottle or package should bear the chemist's name and address and be clearly labelled 'poison' to alert the consumer to use the product with caution.[27] The Act thus provided a legislative regime of public protection against the indiscriminate sale of poisons, which was certainly robust in contrast to the total lack of control which had hitherto existed.

Proprietary medicines containing poisons, however, were expressly excluded from the fundamental provision of the Act that a scheduled poison could be sold only by a qualified chemist. Section 16 provided that the restrictions did not apply to 'the making or dealing in Patent Medicines'. The exemption ostensibly left the trade in toxic proprietary medicines untouched, to proceed as it always had: namely that even if they contained scheduled poisons they could be sold by anyone who chose to do so, even if unqualified, in open shop, with no labelling or caution.

[22] Between 1848 and 1854 there were some 3,000 recorded deaths from poisoning, averaging in the region of 400 a year, a figure which continued to reflect the number of deaths recorded in 1864: 'Eighteenth Annual Report of Births, Marriages and Deaths in England', *HCPP* (1857 session 2) (2260) xxii 279, 440–41, 472–73, 492–94; 'Twenty-seventh Annual Report of Births, Marriages and Deaths in England', *HCPP* (1866) (3712) xix 1, 5, 196–97, 200–01.

[23] Pharmacy Act 1868 (31 & 32 Vict c 121). The sale of arsenic was the first to be regulated: Sale of Arsenic Regulation Act 1851 (14 & 15 Vict c 13).

[24] Pharmacy Act 1868, ibid s 1.

[25] ibid s 2.

[26] ibid s 17.

[27] ibid.

In light of the size of the trade, and the policy of the Act, this apparently sweeping exemption was remarkable. Nevertheless, when the Pharmacy Bill 1868 was debated in committee, the exempting clause was not raised,[28] and it hardly figured in the discussion in the professional press immediately following the enactment.[29] The driving force behind the inclusion of the exemption was accordingly not a matter of public record, but there is evidence to suggest that, unsurprisingly, it was the work of vested interests, namely the proprietors and vendors of commercial medicines, anxious to ensure that they were not denied a share of a very lucrative trade.[30] They already constituted a powerful lobby in opposition to the underlying ethos of the Pharmacy Act that poisons could only be sold by qualified chemists.[31] That the exemption was the price to be paid for ensuring the passage of the Act was certainly the firmly held view of those agitating for reform over a decade later and beyond.[32]

IV. The Tax Confusion

Ostensibly the facts that all proprietary medicines were subject to stamp duty, and that 'patent medicines' containing scheduled poisons were exempt from the regulations that applied to all other scheduled poisons, were entirely unconnected. The first concerned the public revenue, the second the regulation of dangerous substances in the public interest. However, the taxation of poisonous proprietary medicines gave rise to a widespread confusion which was deliberately used to evade the poisons legislation for commercial ends, with serious consequences for the public health enduring for some 25 years from 1868 to 1893. The confusion lay in the loose wording of the exemption in the poisons legislation, and the unwarranted importation of the tax legislation to address it.

The scope and efficacy of the exemption of poisonous proprietary medicines from poisons controls in the Pharmacy Act 1868 depended entirely on the meaning of the phrase 'patent medicines', a phrase the Act left undefined. Nomenclature had always been fluid. In the eighteenth century the terms quack, proprietary, secret, patent, nostrum and empiric were used interchangeably to describe medicines

[28] 'Debates on the Pharmacy Bill' (1868–69) 10 *Pharmaceutical Journal* (series 2) 57. See *Parliamentary Debates* (hereafter *Parl Deb*), vol 192, series 3, cols 1554–56, 1629–30, 1744–48, 15–18 June 1868 HL; *Parl Deb*, vol 193, series 3, cols 1214–20, 15 July 1868 HC.

[29] See, eg, 'The Sale of Poisons under the Pharmacy Act of 1868' (1868–69) 10 *Pharmaceutical Journal* (series 2) 331; 'The Pharmacy Act of 1868' (1862) 92 *The Lancet* 649.

[30] DC on Poisons, Minutes, 1903 (n 18) q 3741 (WJ Leggett).

[31] See 'Report of the Departmental Committee on Schedule A to the Pharmacy Act 1868', *HCPP* (1903) (Cd 1442) xxxiii 1, Minority Report, II 12.

[32] *Parl Deb* vol 269, series 3, col 596, 12 May 1882 HC (Charles Warton); 'Pharmaceutical Society v Piper and Co' (1892–93) 23 *Pharmaceutical Journal* (series 3) 495. See too DC on Poisons, Minutes, 1903 (n 18) q 3937 (WJ Leggett); J Ingham, 'Proprietary Medicines Containing Poison' (1892–93) 23 *Pharmaceutical Journal* (series 3) 883.

sold commercially in which individuals claimed a degree of proprietary interest, though ultimately the terms used reflected a distinction of scale. The term 'proprietary medicines' was therefore an appropriate name for all medicines of this kind. Calling proprietary medicines 'patent medicines' stemmed from the beginnings of the trade when it was a common practice to apply for and obtain formal royal letters patent for a medicine so as to acquire a monopoly on its manufacture and sale.[33] When it became too cumbersome and expensive to do so, proprietors and vendors began falsely to claim patented status to enhance the prestige of their product and give it a measure of respectability. They did so openly in the fulsome advertising on which their trade depended. Gradually the term 'patent medicines' came to be understood as reflecting the character of all such medicines, notably remedies with a secret composition, extravagantly promoted, and subject to proprietary claims. It was the term invariably employed by vendors and customers alike.

The use of such a loose expression in a formal statute was described as 'curious' in later litigation, 'a very slovenly slipshod mode of expression'.[34] It is possible that the intention was indeed to reflect the popular meaning of the term and exempt all proprietary medicines from the poisons regulation, but had the draftsmen so intended, they could have expressed this precisely, even referencing the categories set out in the medicine stamp duty legislation. Rather than adopt this cumbersome model, their successors may have decided it was easier to adopt the popular nomenclature of 'patent medicines' which everyone understood, even though it was both inaccurate and could lead to confusion. This is unlikely for two reasons. First, those who drafted legislation were fully aware of the need for precise language in view of the prevailing canons of statutory interpretation, and popular language was avoided. Secondly, it will be seen that the courts ultimately found that Parliament had not intended the exemption to carry the broader meaning because it quite clearly undermined the policy of the Pharmacy Act. It is more likely that the use of the term was simply an example of poor drafting, but whatever the motive in 1868, the phrase 'patent medicines' was employed in the statutory exemption and became accepted as carrying the broad popular meaning in relation to the law regulating poisons, and thereby to a large extent undermining the objective of the Act.

Vendors sought to move beyond popular nomenclature and to give this interpretation a legal basis. For this they looked to the medicine stamp duty both in its substance and its process. Despite the medicine stamp duty legislation carefully avoiding the phrase 'patent medicines', the term was almost universally adopted to describe all medicines brought within the purview of the tax. The reason was twofold: first, that virtually every kind of proprietary medicine in existence was brought into charge under the stamp duty legislation. Secondly, that they all had

[33] See generally Alan Mackintosh, 'Authority and Ownership: The Growth and Wilting of Medicine Patenting in Georgian England' (2016) 49 *British Journal for the History of Science*, 541.

[34] 'Pharmaceutical Society v Piper and Co' (1892–93) 23 *Pharmaceutical Journal* (series 3) 494 (Mr Bonsey).

to bear a revenue stamp and all vendors had to be licensed. Vendors of proprietary medicines, and their customers, took the view that liability to the tax and its physical manifestation in the stamp and licence gave a degree of official approval of the proprietary medicine analogous to that bestowed by a formal royal patent, and that accordingly such medicines were 'patent medicines' within the exemption and so not subject to the poisons controls.

The reasoning was entirely spurious. A patented medicine was one which had been granted a royal patent of monopoly and was protected from competition for 14 years. Whether a medicine was formally patented or not was a matter of record, and so an erroneous claim could be refuted with immediate and indisputable proof. Liability to the medicine stamp duty reflected the inherent character of the medicine, including its proprietary nature, but it did not, and could not, impress the medicine with the character of a formally patented medicine. The presence of the revenue stamp on a proprietary medicine was no more, and no less, than proof that the medicine stamp duty had been paid. The revenue officers were bound to issue the stamp to any proprietor of a dutiable medicine who paid for it. The stamp carried with it no more sanction or approval of the container's contents than a postage stamp did of the contents of a letter. The medicines were not examined by the revenue department of central government to assess their safety or efficacy, and officers neither knew nor cared whether the medicine was effective, benign or toxic, as long as the duty was paid. Analysis, when it was undertaken, was only to determine whether a particular medicine came within the charge to the tax. Similarly, the licence that all vendors of chargeable medicines had to obtain before they were permitted to sell them could be obtained by anyone on payment of a small sum. There was no examination of the fitness of the individual to sell medicines, or even of their honesty, the licence serving purely as an administrative framework to assist in the implementation of the medicine stamp duty by providing a record of medicine vendors and their trading premises. Any link between liability to the medicine stamp duty and the protection of a formal patent was illusory. As the editors of *The Law Journal* observed, '[T]he owner of a proprietary medicine should not be permitted, on the slender authority of a Government medicine stamp, to pose before the world as a patentee'.[35] The medical press, too, understood it was a 'fallacious contention' to evade the poisons legislation,[36] with the *British Medical Journal* in particular showing a consistently sound understanding of the issues involved, with accurate and well-considered commentary.[37]

Purchasers of proprietary medicines, however, accepted the notion wholeheartedly.[38] They regarded the stamp as a mark of official recognition,

[35] 'Patent Medicines' (1893) 28 *The Law Journal* 122.

[36] 'The Irregular Sale of Poisons' (1892) 1 *BMJ* 1 978, 978. See too 'Patent Medicines' (1892–93) 23 *Pharmaceutical Journal* (series 3) 694; 'The Illegal Sale of Poison' (1892) 2 *BMJ* 416.

[37] See, eg, 'Patent Medicines, So-Called' (1884) 2 *BMJ* 125.

[38] Confusion was seen at the most informed level: see *Parl Deb* vol 269, series 3, col 595, 12 May 1882 HC.

interpreted not just as indicating government sanction, but also as a guarantee of effectiveness and purity.[39] '"Oh!" say the artisan, the small tradesman's wife, and many others in a higher position in society, "this must be a good remedy, it is protected by Royal Letters Patent"'.[40] In giving a medicine an aura of respectability, legitimacy and credibility, it had immense commercial power, and it was no surprise that vendors made extensive use of the stamp in their advertisements, exploiting and fostering this perception to the full. It was, for example, usual to advertise medicines with the words 'none genuine unless guaranteed by the Government stamp', and some products which were not even liable to the tax went so far as to bear an imitation stamp to increase their appeal to customers.

Had the medicines in question been harmless, then the damage such a perception caused would be limited to some extent. In the case of medicines containing poisons, the danger was potentially both real and extensive. As was remarked in the House of Commons in 1884, it was absurd that the sale of ordinary poisons was strictly regulated, but 'anyone could, by putting a Government stamp on the bottle, sell any farrago of poisonous stuff'.[41] The editor of *Health News* argued that the damage done to the public by stamping proprietary medicines was 'incalculable'. The medicine stamp was regarded, essentially, as a 'government passport' for the sale of poisonous proprietary medicines.[42]

The perception, however, went further than an official-looking stamp, strengthening the false analogy drawn between the presence of the stamp and the granting of a formal patent. The wording of a normal medicine duty stamp in the middle years of the nineteenth century did not suggest any personal nexus between the product and the proprietor, because it only bore the words 'Inland Revenue', 'Medicine Label' and the amount of the duty, though its presence on a bottle or packet which itself invariably bore the name of the maker or vendor of the medicine sufficed to make the connection in the public mind. However, an unequivocal personal connection between apparent government sanction and a medicine's proprietor or vendor was demonstrated by what were known as 'appropriated stamps'. These were revenue stamps upon which the medicine proprietor's name and that of the product were printed, and they were entirely legitimate and purchased from the Inland Revenue. They were extremely popular.[43] Traders believed they gave them some security from competition because they would only be supplied to the individual who paid for them and so it demonstrated that the medicine in question was, at least, their

[39] See Editorial (1884) 124 *The Lancet* 21, 22; 'On the Professional Character of the Pharmaceutical Chemist' (1842) 2 *Pharmaceutical Journal* (series 1) 1, 2–3; *Parl Deb* vol 290, series 3, col 970, 14 July 1884 HC.

[40] Anon, *Exposures of Quackery* (London, Savoy Press, c 1897) vol 1, ch 1, 13. See too Wippell Gadd, 'How Far can the Abuse of Drugs be Prevented by Law?' (1910–11) 8 *Transactions of the Medico-Legal Society* 74, 81.

[41] *Parl Deb*, vol 286, series 3, col 804, 26 March 1884 HC (Robert Farquharson).

[42] Henry W Hubbard, 'The Poisons of the Day: A New Social Evil' (1882) 46 *Macmillan's Magazine* 238, 241; Anon, *Exposures of Quackery* (n 40) 24.

[43] For a full list of appropriated stamps in force in 1936, see TNA, CUST 118/366, 182–88.

own genuine one.[44] It was as marketing tools that appropriated stamps were used so enthusiastically, and shamelessly,[45] over the range of proprietary medicines, and those containing toxic or addictive ingredients were no exception. The proprietor of *Dr J. Collis Browne's Chlorodyne*, for instance, purchased an appropriated stamp. Being personalised in this way, appropriated stamps could even more readily be taken in the public mind as formal recognition of a specific medicine, and in this sense to resemble a grant of letters patent. Such was the potency of this perception that the revenue authorities felt it necessary to state that appropriated stamps did not 'have the effect of Letters Patent, the only security afforded being that they are supplied solely to the person for whom the special Plate was engraved, or to his authorised Agent'.[46] It appears that the Patent Office too felt the need to explain that the use of appropriated medicine duty stamps did not have the effect of letters patent, and that all communications with regard to the stamps were to be addressed to the Inland Revenue at Somerset House.[47]

Within a decade of the passing of the Pharmacy Act 1868, the practical exemption of all proprietary medicines from any legislative control of their poison content was causing very real problems. The traditional demand for self-medication continued unabated and indeed grew significantly, as did, inevitably, the trade in such products.[48] The unchecked and indiscriminate use of toxic ingredients in the composition of popular proprietary medicines, themselves freely available through a range of outlets with no regulation,[49] was condemned for its 'deplorable results'.[50] That it caused serious illness, addiction and all too often death, was widely accepted in medical, pharmaceutical and governmental circles. One writer in the *British Medical Journal* said that it had been stated 'on good authority' that there were 150,000 deaths per annum from patent medicines.[51]

Chlorodyne was notorious for causing deaths, and reports of chlorodyne poisoning abounded in the press, usually in the reports of coroners' inquests across the country. Deaths were either from accidental overdose when taken for

[44] It was regarded as protection akin to that given by the registration of a trade mark, and better in that forging a trade mark was a mere misdemeanour, while forging a revenue stamp was a felony which the Crown would always prosecute. See generally Lionel Bently, 'The Making of Modern Trade Mark Law: The Construction of the Legal Concept of Trade Mark (1860–1880)' in Lionel Bently, Jennifer Davis, and Jane C Ginsburg (eds), *Trade Marks and Brands* (Cambridge, Cambridge University Press, 2008).

[45] See 'Patent Medicines, So-Called' (n 37) 126.

[46] TNA, IR 83/61, 'Taxes, Precedent Book, 1892–1910'.

[47] Henry W Hubbard, 'Homicide, as a Misadventure' (1890) 16 *The National Review* 183, 187.

[48] In 1868 over 11,000 licences and over eight million stamps were issued. By 1884, just under 20,000 licences and over 19 million stamps were issued: 'Twenty-Seventh Annual Report of the Commissioners of Inland Revenue', *HCPP* (1884) (C 4088) xxiii 45, 111.

[49] In the course of an inquest regarding the death of a nine year old boy from ingesting *Indian Tincture*, a medicine containing Indian hemp, it emerged that in St Helens alone there were 93 shopkeepers who sold such compounds, and between 30 and 40 within a radius of one mile at Wigan: TNA, PC 8/310.

[50] *Parl Deb*, vol 269, series 3, col 597, 12 May 1882 HC.

[51] 'Poisoning by Chlorodyne' (1885) 1 *BMJ* 38, 39. See too 'Preventable Poisoning' (1889) 1 *BMJ* 424.

the relief of coughs or sleeplessness, overdose due to addiction, or from deliberate ingestion as an instrument of suicide.[52] It was also well known that chlorodyne was used as a stimulant by individuals who abstained from alcohol. *Hunter's Solution of Chloral* was regarded as equally hazardous, and its exemption from the poisons regulations was a dangerous absurdity. Only a registered chemist was permitted to sell unbranded solution of chloral, because it was a poison within the schedule to the Pharmacy Act 1868, but any unqualified individual could sell *Hunter's* even though it was significantly stronger and therefore potentially more harmful. Deaths of infants from toxic proprietary medicines were particularly prominent in the press. The opium content of medicines directed at children was particularly concerning, and it was said that in some districts *Daffy's Elixir* and *Godfrey's Cordial* were widely used to keep children quiet, and sometimes deliberately to cause their deaths.[53] The *Pharmaceutical Journal* regularly reported the deaths of young children from narcotic poisoning having taken cough preparations: *Budden's Compound Balsam of Horehound* and *Kay's Compound Essence of Linseed* were particularly condemned.[54]

The scale of deaths directly attributable to proprietary medicines containing poisons and the considerable degree of public attention afforded them led to pressure from medical and pharmaceutical professionals to address the exemption of toxic medicines from the legislative controls which existed. In giving evidence at an inquest into a suicide by chlorodyne, the chemists who had sold the medicine admitted they knew it contained morphia, chloroform, Indian hemp and prussic acid, 'but did not consider that it was a poison because it was a patent medicine'.[55] Indeed it was observed that 'chlorodyne and other patent medicines are supplied by some local chemists to all comers, in, practically, unlimited quantities'.[56] The coroner agreed with the jury that representations should be made to the effect that chlorodyne and other potent patent medicines should be brought within the poisons regulations.[57] At the very least, demanded coroners, such medicines should be labelled 'poison'. When coroners' juries called for deaths from poisonous proprietary medicines to be formally raised, the Privy Council was informed. For example, the jury asked the Home Secretary to consider the restriction of such medicines after an inquest found that two infants died from ingesting *Holt's*

[52] See, eg, 'Alleged Death from Chlorodyne' (1865) 6 *Pharmaceutical Journal* (series 2) 39; 'Case of Poisoning by Chlorodyne' (1885) 1 *BMJ* 906; 'Poisoning by Chlorodyne' (1892) 1 *BMJ* 515; DC on Poisons, Minutes, 1903 (n 18) q 1556 and Appendix V, 172.

[53] 'Report and Minutes of Evidence, Select Committee of the House of Lords on the Sale of Poisons Bill', *HCPP* (1857 session 2) (294) xii 551, qq 362–63.

[54] 'Alleged Acceleration of the Death of a Child by a Patent Medicine' (1881) 12 *Pharmaceutical Journal* (series 3) 532; 'Alleged Poisoning by a Proprietary Medicine' (1872) 2 *Pharmaceutical Journal* (series 3) 837. See too 'The Sale of Patent Medicines Containing Poisons' (1882) 13 *Pharmaceutical Journal* (series 3) 339; 'Poisoning by Patent Medicines' (1875) 2 *BMJ* 647–48; *Parl Deb*, vol 284, series 3, col 176, 7 February 1884 HC.

[55] 'Poisoning by Chlorodyne' (n 51) 39.

[56] ibid 38.

[57] ibid 39.

Whooping Cough Specific, which contained antimony. Similar cases drawn to the attention of the Privy Council included the death of a nine year old boy from *Indian Tincture* containing Indian hemp and that of an elderly lady having taken *Martin's Pectoral Balsam* containing opium.[58] The medical profession too called for greater restrictions on the sale of poisonous proprietary medicines, notably the Royal College of Surgeons and the Royal College of Physicians.[59] The *British Medical Journal* urged that chlorodyne be labelled as 'poison'.[60] This pressure to bring toxic proprietary medicines into the poisons regulations reached its height in the early 1880s.

V. Attempts at Reform

In 1882 an official memorandum described the exemption of poisonous proprietary medicines from the operation of the Pharmacy Act as a clear defect of the law regulating poisons.[61] The blatant and entirely unfounded use of the medicine stamp duty mechanism to argue a theoretical, and effect a practical, circumvention of the poisons legislation was harmful to the public and had to be addressed. The problems caused by the exemption could have been addressed in a number of ways. Broadly, the choice lay between reforming the medicine stamp duty or reforming the poisons legislation. The first option was problematic because the difficulty did not lie with the tax legislation as such, but rather with a misguided popular understanding of the significance of the revenue stamp. The stamp could not be dispensed with as it constituted proof of payment of the tax and was essential to the administration of the stamp duty. The tax itself would never be abolished merely on the basis of an inaccurate public perception of the stamp, which was a cultural issue and not a legal one. That was understood, and it was rarely suggested. The only realistic reform would be to change the appearance of the stamp to modify the public perception of it, but that did not address the real issue in question. It was, therefore, the second option which had to be adopted, namely the reform or clarification of the poisons legislation. That suggested two possibilities: a straightforward abolition of the exemption for 'patent medicines' in the Pharmacy Act 1868, or the establishment of a strict interpretation of the phrase either in reforming legislation or through judicial pronouncement.

After more than a decade of concern forcibly expressed in the medical and pharmaceutical press, with the more sensational cases of poisoning to be found in the general newspapers too, the pressure to reform began to bear fruit. A draft bill of 1883 purported to remove the exemption for proprietary medicines containing

[58] TNA, PC 8/310.
[59] ibid.
[60] See TE Amyot, 'Lawful Poisoning' (1881) 2 *BMJ* 691.
[61] TNA, PC 8/268.

scheduled poisons and proposed that such medicines be labelled accordingly with an instruction to use with caution.[62] The bill came to nothing, but is of interest in that rather than using the term 'patent medicines' in the body of the bill, the reference was to any medicine liable to stamp duty and containing a scheduled poison,[63] a much broader definition. A more successful initiative was taken by Charles Warton, the Member of Parliament for Bridport, in the following year. A barrister with no known medical affiliations, Warton initiated a vigorous parliamentary campaign to have the legislation amended. He had first raised the matter in Parliament in 1882,[64] and in 1884, exasperated by the Government's lack of action, produced his bill for restricting the sale of proprietary medicines – which, ironically, he too called 'patent' medicines – containing poisons.[65] The bill proposed to abolish the exemption in section 16 of the Pharmacy Act 1868,[66] and ensure that the Pharmaceutical Society analyse proprietary medicines and bring poisonous ones within the poisons regulations.[67] The bill survived only a week. It was rejected by the House of Commons without a division on the order for a second reading, the Government announcing that it intended to address the matter more broadly in due course. Despite considerable interest in the bill, it failed principally because the vested interests of the trade proved too strong and the Government deemed the scheme unworkable.[68] To require all proprietary medicines to undergo analysis however small the poison content would amount to 'harassing legislation'.[69] Warton did have some success in addressing the encouragement given to the trade in proprietary medicines by the appearance of the medicine duty stamp. He secured reform to the wording of the stamp, because it led the Chancellor of the Exchequer to discuss the matter with the Board of Inland Revenue, and in 1885 it was announced that the stamp would be modified 'so as to show clearly and make it plain that there is no Government guarantee of the medicine'.[70] Two months later new stamps were introduced, bearing the words 'This stamp implies no Government guarantee of the medicine', later shortened to 'No Government guarantee'. Unfortunately, such was the potency of the Government stamp that the disclaimer had little effect and the stamp retained its delusive character in the public mind.[71]

When a new Poisons Bill was finally introduced in the House of Lords in the following year, it made no express mention of 'patent' medicines and so by

[62] TNA, PC 8/299, 'A Bill to regulate the Sale of Poisons and Patent Medicines, 46 & 47 Vict. (1883)'.
[63] ibid cll 8 and 9.
[64] *Parl Deb*, vol 269, series 3, col 595, 12 May 1882 HC.
[65] 'Bill to Restrict the Sale of Patent Medicines', *HCPP* (1884) (Bill no 9) vi 31.
[66] ibid cl 5.
[67] *Parl Deb*, vol 286, series 3, cols 801–04, 26 March 1884 HC.
[68] ibid cols 807–10.
[69] ibid col 810 (Sir Henry James AG).
[70] *Parl Deb*, vol 299, series 3, col 428, 13 July 1885 HC. See 'Report and Minutes of Evidence from the Select Committee on Patent Medicines', (hereafter 'SC on Patent Medicines, 1914') *HCPP* (1914) (Cd 414) ix 1, q 257.
[71] 'The Law and the Sale of Poisons' (1899) 154 *The Lancet* 1177, 1177.

implication repealed the exemption of 1868 and brought such medicines containing poisons within the controls imposed by the bill on all poisons.[72] The only concession was that where a medicine contained a scheduled poison in such amount that it would not be poisonous if the medicine were taken as directed, it sufficed if the bottle was labelled 'to be used with caution'.[73] However the bill was unclear and ambiguous and was unanimously opposed by the Pharmaceutical Society on the grounds that it was 'so impracticable' that it would not fulfil its intention to protect the public.[74] As to the specific matter of proprietary medicines, the President of the Society understood the bill to allow even the most potent proprietary medicine to be sold, with a cautionary label, but otherwise outside the regulations of the Act, while others were unclear whether their sale was also confined to qualified individuals.[75] This bill too progressed no further.

VI. The Courts Intervene

With all attempts at legislative reform having failed, it fell to the courts to address the problem if and when a case in point came before them. In 1881 a police report following an accidental and fatal overdose of *Hunter's Solution of Chloral* marked the beginning of a series of prosecutions to establish the limits of the exemption from the poisons regulations of 'patent medicines'. The medicine, it said, was sold as a patent medicine bearing the Government stamp, and was available all over the country. It was not labelled 'poison', it being found on inquiry that chemists supposed the Government stamp overrode the provisions of the Pharmacy Act.[76] Indeed, it was a 'recognised trade custom' not to label them 'poison'.[77] The Home Office, informed by the opinions of the Institute of Chemistry, the College of Surgeons, the College of Physicians and the Pharmaceutical Society, took the view that this was erroneous, and that section 16 did not exempt medicines containing poisons from the operation of section 17 of the Pharmacy Act 1868, namely the provision setting down all the controls on the sale of poisons other than the requirement for the sale to be by a qualified chemist. For poisons in the second part of the schedule, the requirements were that the article should be labelled 'poison' and bear its name and the name and address of the supplier. On that basis, and under increasing pressure from the British Medical Association and coroners, it called for a test case to be brought to determine the point.[78] The prosecution, brought in early 1882 at the instance of the Director of Public Prosecutions, revealed that

[72] Poisons Bill, *HCPP* (1885) (Bill no 33) v 1 (HL).
[73] ibid cl 9(1).
[74] 'The New Poisons Bill' (1884–85) 15 *Pharmaceutical Journal* (series 3) 835.
[75] ibid.
[76] TNA, HO 45/9605/A1638, 'Police Report', 16 November 1881.
[77] 'Patent Medicines containing Poison' (1892) 1 *BMJ* 1102.
[78] TNA, HO 45/9605/A1638.

Hunter's Solution of Chloral had been sold without being labelled 'poison' in breach of section 17 of the Pharmacy Act 1868, chloral having been added to the second part of the schedule by order in council in 1877. On analysis it was found that a small amount of the medicine could be fatal. The defence counsel's argument that 'directly the Government stamp was placed upon it, the solution no longer came within the operation of the Act' was rejected by the magistrate and judgment was given for the Crown.[79] Leave to appeal was given, but the case was taken no further.

A second Treasury prosecution in 1889, concerning a child who died as a result of drinking a cough linctus containing morphine which was not labelled 'poison', was again brought with the intention of correcting the prevailing view, even among chemists, that the medicine stamp negated the need to label scheduled poisons. The point was neatly made by counsel for the prosecution, who observed that 'a proprietary preparation is not turned into a patent medicine by simply placing on it a medicine duty stamp'.[80]

In 1892 the matter was raised again in a third Treasury prosecution, instituted by the Parliamentary Bills Committee of the British Medical Association. JT Davenport, the manufacturer of *Dr J. Collis Browne's Chlorodyne*, had sold a bottle of the medicine containing morphine and chloroform, both scheduled poisons, without labelling it as a poison.[81] The Solicitor to the Treasury had selected this chlorodyne as the subject of this test case as it was the best known, most widely used proprietary medicine containing significant poisons and had caused a large number of deaths through its unusually toxic composition. Indeed, said counsel for the prosecution, it was 'common knowledge' that fatal results from taking chlorodyne were frequent.[82] The bottles of *Collis Browne's Chlorodyne* in evidence all displayed the Government stamp, the name of the article, the manufacturer's name and address, and the sentence 'None genuine without Dr J Collis Browne's name on the Government stamp'. Counsel for the defence pleaded the exemption for 'patent medicines' but the magistrate found for the Crown on the basis that the term 'patent medicines' in section 16 meant those possessing a formal patent. He arrived at that conclusion by looking to the medicine stamp duty legislation, where he observed that patent medicines were distinguished from all other proprietary medicines and thus formed a distinct class. Not being formally patented, *Collis Browne's Chlorodyne* did not come within the exemption, and as it contained a scheduled poison, it had to be labelled with the name of the article as sold, the word 'poison' and the name and address of the seller.[83]

It was the case of *R v Davenport* which marked the beginning of the resolution by the courts of the problem of the unrestricted sale of poisonous

[79] The case was reported in *The Times* (25 January 1882) 4.
[80] 'Poisons in Proprietary Preparations' (1890) 1 *BMJ* 734.
[81] For a report of the case, see 'Patent Medicines Containing Poison: Government Prosecution' (1892) 1 *BMJ* 995.
[82] ibid 995 (Mr Gill).
[83] ibid 995–96 (Mr Lushington). See SC Patent Medicines, 1914 (n 70) qq 8378–79.

proprietary medicines. After Davenport's conviction, Ernest Hart, the chairman of the Parliamentary Bills Committee of the British Medical Association who had been instrumental in initiating the prosecution, urged the Pharmaceutical Society to take proceedings against offending retailers. It was notable that since the passing of the Pharmacy Act in 1868 the Pharmaceutical Society had not used its statutory power to bring judicial proceedings against unqualified individuals selling poisonous proprietary medicines. In view of the repeated failure of attempts at legislative reform, such inactivity was surprising, but it appears that the Society had abided by guidance from the Privy Council to the effect that it could safely assume that a compound which was in itself harmless, even though it contained a scheduled poison, did not come within the Act.[84] It was of course possible to consume compounds of this nature in such large quantities that death resulted, but these were extreme cases and the Pharmaceutical Society could proceed on the reasonable basis outlined by the Privy Council.[85] The guidance was neither precise nor binding, but the Society's reliance on it would explain why no action was taken for so long in respect of chlorodyne and similar medicines. *Davenport*, however, proved the catalyst, and by the middle of 1892 penalties had been paid in nine cases, and several other cases were standing over for hearing. Proceedings had been authorised in another 33 cases.[86]

A judicial ruling that medicines containing scheduled poisons had to be appropriately labelled was not of great concern to vendors. It had always been clear from a careful reading of the Pharmacy Act that even if the medicine came within section 16, it was not exempt from the labelling requirements in section 17.[87] Furthermore, labelling poisonous proprietary medicines would rarely materially affect a retailer's business and many of the large dealers, including Davenport himself, quietly paid the penalties and then labelled their goods, often ensuring the caution was not too obvious.[88] Of far greater concern to medicine proprietors and vendors would be a definitive judicial ruling that the term 'patent medicine' in the exemption did not include all proprietary medicines, a finding underlying the *Davenport* decision but subsumed by the labelling point, for that would mean only qualified chemists could sell them and that would severely damage their highly lucrative trade. As a result, some vendors showed 'a distinctly defiant attitude' to the *Davenport* decision,[89] and indeed the owners of proprietary medicines formed the Patent Medicine Vendors' Association specifically to protect themselves in this activity.[90]

[84] TNA, PC 8/153, 'Law Officers' Opinion on the Pharmacy Act 1868', 5 March 1869. A draft bill of 1883 provided to the contrary, but a handwritten marginal note observed that this would raise questions which were 'not at all easy, and involve many technical considerations': TNA, PC 8/299.

[85] 'Pharmaceutical Society v Piper and Co.' (1892–93) 23 *Pharmaceutical Journal* (series 3) 493.

[86] 'Restriction of the Sale of Poisons' (1892) 2 *BMJ* 376.

[87] Because the exemption in s 16 was from what is 'hereinbefore contained' in the Act.

[88] 'Restriction of the Sale of Poisons' (n 86).

[89] 'The Illegal Sale of Poisons' (1892) 2 *BMJ* 807, 808.

[90] DC on Poisons, Minutes, 1903 (n 18) q 3739 (WJ Leggett); 'The Sale of Proprietary Medicines Containing Poison' (1892) 2 *BMJ* 601.

In 1892 the Pharmaceutical Society sought to obtain an authoritative decision on the scope of the section 16 exemption and brought proceedings against a firm of grocers for selling a bottle of *Dr J. Collis Browne's Chlorodyne* in open shop when unqualified. The case of *Pharmaceutical Society v Piper & Co* was heard in the Bloomsbury County Court[91] then, some two months later, on appeal in the Divisional Court. The bottle contained one grain of morphine, and medical experts asserted that a hundredth part of a grain would kill an infant, while eight-tenths could kill an adult. *Collis Browne's Chlorodyne* was admitted to be a popular and useful medicine which had been on the market for many years, but it was not, and never had been, protected by letters patent.

Two points were at issue before the Court in the *Piper* litigation: first, whether *Collis Browne's Chlorodyne* was a poison within the meaning of the Act; and second, whether, if it were so found, it came within the exemption for 'patent medicines'. The case was closely argued in the County Court before Bacon J by counsel for the grocers, HD Bonsey, who frequently acted for the Patent Medicine Vendors' Association, and TR Grey, for the Pharmaceutical Society. Counsel for the grocers argued first that *Collis Browne's Chlorodyne* was not a poison within the meaning of the Act because it was a mixture, and that the presence of some poison did not make the whole mixture a poison. To find otherwise would cause real hardship to the trade and to those who relied on these simple remedies for everyday conditions because virtually all such medicines did contain poisons, but in such small quantities that when taken properly they would cause no harm.[92] Even if it were a poison within the Act, he continued, as an exempt patent medicine it could be sold by an unqualified individual as long as it was labelled as 'poison'. A number of witnesses appeared for the grocers to demonstrate that the words 'patent medicine' had always been understood by the trade to include all proprietary medicines.[93] It was also clear that they equated stamped medicines with 'patent' medicines.[94] That popular meaning, argued counsel, was both reasonable and most probably the intention of the legislature at the time the Act was passed, when no formally patented medicines existed in contrast to thousands of proprietary medicines.[95] Had the legislators intended to include only formally-patented medicines within the exemption, they would have used the usual legal mode of expression, as used in the Stamp Acts, namely medicines sold under 'Her Majesty's Letters Patent under the Great Seal'. Any other interpretation would be 'strained'.[96]

Mr Grey, counsel for the Pharmaceutical Society in the County Court, would have none of it. *Collis Browne's Chlorodyne* was a poison because it contained a scheduled poison and, if taken in large quantities, could prove fatal. It did not

[91] The full report of the proceedings is in (1892–93) 23 *Pharmaceutical Journal* (series 3) 489–503 (County Court) and 656–62 (Divisional Court).

[92] ibid 492–94.

[93] ibid 494, 496–98.

[94] ibid 497, 500, 658.

[95] ibid 495, 676.

[96] ibid 679.

come within the exemption for 'patent medicines' because when the term was used in an Act of Parliament it could only mean medicines for which a formal patent had been taken out. The medicine stamp duty legislation made a clear distinction between formally-patented medicines and other classes of proprietary medicines, as did the food and drugs legislation.[97] To open the exemption to all stamped medicines would mean that anyone could include as much poison in a medicine as they wished, and sell it on the open market with no restrictions beyond a label of 'poison', having only paid a few shillings for a medicine stamp duty licence and affixed the correct stamp to the product.

In the County Court Bacon J found for the Pharmaceutical Society, primarily on the basis of the mischief the Act was intended to address. To allow a poison to escape the controls of the legislation simply by mixing it with another ingredient would render the Act nugatory. A poison did not cease to be a poison simply because it was mixed with something else.[98] Furthermore, *Collis Browne's Chlorodyne* did not come within the exemption for 'patent medicines'. The term 'patent medicines', said the judge, was undoubtedly a 'handy and convenient title,' but '[b]ad as that description is, still it conveys a meaning'.[99] That meaning was medicines sold under letters patent under the great seal and the reason, he said, was obvious. Accepting the argument of counsel for the Pharmaceutical Society, the exemption of a large number of medicines whose composition was unknown and could contain deadly poisons would undermine the policy and purpose of the Act to safeguard the public, while the exemption of those medicines whose composition was well known through a formal patent would not. On that basis, too, he could not hold that every medicine bearing the medicine stamp, namely all proprietary medicines, came within the exemption.[100] *Collis Browne's Chlorodyne* was a poison, and it fell outside the exemption. It could, therefore, be sold only by qualified chemists and had to be labelled 'poison'. When the arguments were reprised on appeal to the Divisional Court in February 1893, in full and considered judgments the Court affirmed Bacon J's decision and reasoning in a case regarded as one of considerable difficulty.[101] 'Patent medicines' meant exactly that – medicines sold under letters patent, confirmed in 1896 to mean a current and valid patent.[102] It was entirely proper that the medicine duty stamp was not a material argument in the course of the litigation. It was discussed only to quash the notion that patent medicines in the exemption meant stamped medicines, and thus recognised that the connection of the tax with the poisons regulation exemption had always been spurious. The decision finally broke any perception of a material connection.

[97] ibid 501. See too ibid 671–72 (Mr Poland, QC); *Pharmaceutical Society v Piper & Co* [1893] 1 QB 686, 689; Food and Drugs Act 1875 (38 & 39 Vict c 63), s 6(2).

[98] 'Pharmaceutical Society v Piper and Co.' (n 85) 502.

[99] ibid 503.

[100] ibid.

[101] ibid 679–83 (Lawrance and Collins JJ). See too *Pharmaceutical Society v Piper* (1893) 68 LT 493.

[102] *Pharmaceutical Society v Fox* (1896) 12 TLR 471.

The decision in the *Piper* case was clear and strong, and was taken no further. Indeed its reasoning was adopted in its entirety by the Court in *Pharmaceutical Society v Armson* in the following year.[103] That case affirmed that the words 'patent medicine' were to be construed according to the ordinary canons of construction, 'in the manner which the Queen's English dictates',[104] to mean medicines for which the owner has obtained a patent under the great seal. Kay LJ saw one clear reason for the exemption: that where the exclusive right to make or sell a medicine had been granted to an individual by letters patent under the great seal, a full description of the product was lodged in the Patent Office, and so any individuals buying the medicine could inform themselves of its ingredients.[105] It would be 'rather hard', he said, to remove from patentees their rights of freely making or selling their product under a patent they had lawfully obtained if, as was likely, they were not qualified chemists.[106]

In the years following the decision in *Piper*, a case understood by the profession to be of considerable importance,[107] the Pharmaceutical Society brought prosecutions against unqualified vendors selling scheduled poisons. Of the 729 prosecutions brought between 1896 and 1901, just over half related to the sale by unqualified individuals of proprietary medicines containing scheduled poisons. The principal medicines in question were *Kay's Essence of Linseed*, various chlorodynes and *Winslow's Syrup*, with cough mixtures containing laudanum also accounting for a significant number.[108]

The grocers inevitably suffered the most financially and commercially from the decision in *Piper* because proprietary medicines formed a considerable portion of their sales.[109] Immediately after the decision the Pharmaceutical Society issued notices to unqualified sellers of proprietary medicines containing poisons informing them it was now unlawful to sell them,[110] and while the editors of *The Law Journal* hoped that the decision would 'check the reprehensible practice' of selling proprietary medicines and claiming exemption from the poisons legislation on the basis that they were 'patent medicines', they also expressed the hope that the Pharmaceutical Society would allow grocers time to clear their existing stocks before proceeding against them.[111] In general, the unqualified vendors of proprietary medicines appear, in large towns at least, to have ceased to sell poisonous

[103] *Pharmaceutical Society v Armson* (1894) 10 TLR 443, [1894] 2 QB 720.
[104] *Pharmaceutical Society v Armson* [1894] 2 QB 720, 728 (AL Smith LJ).
[105] ibid 726.
[106] ibid 726–27.
[107] Michael Carteighe, 'Fifty-second Annual Meeting of the Pharmaceutical Society' (1892–93) 23 *Pharmaceutical Journal* 953.
[108] DC on Poisons, Minutes, 1903 (n 18) Appendix vii, 176, 195.
[109] For the practical difficulties faced by chemists, see FA Rogers, 'What Uniform Procedure can be Adopted by Chemists with Regard to the Sale of Scheduled Poisons' (1892–93) 23 *Pharmaceutical Journal* (series 3) 897.
[110] Carteighe (n 107) 953.
[111] 'Patent Medicines' (n 35) 191.

proprietary medicines.[112] Other manufacturers, voluntarily or as a result of legal proceedings, began to remove the poisons from their products and then continued to market them lawfully. The proprietors of *Steedman's Soothing Powders*, a remedy for teething infants which contained a very small amount of opium, knowing that labelling a medicine intended for children as 'poison' would be a commercial disaster, and having received medical advice to the effect that the powders would be almost as effective without the trace amount of opium, removed it from its formulation.[113] Similarly, morphine was removed from *Owbridge's Lung Tonic*,[114] *Beecham's Cough Pills*,[115] *Powell's Balsam of Aniseed* and *Winslow's Soothing Syrup*.[116] By the time the British Medical Association published its expert analysis of the most common proprietary medicines in 1909, most contained no scheduled poisons, or only a trace thereof.[117]

The more recalcitrant proprietors of medicines containing scheduled poisons sought to evade the decision in *Piper* by applying for a formal patent, but where the Pharmaceutical Society suspected this, it took action and immediately following the ruling in 1893 it succeeded in having nine patents revoked and a further 42 applications for patents abandoned.[118] In one case reported in the legal press the Society petitioned for the revocation of a patent for a cough mixture containing two scheduled poisons, namely morphine and chloroform. The grounds for revocation were an absence of novelty, and that on the face of the specification the article was not a proper one for the grant of a patent. The Society maintained the patent was 'indefensible', and since the patentee offered no defence, it was duly revoked. The case highlighted the concern that such patents had been granted to the detriment of the public health and safety and clearly undermining the intent of the Pharmacy Act 1868. It was said that the Court of Chancery gave great weight to the argument that the effect of a patent would be to enable the patentee to freely sell a medicine which, had it not been formally patented, would have been considerably restricted in its sale.[119] As the editors of *The Law Journal* observed in reporting the matter, '[i]t is certainly desirable that compounds containing a deadly amount of poisonous ingredient should not be allowed, under the protection of a worthless patent, to be thrown broadcast over the country'.[120]

[112] Carteighe (n 107) 953.
[113] SC on Patent Medicines, 1914 (n 70) qq 9916–26.
[114] DC on Poisons, Minutes, 1903 (n 18) q 548.
[115] SC on Patent Medicines, 1914 (n 70) q 8982.
[116] ibid q 2971.
[117] British Medical Association, *Secret Remedies: What they Cost and what they Contain* (London, British Medical Association, 1909).
[118] SC on Patent Medicines, 1914 (n 70) q 12390. See too 'Patents and the Sale of Poisons' (1893) 2 *BMJ* 1066; 'Patent Medicines' (1894) 1 *BMJ* 1281.
[119] Wippell Gadd, 'How Far can the Abuse of Drugs be Prevented by Law?' (1910–11) 8 *Transactions of the Medico-Legal Society* 74, 82.
[120] 'Proprietary and Patent Medicines' (1893) 28 *The Law Journal* 851, 852. See *Re Rendell's Patent* (1894) 96 LT 607.

Following the *Piper* decision, the exemption in section 16 of the Pharmacy Act 1868 applying only to medicines bearing a formal patent which was still in force, was so narrow that it was essentially of no practical importance since no formally patented medicines were in existence. There was thus no urgency to repeal the clause, and indeed the Poisons and Pharmacy Act 1908,[121] which retained the Pharmacy Act 1868 as the primary legislation, left the exemption for 'patent medicines' untouched. Not until 1933 was the exemption finally removed, in an Act which considered the whole law regulating the complicated and increasingly outdated relationship between poisons and the practice of pharmacy.[122] Patent and proprietary medicines were not mentioned by name in the extensive debates on the bill, but as the Act repealed the existing legislation relating to the sale of poisons other than the Dangerous Drugs Act 1920, the exemption for formally-patented medicines was effectively abolished. It was striking that the medicine stamp duty did not appear in any of the debates reported, suggesting the fallacious connection had been exposed once and for all, and that the discourse had moved on.[123] From 1933, therefore, all proprietary medicines, including formally patented ones, were subject to the poisons regulations if they contained a scheduled poison.

VII. Conclusion

For the last quarter of the nineteenth century, when Britain was still ravaged by epidemic and endemic diseases and self-medication was widespread, the regulation of popular proprietary medicines containing poisons was significantly undermined. Vested interests exploited poor statutory drafting by cynically misusing the medicine stamp duty and its legislative code, and promoting a cultural misunderstanding of the nature of the medicine duty stamp itself. In this way toxic or addictive medicines escaped legislative attempts at regulation in 1868 and were freely available throughout the century. The number of deaths, particularly of infants, and a growing awareness within medical circles of the problems of addiction caused by this practice constituted the imperative for change, and ultimately provoked a legal response. Other factors were clearly at play, not least the tensions in the medical and pharmaceutical sectors fighting for professional recognition and monopoly in their activities, but essentially it was the public health crisis that drove the reform of the poisons legislation.

While the legislative response failed, largely because of the power of commercial imperatives, the judicial response was strikingly effective. The construction of the poorly drafted exemption provision in the Pharmacy Act 1868 by the judges

[121] 8 Edw VII c 55.
[122] Pharmacy and Poisons Act 1933 (23 & 24 Geo V c 25).
[123] *Parl Deb*, vol 86, series 5, cols 1035–78, 7 March 1933 HL.

in *Piper* took poisonous proprietary medicines out of circulation, and thereby rendered the consuming public significantly safer. It allowed the Act to operate as it had always been intended. It was a decision of real significance, because it constituted the very first legal control over proprietary medicines of any kind in Britain. It is true that the exemption survived until 1933, but its construction was so narrow, and in any event the poison content of most proprietary medicines had been removed in the years following the *Piper* decision, that its presence in the legislation did not endanger the public health.

While the decision in *Piper* made it clear that the long-standing connection between formally-patented medicines and stamped medicines was entirely specious, and therefore irrelevant to the poisons regulations, the decision could not address the outstanding problem in relation to the medicine stamp duty. The tax itself did no harm. Indeed, it was beneficial to some degree in that it could be said to impose a commercial restraint on the potentially harmful practice of self-medication by making the medicine more expensive for the customer and imposing an administrative burden on the vendors. Its necessary physical expression, the stamp, however, did do harm. The perception of the stamp as an official government guarantee of quality continued unabated.[124] The danger to the public health of this was no longer so acute, because after *Piper* stamped proprietary medicines sold in open shop were those which were generally regarded as benign, but it was still undesirable in that it encouraged self-medication and the avoidance of professional medical care. This was a cultural, not a legal, issue and the tax legislators could do little in the way of effective response. It has been seen that tax law permitted only a change of wording on the stamp, which in practice made no difference. The problem would have been instantly solved by abolishing the medicine stamp duty altogether, but this the legislators were unwilling to do. Whatever the unfortunate indirect effect of the medicine stamp duty on the general public's health and its exploitation of public credulity, in the nineteenth century, and well into the twentieth, legislators would abolish a tax only when it ceased to yield sufficient revenue, and administration costs outweighed any gain. In 1884 the Chancellor of the Exchequer, Hugh Childers, said he could 'hold out no hope of repealing this tax, which brings in £160,000 a year'[125] and as late as 1935 Neville Chamberlain said that the repeal of the medicine stamp duty was 'out of the question because of the loss of revenue … it would involve'.[126] Tax law staunchly maintained the orthodox position that any undesirable social effects of a tax would be ignored if the yield was maintained, and this dominance of financial imperatives was unmoving. Governments had no interest in the integrity of medicines and were largely indifferent to the social effect of the medicine duty stamp, just as they had been for over 20 years to the impact on public health of

[124] TNA, CUST 118/366, 43.
[125] *Parl Deb*, vol 292, series 3, col 93, 7 August 1884 HC.
[126] TNA, CUST 118/367, 117.

the window tax.[127] Taxes were instruments of revenue and were not regarded as an appropriate vehicle for the regulation of undesirable social practices. With the notable exception of customs duties, this was the policy underlying all nineteenth century taxation and even the public health crisis caused by poisonous proprietary medicines did not change it. The medicine stamp duty was eventually abolished in 1941, not because of any damage to the public health, but because it had become legally untenable.[128] With its abolition, however, the problematic stamp with its cultural perceptions disappeared.

[127] Chantal Stebbings, 'Public Health Imperatives and Taxation Policy: The Window Tax as an Early Paradigm in English Law' in John Tiley (ed), *Studies in the History of Tax Law*, vol 5 (Oxford, Hart Publishing, 2011).

[128] Pharmacy and Medicines Act 1941 (4 & 5 Geo VI c 41) s 11; Stebbings (2018) (n 8) 185–217.

11

Private Offence, Public Wrong: Prosecuting Disease Transmission by Medical Professionals in Nineteenth-Century England

KATHERINE D WATSON

I. Introduction

In the late twentieth century, the HIV epidemic in the United States triggered calls for the criminal prosecution of individuals who knowingly communicated the disease to another person, and by 1990 several people had been convicted.[1] This trend prompted public health historian Gregg S Meyer to note the parallels to an earlier debate 'occasioned by another potentially lethal sexually transmitted disease, syphilis'.[2] In an article that examined the period 1880–1913, Meyer found evidence that in sixteenth-century Europe the transmission of syphilis could have been regarded as a criminal offence, but that more than three centuries had then passed before actual laws to punish it emerged. Such laws generally focused on women, particularly prostitutes, because doctors believed that women – in whom the signs of venereal disease were less easily recognised – were its 'chief carriers'.[3] By the turn of the twentieth century, the need for a public health 'war on syphilis' had gained international traction in the medical profession.[4] Simultaneously, the poisonous impact of venereal disease on marriage had been taken up by English

[1] Lawrence O Gostin, 'The AIDS Litigation Project: A National Review of Court and Human Rights Commission Decisions, Part I: The Social Impact of AIDS' (1990) 263 *Journal of the American Medical Association* 1961.

[2] Gregg S Meyer, 'Criminal Punishment for the Transmission of Sexually Transmitted Diseases: Lessons from Syphilis' (1991) 65 *Bulletin of the History of Medicine* 549.

[3] Keir Waddington, *An Introduction to the Social History of Medicine: Europe Since 1500* (Basingstoke, Palgrave Macmillan, 2011) 68.

[4] Meyer (n 2) 550–51.

feminists as a means of critiquing the sexual double standard,[5] since the repeal in 1886 of the infamous Contagious Diseases Acts (1864, 1866, 1869) had ended the forcible medical examination of suspected prostitutes but had done nothing to protect a woman who found herself married to a man suffering from venereal disease.[6]

The advent of World War I led to renewed attempts to criminalise female sexuality, as a means of protecting soldiers' health. In England this culminated in the short-lived Regulation 40D, introduced as an amendment to the Defence of the Realm Act in March 1918 but repealed just six months later. This Regulation applied only to women, who could be subjected to a forced medical examination and imprisoned for soliciting or having sex with a member of the armed forces if she was suffering from venereal disease. In this situation, 'the transmission of VD to a soldier was seen as a crime against the state, by weakening the armed forces both physically and morally'.[7] While American women remained subject to potential detention and examination, especially in wartime,[8] in the United Kingdom public health campaigns focused on prevention until the HIV/AIDS epidemic precipitated renewed interest in the criminalisation of disease transmission. In England and Wales, it has been possible to prosecute people for the reckless or intentional transmission of HIV since 2001 and, according to Kat Smithson's calculation in 2023, 'To date there have been more than thirty people convicted of reckless HIV transmission, and one person of intentionally transmitting HIV. There has also been one especially contentious case of transmission of Herpes.'[9]

Other prosecutions have been brought for transmission of gonorrhoea and hepatitis B and C.[10]

Transmission of HIV is typically criminalised in one of two ways: under a country's general law concerning offences against the person, as in England and Wales; or under HIV- or disease-specific legislation.[11] According to the National Aids Trust, prosecutions 'are complex in nature, in part because they are based

[5] Gail Savage, '"The Wilful Communication of a Loathsome Disease": Marital Conflict and Venereal Disease in Victorian England' (1990) 34 *Victorian Studies* 35.

[6] ibid 38.

[7] Laura Lammasniemi, 'Regulation 40D: Punishing Promiscuity on the Home Front During the First World War' (2017) 26 *Women's History Review* 585.

[8] John Parascandola, 'Quarantining Women: Venereal Disease Rapid Treatment Centers in World War II America' (2009) 83 *Bulletin of the History of Medicine* 431; Scott W Stern, 'America's Forgotten Mass Imprisonment of Women Believed to Be Sexually Immoral' (*History*, 21 July 2019), available at www.history.com/news/chamberlain-kahn-act-std-venereal-disease-imprisonment-women.

[9] Kat Smithson, 'New Crown Prosecution Service Guidance on HIV Transmission Cases is Clear that U=U' (*National Aids Trust Blog*, 29 March 2023), available at www.nat.org.uk/blog/new-crown-prosecution-service-guidance-hiv-transmission-cases-clear-uu.

[10] Lisa Power, *Understanding Criminal Prosecutions for Sexual Transmission of Infection* (London, Terrence Higgins Trust, 2018) 3, available at www.tht.org.uk/hiv-and-sexual-health/living-well-hiv/legal-issues/views-prosecutions.

[11] Matthew Weait, 'HIV and the Meaning of Harm' in Catherine Stanton and Hannah Quirk (eds), *Criminalising Contagion: Legal and Ethical Challenges of Disease Transmission and the Criminal Law* (Cambridge, Cambridge University Press, 2016).

upon law which was not designed for this purpose (Offences Against the Person Act 1861)'.[12] This brings out two important aspects of the history of the prosecution of disease transmission in England: it has largely been focused on sexually transmitted diseases, and even today it continues to rest on a Victorian statute.[13]

In the rest of this chapter, the broad outlines of the historiography relating to the prosecution of venereal disease transmission will be sketched briefly, before turning to consider a different aspect of the topic: what criminal penalties, if any, should be applied to medical practitioners – doctors and midwives – who infected their patients with a disease they knew they had contracted? The Offences Against the Person Act 1861 opened up new options for prosecution, but in order to understand why and how these could be deployed, we must first consider the legal expectations placed upon doctors and midwives. Textbooks of forensic medicine provide the ideal means of doing this. Written for both doctors and lawyers, they contain discussions of the law and its interpretation in the civil and criminal courts, and summaries of the legal duties owed by medical professionals which were periodically revised not only in the light of new case law but also following new medical and scientific discoveries, such as antisepsis and germ theory. The chapter will then examine a series of prosecutions of medical practitioners accused of transmitting an infectious disease, to consider their success or failure in the light of wider debates about public health, professional responsibility, and harm.

II. Victorian Prosecutions for the Transmission of Venereal Disease

At about the same time that Meyer published his work on prosecutions for the transmission of syphilis, Gail Savage examined the Victorian debate about the sexual double standard from the perspective of English divorce law. Under the Divorce and Matrimonial Causes Act 1857,[14] women could sue for divorce only on the grounds of adultery, plus one other offence of bigamy, incest, cruelty or desertion. Allegations of cruelty in divorce proceedings most often focused on physical abuse,[15] but lawyers acting on behalf of wives also recognised that citing the transmission of venereal disease as a form of cruelty offered the divorce court a persuasive argument. The total number of divorce suits in which it was used was relatively small, just 107 in the period 1858–1901, but it was employed more frequently by wives than by husbands and these wives' suits enjoyed a higher success rate – 94.4 per cent versus 57.9 per cent for husbands. Success lay in the

[12] Smithson (n 9).

[13] 24 & 25 Vict c 100; in force from 6 November 1861. The law in Scotland was and remains different and will not be discussed in this chapter.

[14] 20 & 21 Vict c 85; in force from 1 January 1858.

[15] Jennifer Aston, 'Petitions to the Court for Divorce and Matrimonial Causes: A New Methodological Approach to the History of Divorce, 1857–1923' (2022) 43 *Journal of Legal History* 162, 178.

reversal of the sexual double standard, by proving that the man had wilfully introduced venereal disease into the home following acts of adultery.[16] And as James Hammerton has written, by the late eighteenth century there was a

> general acceptance of 'wilful communication' of venereal disease as legal cruelty, which required proof that the offending spouse was aware of the infection, the disease was actually communicated, and the victim was unaware of the offender's condition.[17]

The links between marital cruelty and disease transmission were thrust under a legal spotlight in *R v Clarence*,[18] where the defendant's criminal conviction for infecting his wife with gonorrhoea was quashed by the Court for Crown Cases Reserved. Lois Bibbings has characterised the case as an unsuccessful attempt to legally categorise Clarence's act as 'a form of *non-sexual* violence'.[19] She places her analysis of the legal arguments and views of the judges at different court levels (who split nine to four) in the context of wider anxieties about male sexual conduct that were circulating in the late Victorian era.[20] Both her work and the examination of this case by Kate Gleeson show that the legal decision-making revolved around the defendant's status as a husband, who in normal circumstances had every right to have sex with his wife.[21] However, both scholars note, albeit very briefly, that although the focus in the case turned to 'sexual propriety and morality', the Crown had actually 'charged specifically nonsexual assaults'.[22]

This was done under the Offences Against the Person Act 1861. Section 20 provided that inflicting grievous bodily harm, with or without a weapon, was a misdemeanor punishable by up to three years' penal servitude; while section 47 provided that assault occasioning actual bodily harm could be prosecuted on indictment and similarly punished by up to three years in a convict prison. Clarence was charged with both offences. A key question on which his conviction might have turned was whether infection by gonorrhea fell within the legal interpretation of 'harm' for the purposes of each offence. However, this issue was overshadowed by Clarence's status as the victim's husband and by the argument made in his defence that she had therefore consented to sexual intercourse. The prosecution argued that she would not have submitted to sexual intercourse if

[16] Savage (n 5) 47–50.

[17] A James Hammerton, *Cruelty and Companionship: Conflict in Nineteenth-Century Married Life* (London, Routledge, 1992) 97.

[18] *R v Clarence* (1888) 22 QBD 23. See also *Old Bailey Proceedings Online* (www.oldbaileyonline.org, version 9.0, April 1888). Trial of Charles James Clarence (28) (t18880423-429a).

[19] Lois S Bibbings, *Binding Men: Stories About Violence and Law in Late Victorian England* (Abingdon, Routledge, 2014) 112.

[20] ibid 119–32.

[21] ibid 132–38. See too Kate Gleeson, 'Sex, Wives, and Prostitutes: Debating *Clarence*' in Judith Rowbotham and Kim Stevenson (eds), *Criminal Conversations: Victorian Crimes, Social Panic, and Moral Outrage* (Columbus, OH, Ohio State University Press, 2005).

[22] Gleeson, 'Sex, Wives, and Prostitutes' (n 21) 220.

she had known that her husband was infected with gonorrhea: by concealing his illness, he had therefore 'obtained consent by fraud, which was no consent at all'.[23] However, this was rejected by a majority of the judges who quashed his convictions on the basis that he could plead consent. Further, concealment of his condition was not itself an illegal act: in the words of Pollock B,

> the real offence is not an assault but the suppression or concealment of that which ought to have been communicated; and … if it be desirable to bring it within the criminal law it should be done by legislation.[24]

Clarence remains a leading case that is much discussed in English legal textbooks on sexual offences in connection with the issues of deception and consent in sexual relations,[25] and in 2004 it was revisited in *R v Dica*.[26] That concerned the conviction of an HIV-positive defendant on two charges of causing grievous bodily harm under section 20. Mohammed Dica had concealed his HIV positive status from two sexual partners with whom he had had unprotected sex, infecting them with HIV. Dica's counsel argued at trial that they had consented to sexual intercourse and hence that Dica could not be convicted, following *Clarence*. However, the judge let the case proceed, holding that HIV infection was a form of harm that could fall within section 20 and withdrawing the defence of consent from the jury. On Dica's appeal against conviction, the Court of Criminal Appeal accepted that HIV infection could come within section 20, but held that the judge had been wrong to withdraw the factual question from the jury, of whether Dica's victims had agreed to run the risk of infection. The convictions were therefore quashed and a retrial was ordered.[27]

Legal scholars and human rights activists may consider current uses of the criminal law to prosecute the transmission of HIV to be inappropriate or poorly conceptualised,[28] but their Victorian counterparts were clearly seeking ways to widen the applicability of the concept of harm, away from its long-time association with physical wounding. Might a prosecution have succeeded where the transmission of a communicable disease occurred via nonsexual means and/or between

[23] See, eg, Peter Rook and Robert Ward, *Rook and Ward on Sexual Offences*, 6th edn (London, Sweet & Maxwell, 2021) 1.363.

[24] *Clarence* (n 18) 64.

[25] Karl Laird, 'Rapist or Rogue? Deception, Consent and the Sexual Offences Act 2003' [2014] *Criminal Law Review* 492; Shivam Kaushik, 'The Impossible Trinity of Deception, Sex and Consent' (2021) 85 *Journal of Criminal Law* 416.

[26] *R v Dica* [2004] EWCA Crim 1103, [2004] QB 1257.

[27] *Rook and Ward* (n 23) 1.364–1.365.

[28] See, eg, Weait (n 11); J Chalmers, 'The Criminalisation of HIV Transmission' (2002) 28 *Journal of Medical Ethics* 160; Damian Warburton, 'A Critical Review of English Law in Respect of Criminalising Blameworthy Behaviour by HIV+ Individuals' (2004) 68 *Journal of Criminal Law* 55; Kate Gleeson, 'The Problem of *Clarence*, Brutal at His Best: James Fitzjames Stephen and the Doctrine of Sexual Inequality' (2005) 14 *Nottingham Law Journal* 1; Sophie Matthiesson, 'Should the Law Deal with Reckless HIV Infection as a Criminal Offence or as a Matter of Public Health?' (2010) 21 *King's Law Journal* 123.

individuals unrelated to one another? And in cases involving non-consensual sex in which a disease was communicated to the victim, it *was* possible to secure a conviction under the 1861 Act. For this proposition, Lois Bibbings cites two cases of the 1860s: *R v Bennett* (1866) and *R v Sinclair* (1867).[29] In the latter, the defendant was charged with the same offences as those with which Clarence was charged 20 years later, but the judge noted that the question of consent to the sexual contact

> might be vitiated by the prisoner's behaviour if the jury found four elements to have existed: first, that he knew of his condition; secondly, that he knew of the likely consequences of engaging in intercourse; thirdly, that he did not tell the girl; and, finally, that she would not have consented had she been in possession of all the facts. Here 'the deceit practised upon her' would entail that she had not consented in the context of non-sexual offences against the person and the disease transmission would constitute an assault.[30]

In *Clarence*, however, Manisty J declined to follow these decisions and declared it to be 'contrary to common sense to describe the act of the prisoner in this case as an assault'.[31] It is evident, therefore, both that prosecutors recognised the *potential* offered by the 1861 Act and that, for a couple of decades at least, it was *in theory* possible to charge defendants with offences in cases involving bodily harm caused when a disease was transmitted to an unwitting victim. Thus, in *Sinclair* the defendant was acquitted of rape but found guilty of assault.[32]

The next part of this chapter examines the possibilities that existed for prosecuting the non-sexual transmission of a communicable disease, using the example of the medical profession as a means of illuminating the arguments that pertained in cases involving other vectors of transmission. In criminal law the role of intent is central to establishing *mens rea*, the intention or knowledge of wrongdoing that constitutes part of a crime, as opposed to the action or conduct of the accused. At a time when epidemics were commonplace but the scientific understanding of how diseases spread was evolving, medical practice would appear to be a prime example of a scenario where the necessary *mens rea* might be established, on the grounds that medical professionals were, or should have been, aware of the risk of transmitting diseases to their patients and could have taken steps to avoid this. In such cases they could be accused of negligence and sued for tortious damages in civil proceedings or prosecuted in a criminal court upon allegations of recklessness.

[29] Bibbings (n 19) 130–131.

[30] ibid 131.

[31] *Clarence* (n 18) 56.

[32] *Old Bailey Proceedings Online* (www.oldbaileyonline.org, version 9.0, August 1867). Trial of William Henry Sinclair (18) (t18670819-776) and (t18670819-777).

III. Medical Practice, Negligence, and the Concept of Bodily Harm

Leading nineteenth-century textbooks on forensic medicine, written by recognised authorities of the day, provided their readers with information on disease transmission as a potential medico-legal issue. Studying these texts reveals that their authors did not consider disease transmission to be a form of professional conduct that might lead to a charge of malpractice (on grounds of negligence, gross ignorance or carelessness) and a suit for damages. The wording of the Offences Against the Person Acts of 1828, 1837 and 1861 underpinned the authors' view that physical harms alone were capable of triggering legal liability. The 1837 statute introduced the term 'grievous bodily harm',[33] and the 1861 statute criminalised a wider range of violent acts, moving beyond wounds inflicted by the use of some weapon or instrument, which is how judges interpreted the 1837 Act. Its successor included firstly 'acts causing or tending to cause danger to life or bodily harm', followed by another lengthy section devoted entirely to assaults.[34]

According to Michael Ryan, who was among the earliest academic authors on forensic medicine in England, 'ignorant malpractice' was 'a great misdemeanour at common law, whether in a licensed or unlicensed practitioner. The party injured suffers a private wrong, and may bring an action for damages adequate to the loss he has sustained'.[35] This book did not refer to grievous bodily harm, as it predated the 1837 Act, but Ryan's work was quickly superseded by the textbooks of Alfred Swaine Taylor (1806–80), William Guy (1810–85) and John Dixon Mann (1840–1912).

In 1844 William Guy stated that the 1837 statute seemed

> to meet every possible mischief which the malice of man can inflict; and hence it becomes less necessary than formerly for medico-legal purposes, to define the term *wound*. … The law provides punishment for all such injuries by the insertion of the words 'or shall by any means whatever cause to any person any bodily injury dangerous to life'.[36]

Thus, although the wording was broad enough, in theory, to encompass the transmission of disease – assuming that the effects of this could be considered an injury – it is clear that doctors and lawyers did not conceive of the law in such terms. Common sense tells us that syphilis and scarlatina are dangerous to life,

[33] An Act to amend the Laws relating to Offences against the Person, 17 July 1837, 1 Vict c 85, s 4.

[34] Offences Against the Person Act 1861, sub-heading under which ss 17–35 appeared. Sections 36–47 appeared under the sub-heading 'assaults'.

[35] Michael Ryan, *A Manual of Medical Jurisprudence, and State Medicine*, 2nd edn (London, Sherwood, Gilbert, and Piper, 1836) 176.

[36] William A Guy, *Principles of Forensic Medicine* (London, Renshaw, 1844) 344.

but there was not yet a legal acknowledgement of this possibility, because of the longstanding assumption that bodily harms were inflicted with weapons. In the fourth edition of Taylor's *Medical Jurisprudence* (1852), the term 'grievous bodily harm' was thought to have a 'vague signification' but was clearly assumed to relate to wounds caused by some kind of weapon.[37] A fatal disease incurred as a result of hospitalisation following an assault had led to a successful prosecution (for murder or manslaughter, it is unclear which) in 1839,[38] but Taylor did not consider the transmission of disease between practitioner and patient.

Later editions of these books also failed to include the concept of disease transmission as a form of harm, but did acknowledge the expectation that medical persons should attend to the prevention as well as the cure of disease, and might be sued for careless or unskillful medical or surgical treatment. However, even as late as 1891 another of Taylor's textbooks focused on cases where the negligence was physical in nature, using the example of childbirth where the mother or child died from violence or blood loss.[39] He noted however that Baron Pollock had stated on one occasion that grievous bodily harm would reasonably apply to such an injury as would render medical treatment necessary.[40] In 1898 Dixon Mann discussed medical negligence and presented different scenarios in which claims for damage could be made against doctors; but he did not include transmission of disease.[41] Neither author seemed to consider that a disease might constitute an injury requiring medical treatment. It was not until 1910 that a medico-legal author included this possibility, in a section titled 'Wounds in their relation to danger to life', when he cited the case of a midwife who had been convicted in 1883.[42] I consider her case below.

IV. Prosecutions for Transmitting an Infectious Disease

To identify prosecutions of medical practitioners accused of infecting one or more of their patients with a transmissible disease, the After-Trial Calendar of Prisoners, 1855–1931 database at *The National Archives* was searched using keywords for the occupation of the accused: 'midwife', 'doctor', 'surgeon', and 'medical'. This database holds details of prisoners tried at the Central Criminal Court,[43] and yielded only three cases, those of midwives Elizabeth Sarah Berry (1891),

[37] Alfred S Taylor, *Medical Jurisprudence*, 4th edn (London, John Churchill, 1852) 191.

[38] ibid 280.

[39] Thomas Stevenson (ed), Alfred S Taylor, *A Manual of Medical Jurisprudence*, 12th edn (London, Churchill, 1891) 314–15.

[40] ibid 235.

[41] J Dixon Mann, *Forensic Medicine and Toxicology* (London, Charles Griffin, 1898) 324.

[42] John Glaister, *A Text-book of Medical Jurisprudence and Toxicology* (Edinburgh, Livingstone, 1910) 248.

[43] The National Archives, CRIM 9, Central Criminal Court, After Trial Calendars of Prisoners, https://discovery.nationalarchives.gov.uk/details/r/C5521.

Mildred Mary Rake (1895), and Angelina Sore (1900). Next, the *British Newspaper Archive* was searched using a number of key phrases: 'midwife disease harm', 'doctor disease harm', 'doctor disease assault', 'medical disease negligence', 'medical disease assault', 'infected by doctor'. These identified just one criminal prosecution, that of Martha Schofield, a Yorkshire midwife (1883), and a civil suit against Dr GB Currie in 1906. Newspaper reports provide the details of each case, summarised below.

A. Martha Schofield: Unlawfully Inflicting Grievous Bodily Harm upon Certain Married Women

In January 1883 Martha Schofield, a widow aged 63 with a large midwifery practice near Sheffield, was charged with having unlawfully and maliciously caused grievous bodily harm to a number of women whom she had attended, and also to their husbands and children. The prosecutions were initiated by the Health Committee of the Town Council, following preliminary investigations made by the Medical Officer of Health, Dr Thomas Whiteside Hime (c 1842–1920), who was known for his zeal and thoroughness.[44] Evidence was given to show that for more than 15 months Schofield had been suffering from a highly contagious disease, syphilis, and that she had been warned by two doctors not to practise.[45] The magistrate committed her to the Leeds Assizes and on 12 February 1883 her trial was held before Day J, one of the four judges who were later to dissent from the majority decision in *Clarence*.

The extensive press reports of her trial provide the gist of the evidence against her and the rationale for the jury's decision. Essentially, Schofield had contracted syphilis 18 months previously, in the course of her duties as a midwife. She had consulted a number of doctors, all of whom told her 'the nature of her complaint, and cautioned that on no account must she attend any patients while the disease remained uncured'.[46] And yet, between late August and early October 1882, she infected three of her patients, two of their husbands, and a newborn infant.[47] She had lied to one doctor about the nature of a finger injury (an external manifestation of the disease) that she attempted to cover with a tip snipped from the finger of a glove.[48] One of the medical witnesses told the Court he had been in practice 42 years, and had seen only four such cases (of disease transmission).

In defence, Schofield's barrister, E Tindal Atkinson, objected to the indictment on the grounds that there were three counts under the 1861 statute and three under

[44] 'Obituary: Thomas Whiteside Hime, BA, MD Dubl., LRCS Edin' *British Medical Journal* 27 November 1920, 843.

[45] *Western Daily Press* (18 January 1883) 7.

[46] *London Evening Standard* (13 February 1883) 3.

[47] 'The Epidemic of Syphilis Caused by a Midwife at Sheffield' *The Lancet* (17 February 1883) 293–94.

[48] For the finger injury, see *Derby Daily Telegraph* (14 February 1883) 2 and *Sheffield Independent* (13 February 1883) 8.

the common law, but did not deny that she had knowingly infected and injured the victims. Instead, he argued that the law did not cover her acts. At common law, the indictments were for being a common nuisance, but for this a wrong had to have been committed against some public authority and in some public place and here the complaint concerned a wrong committed against a private individual. Under the statute, meanwhile, it had to be proven against her that an actual assault against the person had occurred.[49]

In reply, the judge revealed the thinking that would, more or less, be reiterated in his *Clarence* decision:

> It would shock him if he could think that a person might communicate such a disease as the one in question, however unintentionally; and was it to be held not to be an offence because the victim had not died? … Was not the spreading of such a disease as this an injury to the public?

To the jury, he noted that even if Schofield had not been warned at all about the risk of infecting her patients, he would still have held that she was criminally liable,

> for it was beyond all question that she had attended at least upon one of the women who had complained that day … after she had been made aware that already others whom she had attended were suffering from it.[50]

A different newspaper reported the following exchange between Atkinson and Day J in even more illuminating detail:

> His Lordship said he could not conceive that it was not an offence at common law to communicate a disease. Could it be said that in a case where death ensued a person could be hanged for murder, that if death did not ensue such a person would not be punishable? Mr Atkinson replied that an individual wrong could not be made into a criminal offence. His Lordship: It must be a public offence, not in the sense of injuring many people, but in the sense of its character. An assault and battery is necessarily a private offence, but it is also a public wrong. Mr Atkinson: There you have a breach of the peace. His Lordship: There is the case of administering poison with intent to kill; show me that is not an indictable offence, then I will not proceed with this. Mr Atkinson said that for one person to kill another was an offence against the public and the public safety. His Lordship: Surely to attempt to give people grievous bodily disease is against the public interest and safety. The State has an interest in the life, liberty, and good health of its subjects, and a person who injures another would, I should have thought, injured the State, and commits a wrong.[51]

After deliberating for 70 minutes, the jury found Schofield guilty on all counts, 'but unanimously recommended her to mercy on account of her previous good character and her old age, and because they thought she had displayed a great amount of ignorance in the matter'.[52]

[49] *London Evening Standard* (13 February 1883) 3.
[50] ibid. See also *The Lancet* (17 February 1883) 294 for a slightly different version of this comment.
[51] *Sheffield Independent* (13 February 1883) 8.
[52] *London Evening Standard* (13 February 1883) 3.

She was sentenced to 12 months' incarceration in Leeds Prison. According to John Glaister, writing years after the event, 45 persons in all were infected either directly or indirectly by the defendant.[53] This may have been an exaggeration, but there is no doubt that there were a large number of victims: in 1895 a junior house surgeon in Manchester traced 10 children who had been infected at birth by Schofield, and found that many of their parents also had the disease.[54]

B. Elizabeth Sarah Berry: A Singular Charge of Manslaughter

Elizabeth Berry had an extensive midwifery practice among the poor of Tooting. On 12 January 1891 she was called upon to attend Emma Spicer, who died from puerperal fever four days later. Berry was then prosecuted for manslaughter by the Director of Public Prosecutions (DPP), because in December she had been told by a doctor that one of her patients had puerperal fever, a very infectious and dangerous disease, that she was likely to infect any other woman she might attend, and that she therefore ought not to practise for two or three months. The case for the prosecution was that in spite of this warning (ie wilfully and carelessly), Berry persisted in attending other women in labour. Berry's version of the story was that there was nothing wrong with her when she attended Emma Spicer and that she did not know she was doing anything wrong. It also appeared she was under the impression that she had performed a sufficient period of quarantine before she attended the dead woman. In the course of the trial it was stated that there were very bad smells in the cottage where Berry and her husband lived, which might have contributed to cause the disease. The jury seem to have been strong supporters: they acquitted her, 'at the same time stating that the prisoner left the court without the slightest stain on her character'.[55]

This acquittal is interesting because although the jury did not believe Elizabeth Berry had been negligent in regard to communicating puerperal fever to Emma Spicer, they seem to have seen the possibility that she might have been the origin of another vector of transmission – via 'bad smells' – as a purely mitigating factor. A different jury might perhaps have interpreted this as further evidence of a disregard for hygiene, but her identification by the press as 'a respectable looking woman' adds to the sense that she made a positive impression in court. Berry did not fit the stereotype of the ignorant and thus possibly criminal midwife, particularly as she had apparently abstained from seeing patients for what she believed was a sufficient length of time – even though it was clearly not the two or three months the doctor had recommended.

[53] Glaister (n 42) 248.

[54] FD Fisher, 'Syphilis Acquired in Childbed' *The Lancet* (16 February 1895) 400–402. Schofield was still alive at this time.

[55] *Marlborough Times* (21 February 1891) 3. See too *Old Bailey Proceedings Online* (www.oldbaileyonline.org, version 9.0, February 1891). Trial of Elizabeth Sarah Beery (sic) (t18910209-242).

The Lancet reported this trial in more detail, revealing several interesting facts.[56] Firstly, Berry was prosecuted by Forrest Fulton (1846–1925), the same barrister who had represented Charles Clarence at his appeal in 1888. Fulton argued that Berry was criminally responsible for the death of her patient due to gross and culpable negligence, whereas in *Clarence* he had argued that there was no criminal harm due to the wife's 'consent' to the sexual activity which caused the harm.[57] In other words, the nature of the disease transmission, sexual or nonsexual, and the relationship between the parties, were of great legal significance, even before the victim's death was factored into consideration. Furthermore, two expert witnesses were called. The renowned police surgeon Dr Thomas Bond (1841–1901) had performed a post-mortem examination and confirmed the cause of death as blood poisoning resulting from puerperal fever. Dr WC Grigg, physician to Queen Charlotte's Lying-in Hospital, then stated that the evidence suggested the infection was probably caught from the victim's surroundings rather than her attendant. Finally, the judge noted that he did not agree with the inquest jury who had found Berry guilty of manslaughter through 'gross and criminal negligence'.[58]

C. Mildred Mary Rake: Warned not to Visit Patients

Rake, a 36-year-old midwife practising in Kentish Town, London, was tried for the manslaughter of two women who died from puerperal fever allegedly caught from her, and it is clear that the DPP was again keen to get involved in a case of disease transmission: the evidence against her in police court was presented by Archibald Bodkin (1862–1957) on behalf of the Treasury.[59] She was tried at the Old Bailey in early April 1895, where the allegation was that she communicated puerperal fever to patients whom she visited after being warned not to visit them until all danger of infection had passed from herself. However, the jury were unable to agree a verdict and Rake was released on bail.[60] She was tried again three weeks later, but no evidence was offered on the two indictments for manslaughter and she was acquitted.[61] It seems that although the DPP wanted to prosecute a case of disease transmission, it was forced to give up the effort as a more or less lost cause, most likely because the evidence of direct responsibility for death resulting from negligence was not strong enough. However, the fact that Rake was not acquitted outright by a jury suggests that at least some of the legal arguments in favour of her guilt were persuasive. If the victims had survived, perhaps the midwife might have been convicted of assault.

[56] 'Medical Trial: Regina *versus* Berry' *The Lancet* (21 February 1891) 463–64.
[57] Gleeson, 'The Problem of *Clarence*' (n 28) 4.
[58] *The Lancet* (21 February 1891) 464.
[59] *The People* (3 March 1895) 11.
[60] *Stratford-upon-Avon Herald* (5 April 1895) 6.
[61] *Old Bailey Proceedings Online* (www.oldbaileyonline.org, version 9.0, April 1895). Trial of Mildred Mary Rake (36) (t18950422-380).

D. Angelina Sore: Neglect and Reckless Conduct

In July 1900 another London midwife was committed for trial at the Old Bailey, after an inquest jury found her to be guilty of the manslaughter of a woman to whom she had communicated 'the contagion of puerperal fever' through gross negligence. Angelina Sore, known as Murray, was then arrested on the coroner's warrant.[62] The evidence was presented a second time at the Westminster Police Court:

> Briefly stated, the case against the accused was that she attended a woman who died on June 10 from puerperal fever and peritonitis. She was afterwards cautioned not to attend another midwifery case for at least six weeks. It was alleged that notwithstanding that she attended Mrs Jones on July 2, with the result that suppurative peritonitis – really a form of puerperal malady – supervened with fatal results. … Mr Francis remanded the accused, offering to accept bail, and intimated that the Treasury would be communicated with to prosecute.[63]

However, this prosecution did not go forward, despite the fact that Sore had been warned in June, by the coroner and parochial officials, not to see other patients following the first death. She did so in defiance of that warning, and her next patient caught the disease and died. However, at her next appearance in police court the magistrate was forced to release her, 'as there could be no proof that the fatal disease was actually communicated by her'.[64]

The legal argument was summarised by the press:

> The case for the prosecution was that the neglect and reckless conduct of the accused made her responsible for the death of Mrs Jones. Mr Langton argued that unless it could be absolutely shown that the puerperal malady of which Mrs Jones died was incurred through infection communicated by the accused no charge of manslaughter could be sustained. It was, he thought, impossible for anyone to positively say how the disease originated. There were cases on all fours with this one, and in them the judge had directed an acquittal. Mr Francis [the magistrate] said it had not been shown that death was attributable to the accused. Mr Bodkin appreciated the difficulty, and said he could not carry the case further than the doctor did when he said that were no means of showing that the disease was communicated by a given person.[65]

Of course, Sore still had to appear at the Old Bailey to answer the charge of manslaughter on the coroner's inquisition, but the outcome was a foregone conclusion: counsel for the prosecution offered no evidence and she was acquitted.[66]

This case reveals that the public (coroner and inquest jury) and the DPP still perceived criminality in the transmission of disease through negligence, but

[62] *Nantwich Guardian* (1 August 1900) 8.
[63] *South Western Star* (27 July 1900) 5.
[64] *Lloyd's List* (9 August 1900) 14.
[65] *South Western Star* (10 August 1900) 5.
[66] *Old Bailey Proceedings Online* (www.oldbaileyonline.org, version 9.0, September 1900). Trial of Angelina Sore (47) (t19000911-612).

were again confounded by the fact that the victim had died: establishing a chain of evidence between Angelina Sore and the victim that was sufficiently strong to support a charge of manslaughter was beyond the capabilities of medicine at that time. Thus, the magistrate noted what seemed to him a peculiar state of the law with regard to the spread of infectious disease: people who were suffering from infectious diseases yet wilfully exposed others were liable under the Public Health Act 1875, but it seemed that medical practitioners who attended infectious cases could mix with the community without incurring any penalty.[67]

E. *William Fletcher Crier v Dr George Hope and Dr George Burnett Currie*: Negligence and Assault

In early March 1906 William Fletcher Crier, an estate agent, and his wife Mary brought an action in the High Court to recover £1000 damages for negligence and assault from George Hope and George Burnett Currie,[68] two doctors practising together in Hanwell and Ealing. Crier had engaged Dr Currie to attend his wife's labour on 15 November 1904, and during Currie's visit, it was alleged, he had infected Mary with scarlet fever. When asked if he had previously attended any scarlet fever case, Currie said he had not, but on inquiry it was found that he had:[69] he had visited a house where two children of a Mrs Miller had the disease, earlier on the day that he visited Mary Crier.[70] For the plaintiffs, a doctor who attended Mary in April 1905 said he found her suffering from debility, consistent with having passed through serious illness, and claimed that after attending an infectious case he himself always had a bath and a thorough course of disinfection. Cross-examined, he admitted that he might not always wash and disinfect himself before proceeding on his rounds. But another medical witness then said he would not have gone to visit a woman in labour two hours after treating scarlet fever patients.[71]

The alleged negligence was clear – the careless transmission of scarlet fever from one patient to another. But what constituted the assault? In this case, it seems to have been both the disease itself and its effects on Mary Crier, who had to have an operation and was so weakened that she was sent away to convalesce. According to her husband, she was now 'a wreck'.[72] Moreover, William Crier was adamant that

[67] *South Western Star* (10 August 1900) 5; Public Health Act 1875, s 126.

[68] For a brief résumé of Currie's distinguished career, see *Aberdeen Press and Journal* (17 August 1937) 8.

[69] *Manchester Courier* (3 March 1906) 7.

[70] *Birmingham Daily Gazette* (3 March 1906) 7; *Manchester Courier* (6 March 1906) 9.

[71] *Daily Mirror* (6 March 1906) 5; *Leominster News and North West Herefordshire & Radnorshire Advertiser* (9 March 1906) 2.

[72] *Globe* (3 March 1906) 3.

> On one occasion, when he charged Dr Currie with having actually attended scarlet fever cases at the time ov [sic] visiting his wife, Dr Currie replied, 'Well, what can a medical man do if he would keep his practice?' 'If I had known that,' said plaintiff, 'I would have given you £200, to stay away from my house while my wife was ill.'[73]

Currie denied that he asked Mrs Miller to say that he had not touched her children, and a Harley Street doctor 'expressed the opinion that there was hardly any risk in attending a confinement two or three hours after a doctor had seen a scarlet fever patient'.[74] Currie's principal defence was that before going to see Mrs Crier, he thoroughly washed himself and changed his coat;[75] the press described this as 'all reasonable precautions'.[76] The case report in *The Lancet* reveals that a total of seven medical witnesses were called, of whom five testified that Dr Currie had taken precautions variously identified as necessary, effective or reasonable.[77] As Alannah Tomkins has shown, it was quite usual for the Victorian medical profession to defend its own against allegations of serious physical assault, including rape and murder,[78] whereas unwillingness to censure fellow doctors in cases of neglect and manslaughter was less uniform.[79] The case against Dr Currie seems to reflect this sort of professional disagreement about acceptable practice.

The judge's instruction to the jury is thus worth reproducing in full, as it no doubt tipped the balance of opinion and added to the pressure on jurors to acquit:

> His Lordship, in the course of his summing up, dealt with the means by which scarlet fever infection might be conveyed. The methods of infection were, he said, most obscure. The period of incubation of the germ was about eight days, and in this case infection might have been communicated on any day after November 11, as the symptoms of it became apparent on the 19th. During the interval any person going into Mrs Crier's room, or anything brought into it, might have brought the infection to her. The jury must consider the circumstances as well as the fact that Dr Currie, shortly before he was called to Mrs Crier, had seen a scarlet fever patient. It must, moreover, be remembered that there was an epidemic of scarlet fever in Ealing at the time. The Jury, after deliberating for over an hour, returned a verdict for the defendants, holding that Dr Currie took the usual precautions.[80]

In other words, the jury found that Currie had not been negligent and therefore was not liable to pay damages for the harm he had caused. This is not to say that he did not infect Mary Crier, for almost certainly he did; but the evidence was not

[73] ibid. See also *Leominster News and North West Herefordshire & Radnorshire Advertiser* (9 March 1906) 2.
[74] *Daily News* (London) (7 March 1906) 2.
[75] *Globe* (6 March 1906) 9.
[76] *Morning Leader* (9 March 1906) 5.
[77] 'Crier and Wife *v.* Hope and Currie' *The Lancet* (17 March 1906) 783–84. This report states that the Criers were claiming £500 for 'special damage'.
[78] Alannah Tomkins, *Medical Misadventure in an Age of Professionalisation, 1780–1890* (Manchester, Manchester University Press, 2017) ch 4.
[79] ibid ch 3.
[80] *Morning Post* (9 March 1906) 10.

strong enough to support the conclusion that he had been careless on the 'balance of probabilities' test for civil liability. This suggested that the evidence was not strong enough to convict him of a criminal offence either, but the plaintiffs' counsel would not drop the question of assault. Following the jury decision, Crier's barrister asked the judge to

> request the jury to answer the question as to whether Dr Currie had not committed a legal assault upon Mrs Crier … by examining her after leading her to believe he was not attending any scarlet fever patients.[81]

After some deliberation the jury indicated that they were unable to agree and were discharged. The judge was then asked to separate the claims, but replied that 'On reflection I do not think I ought to have allowed the second question to go to the jury'.[82] He then granted a stay of execution, with a view to an appeal; but no appeal was subsequently reported.

This case was argued in a manner consistent with the criminal prosecutions for disease transmission first seen in the *Sinclair* case of 1867. The plaintiffs' legal team tried to show that Dr Currie knew (or suspected the likelihood) of being infectious because he repeatedly denied seeing scarlet fever cases; secondly, that he (as a doctor) knew the likely consequences of going from a fever case to a parturient woman; thirdly, that he did not tell the Criers of his prior case; and, finally, that Crier would not have consented to have him treat Mary had he been in possession of all the facts. For doctors, however, the most important question concerned risk and the appropriate means to manage it. In reflecting on the importance of this case to medical practitioners, an editorial in *The Lancet* opined that the danger of being sued would remind a doctor not to relax his vigilance, as

> constant familiarity with such risks and long immunity from an accident may tend to lessen his sense of the danger of infection to which his patients inevitably must be subjected from time to time.[83]

V. The Infectious Disease Notification Act 1889

A search of the *British Newspaper Archive* using the phrase 'doctor communicated disease' returned a number of articles concerning the Infectious Disease Notification Act 1889 and sporadic reflections upon the role played by doctors as carriers of disease. The Act had its first reading in the House of Commons at the end of June and received Royal Assent on 30 August 1889. It was permissive, and designed to assist local authorities in England, Wales, Scotland and Ireland in preventing the spread of infectious disease, by enabling them to obtain early and

[81] 'Crier and Wife *v.* Hope and Currie' (n 77) 784.
[82] ibid.
[83] 'Crier and Wife *v.* Hope and Currie' (n 77) 773.

accurate information about the cases that occurred in their districts. But it did not impose any penalties upon doctors who transmitted disease. This prompted a letter to *The Times* from notable social reformer and activist Frances Power Cobbe (1822–1904) which asked, not for the first time, why

> the zeal recently directed to the protection of the public from infectious diseases should have stopped short at isolating the patients (who at worst are passive in their sick beds) and have taken no account of the doctors, who run all over the town, carrying – according to their own theories – millions of disease germs on their persons and clothing.[84]

Most of the letters published in response to Cobbe's were supportive, as was the *Liverpool Echo*:

> Even granting that the majority of medical practitioners take proper and reasonable precautions, there are others who, either from carelessness, want of time, or pressure of work, expose those whom they attend to great risk of infection. Cases in which death is brought into the house by the doctor may not be numerous, but that the germs of fever and disease are occasionally carried from patient to patient by the practitioner in his hurried rounds there is only too much reason to believe.[85]

An editorial in the *Cork Constitution* thought her suggestions worthy of trial, since

> neither the overcrowded state of the medical profession, the advancement of sanitary science, nor yet legislation in the interest of the public health, appear to have made much headway in combatting disease and its causes.[86]

The *Saffron Walden Weekly News* suggested that the issue Cobbe had raised had 'long been a source of anxiety to many people'.[87] Dr James Turle, Medical Officer of Health for North Finchley, thought that handwashing was equally important to limiting the time that doctors spent with infectious patients; but he admitted that negligent doctors had caused loss of life, 'chiefly in former years'.[88]

However, other newspapers pointed out the impracticality of her suggestions:

> After visiting a case of infectious disease, the doctor is recommended (1) to use disinfectants, (2) to wash his hands, face, hair, and beard, and (3) to change all his clothing. How does Miss Cobbe think that doctor would get through his day's work if he had to change all his clothing every time that he saw an infant suspected of measles or a small boy convicted of scarlatina? He would require the wardrobe of a Prince of Wales and the rapidity of a Lightning-Change-Artist.[89]

[84] *Liverpool Echo* (16 November 1889) 3. See Frances Power Cobbe, 'The Notification of Infectious Doctors' *The Times* (15 November 1889) 13.

[85] *Liverpool Echo* (16 November 1889) 3.

[86] *Cork Constitution* (19 November 1889) 4.

[87] *Saffron Walden Weekly News* (23 November 1889) 4.

[88] *Cork Constitution* (27 December 1889) 6.

[89] *St James's Gazette* (15 November 1889) 13.

In the view of *The Lancet*, reported in the *Eastern Morning News*, 'any legislation having … the notification of doctors as its object would be futile and superfluous'.[90] The *British Medical Journal* responded that doctors did take effective precautions, for instance by sending their assistant to ensure the safety and welfare of a patient.[91]

This correspondence is undoubtedly revealing of prevailing attitudes among the medical profession and interested public, but of more direct relevance to this chapter is the question of whether or not any medical professionals were prosecuted under the terms of the 1889 Act. Certainly some were, though I have not found examples of cases where medical professionals were found to have acted negligently in communicating a disease and therefore convicted of an offence. In 1906 a doctor in Derbyshire was fined the maximum 40 shillings plus costs for failing to notify the district Medical Officer of Health about a fatal case of puerperal fever. His explanation was that he forgot, and that the certified midwife ought to have known that she should not afterward attend anyone else. The prosecutor, on behalf of the Chesterfield Rural District Council, stated that the doctor should have *told* her not to attend anyone else *and* sent a formal notification of the death immediately.[92] It is to the midwife's credit that the next seven patients she saw all remained healthy, given how highly contagious puerperal fever was and its high mortality; and indeed the possibility that she could have infected others was part of why the bench considered this such a serious case.[93]

VI. Conclusion

Doctors were well aware of the dangers that attended surgery and hospitalisation; eighteenth-century practitioners understood that a disease like gaol fever could be spread from one person to another. The medico-scientific understanding of disease transmission then increased considerably during the course of the nineteenth century. In the 1840s Ignaz Semmelweis showed the likely vector of infection in midwifery cases, publishing a book on the topic in 1861. Joseph Lister published the initial results of his antiseptic procedures in 1867. Germ theory was developed from the late 1850s to the 1880s, most prominently via the research of Louis Pasteur and Robert Koch. Yet, textbooks of forensic medicine did not address the transmission of a disease from a doctor or midwife to a patient as a public wrong, or even as a possibility. Only Glaister, in 1910, mentioned the possibly sole case of a midwife who was successfully prosecuted, Martha Schofield.

The comment made by one of the medical witnesses at her trial, who told the Court he had seen four cases of disease transmission by a midwife in his career

[90] *Eastern Morning News* (25 November 1889) 2.
[91] *Cambridge Daily News* (20 December 1889) 2.
[92] *Derbyshire Courier* (4 August 1906) 7.
[93] *Derbyshire Courier* (31 July 1906) 3.

of 42 years, together with the responses to the suggestions made by Frances Power Cobbe, suggests that the transmission of infectious diseases by medical professionals occurred fairly regularly, but was not typically subject to legal proceedings. Incidents may well have led to civil suits for damages (by middle class victims who had the funds to take a doctor to court), but seem unlikely to have resulted in many criminal prosecutions. Further research might reveal more prosecutions, particularly in the 1880s following Schofield's conviction, as the example of London shows that legal officials tried to prosecute cases when they occurred. The involvement of the DPP is indicative of a legal recognition that a private offence constituted a public wrong in such cases. But the failed attempts by prosecutors at the Old Bailey indicate the problems that were likely to ensue in cases where the patient had died, not least the fact that it was difficult – medically and scientifically – to prove a direct connection between the accused practitioner and the patient's disease when pathways to infection were not well understood. Moreover, in the absence of well-defined recklessness it was equally difficult to demonstrate the *mens rea* required to sustain a criminal prosecution.

Even more importantly, there remained a legal suspicion that disease transmission did not constitute 'harm' for the purposes of the Offences Against the Person Act 1861. This may explain why others were not prosecuted as Martha Schofield was. While it cannot be said for certain that *Clarence* was the end of the road for the innovatory use of the 1861 Act to prosecute disease transmission, it must have been a factor in lawyers' minds if and when they were asked to consider such cases. Finally, the fact that the Infectious Disease Notification Act 1889 did not encompass this type of public harm suggests that lawmakers were not alert to the possibility, which of course the powerful medical lobby would not have wished to publicise.

INDEX

For specific legislation from the United Kingdom, *see* legislation below. Legislation from other places is included under the index entry for that place.

www.ingramcontent.com/pod-product-compliance
Ingram Content Group UK Ltd.
Pitfield, Milton Keynes, MK11 3LW, UK
UKHW020249290926
15470UKWH00002B/832

9 781509 984442